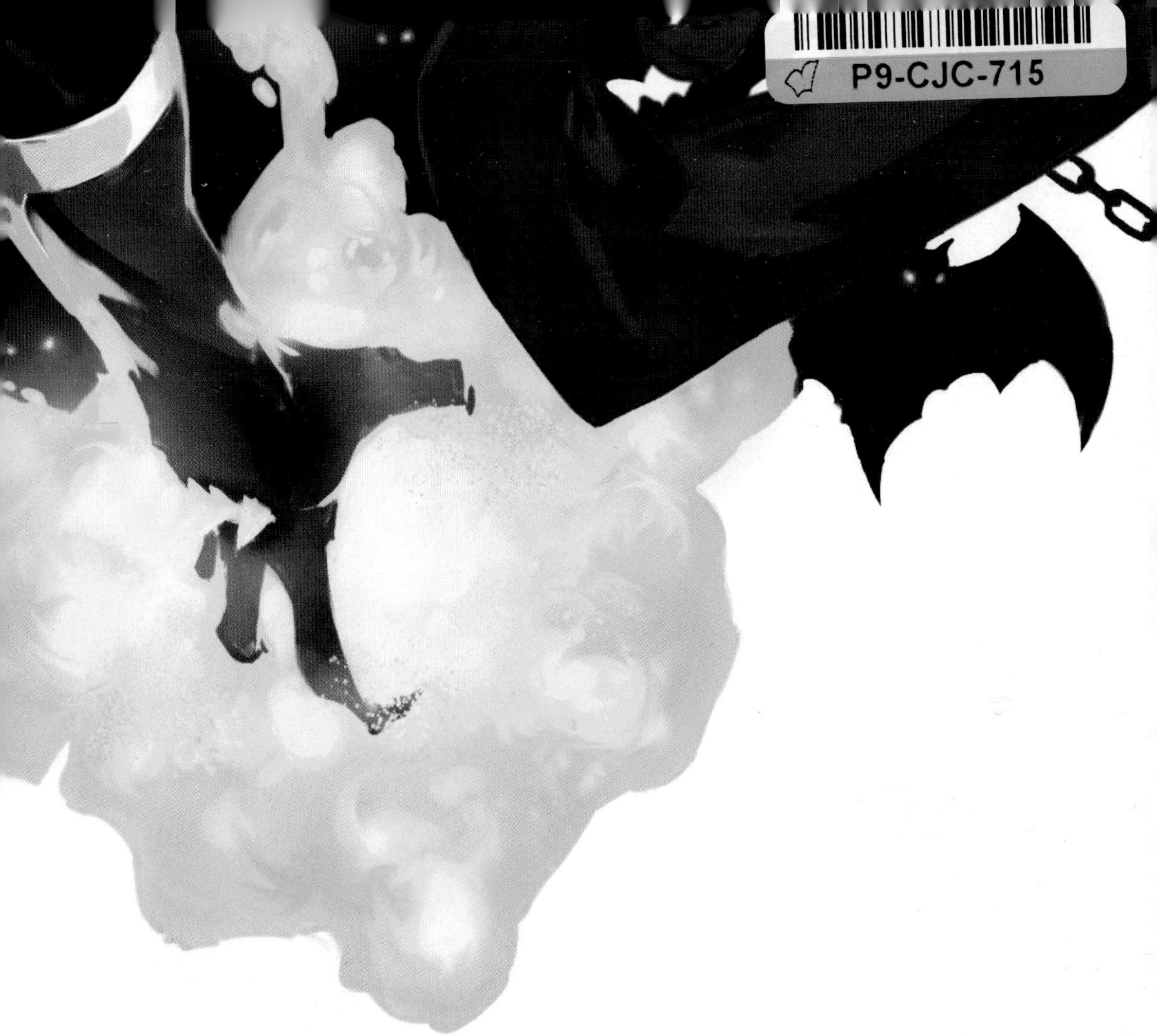

SPAWN®

ORIGINS
COLLECTION

VOLUME 1

COLLECTING
ISSUES 1-6

BEN TIMMRECK, JENNIFER CASSIDY, TYLER JEFFERS MANAGING EDITORS

BEN TIMMRECK, JERRY POTEET ART DIRECTION

ERIC STEPHENSON PUBLISHER FOR IMAGE COMICS

SPAWN CREATED BY TODD McFARLANE

image

TODD McFARLANE
P R O D U C T I O N S
McFARLANE.COM

SPAWN ORIGINS COLLECTION VOLUME 1. Fifth Printing. April 2016. Published by IMAGE COMICS, 2001 Center Street, Sixth Floor, Berkley, CA 94704 USA. Originally published in single magazine form as Spawn, Issues 1-6. Spawn, its logo and its symbol are registered trademarks © 2016 Todd McFarlane Productions, Inc. All other related characters are ™ and © 2016 Todd McFarlane Productions, Inc. All rights reserved. The characters, events and stories in this publication are entirely fictional. With exception of artwork used for review purposes, none of the contents of this publication may be reprinted without the permission of Todd McFarlane Productions, Inc. Printed in the USA. For information regarding the CPSIA on this printed material call: 203-595-3636 and provide reference #EAST – 677804.

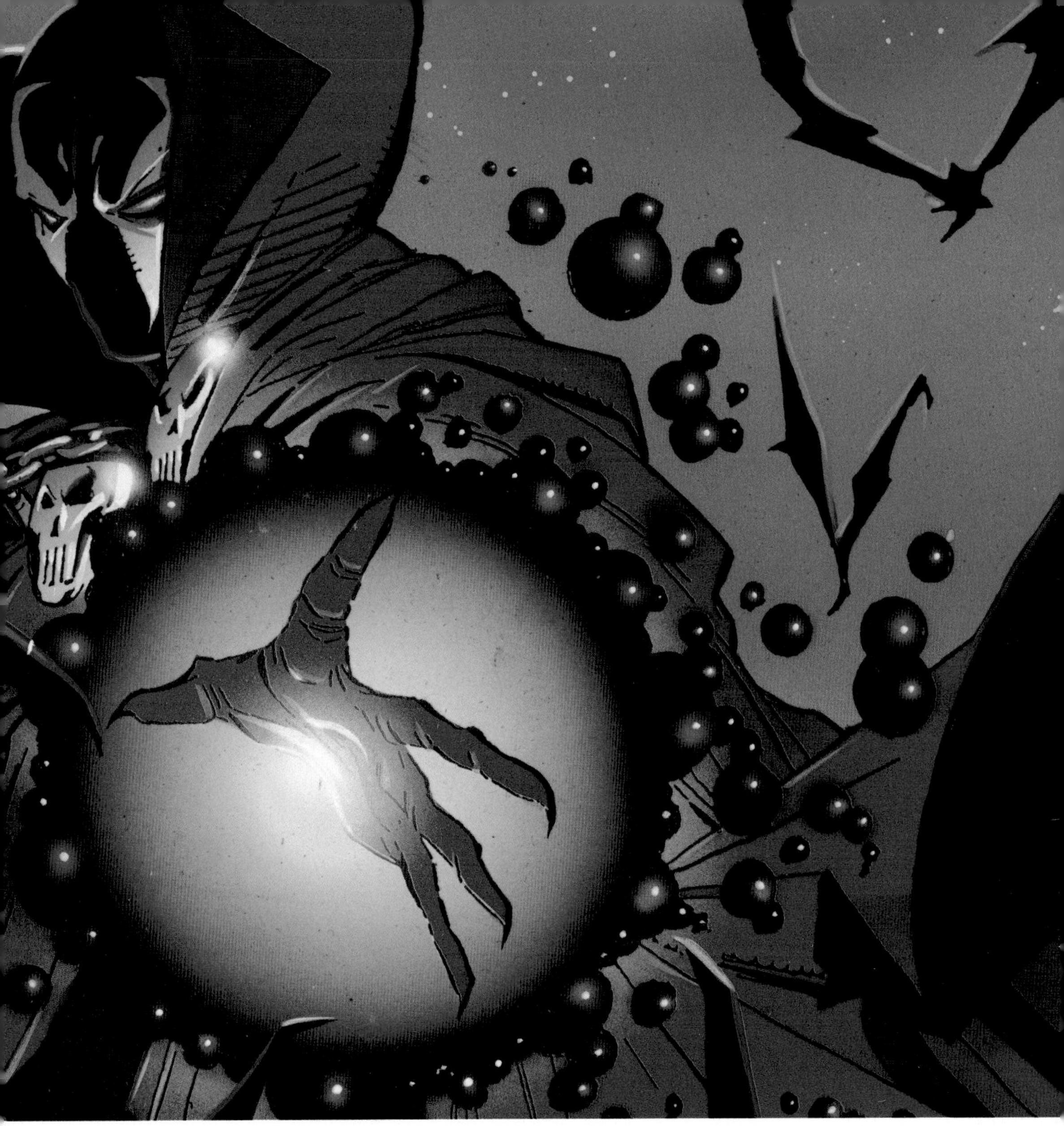

STORIES, PENCILS & INKS TODD McFARLANE

LETTERING TOM ORZECHOWSKI

COLOR STEVE OLIFF, REUBEN RUDE & OLYOPTICS

COVERS TODD McFARLANE

TRADE PAPERBACK COVER GREG CAPULLO

"I first conceived the idea for the character of Spawn when I was in high school. The original costume I drew is essentially the same, other than the color, which was originally blue. As I gained experience, my drawing became more fluid. Do I have a master plan? Yes. Do I know the end of the story? Yes. Do I hope that I never have to tell it? Yes. I have conceived of the ending of Spawn, but the only way I would tell it is if nobody cared about the character any more. Hopefully, done right, I won't ever have to tell that story. I am hoping that Spawn, sort of like Superman and Batman, will outlive the creator. I've always said that Mickey Mouse is still alive, but Disney isn't. His creative children have surpassed his longevity."

-Todd McFarlane
Interview for Millarworld

1 | **MAY 1992**

"QUESTIONS"

PART ONE

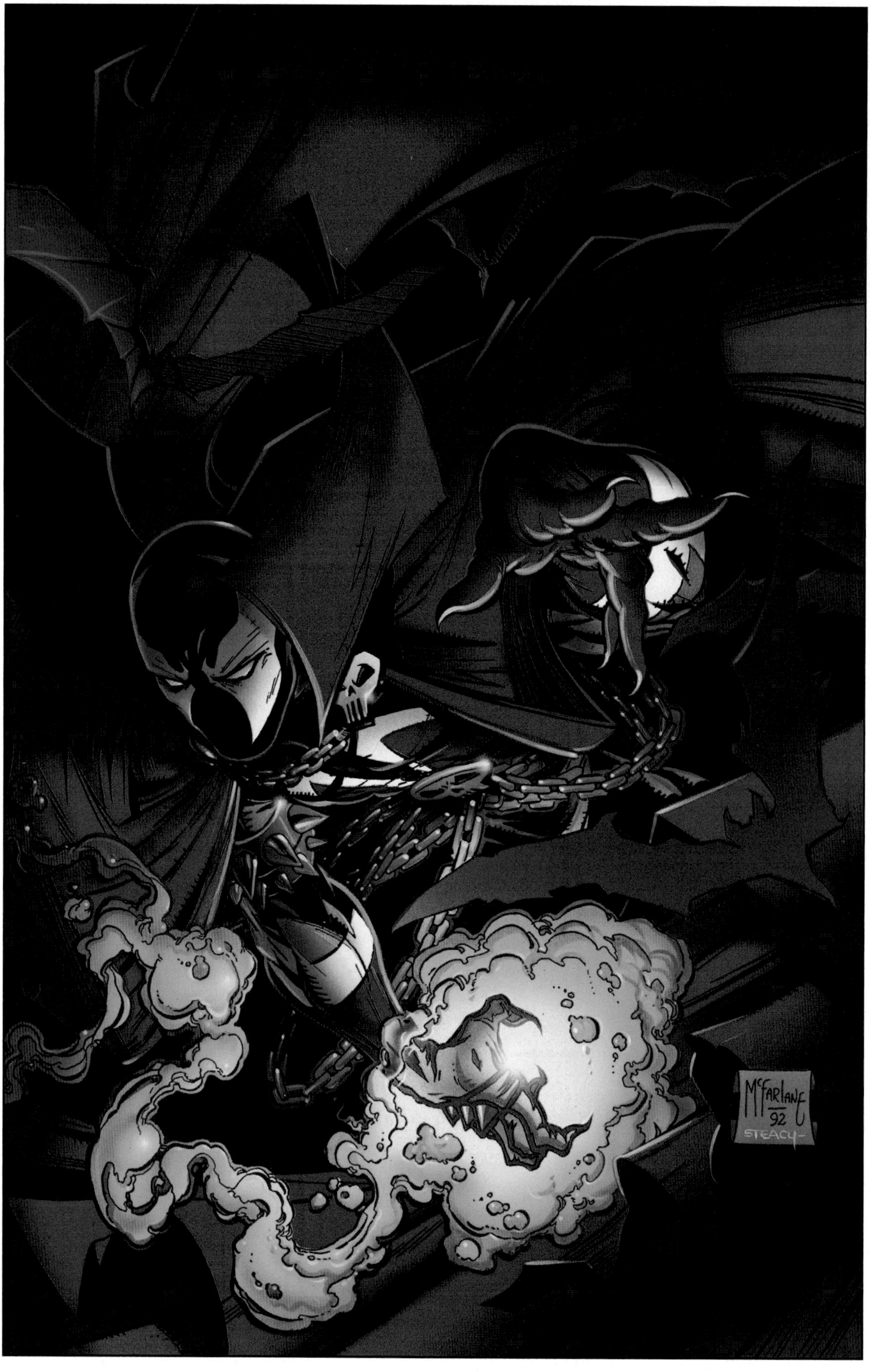
McFARLANE
92
STEACY

Spawn #1, cover

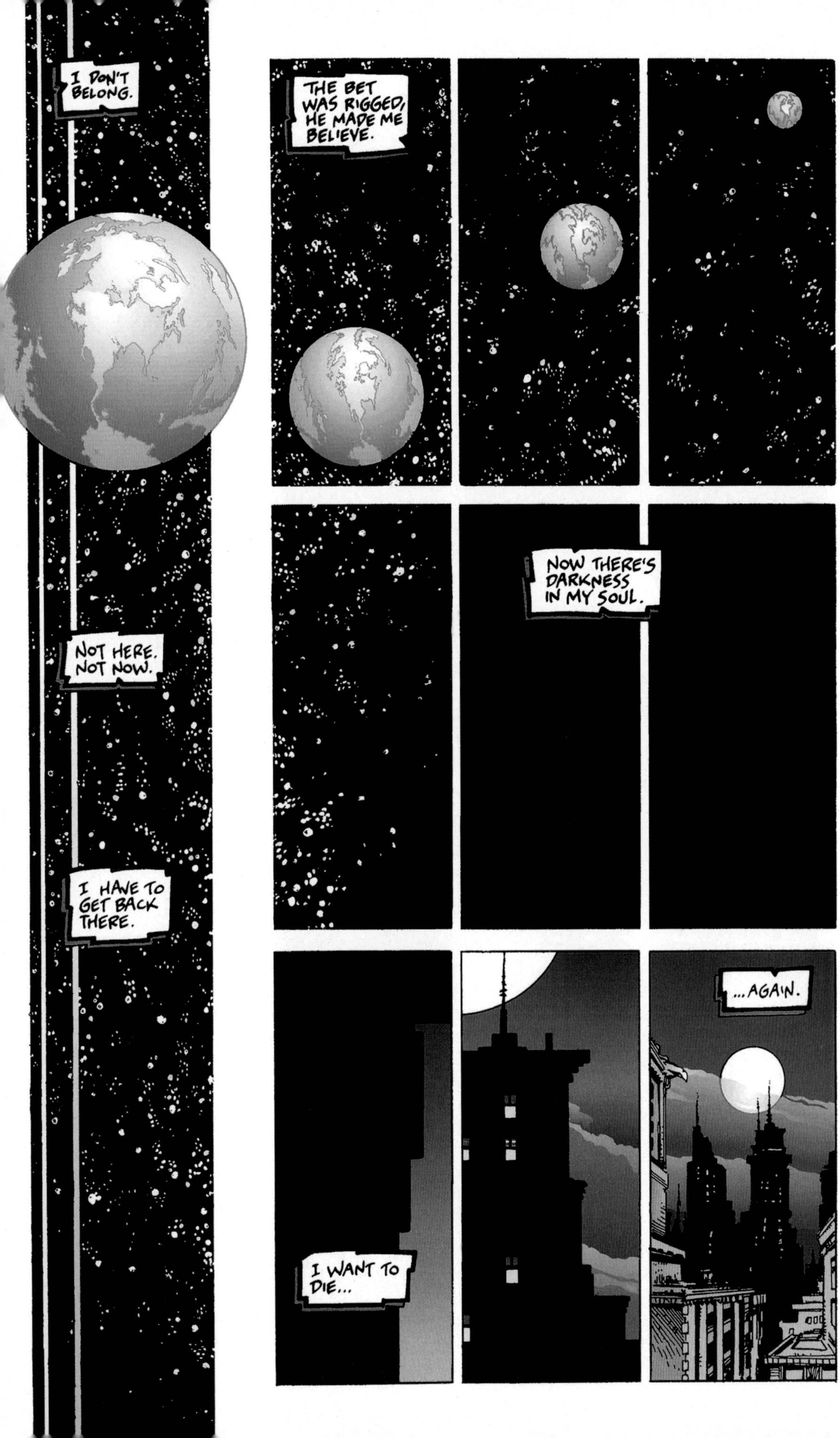
I DON'T BELONG.
NOT HERE. NOT NOW.
I HAVE TO GET BACK THERE.
THE BET WAS RIGGED, HE MADE ME BELIEVE.
NOW THERE'S DARKNESS IN MY SOUL.
I WANT TO DIE...
...AGAIN.

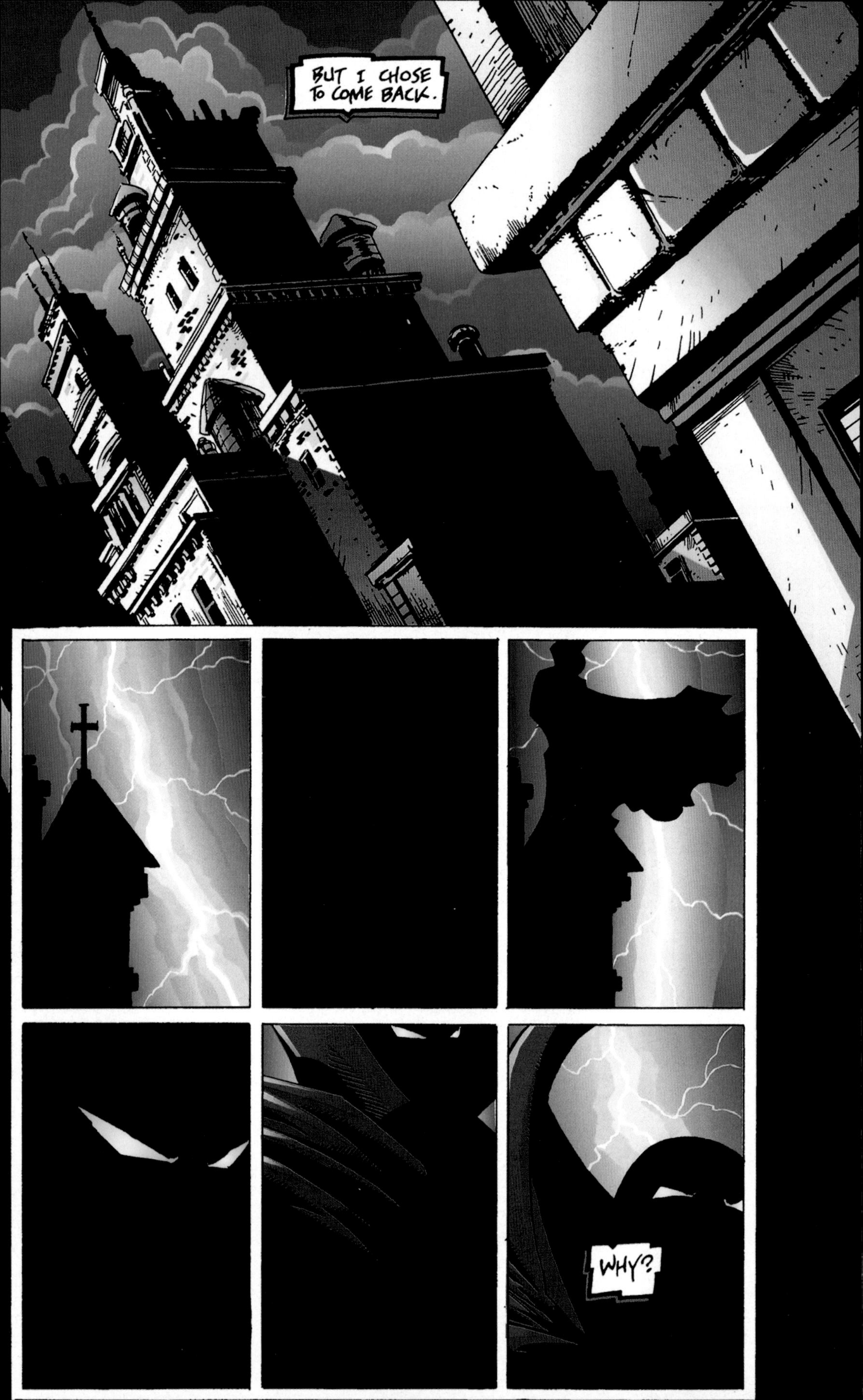
BUT I CHOSE TO COME BACK.
WHY?

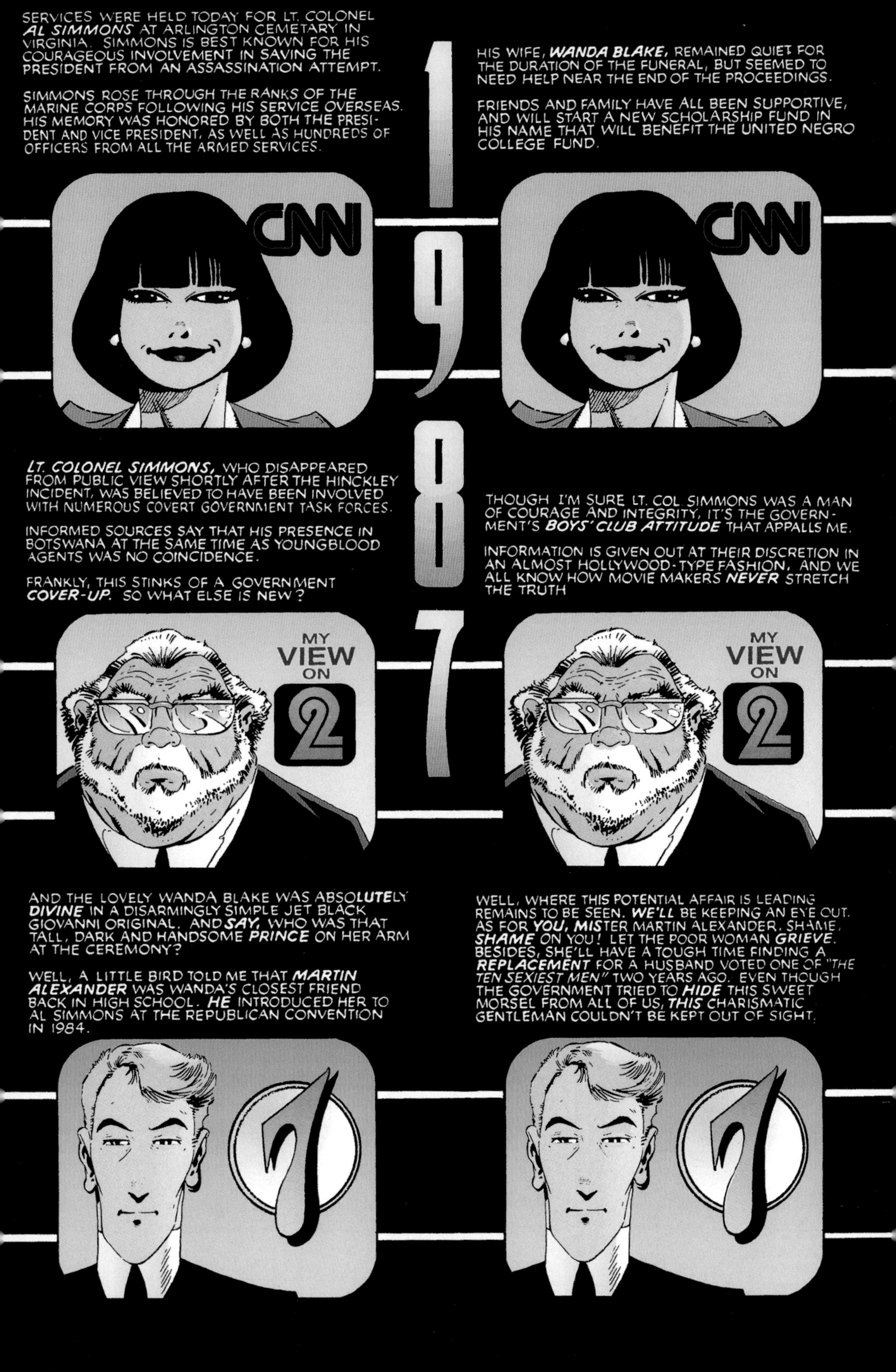
SERVICES WERE HELD TODAY FOR LT. COLONEL AL SIMMONS AT ARLINGTON CEMETARY IN VIRGINIA. SIMMONS IS BEST KNOWN FOR HIS COURAGEOUS INVOLVEMENT IN SAVING THE PRESIDENT FROM AN ASSASSINATION ATTEMPT.
SIMMONS ROSE THROUGH THE RANKS OF THE MARINE CORPS FOLLOWING HIS SERVICE OVERSEAS. HIS MEMORY WAS HONORED BY BOTH THE PRESIDENT AND VICE PRESIDENT, AS WELL AS HUNDREDS OF OFFICERS FROM ALL THE ARMED SERVICES.
HIS WIFE, WANDA BLAKE, REMAINED QUIET FOR THE DURATION OF THE FUNERAL, BUT SEEMED TO NEED HELP NEAR THE END OF THE PROCEEDINGS.
FRIENDS AND FAMILY HAVE ALL BEEN SUPPORTIVE, AND WILL START A NEW SCHOLARSHIP FUND IN HIS NAME THAT WILL BENEFIT THE UNITED NEGRO COLLEGE FUND.
1987
CNN
CNN
LT. COLONEL SIMMONS, WHO DISAPPEARED FROM PUBLIC VIEW SHORTLY AFTER THE HINCKLEY INCIDENT, WAS BELIEVED TO HAVE BEEN INVOLVED WITH NUMEROUS COVERT GOVERNMENT TASK FORCES.
INFORMED SOURCES SAY THAT HIS PRESENCE IN BOTSWANA AT THE SAME TIME AS YOUNGBLOOD AGENTS WAS NO COINCIDENCE.
FRANKLY, THIS STINKS OF A GOVERNMENT COVER-UP. SO WHAT ELSE IS NEW?
THOUGH I'M SURE LT. COL. SIMMONS WAS A MAN OF COURAGE AND INTEGRITY, IT'S THE GOVERNMENT'S BOYS' CLUB ATTITUDE THAT APPALLS ME.
INFORMATION IS GIVEN OUT AT THEIR DISCRETION IN AN ALMOST HOLLYWOOD-TYPE FASHION. AND WE ALL KNOW HOW MOVIE MAKERS NEVER STRETCH THE TRUTH
MY VIEW ON 2
MY VIEW ON 2
AND THE LOVELY WANDA BLAKE WAS ABSOLUTELY DIVINE IN A DISARMINGLY SIMPLE JET BLACK GIOVANNI ORIGINAL. AND SAY, WHO WAS THAT TALL, DARK AND HANDSOME PRINCE ON HER ARM AT THE CEREMONY?
WELL, A LITTLE BIRD TOLD ME THAT MARTIN ALEXANDER WAS WANDA'S CLOSEST FRIEND BACK IN HIGH SCHOOL. HE INTRODUCED HER TO AL SIMMONS AT THE REPUBLICAN CONVENTION IN 1984.
WELL, WHERE THIS POTENTIAL AFFAIR IS LEADING REMAINS TO BE SEEN. WE'LL BE KEEPING AN EYE OUT. AS FOR YOU, MISTER MARTIN ALEXANDER. SHAME, SHAME ON YOU! LET THE POOR WOMAN GRIEVE. BESIDES, SHE'LL HAVE A TOUGH TIME FINDING A REPLACEMENT FOR A HUSBAND VOTED ONE OF "THE TEN SEXIEST MEN" TWO YEARS AGO. EVEN THOUGH THE GOVERNMENT TRIED TO HIDE THIS SWEET MORSEL FROM ALL OF US, THIS CHARISMATIC GENTLEMAN COULDN'T BE KEPT OUT OF SIGHT.

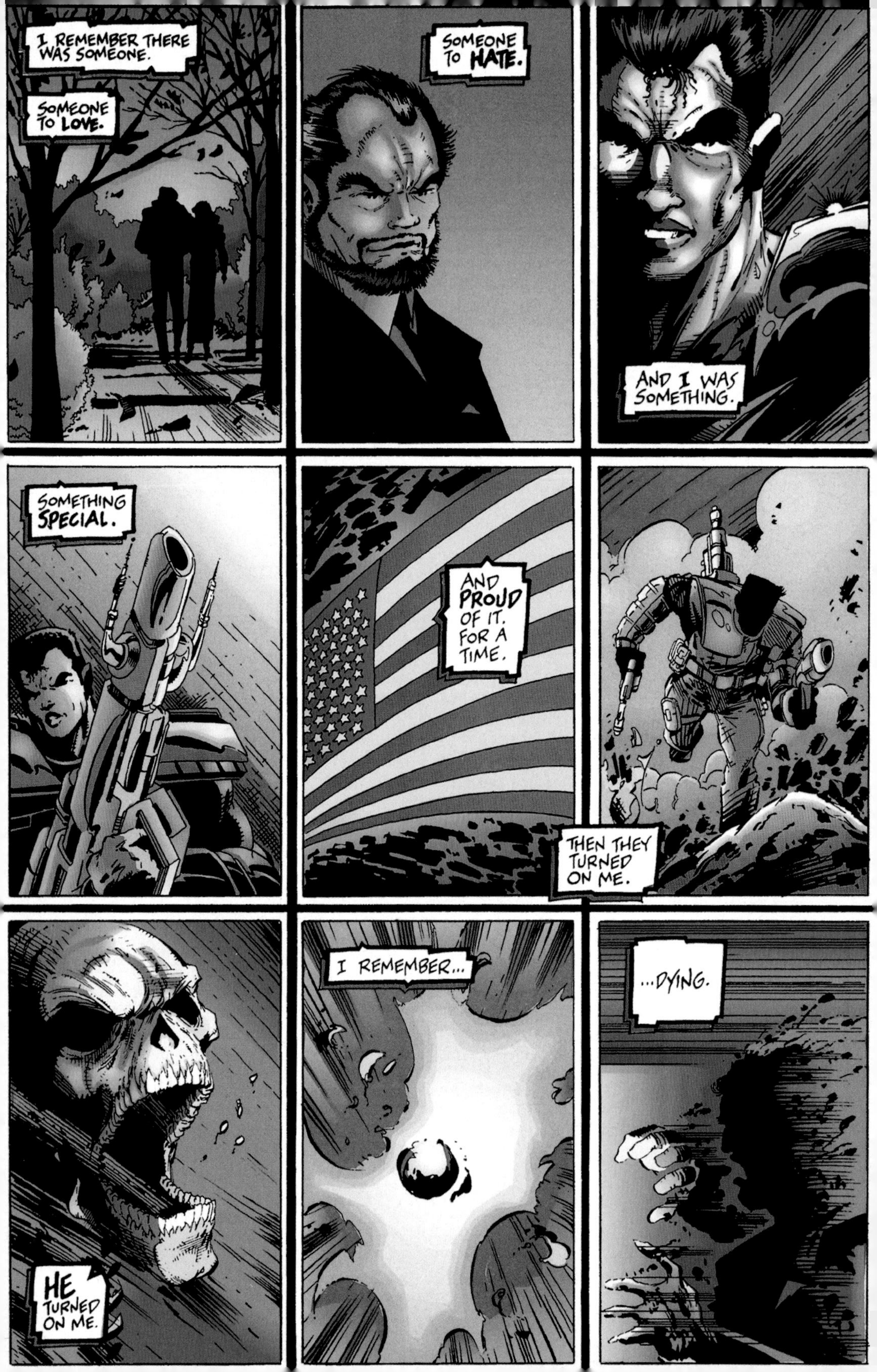
I REMEMBER THERE WAS SOMEONE.
SOMEONE TO LOVE.
SOMEONE TO HATE.
AND I WAS SOMETHING.
SOMETHING SPECIAL.
AND PROUD OF IT. FOR A TIME.
THEN THEY TURNED ON ME.
HE TURNED ON ME.
I REMEMBER...
...DYING.

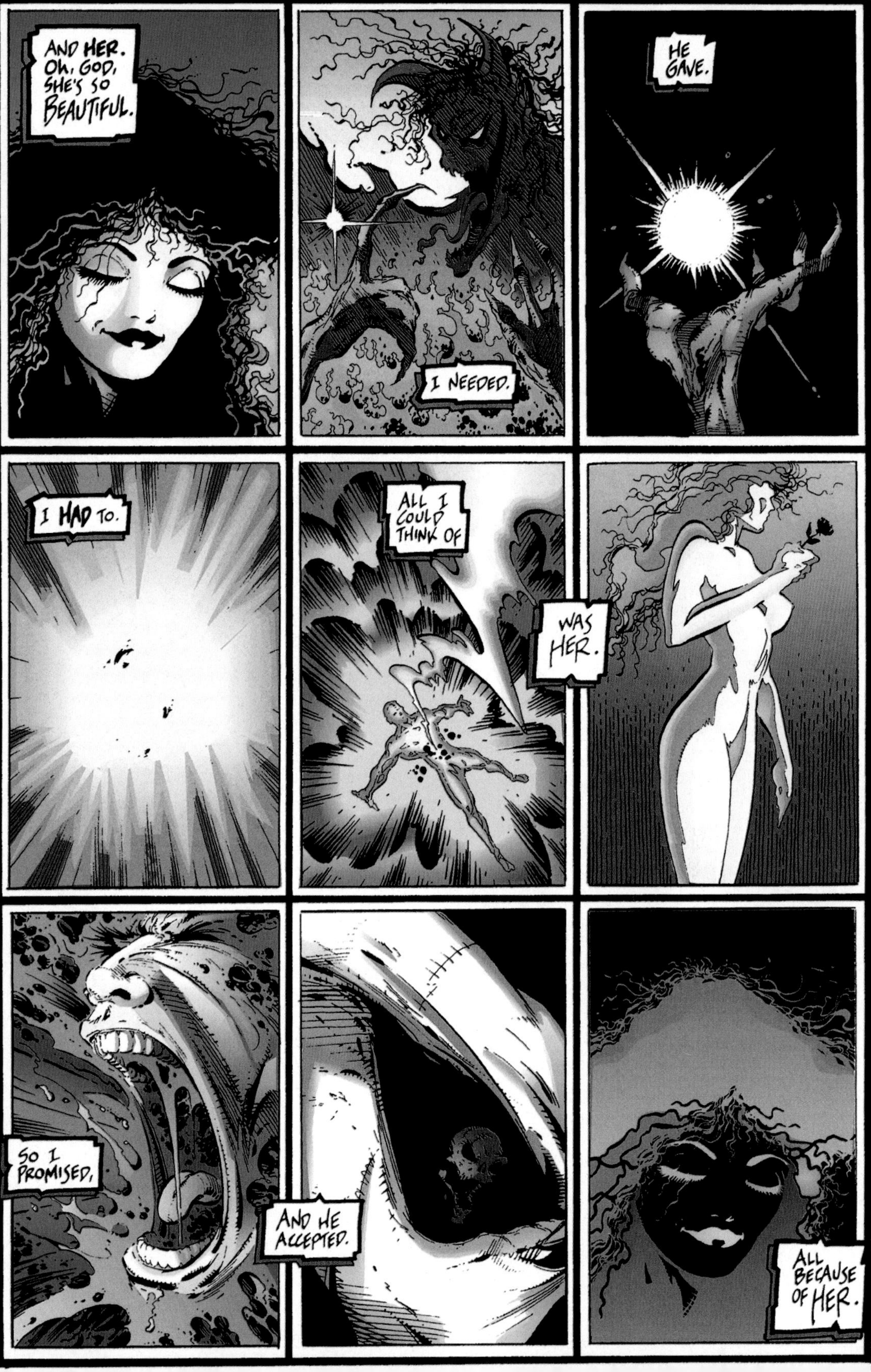
AND HER. Oh, GOD, SHE'S SO BEAUTIFUL.
I NEEDED.
HE GAVE.
I HAD TO.
ALL I COULD THINK OF
WAS HER.
SO I PROMISED,
AND HE ACCEPTED.
ALL BECAUSE OF HER.

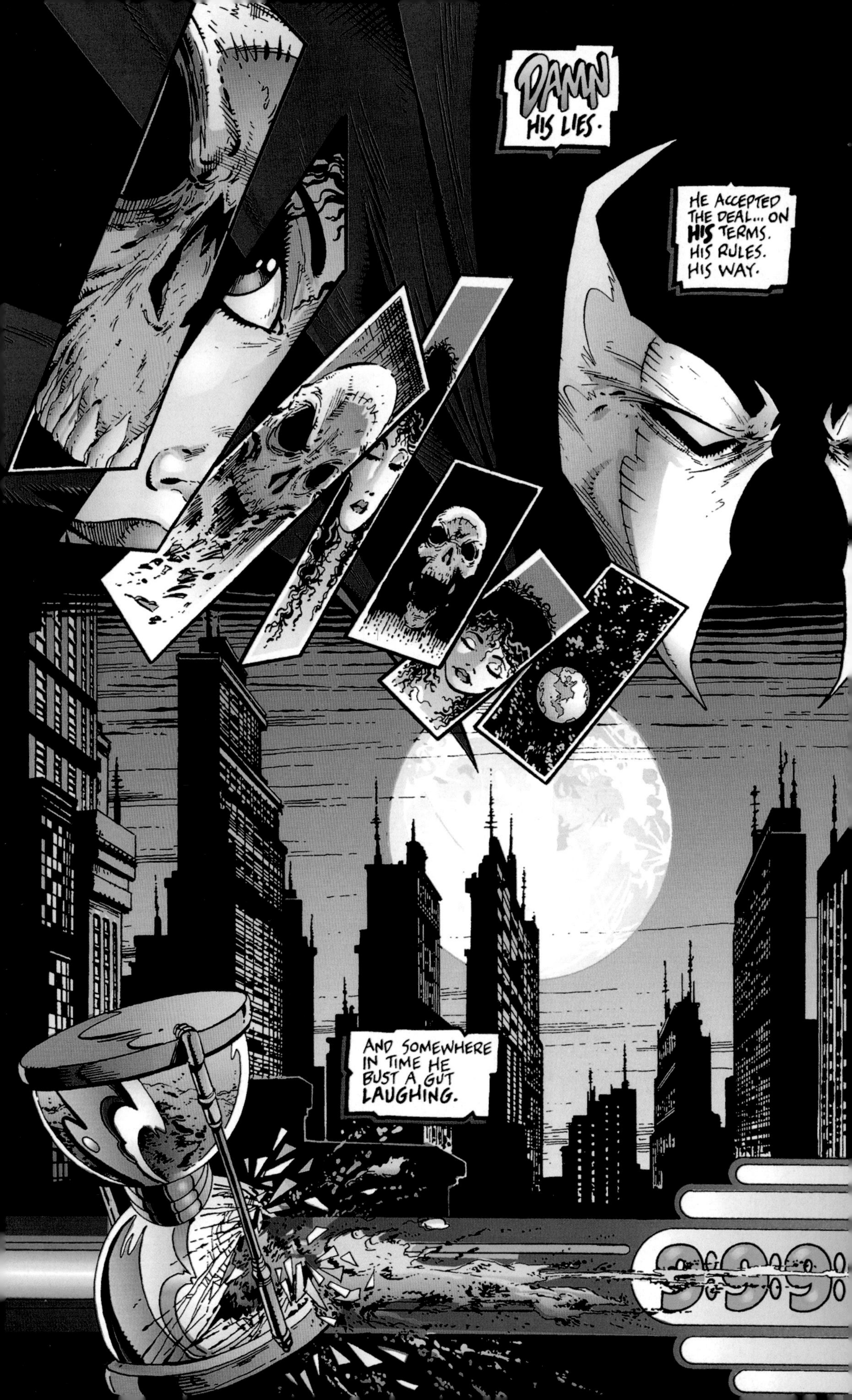
DAMN HIS LIES.
HE ACCEPTED THE DEAL... ON HIS TERMS. HIS RULES. HIS WAY.
AND SOMEWHERE IN TIME HE BUST A GUT LAUGHING.
9999

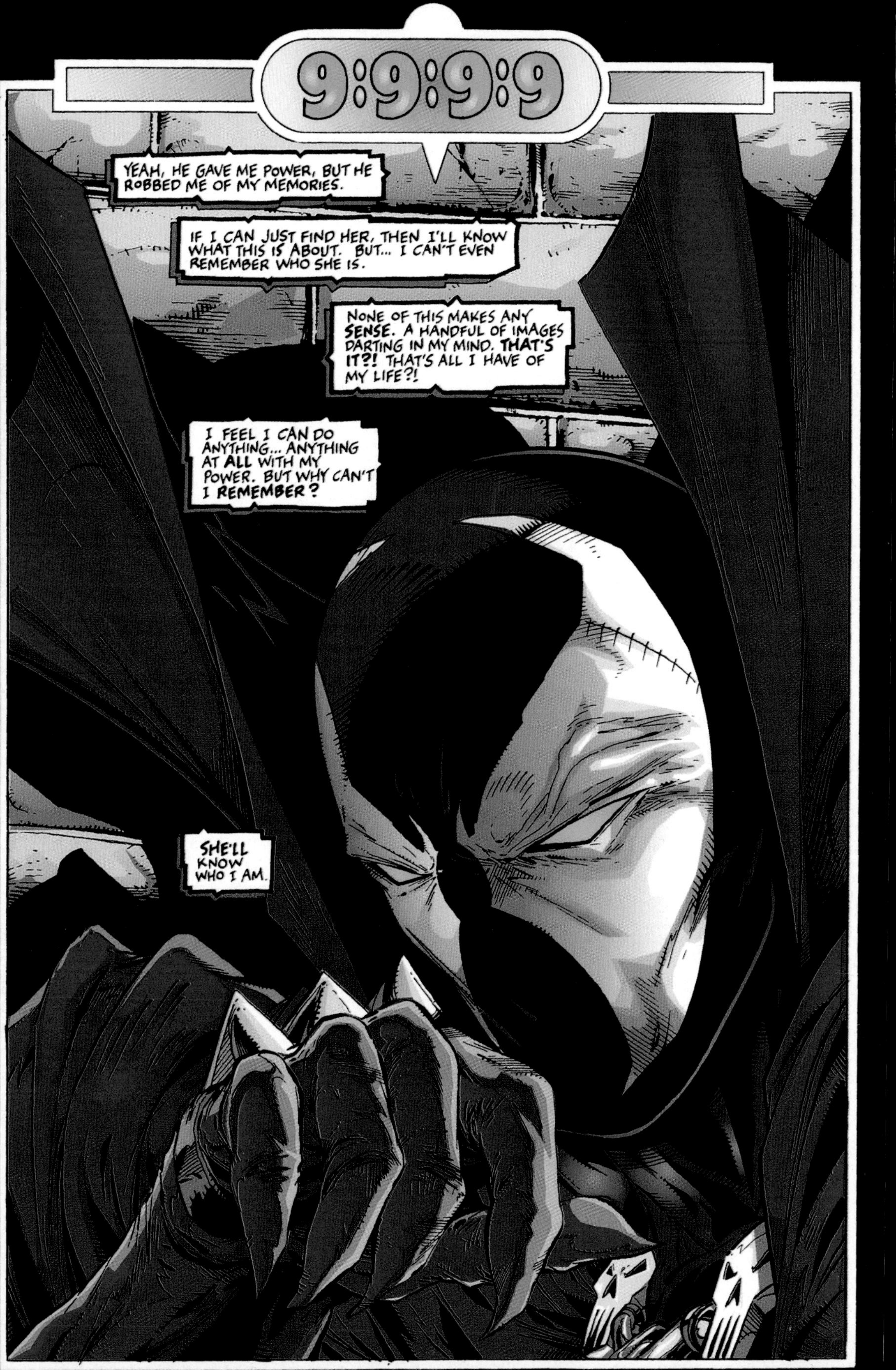
9:9:9:9
YEAH, HE GAVE ME POWER, BUT HE ROBBED ME OF MY MEMORIES.
IF I CAN JUST FIND HER, THEN I'LL KNOW WHAT THIS IS ABOUT. BUT... I CAN'T EVEN REMEMBER WHO SHE IS.
NONE OF THIS MAKES ANY SENSE. A HANDFUL OF IMAGES DARTING IN MY MIND. THAT'S IT?! THAT'S ALL I HAVE OF MY LIFE?!
I FEEL I CAN DO ANYTHING... ANYTHING AT ALL WITH MY POWER. BUT WHY CAN'T I REMEMBER?
SHE'LL KNOW WHO I AM.

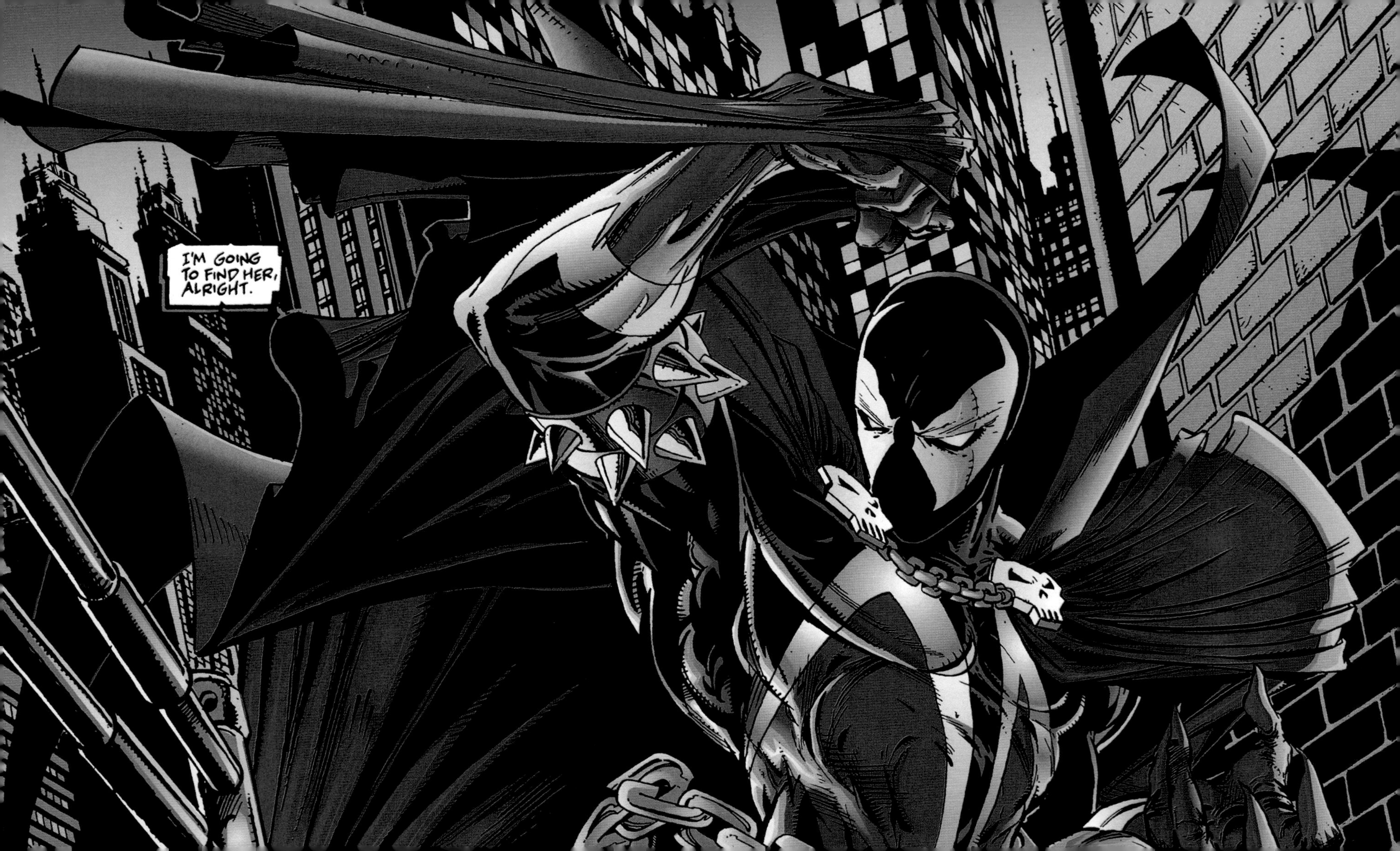
I'M GOING TO FIND HER, ALRIGHT.

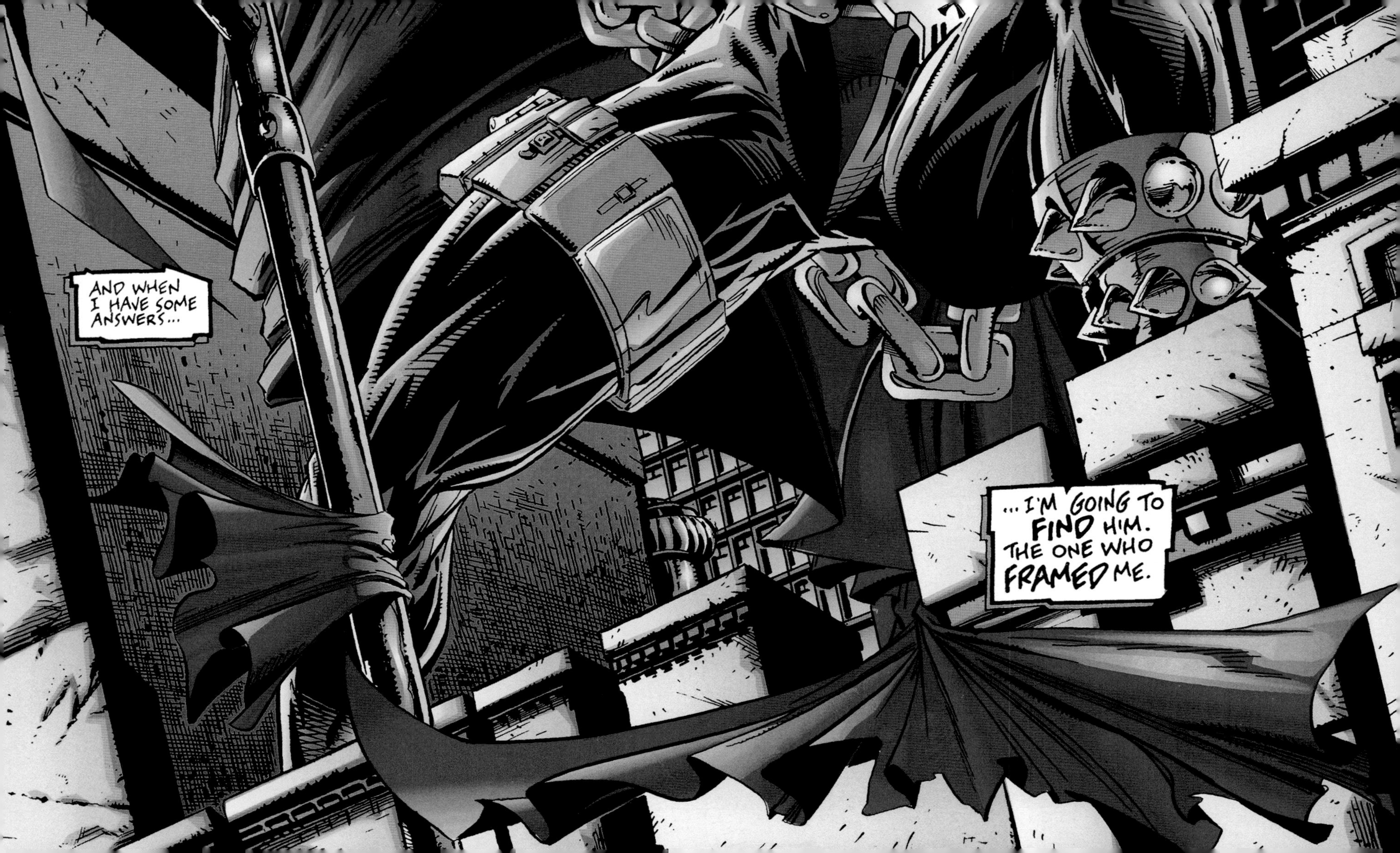
AND WHEN I HAVE SOME ANSWERS...
...I'M GOING TO FIND HIM. THE ONE WHO FRAMED ME.

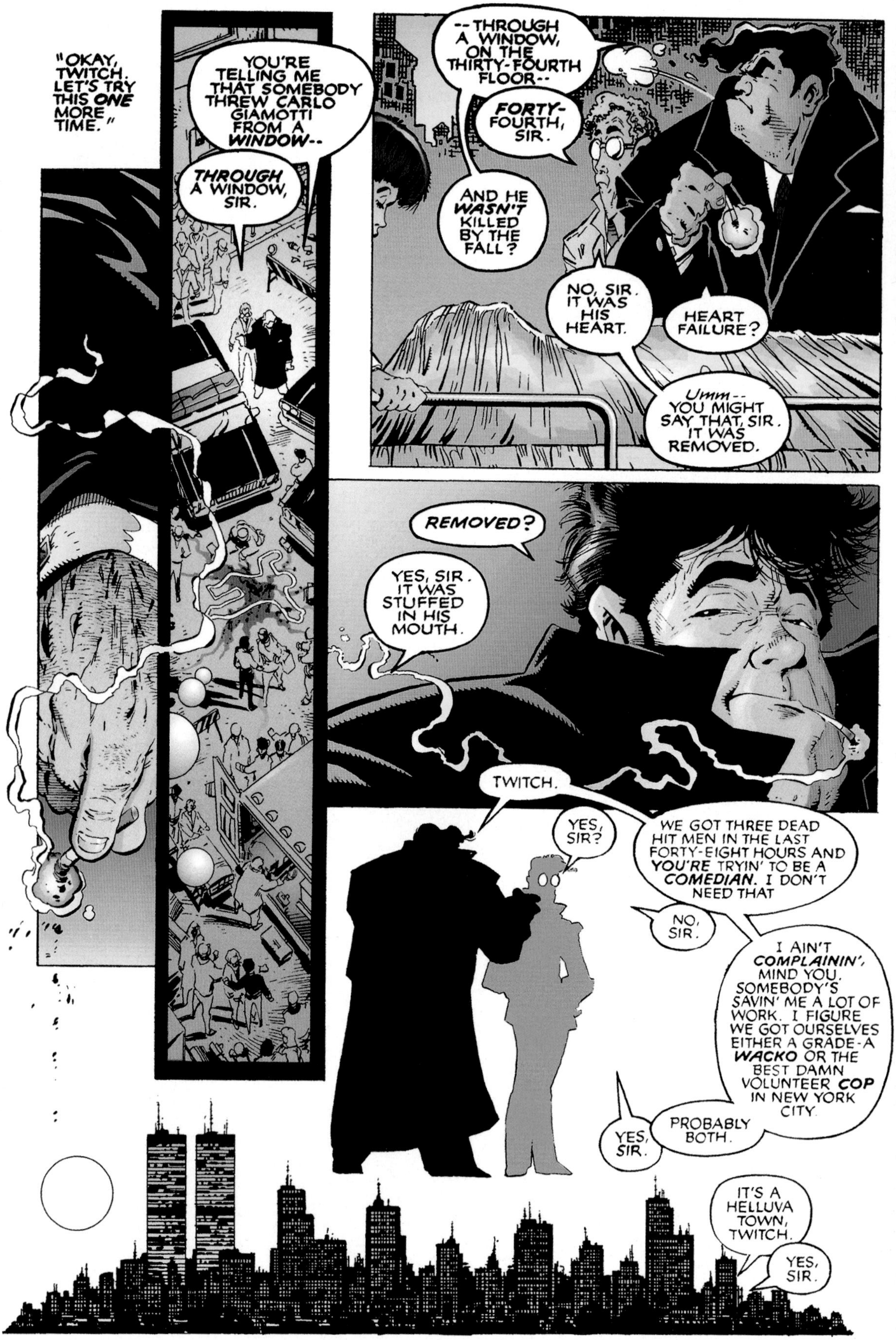
"OKAY, TWITCH. LET'S TRY THIS ONE MORE TIME."
YOU'RE TELLING ME THAT SOMEBODY THREW CARLO GIAMOTTI FROM A WINDOW--
THROUGH A WINDOW, SIR.
--THROUGH A WINDOW, ON THE THIRTY-FOURTH FLOOR--
FORTY-FOURTH, SIR.
AND HE WASN'T KILLED BY THE FALL?
NO, SIR. IT WAS HIS HEART.
HEART FAILURE?
Umm-- YOU MIGHT SAY THAT, SIR. IT WAS REMOVED.
REMOVED?
YES, SIR. IT WAS STUFFED IN HIS MOUTH.
TWITCH.
YES, SIR?
WE GOT THREE DEAD HIT MEN IN THE LAST FORTY-EIGHT HOURS AND YOU'RE TRYIN' TO BE A COMEDIAN. I DON'T NEED THAT
NO, SIR.
I AIN'T COMPLAININ', MIND YOU. SOMEBODY'S SAVIN' ME A LOT OF WORK. I FIGURE WE GOT OURSELVES EITHER A GRADE-A WACKO OR THE BEST DAMN VOLUNTEER COP IN NEW YORK CITY.
YES, SIR.
PROBABLY BOTH.
IT'S A HELLUVA TOWN, TWITCH.
YES, SIR.

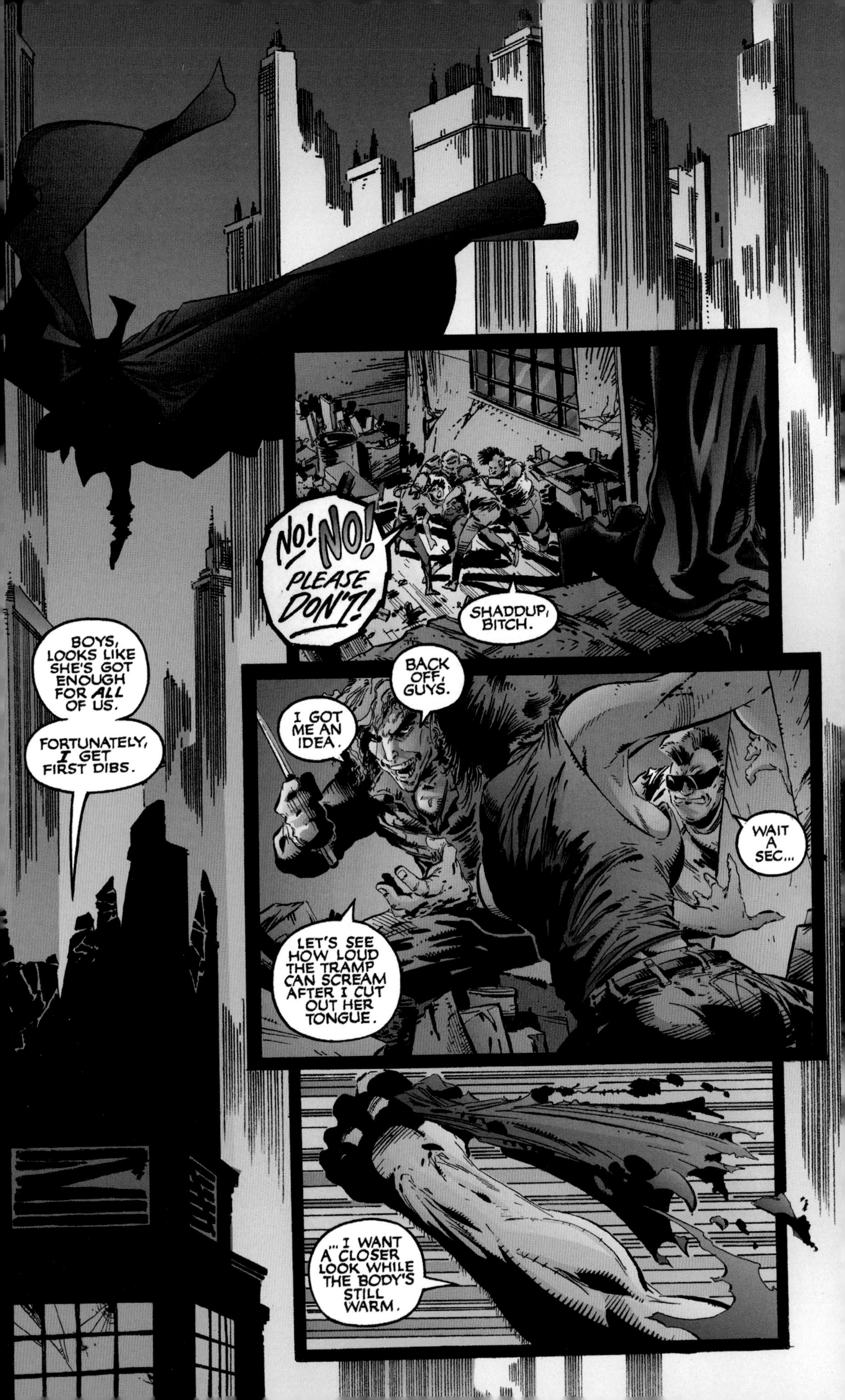
NO! NO! PLEASE DON'T!
SHADDUP, BITCH.
BOYS, LOOKS LIKE SHE'S GOT ENOUGH FOR ALL OF US.
FORTUNATELY, I GET FIRST DIBS.
BACK OFF, GUYS.
I GOT ME AN IDEA.
LET'S SEE HOW LOUD THE TRAMP CAN SCREAM AFTER I CUT OUT HER TONGUE.
WAIT A SEC...
...I WANT A CLOSER LOOK WHILE THE BODY'S STILL WARM.

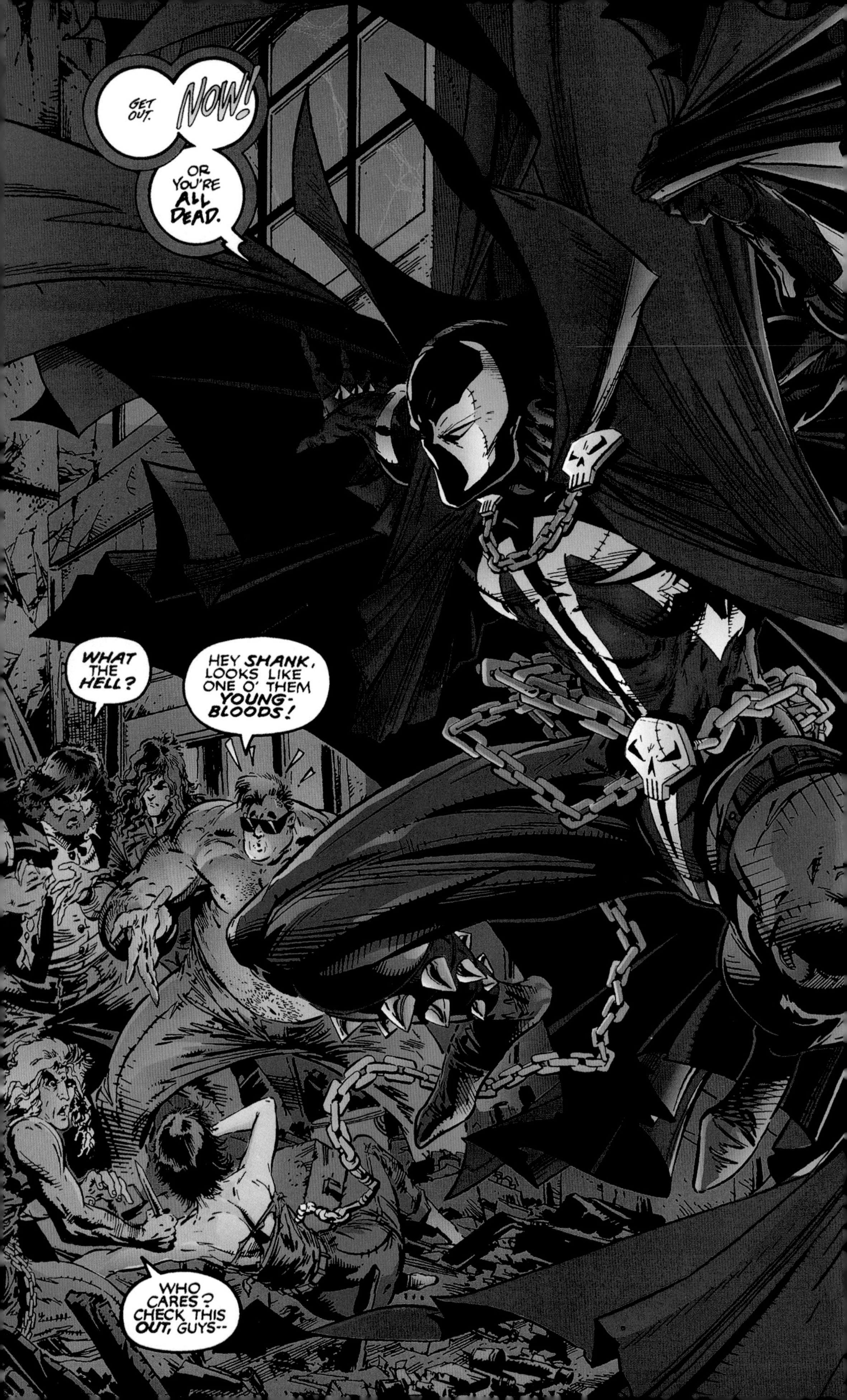
GET OUT. NOW!
OR YOU'RE ALL DEAD.
WHAT THE HELL?
HEY SHANK, LOOKS LIKE ONE O' THEM YOUNG-BLOODS!
WHO CARES? CHECK THIS OUT, GUYS--

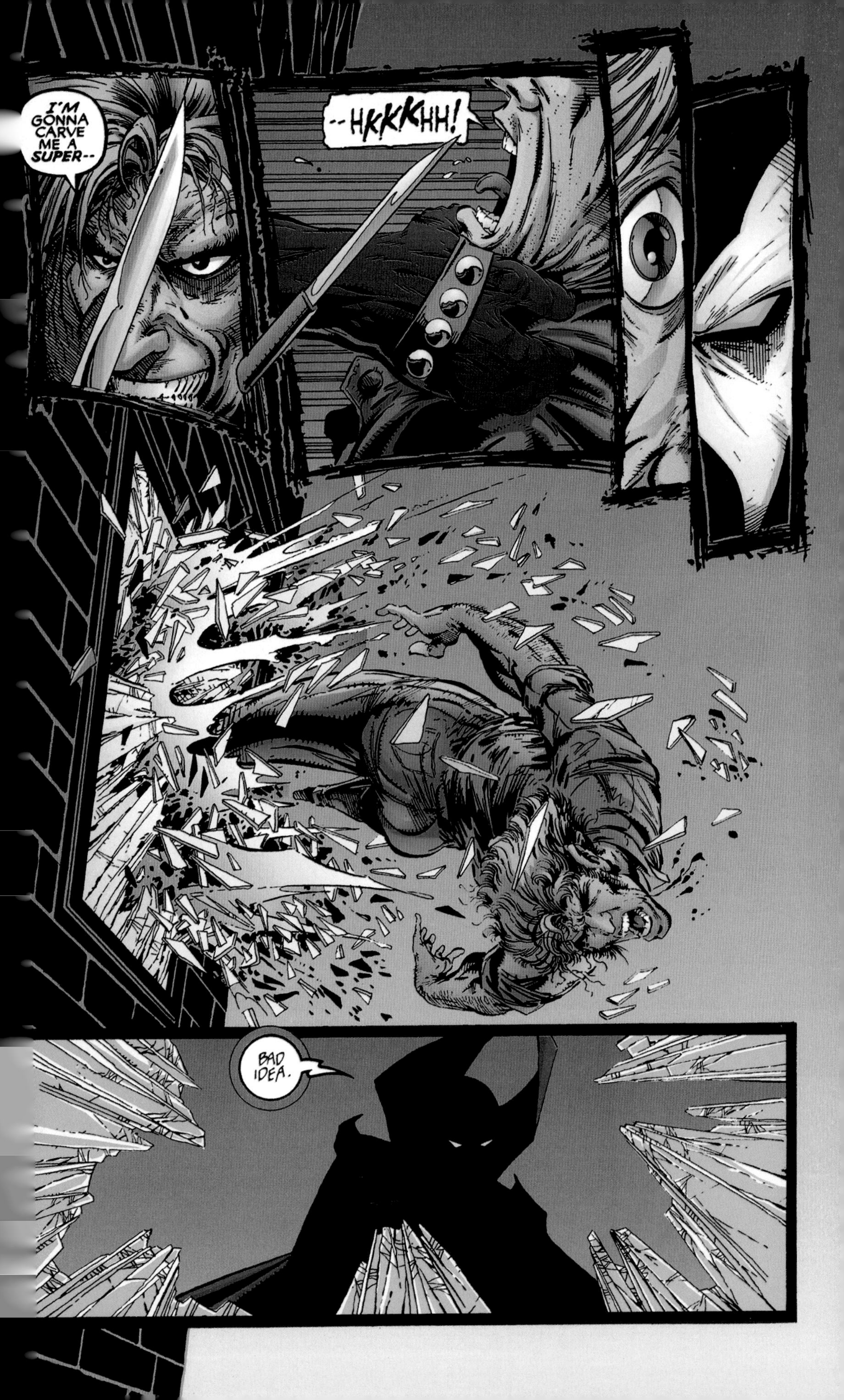
I'M GONNA CARVE ME A SUPER--
--HKKKHH!
BAD IDEA.

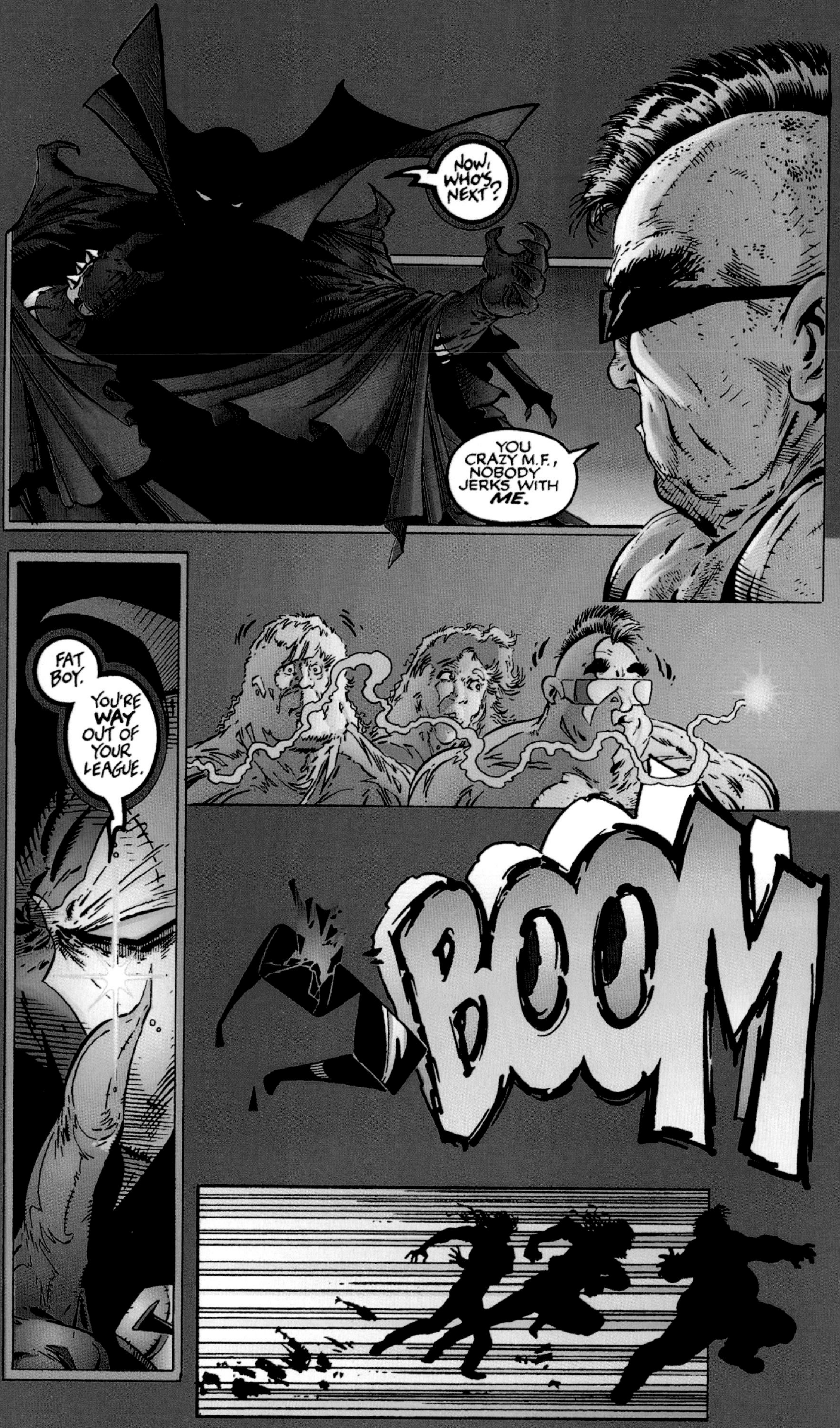
NOW, WHO'S NEXT?
YOU CRAZY M.F., NOBODY JERKS WITH ME.
FAT BOY.
YOU'RE WAY OUT OF YOUR LEAGUE.
BOOM

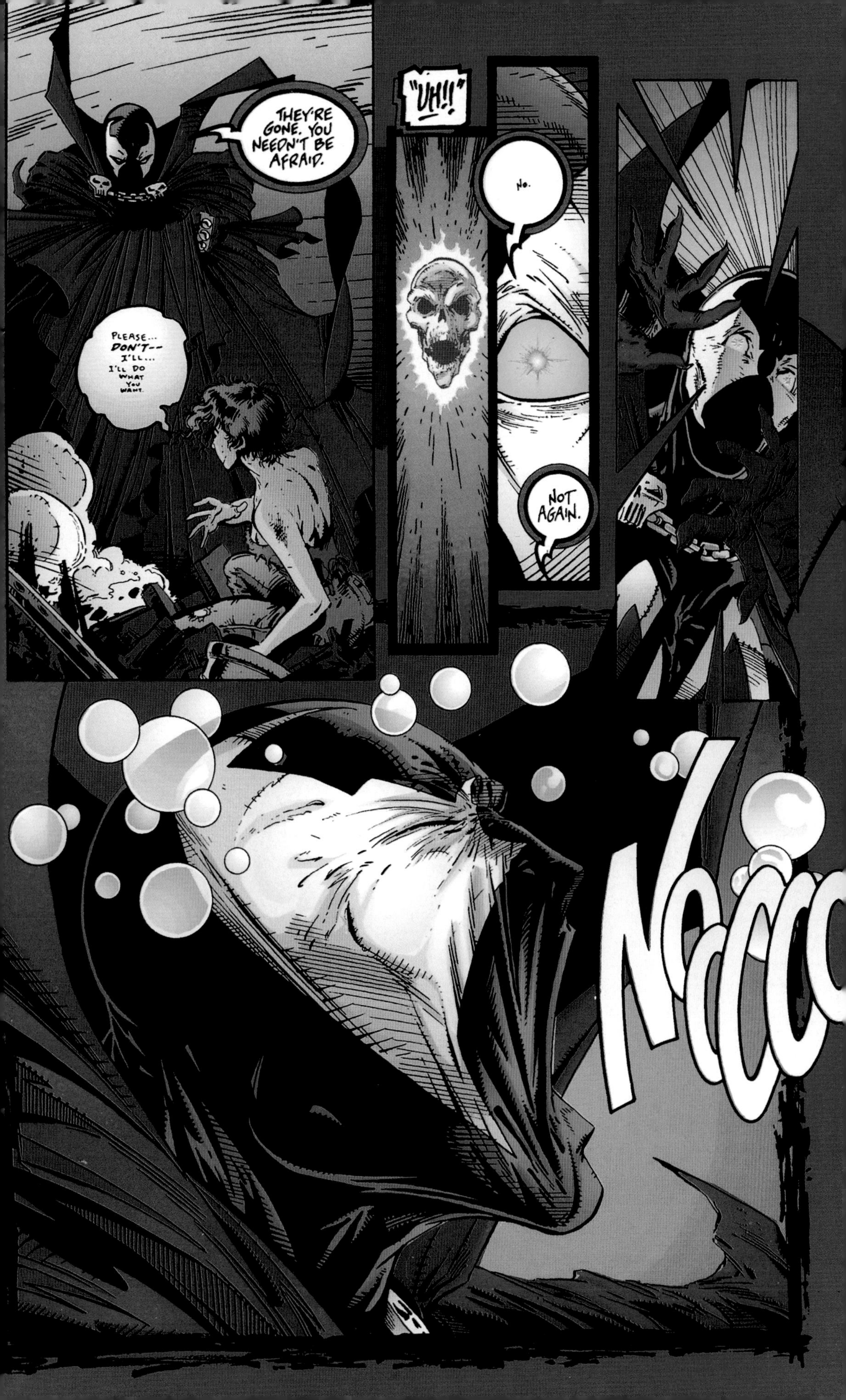
THEY'RE GONE. YOU NEEDN'T BE AFRAID.
PLEASE... DON'T-- I'LL... I'LL DO WHAT YOU WANT.
"UH!!"
NO.
NOT AGAIN.
NOOOO

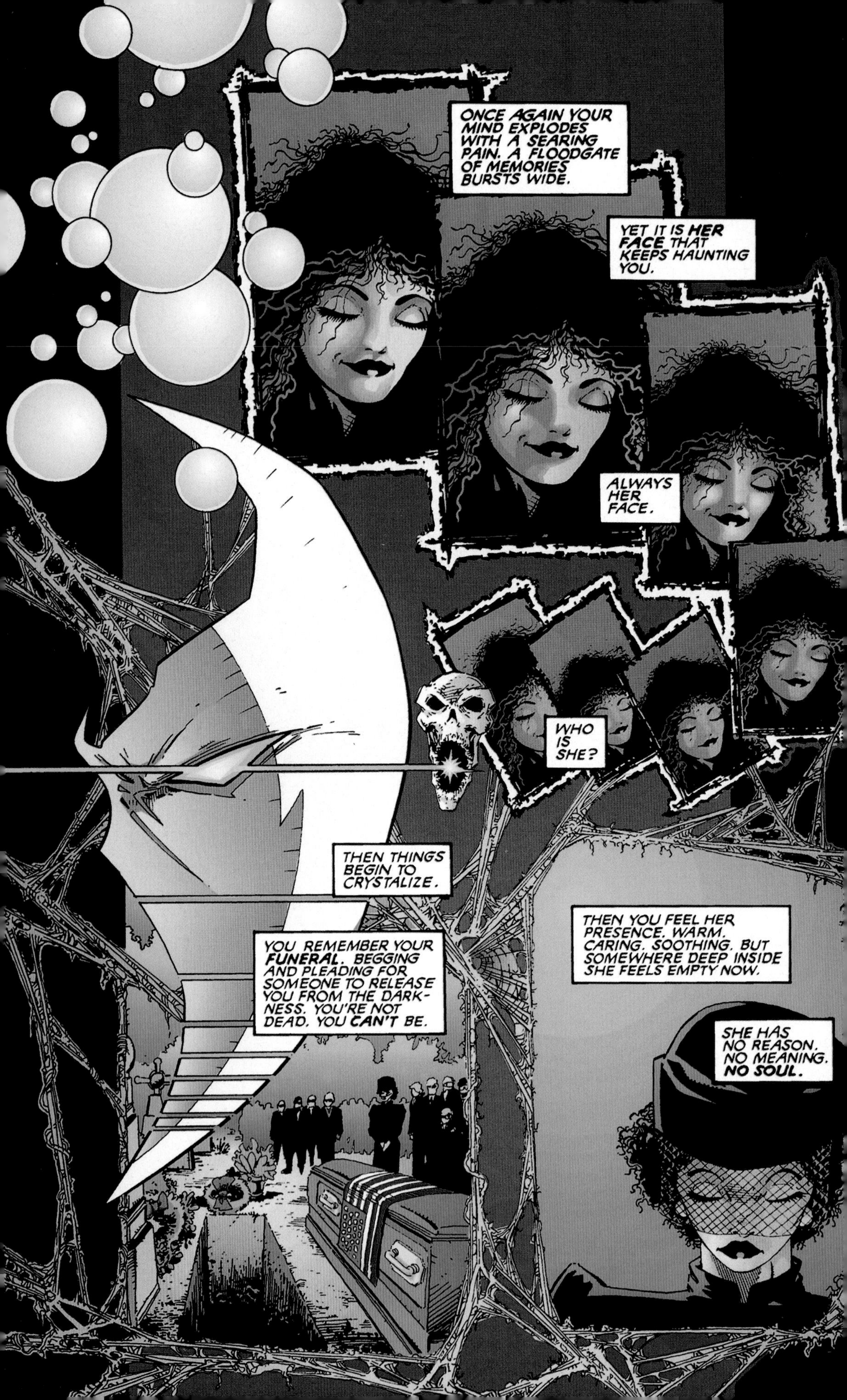
ONCE AGAIN YOUR MIND EXPLODES WITH A SEARING PAIN. A FLOODGATE OF MEMORIES BURSTS WIDE.
YET IT IS HER FACE THAT KEEPS HAUNTING YOU.
ALWAYS HER FACE.
WHO IS SHE?
THEN THINGS BEGIN TO CRYSTALIZE.
YOU REMEMBER YOUR FUNERAL. BEGGING AND PLEADING FOR SOMEONE TO RELEASE YOU FROM THE DARK-NESS. YOU'RE NOT DEAD. YOU CAN'T BE.
THEN YOU FEEL HER PRESENCE. WARM. CARING. SOOTHING. BUT SOMEWHERE DEEP INSIDE SHE FEELS EMPTY NOW.
SHE HAS NO REASON. NO MEANING. NO SOUL.

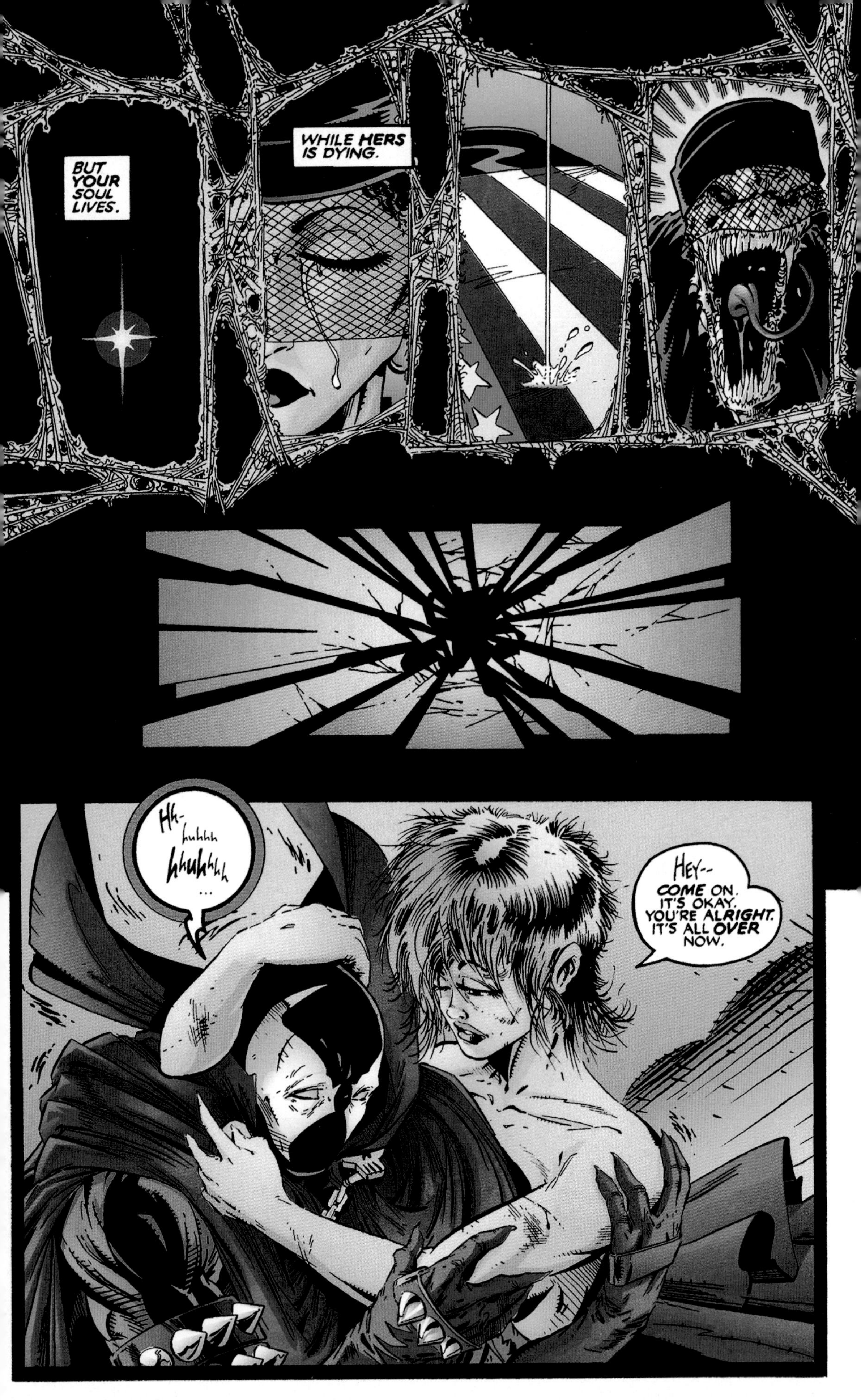
BUT YOUR SOUL LIVES.
WHILE HERS IS DYING.
Hh-huhhh hhuhhhh...
HEY-- COME ON. IT'S OKAY. YOU'RE ALRIGHT. IT'S ALL OVER NOW.

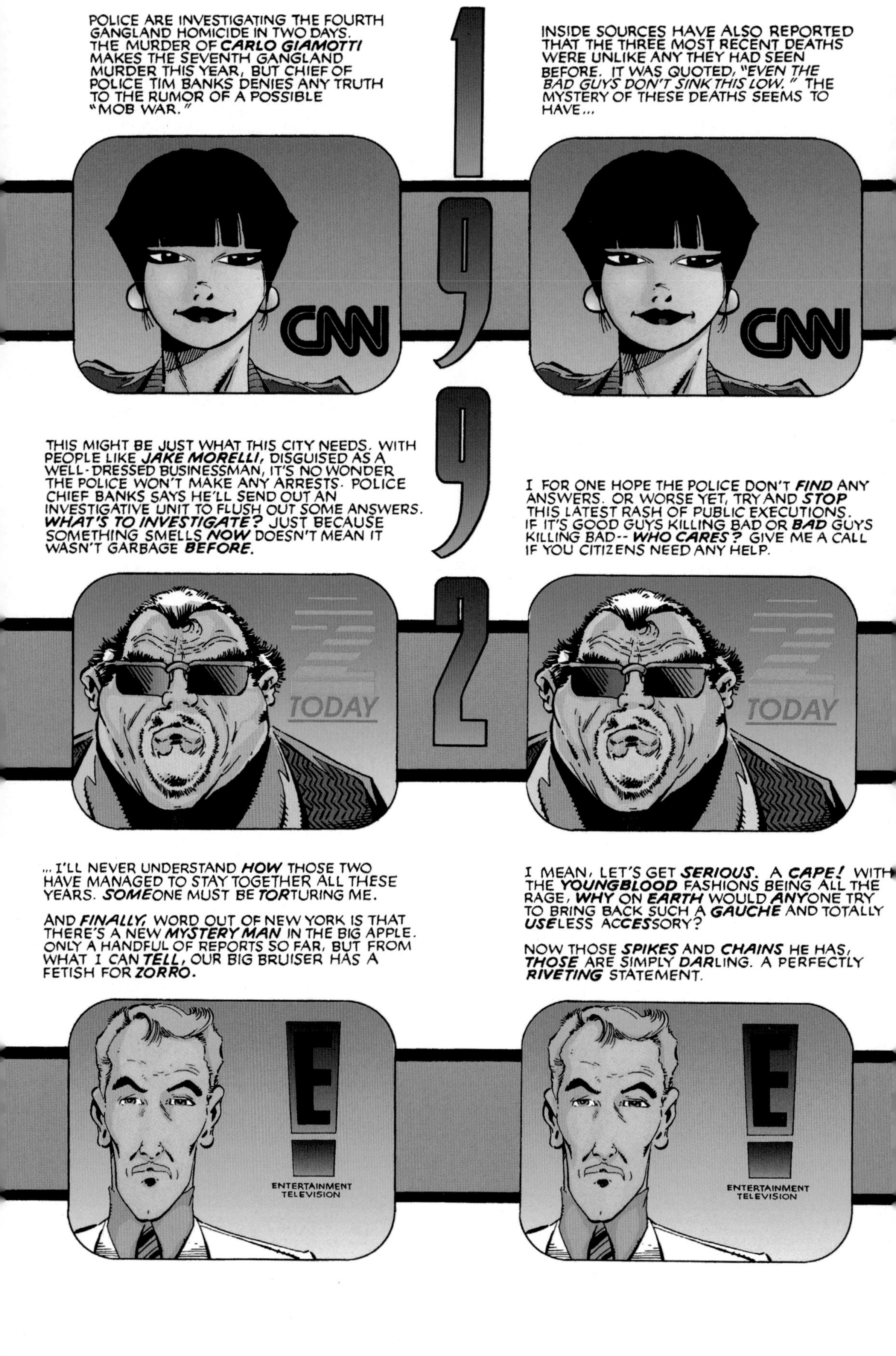

1992
POLICE ARE INVESTIGATING THE FOURTH GANGLAND HOMICIDE IN TWO DAYS. THE MURDER OF CARLO GIAMOTTI MAKES THE SEVENTH GANGLAND MURDER THIS YEAR, BUT CHIEF OF POLICE TIM BANKS DENIES ANY TRUTH TO THE RUMOR OF A POSSIBLE "MOB WAR."
CNN
INSIDE SOURCES HAVE ALSO REPORTED THAT THE THREE MOST RECENT DEATHS WERE UNLIKE ANY THEY HAD SEEN BEFORE. IT WAS QUOTED, "EVEN THE BAD GUYS DON'T SINK THIS LOW." THE MYSTERY OF THESE DEATHS SEEMS TO HAVE...
CNN
THIS MIGHT BE JUST WHAT THIS CITY NEEDS. WITH PEOPLE LIKE JAKE MORELLI, DISGUISED AS A WELL-DRESSED BUSINESSMAN, IT'S NO WONDER THE POLICE WON'T MAKE ANY ARRESTS. POLICE CHIEF BANKS SAYS HE'LL SEND OUT AN INVESTIGATIVE UNIT TO FLUSH OUT SOME ANSWERS. WHAT'S TO INVESTIGATE? JUST BECAUSE SOMETHING SMELLS NOW DOESN'T MEAN IT WASN'T GARBAGE BEFORE.
TODAY
I FOR ONE HOPE THE POLICE DON'T FIND ANY ANSWERS. OR WORSE YET, TRY AND STOP THIS LATEST RASH OF PUBLIC EXECUTIONS. IF IT'S GOOD GUYS KILLING BAD OR BAD GUYS KILLING BAD-- WHO CARES? GIVE ME A CALL IF YOU CITIZENS NEED ANY HELP.
TODAY
...I'LL NEVER UNDERSTAND HOW THOSE TWO HAVE MANAGED TO STAY TOGETHER ALL THESE YEARS. SOMEONE MUST BE TORTURING ME.
AND FINALLY, WORD OUT OF NEW YORK IS THAT THERE'S A NEW MYSTERY MAN IN THE BIG APPLE. ONLY A HANDFUL OF REPORTS SO FAR, BUT FROM WHAT I CAN TELL, OUR BIG BRUISER HAS A FETISH FOR ZORRO.
ENTERTAINMENT TELEVISION
I MEAN, LET'S GET SERIOUS. A CAPE! WITH THE YOUNGBLOOD FASHIONS BEING ALL THE RAGE, WHY ON EARTH WOULD ANYONE TRY TO BRING BACK SUCH A GAUCHE AND TOTALLY USELESS ACCESSORY?
NOW THOSE SPIKES AND CHAINS HE HAS, THOSE ARE SIMPLY DARLING. A PERFECTLY RIVETING STATEMENT.
ENTERTAINMENT TELEVISION

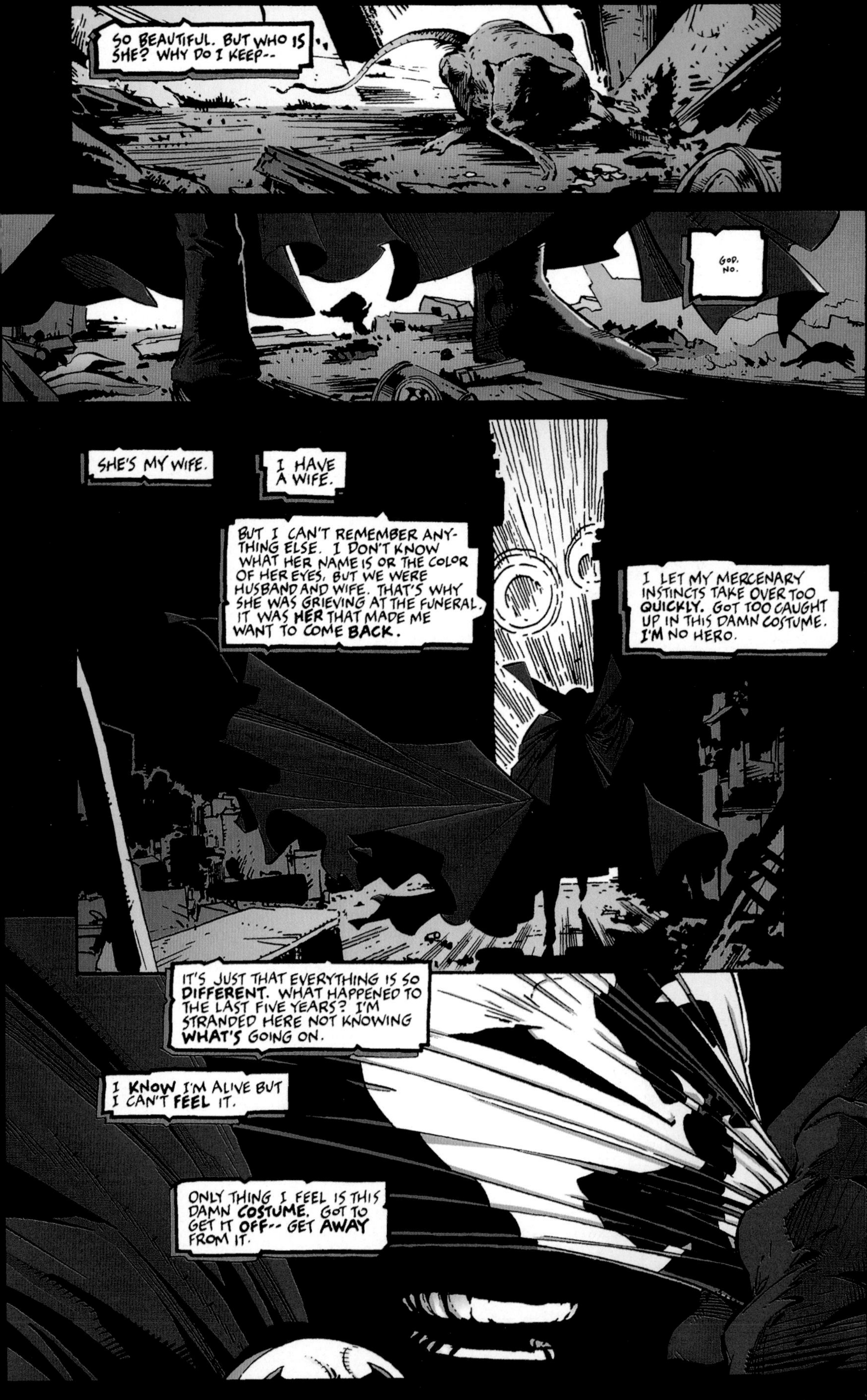
SO BEAUTIFUL. BUT WHO IS SHE? WHY DO I KEEP--
GOD. NO.
SHE'S MY WIFE.
I HAVE A WIFE.
BUT I CAN'T REMEMBER ANYTHING ELSE. I DON'T KNOW WHAT HER NAME IS OR THE COLOR OF HER EYES, BUT WE WERE HUSBAND AND WIFE. THAT'S WHY SHE WAS GRIEVING AT THE FUNERAL. IT WAS HER THAT MADE ME WANT TO COME BACK.
I LET MY MERCENARY INSTINCTS TAKE OVER TOO QUICKLY. GOT TOO CAUGHT UP IN THIS DAMN COSTUME. I'M NO HERO.
IT'S JUST THAT EVERYTHING IS SO DIFFERENT. WHAT HAPPENED TO THE LAST FIVE YEARS? I'M STRANDED HERE NOT KNOWING WHAT'S GOING ON.
I KNOW I'M ALIVE BUT I CAN'T FEEL IT.
ONLY THING I FEEL IS THIS DAMN COSTUME. GOT TO GET IT OFF-- GET AWAY FROM IT.

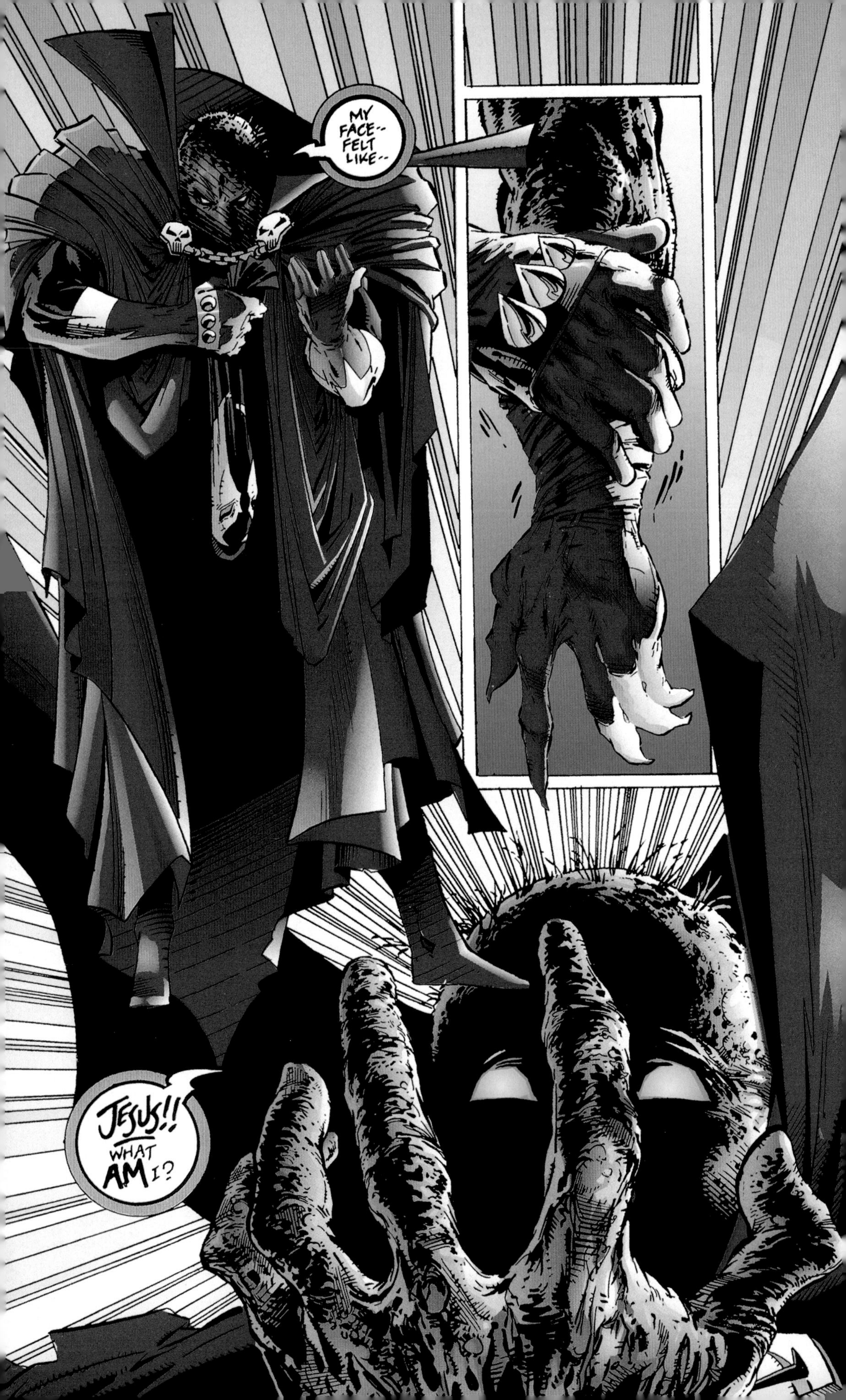
MY FACE-- FELT LIKE--
JESUS!! WHAT AM I?

WHAT AM I?

I DUNNO, TWITCH...

IF IT REALLY *IS* SOME GOVERNMENT HERO GONE WACKO, THEM WASHINGTON STIFFS AIN'T GONNA LET US GET CLOSE. THEM TIGHT ASSES. BUT IF THIS GUY DECIDES HE WANTS TO START SNUFFING OUT "JOE AVERAGE," THEN WE GOT OURSELVES A *SERIOUS* PROBLEM.

AND THE DAMAGE THIS GUY HAS DONE TO THOSE THREE BODIES IS FRIGGIN' *UNREAL*. WONDER HOW MUCH *POWER* THIS GUY HAS IN HIM?

 9:9:9:5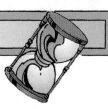

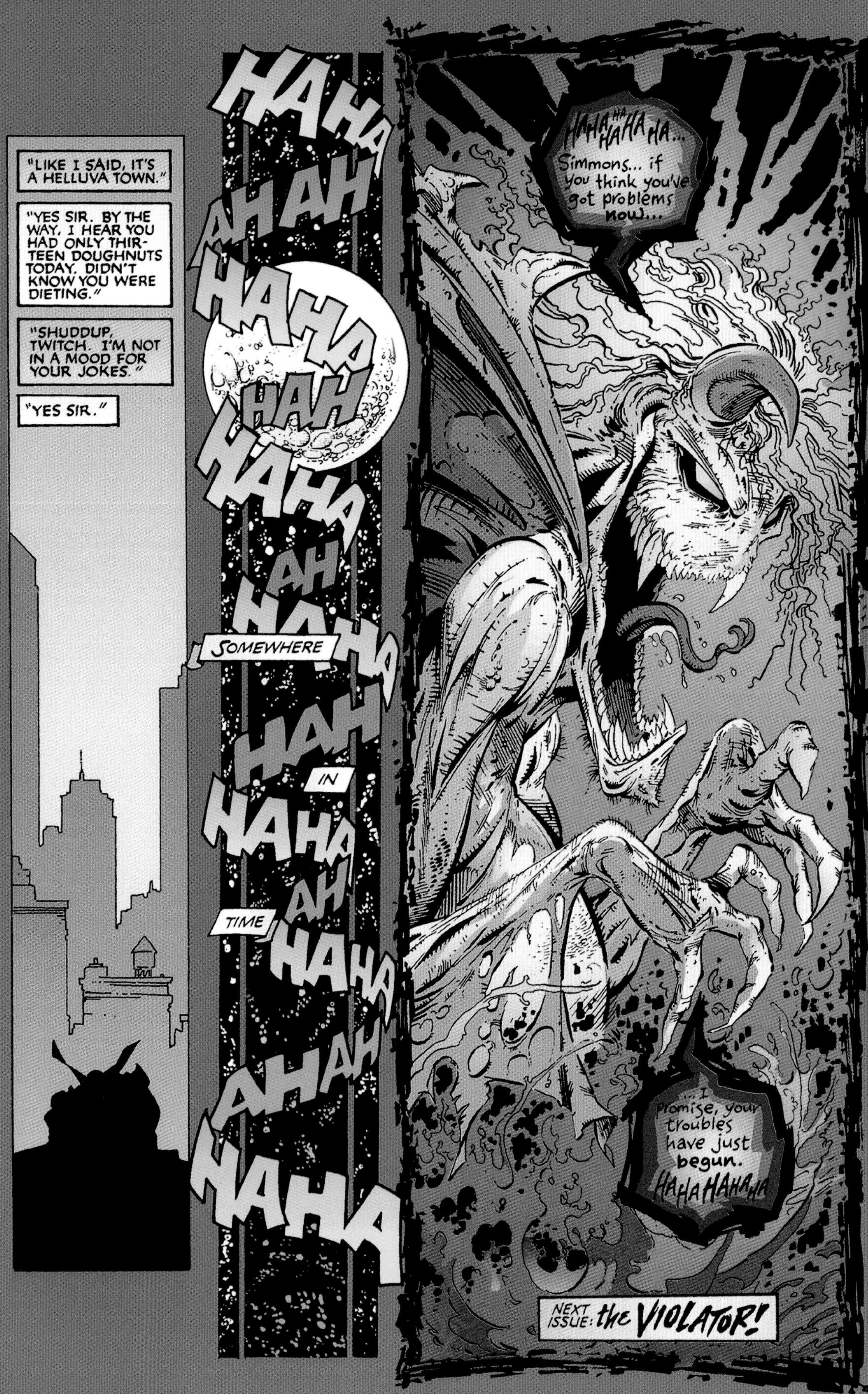

"LIKE I SAID, IT'S A HELLUVA TOWN."
"YES SIR. BY THE WAY, I HEAR YOU HAD ONLY THIRTEEN DOUGHNUTS TODAY. DIDN'T KNOW YOU WERE DIETING."
"SHUDDUP, TWITCH. I'M NOT IN A MOOD FOR YOUR JOKES."
"YES SIR."
HAHA AHAH HAHA HAH HAHA AH HAHA
SOMEWHERE
HAH
IN
HAHA AH
TIME
HAHA AHAH HAHA
HAHAHAHAHAHA... Simmons... if you think you've got problems now...
...I promise, your troubles have just begun. HAHA HAHAHA
NEXT ISSUE: the VIOLATOR!

<table>
<tr><td>2</td><td>JUL
1992</td></tr>
</table>

"QUESTIONS"

PART TWO

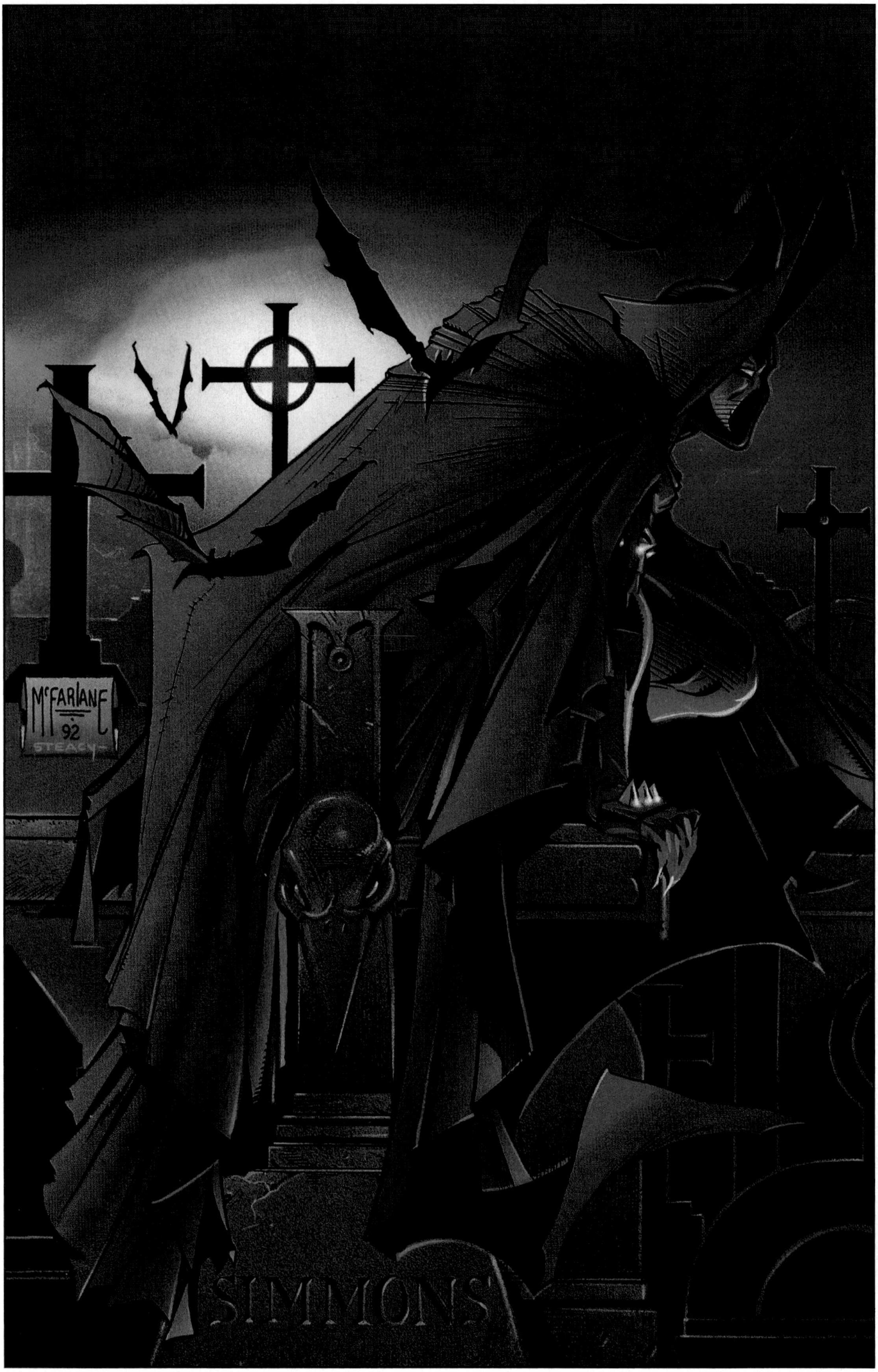
McFARLANE
92
STEACY
SIMMONS

Spawn #2, cover

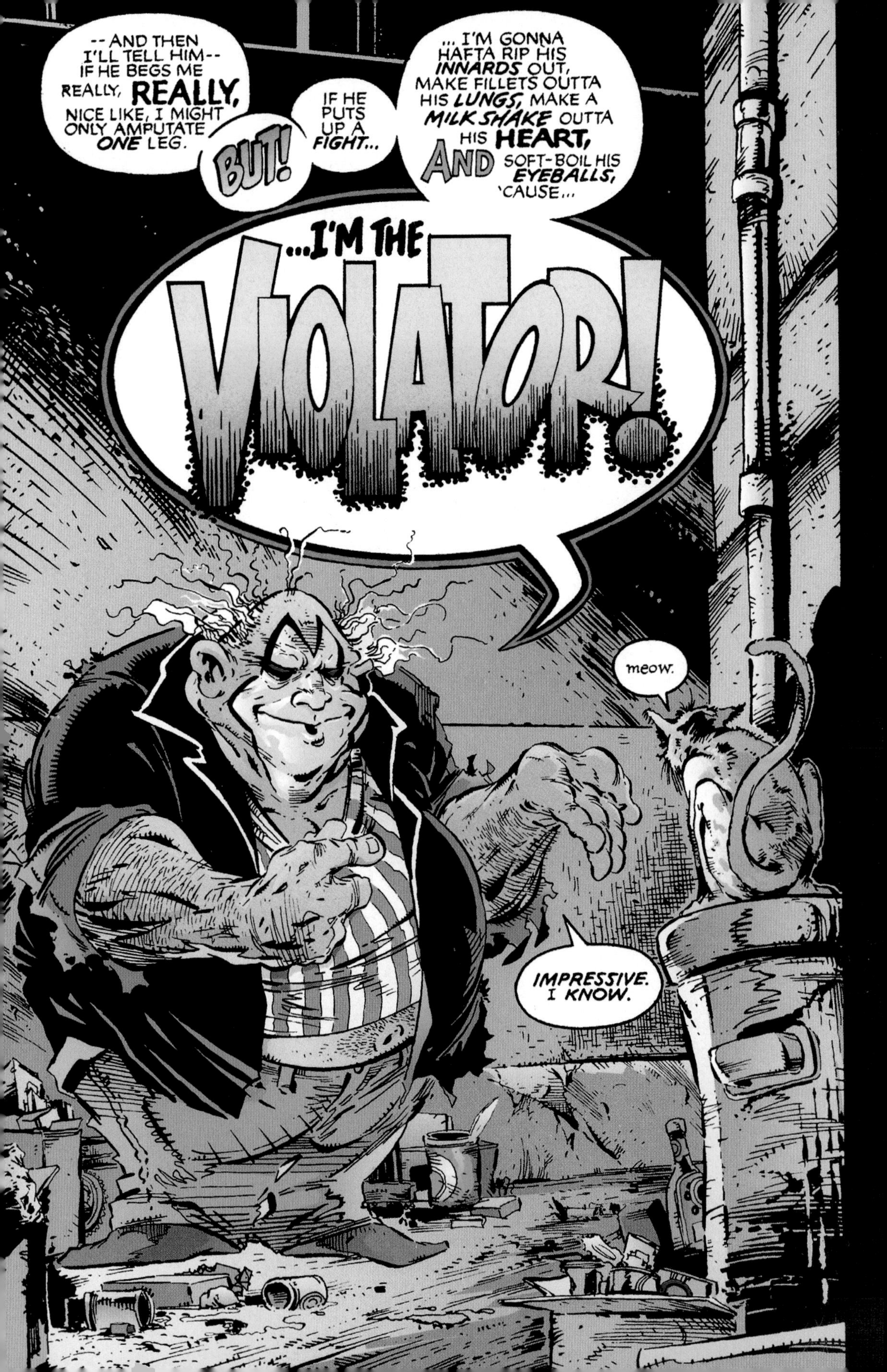
-- AND THEN I'LL TELL HIM-- IF HE BEGS ME REALLY, REALLY, NICE LIKE, I MIGHT ONLY AMPUTATE ONE LEG.
BUT!
IF HE PUTS UP A FIGHT...
... I'M GONNA HAFTA RIP HIS INNARDS OUT, MAKE FILLETS OUTTA HIS LUNGS, MAKE A MILK SHAKE OUTTA HIS HEART, AND SOFT-BOIL HIS EYEBALLS, 'CAUSE...
...I'M THE VIOLATOR!
meow.
IMPRESSIVE. I KNOW.

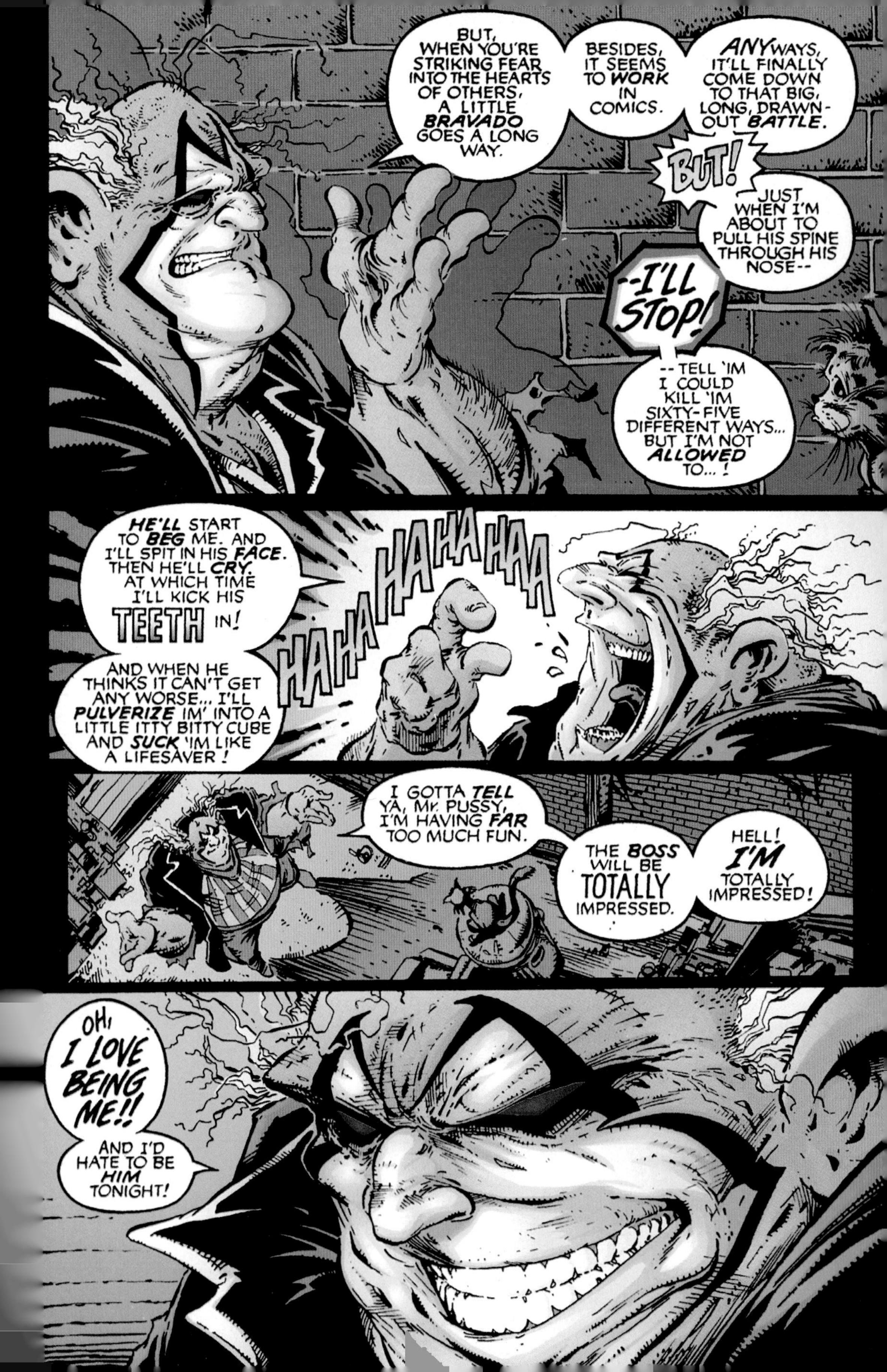
BUT, WHEN YOU'RE STRIKING FEAR INTO THE HEARTS OF OTHERS, A LITTLE BRAVADO GOES A LONG WAY.
BESIDES, IT SEEMS TO WORK IN COMICS.
ANYWAYS, IT'LL FINALLY COME DOWN TO THAT BIG, LONG, DRAWN-OUT BATTLE.
BUT!
JUST WHEN I'M ABOUT TO PULL HIS SPINE THROUGH HIS NOSE--
--I'LL STOP!
--TELL 'IM I COULD KILL 'IM SIXTY-FIVE DIFFERENT WAYS... BUT I'M NOT ALLOWED TO...!
HE'LL START TO BEG ME. AND I'LL SPIT IN HIS FACE. THEN HE'LL CRY. AT WHICH TIME I'LL KICK HIS TEETH IN!
AND WHEN HE THINKS IT CAN'T GET ANY WORSE... I'LL PULVERIZE IM' INTO A LITTLE ITTY BITTY CUBE AND SUCK 'IM LIKE A LIFESAVER!
HAHAHAHAHAHAA
I GOTTA TELL YA, Mr. PUSSY, I'M HAVING FAR TOO MUCH FUN.
THE BOSS WILL BE TOTALLY IMPRESSED.
HELL! I'M TOTALLY IMPRESSED!
OH, I LOVE BEING ME!!
AND I'D HATE TO BE HIM TONIGHT!

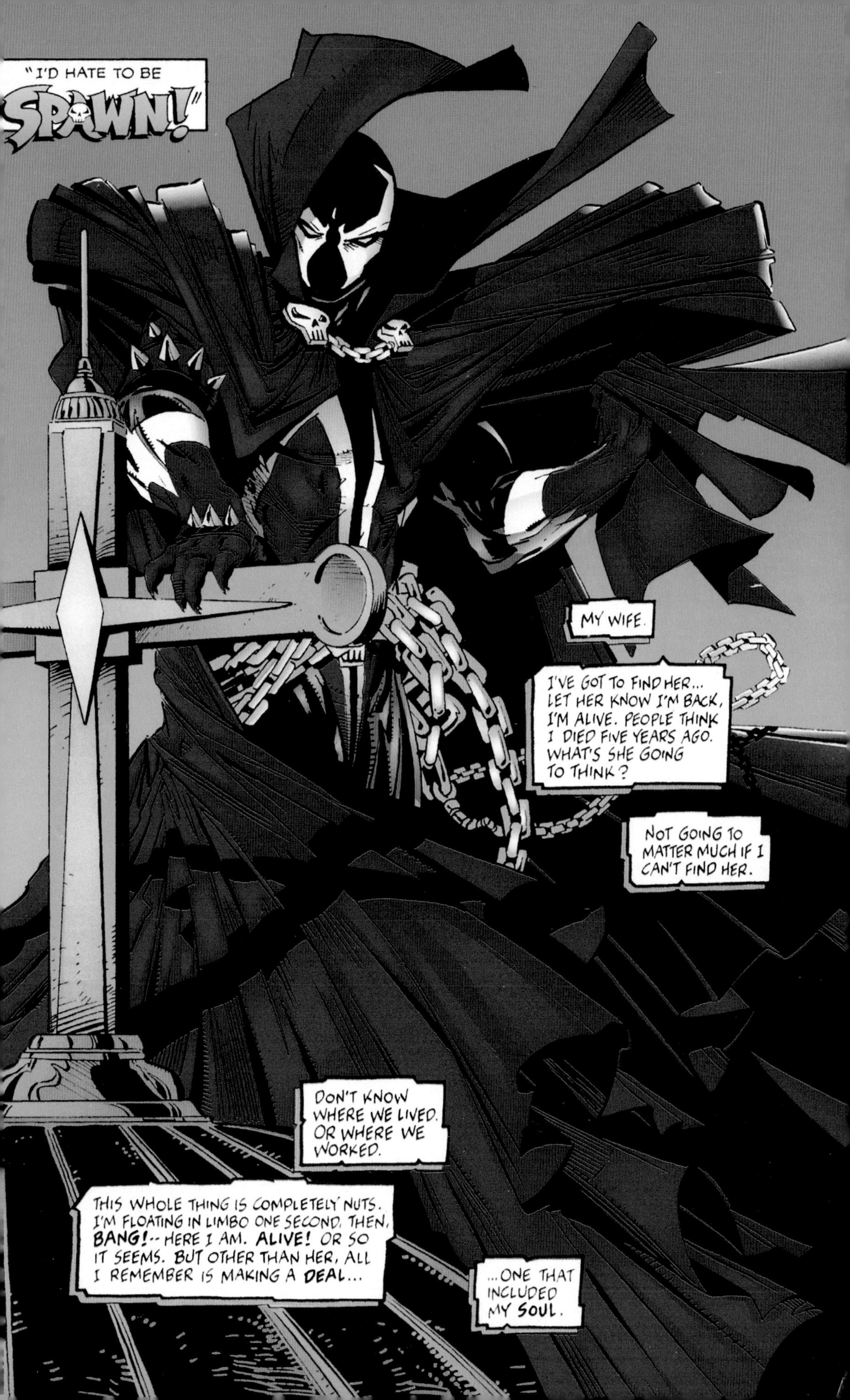
"I'D HATE TO BE
SPAWN!"
MY WIFE.
I'VE GOT TO FIND HER... LET HER KNOW I'M BACK, I'M ALIVE. PEOPLE THINK I DIED FIVE YEARS AGO. WHAT'S SHE GOING TO THINK?
NOT GOING TO MATTER MUCH IF I CAN'T FIND HER.
DON'T KNOW WHERE WE LIVED. OR WHERE WE WORKED.
THIS WHOLE THING IS COMPLETELY NUTS. I'M FLOATING IN LIMBO ONE SECOND. THEN, BANG!-- HERE I AM. ALIVE! OR SO IT SEEMS. BUT OTHER THAN HER, ALL I REMEMBER IS MAKING A DEAL...
...ONE THAT INCLUDED MY SOUL.

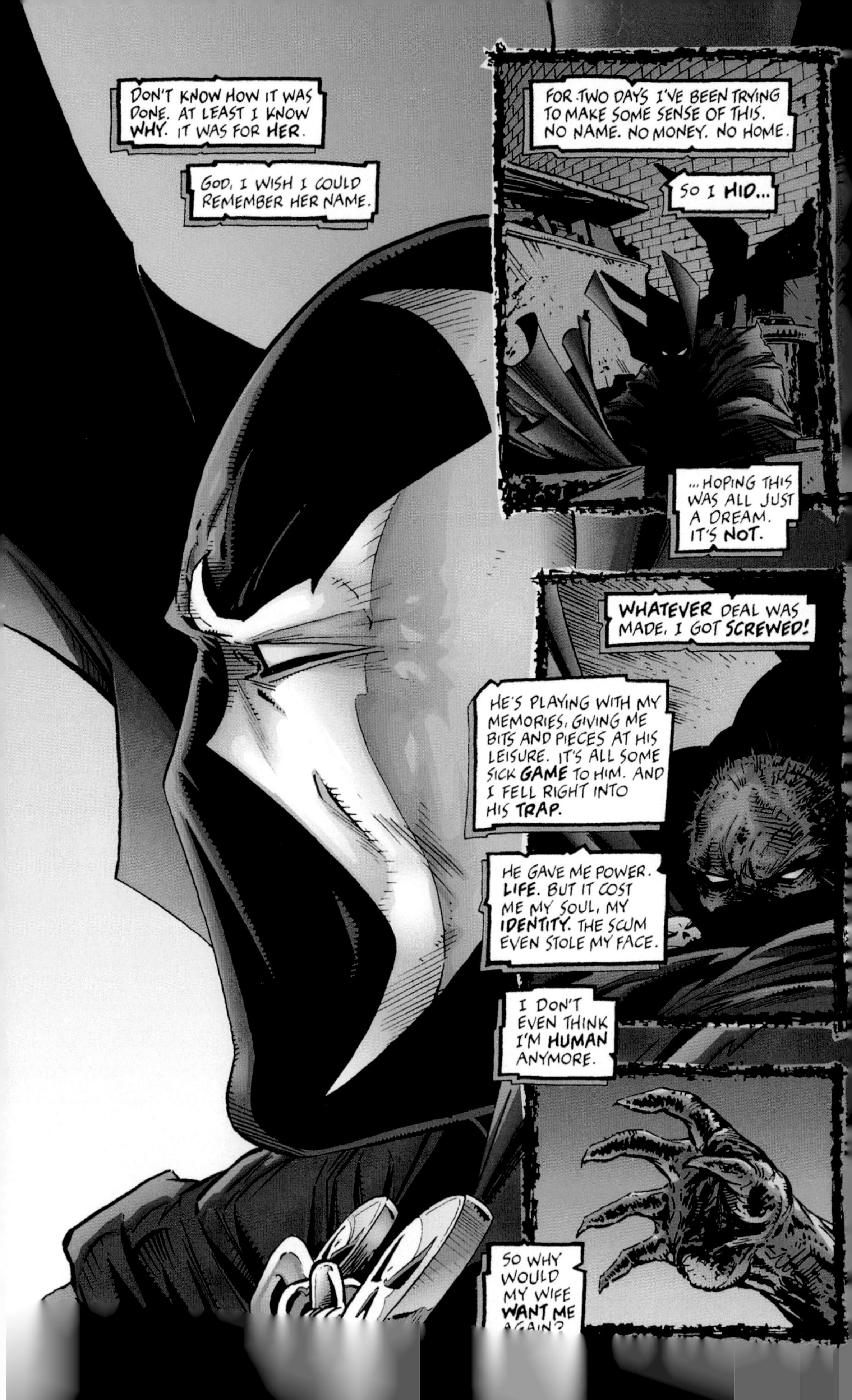

DON'T KNOW HOW IT WAS DONE. AT LEAST I KNOW WHY. IT WAS FOR HER.
GOD, I WISH I COULD REMEMBER HER NAME.
FOR TWO DAYS I'VE BEEN TRYING TO MAKE SOME SENSE OF THIS. NO NAME. NO MONEY. NO HOME.
SO I HID...
...HOPING THIS WAS ALL JUST A DREAM. IT'S NOT.
WHATEVER DEAL WAS MADE, I GOT SCREWED!
HE'S PLAYING WITH MY MEMORIES, GIVING ME BITS AND PIECES AT HIS LEISURE. IT'S ALL SOME SICK GAME TO HIM. AND I FELL RIGHT INTO HIS TRAP.
HE GAVE ME POWER. LIFE. BUT IT COST ME MY SOUL, MY IDENTITY. THE SCUM EVEN STOLE MY FACE.
I DON'T EVEN THINK I'M HUMAN ANYMORE.
SO WHY WOULD MY WIFE WANT ME

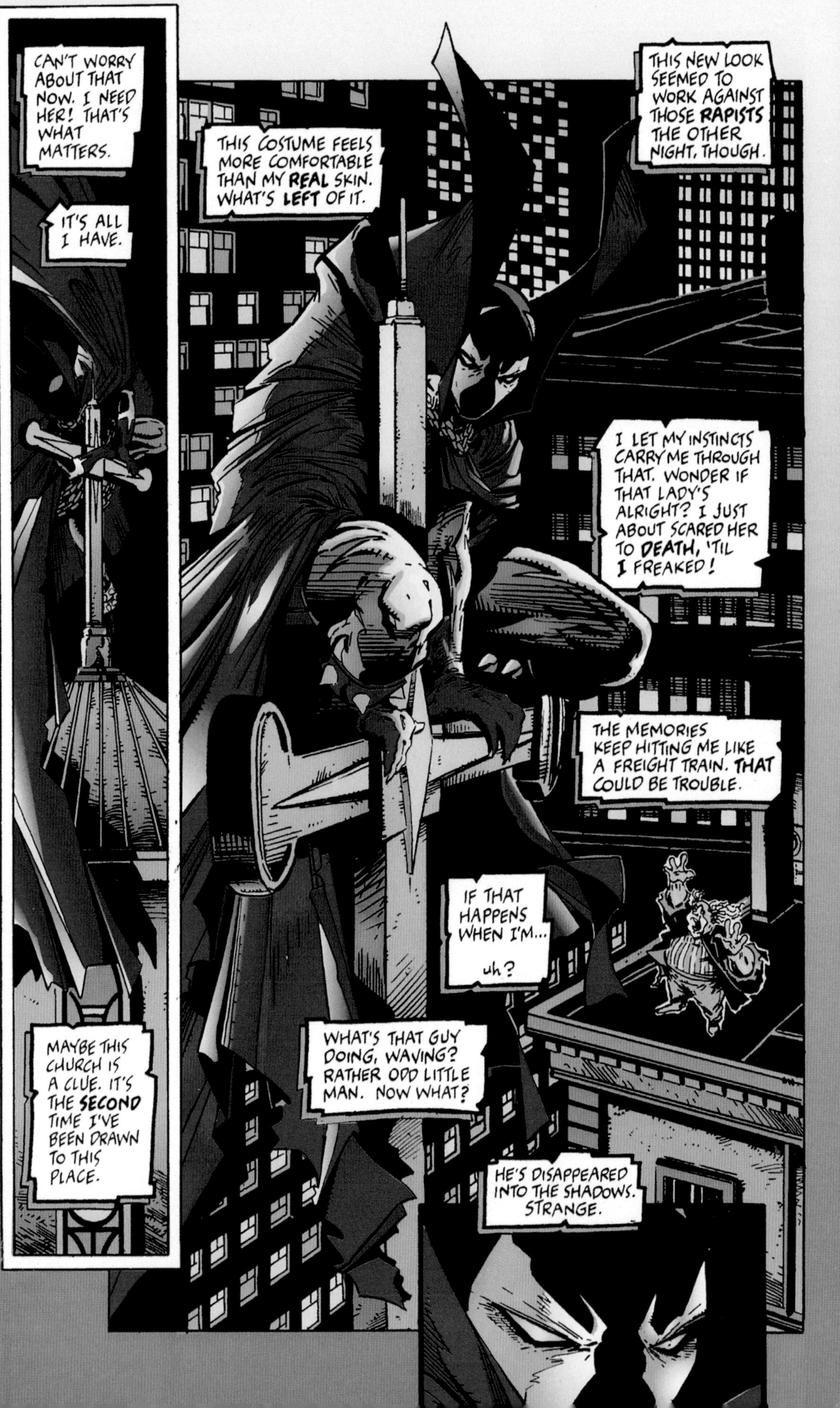
CAN'T WORRY ABOUT THAT NOW. I NEED HER! THAT'S WHAT MATTERS.
IT'S ALL I HAVE.
THIS COSTUME FEELS MORE COMFORTABLE THAN MY REAL SKIN. WHAT'S LEFT OF IT.
THIS NEW LOOK SEEMED TO WORK AGAINST THOSE RAPISTS THE OTHER NIGHT, THOUGH.
I LET MY INSTINCTS CARRY ME THROUGH THAT. WONDER IF THAT LADY'S ALRIGHT? I JUST ABOUT SCARED HER TO DEATH, 'TIL I FREAKED!
THE MEMORIES KEEP HITTING ME LIKE A FREIGHT TRAIN. THAT COULD BE TROUBLE.
IF THAT HAPPENS WHEN I'M...
uh?
MAYBE THIS CHURCH IS A CLUE. IT'S THE SECOND TIME I'VE BEEN DRAWN TO THIS PLACE.
WHAT'S THAT GUY DOING, WAVING? RATHER ODD LITTLE MAN. NOW WHAT?
HE'S DISAPPEARED INTO THE SHADOWS. STRANGE.

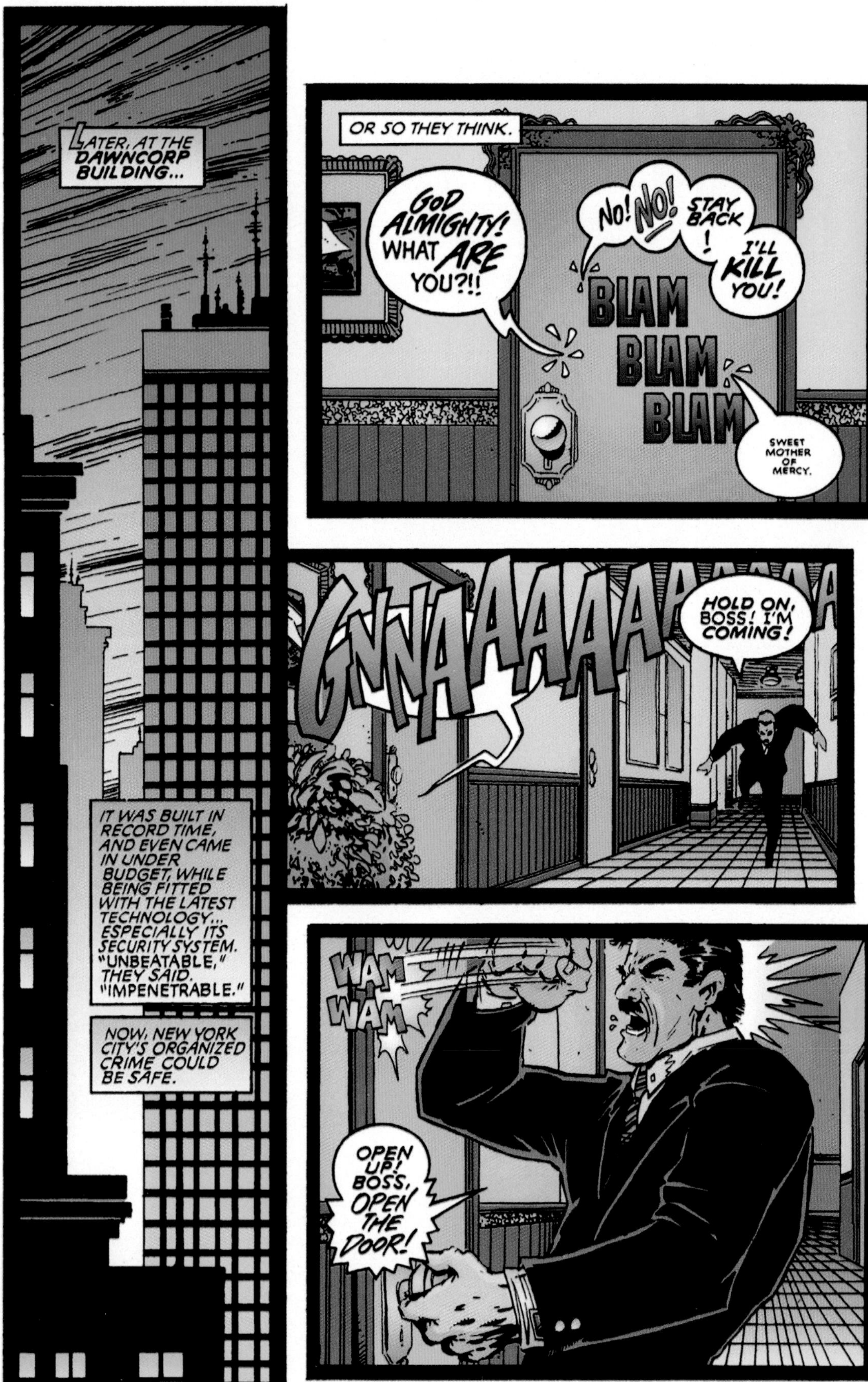
LATER, AT THE DAWNCORP BUILDING...
IT WAS BUILT IN RECORD TIME, AND EVEN CAME IN UNDER BUDGET, WHILE BEING FITTED WITH THE LATEST TECHNOLOGY... ESPECIALLY ITS SECURITY SYSTEM. "UNBEATABLE," THEY SAID. "IMPENETRABLE."
NOW, NEW YORK CITY'S ORGANIZED CRIME COULD BE SAFE.
OR SO THEY THINK.
GOD ALMIGHTY! WHAT ARE YOU?!!
NO! NO! STAY BACK! I'LL KILL YOU!
BLAM BLAM BLAM
SWEET MOTHER OF MERCY.
GNNAAAAAAAAAAA
HOLD ON, BOSS! I'M COMING!
WAM WAM
OPEN UP! BOSS, OPEN THE DOOR!

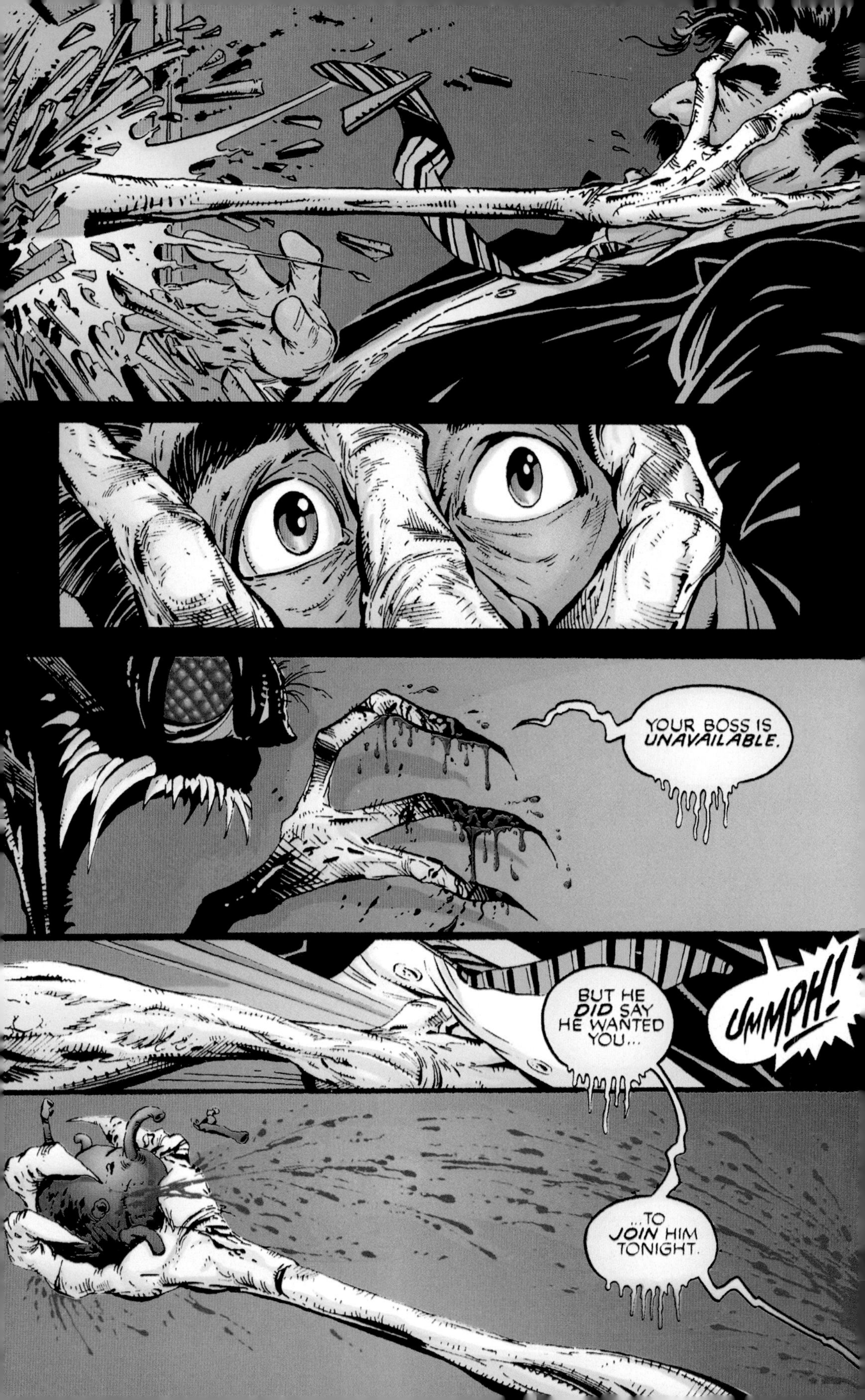
YOUR BOSS IS UNAVAILABLE.
BUT HE DID SAY HE WANTED YOU...
UMMPH!
...TO JOIN HIM TONIGHT.

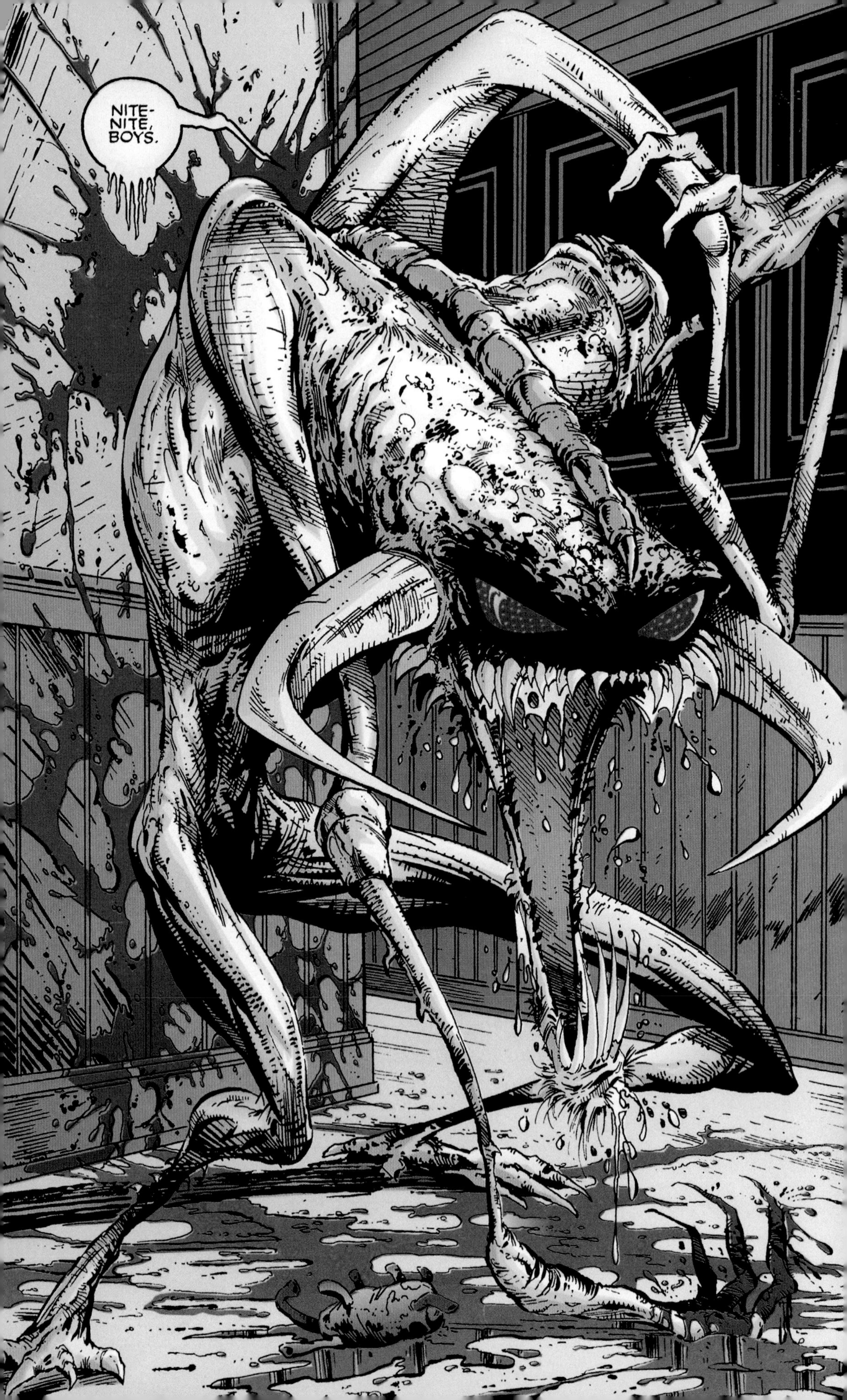
NITE-NITE, BOYS.

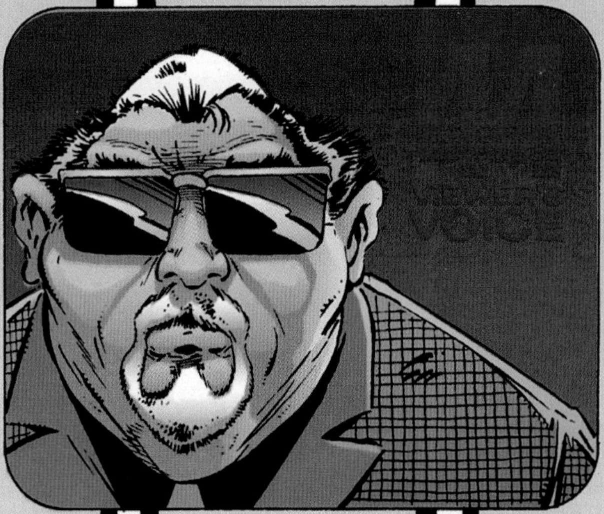

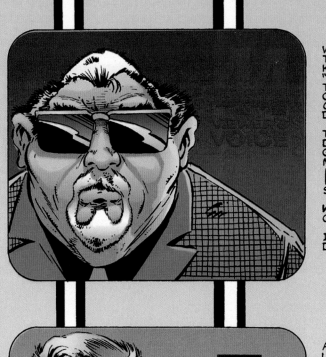

WELL, WELL, WELL. IT BREAKS MY HEART TO REPORT ANOTHER COUPLE OF MAFIA KILLINGS. IT LOOKS LIKE OUR BOY THE "HEART SURGEON" IS AT IT AGAIN. THOUGH THE POLICE HAVEN'T CONFIRMED ANY CONNECTION TO THE ***OTHER*** DEATHS, ONLY THOSE OF US WHO ARE BRAIN-DEAD CAN'T FIGURE ***THIS*** ONE OUT.

THE POLICE ALSO REPORT THAT THEY'VE DOUBLED THE TASK FORCE INVESTIGATING THESE VEG-O-MATIC KILLINGS. MY ONLY QUESTION:

WHY?!! LAST TIME I CHECKED, ***ALL*** SIX OF THEM WERE 'LEG-BREAKERS.'

WHAT'S TO INVESTIGATE? AM I THE ONLY ONE ASKING THIS QUESTION?

I'VE GOT A BETTER IDEA-- LET ME HELP DIG THE GRAVES.

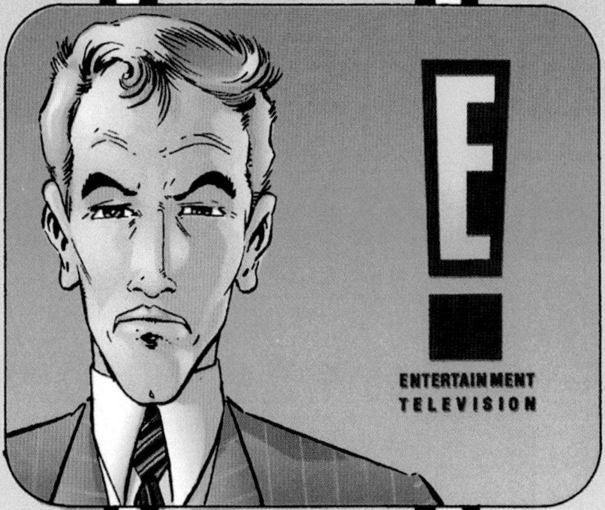
E!
ENTERTAINMENT TELEVISION

AS I'VE STATED BEFORE, RUMORS ARE THE UGLY SIDE OF SHOW BIZ.

THE YOUNGBLOODS, CHANGING THEIR COSTUMES FOR ONE UNIFIED LOOK? ***C'MON,*** IT'S THE MYRIAD COLORS AND ENSEMBLES THAT ***TOOK*** THEM TO THE TOP. ***WHY*** IN HEAVEN'S NAME WOULD THEY WANT TO ALIENATE THEIR FANS ***NOW?***

SEX APPEAL HAS ***AL***WAYS BEEN A BIG PRIORITY TO THE MARKETING GENIUSES BEHIND OUR HEROES IN TIGHTS. 'BLOOD MERCHANDISE IS OVER THE $2.2 ***BIL***LION MARK AL***READY.*** I JUST ***KNEW*** THERE'D BE A DAY THEY'D TOPPLE THOSE PIZZA-EATING TURTLES.

AND ***SPEAKING*** OF GREEN GUYS, CHICAGO IS REPORTING THE APPEARANCE OF A ***DRAGON,*** FIN AND ***ALL***. NOW WOULDN'T ***THAT*** MAKE A GREAT TICKLER.

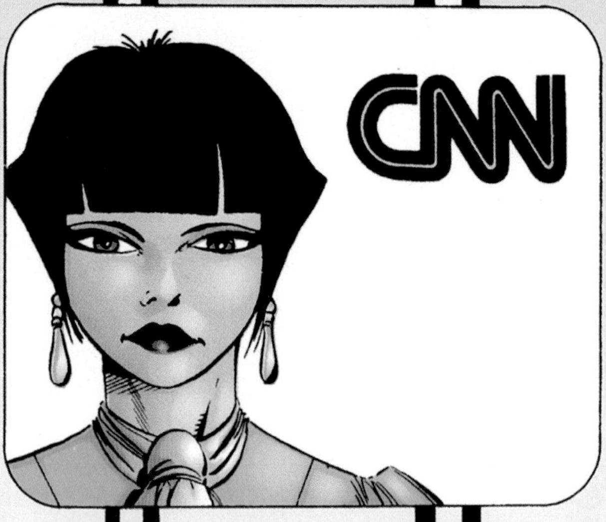
CNN

...SOURCES ALSO INDICATE THAT SINCE TONIGHT'S MURDERS, OVER A DOZEN OF NEW YORK'S MOST POWERFUL MEN HAVE ASKED FOR POLICE PROTECTION. ALL OF THESE MEN HAVE 'ALLEGED' CONNECTIONS TO CRIMINAL AFFAIRS.

ON A MORE POSITIVE NOTE, ***WANDA BLAKE,*** WIDOW OF ***LT. COL. AL SIMMONS,*** HELPED OPEN ANOTHER CARE CLINIC FOR DISABLED CHILDREN.

MONEY GENERATED BY HER LATE HUSBAND'S MEMORIAL FUND HELPED FINISH THE CENTER, WHICH HAD BEEN ON HOLD. THE CURRENT RECESSION IS BLAMED.

THIS IS THE THIRD SUCH PROJECT THAT Ms. BLAKE HAS BEEN INVOLVED WITH.

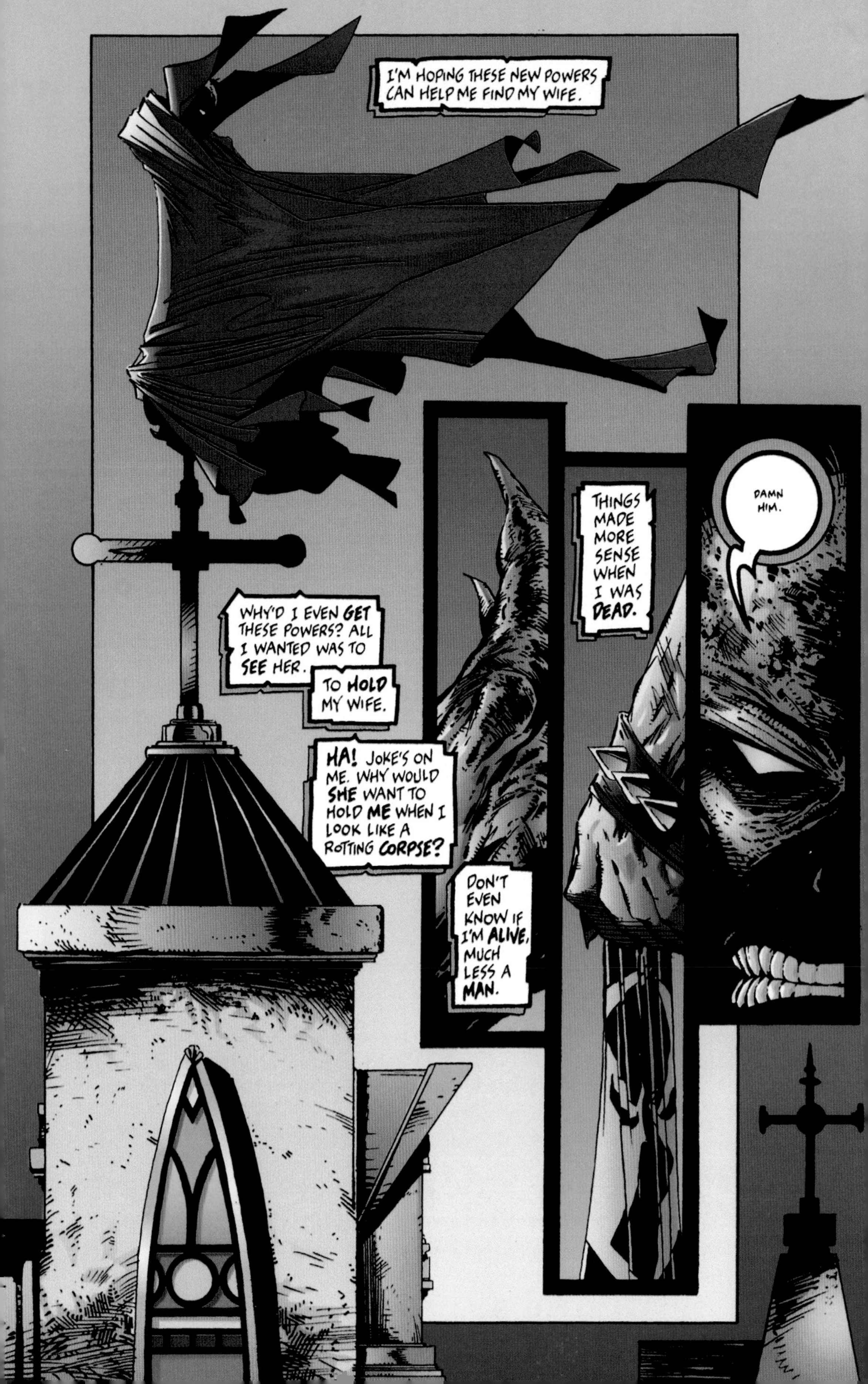

I'M HOPING THESE NEW POWERS CAN HELP ME FIND MY WIFE.
WHY'D I EVEN GET THESE POWERS? ALL I WANTED WAS TO SEE HER.
TO HOLD MY WIFE.
HA! JOKE'S ON ME. WHY WOULD SHE WANT TO HOLD ME WHEN I LOOK LIKE A ROTTING CORPSE?
DON'T EVEN KNOW IF I'M ALIVE, MUCH LESS A MAN.
THINGS MADE MORE SENSE WHEN I WAS DEAD.
DAMN HIM.

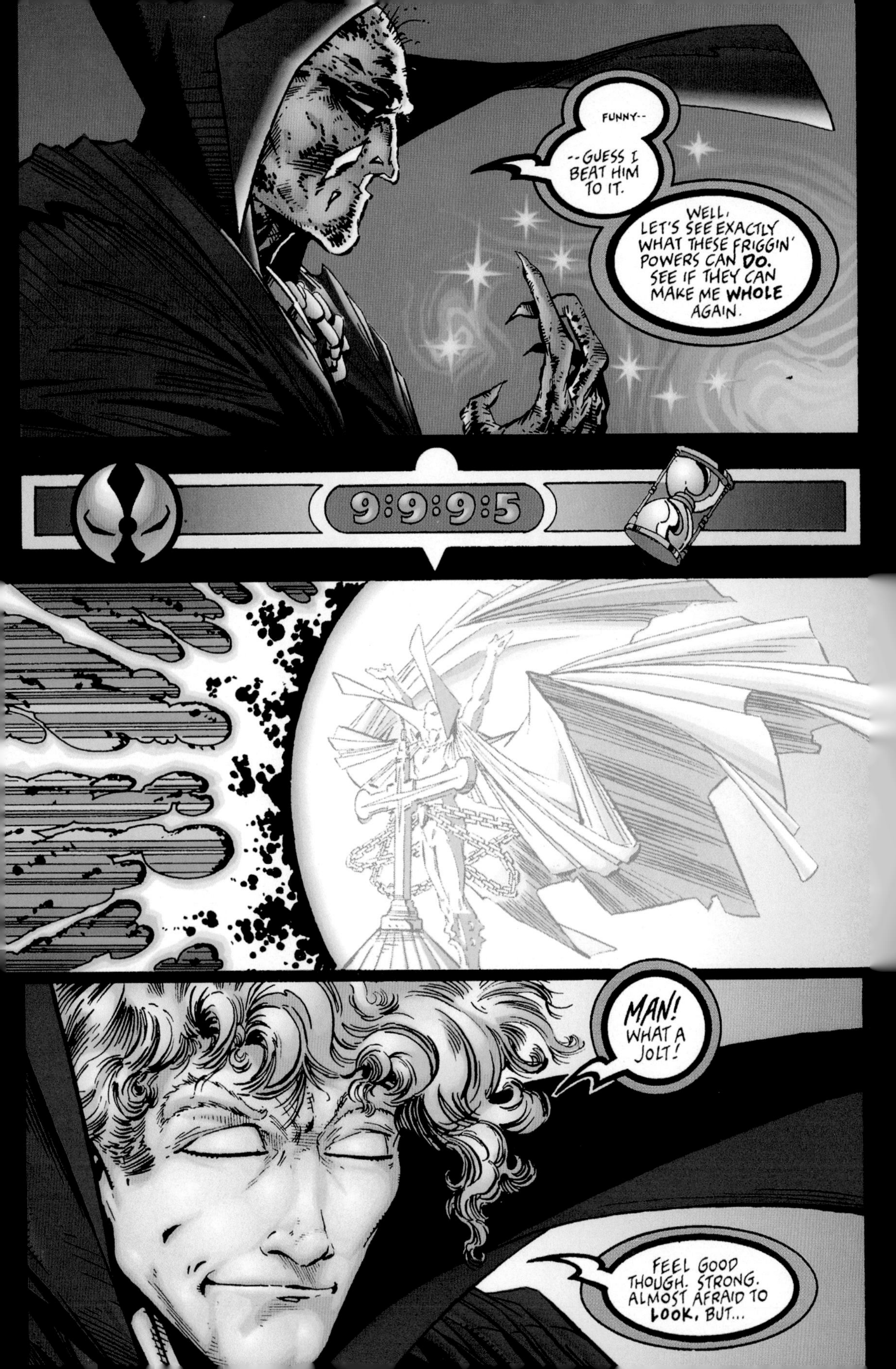

FUNNY--
--GUESS I BEAT HIM TO IT.
WELL, LET'S SEE EXACTLY WHAT THESE FRIGGIN' POWERS CAN **DO.** SEE IF THEY CAN MAKE ME **WHOLE** AGAIN.
9:9:9:5
MAN! WHAT A JOLT!
FEEL GOOD THOUGH. STRONG. ALMOST AFRAID TO **LOOK,** BUT...

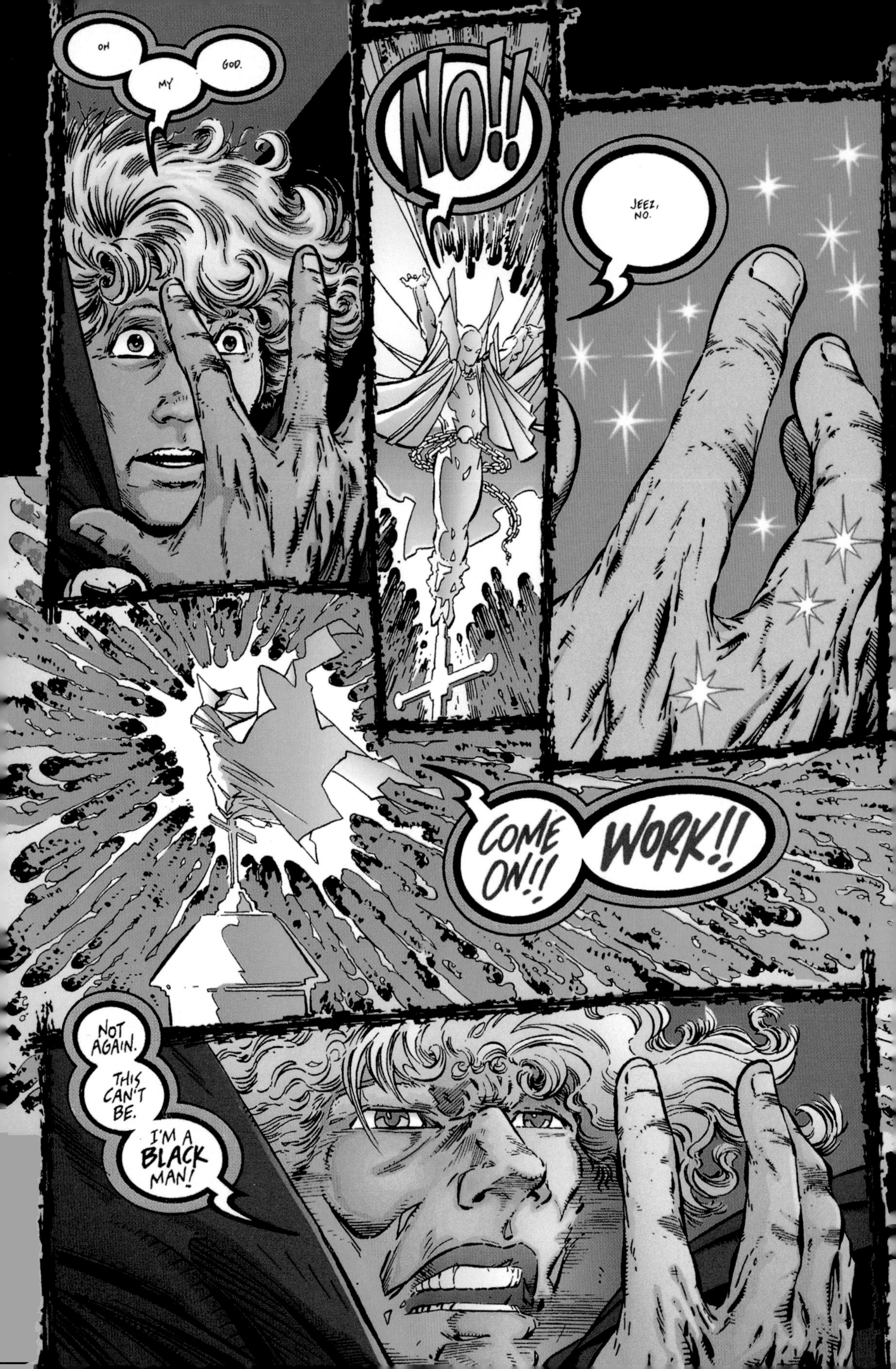
OH
MY
GOD.
NO!!
JEEZ, NO.
COME ON!!
WORK!!
NOT AGAIN.
THIS CAN'T BE.
I'M A BLACK MAN!

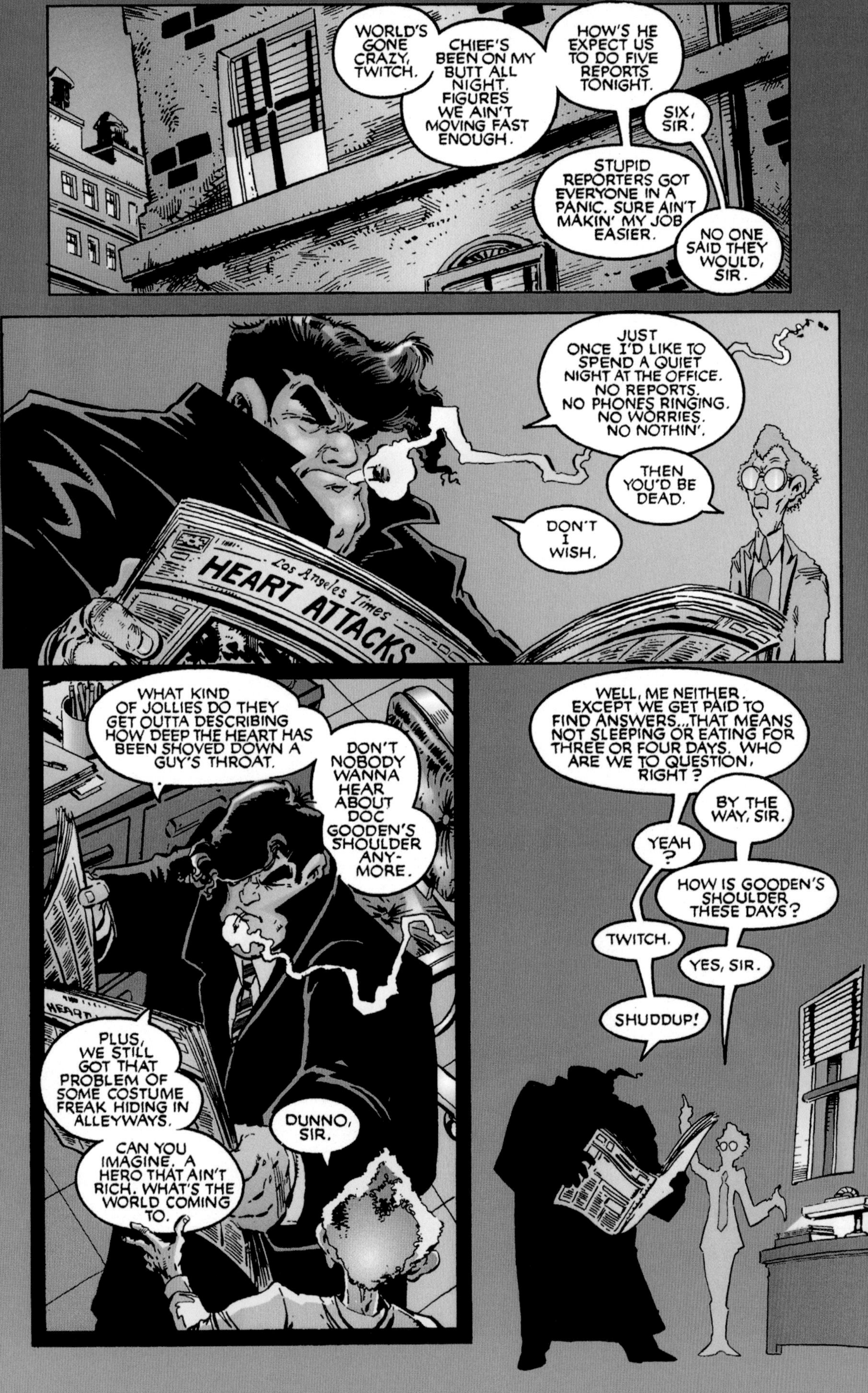
WORLD'S GONE CRAZY, TWITCH.
CHIEF'S BEEN ON MY BUTT ALL NIGHT. FIGURES WE AIN'T MOVING FAST ENOUGH.
HOW'S HE EXPECT US TO DO FIVE REPORTS TONIGHT.
SIX, SIR.
STUPID REPORTERS GOT EVERYONE IN A PANIC. SURE AIN'T MAKIN' MY JOB EASIER.
NO ONE SAID THEY WOULD, SIR.
JUST ONCE I'D LIKE TO SPEND A QUIET NIGHT AT THE OFFICE. NO REPORTS. NO PHONES RINGING. NO WORRIES. NO NOTHIN'.
THEN YOU'D BE DEAD.
DON'T I WISH.
Los Angeles Times
HEART ATTACKS
WHAT KIND OF JOLLIES DO THEY GET OUTTA DESCRIBING HOW DEEP THE HEART HAS BEEN SHOVED DOWN A GUY'S THROAT.
DON'T NOBODY WANNA HEAR ABOUT DOC GOODEN'S SHOULDER ANY-MORE.
PLUS, WE STILL GOT THAT PROBLEM OF SOME COSTUME FREAK HIDING IN ALLEYWAYS.
DUNNO, SIR.
CAN YOU IMAGINE. A HERO THAT AIN'T RICH. WHAT'S THE WORLD COMING TO.
WELL, ME NEITHER. EXCEPT WE GET PAID TO FIND ANSWERS...THAT MEANS NOT SLEEPING OR EATING FOR THREE OR FOUR DAYS. WHO ARE WE TO QUESTION, RIGHT?
BY THE WAY, SIR.
YEAH?
HOW IS GOODEN'S SHOULDER THESE DAYS?
TWITCH.
YES, SIR.
SHUDDUP!

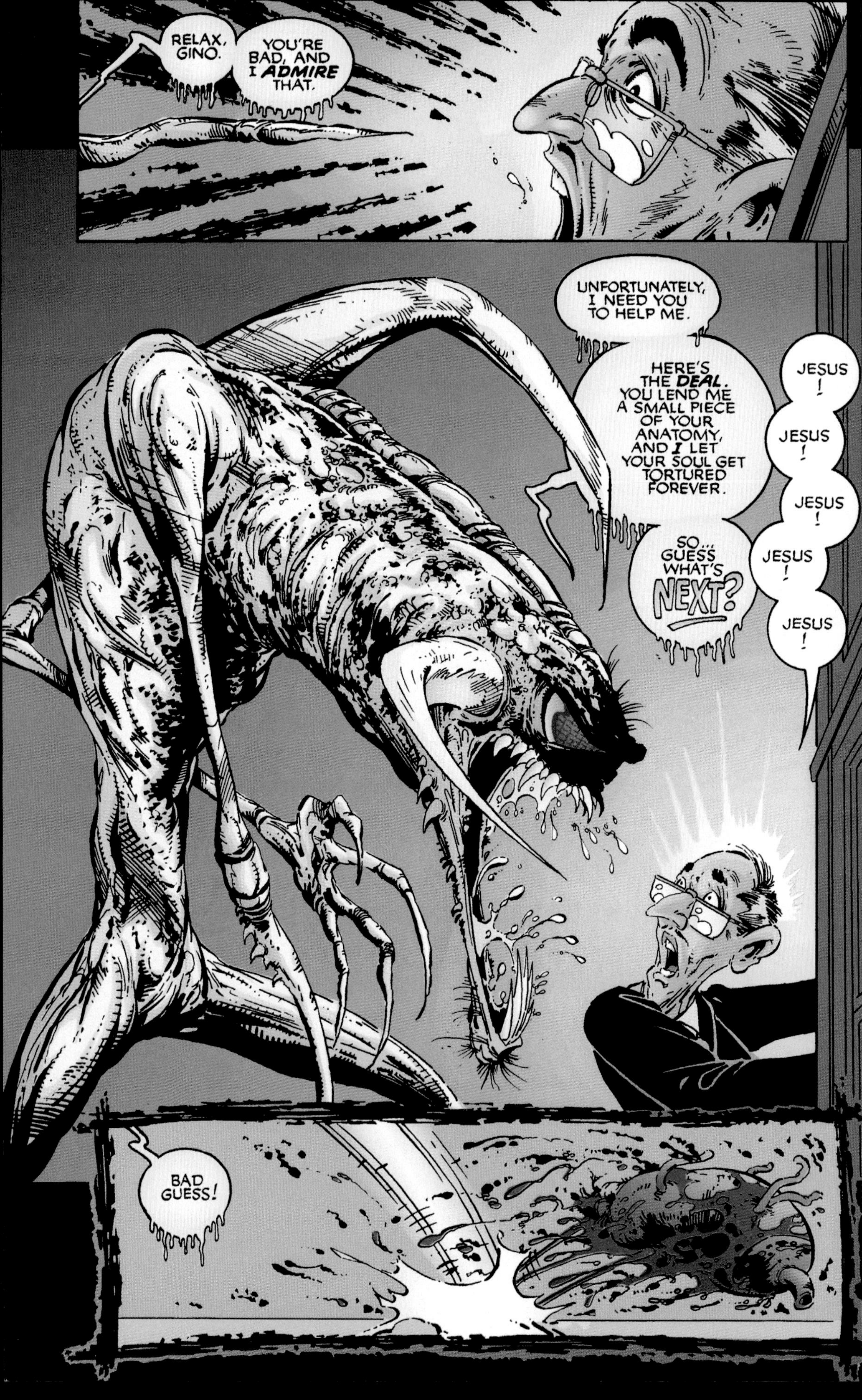
RELAX, GINO.
YOU'RE BAD, AND I ADMIRE THAT.
UNFORTUNATELY, I NEED YOU TO HELP ME.
HERE'S THE DEAL. YOU LEND ME A SMALL PIECE OF YOUR ANATOMY, AND I LET YOUR SOUL GET TORTURED FOREVER.
SO... GUESS WHAT'S NEXT?
JESUS!
JESUS!
JESUS!
JESUS!
JESUS!
BAD GUESS!

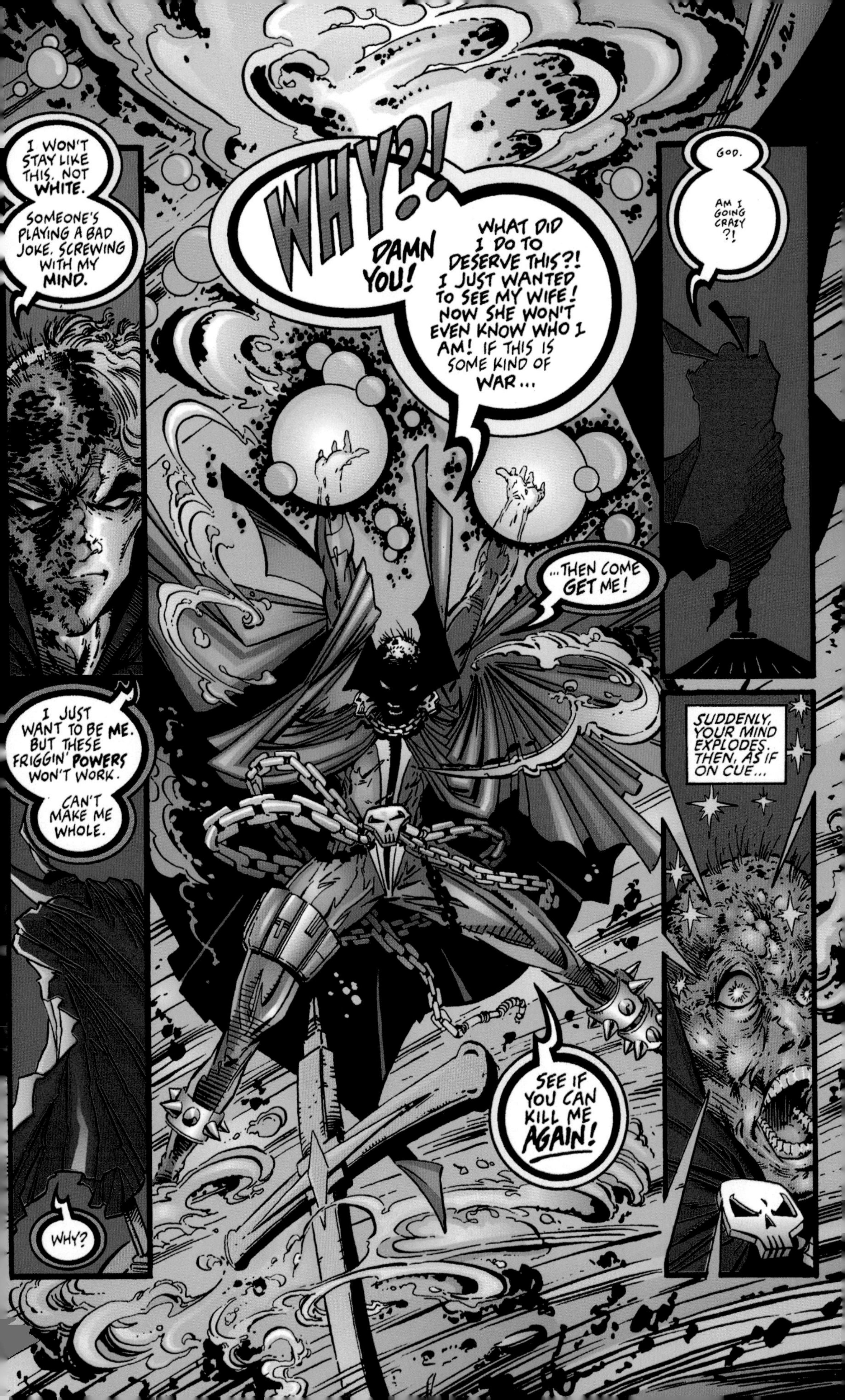
I WON'T STAY LIKE THIS. NOT WHITE.
SOMEONE'S PLAYING A BAD JOKE. SCREWING WITH MY MIND.
WHY?!
DAMN YOU!
WHAT DID I DO TO DESERVE THIS?! I JUST WANTED TO SEE MY WIFE! NOW SHE WON'T EVEN KNOW WHO I AM! IF THIS IS SOME KIND OF WAR...
GOD.
AM I GOING CRAZY ?!
...THEN COME GET ME!
I JUST WANT TO BE ME. BUT THESE FRIGGIN' POWERS WON'T WORK.
CAN'T MAKE ME WHOLE.
WHY?
SEE IF YOU CAN KILL ME AGAIN!
SUDDENLY, YOUR MIND EXPLODES. THEN, AS IF ON CUE...

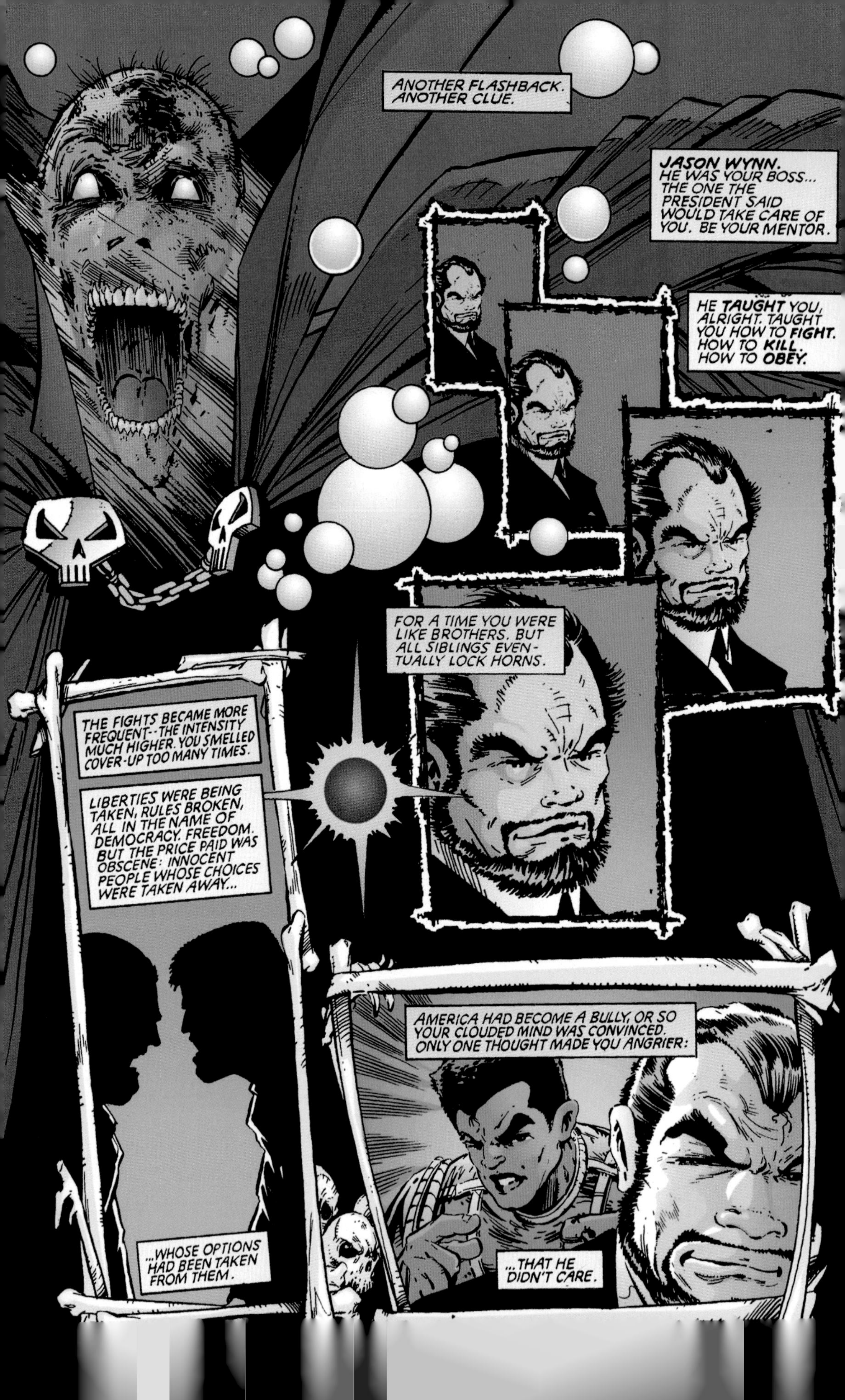

ANOTHER FLASHBACK. ANOTHER CLUE.
JASON WYNN. HE WAS YOUR BOSS... THE ONE THE PRESIDENT SAID WOULD TAKE CARE OF YOU. BE YOUR MENTOR.
HE TAUGHT YOU, ALRIGHT. TAUGHT YOU HOW TO FIGHT. HOW TO KILL. HOW TO OBEY.
FOR A TIME YOU WERE LIKE BROTHERS. BUT ALL SIBLINGS EVEN-TUALLY LOCK HORNS.
THE FIGHTS BECAME MORE FREQUENT--THE INTENSITY MUCH HIGHER. YOU SMELLED COVER-UP TOO MANY TIMES.
LIBERTIES WERE BEING TAKEN, RULES BROKEN, ALL IN THE NAME OF DEMOCRACY. FREEDOM. BUT THE PRICE PAID WAS OBSCENE: INNOCENT PEOPLE WHOSE CHOICES WERE TAKEN AWAY...
...WHOSE OPTIONS HAD BEEN TAKEN FROM THEM.
AMERICA HAD BECOME A BULLY, OR SO YOUR CLOUDED MIND WAS CONVINCED. ONLY ONE THOUGHT MADE YOU ANGRIER:
...THAT HE DIDN'T CARE.

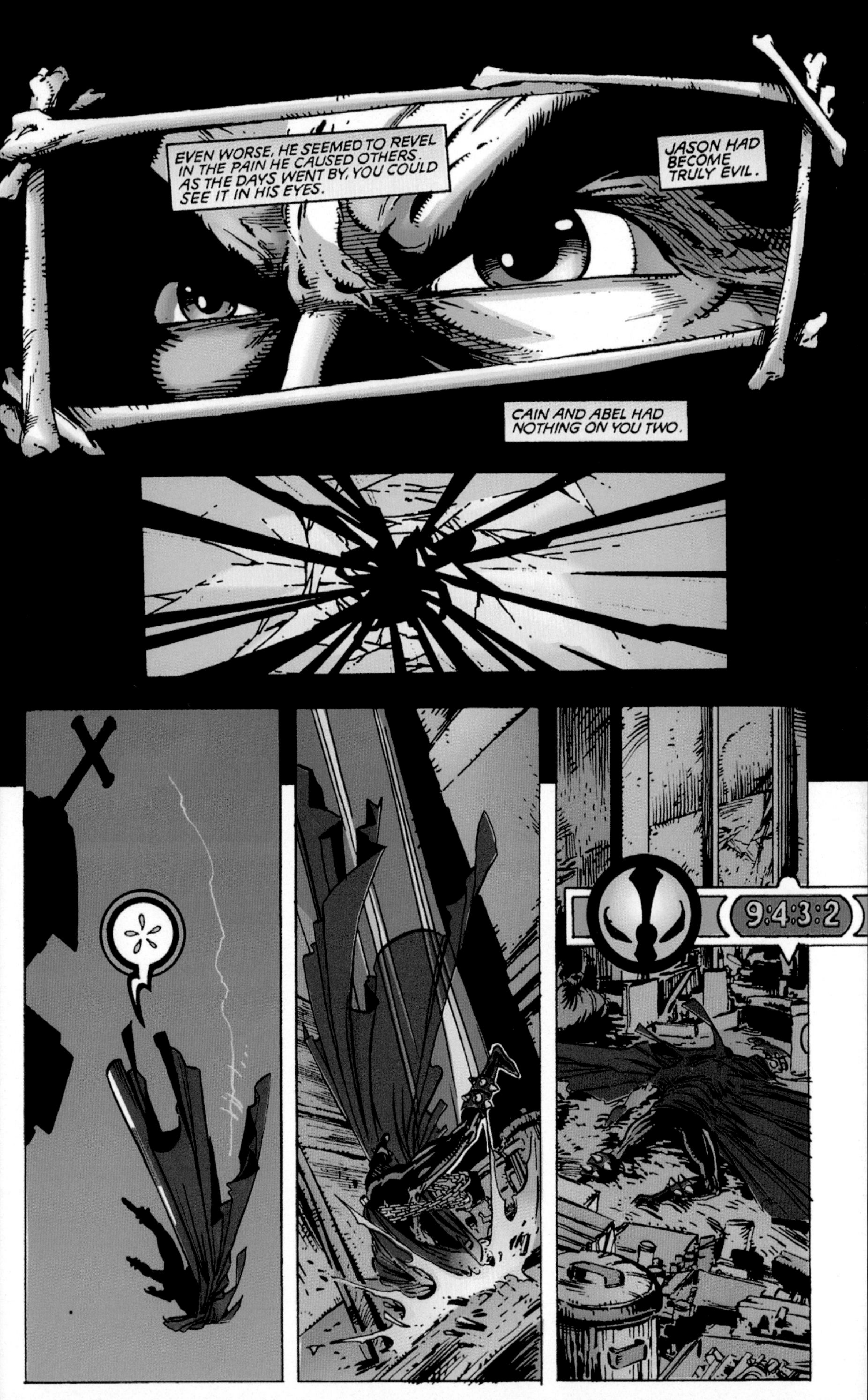
EVEN WORSE, HE SEEMED TO REVEL IN THE PAIN HE CAUSED OTHERS. AS THE DAYS WENT BY, YOU COULD SEE IT IN HIS EYES.
JASON HAD BECOME TRULY EVIL.
CAIN AND ABEL HAD NOTHING ON YOU TWO.
9:4:3:2

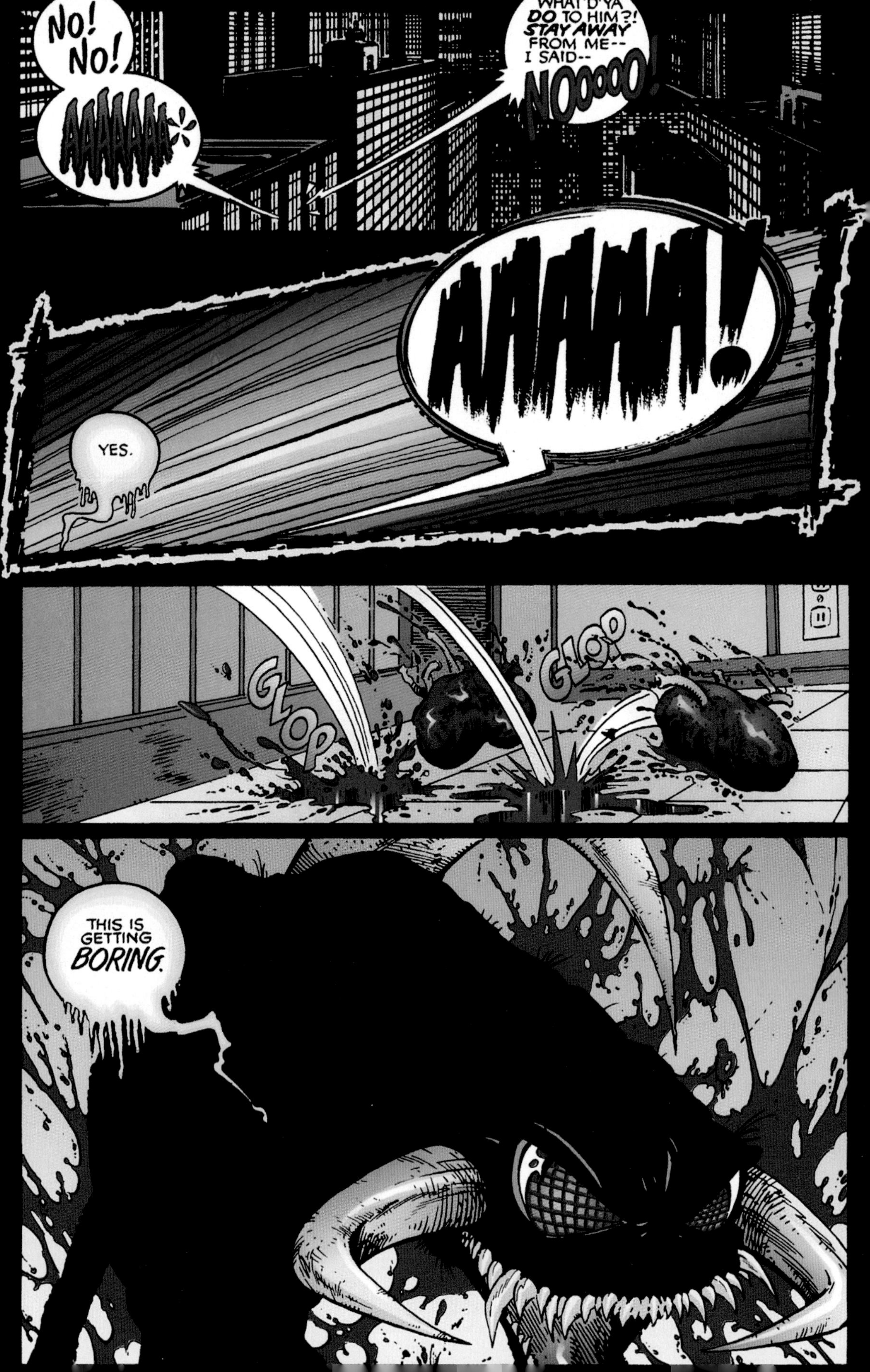
No! No!
AAAAAAA!
WHAT'D'YA DO TO HIM?! STAY AWAY FROM ME-- I SAID--
NOOOOO!
AAAAAA!
YES.
GLOP
GLOP
THIS IS GETTING BORING.

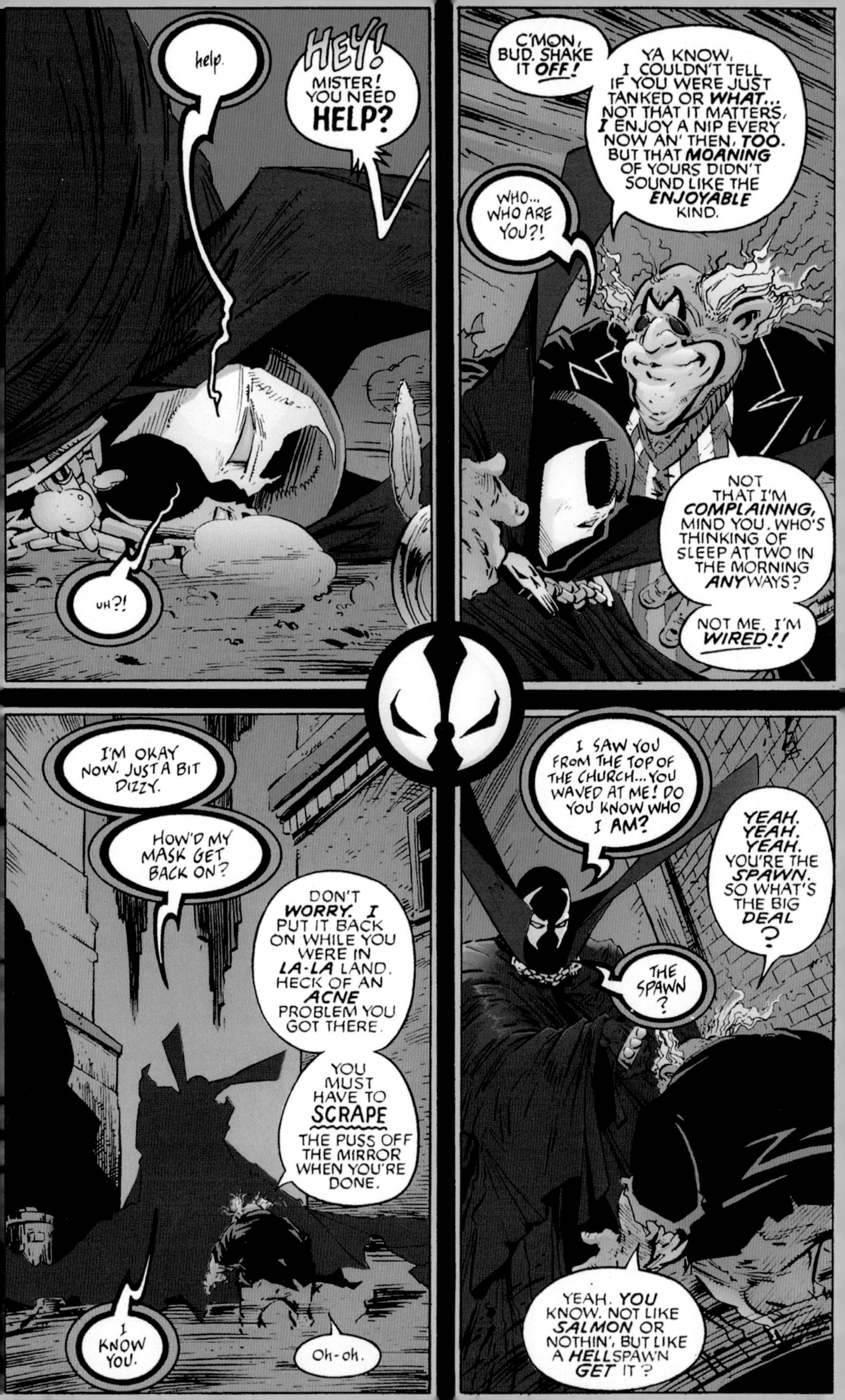
help.
HEY! MISTER! YOU NEED HELP?
UH?!
C'MON, BUD. SHAKE IT OFF!
YA KNOW, I COULDN'T TELL IF YOU WERE JUST TANKED OR WHAT... NOT THAT IT MATTERS, I ENJOY A NIP EVERY NOW AN' THEN, TOO. BUT THAT MOANING OF YOURS DIDN'T SOUND LIKE THE ENJOYABLE KIND.
WHO... WHO ARE YOU?!
NOT THAT I'M COMPLAINING, MIND YOU. WHO'S THINKING OF SLEEP AT TWO IN THE MORNING ANYWAYS?
NOT ME. I'M WIRED!!
I'M OKAY NOW. JUST A BIT DIZZY.
HOW'D MY MASK GET BACK ON?
DON'T WORRY. I PUT IT BACK ON WHILE YOU WERE IN LA-LA LAND. HECK OF AN ACNE PROBLEM YOU GOT THERE.
YOU MUST HAVE TO SCRAPE THE PUSS OFF THE MIRROR WHEN YOU'RE DONE.
I KNOW YOU.
Oh-oh.
I SAW YOU FROM THE TOP OF THE CHURCH... YOU WAVED AT ME! DO YOU KNOW WHO I AM?
YEAH. YEAH. YEAH. YOU'RE THE SPAWN. SO WHAT'S THE BIG DEAL ?
THE SPAWN ?
YEAH. YOU KNOW. NOT LIKE SALMON OR NOTHIN', BUT LIKE A HELLSPAWN GET IT ?

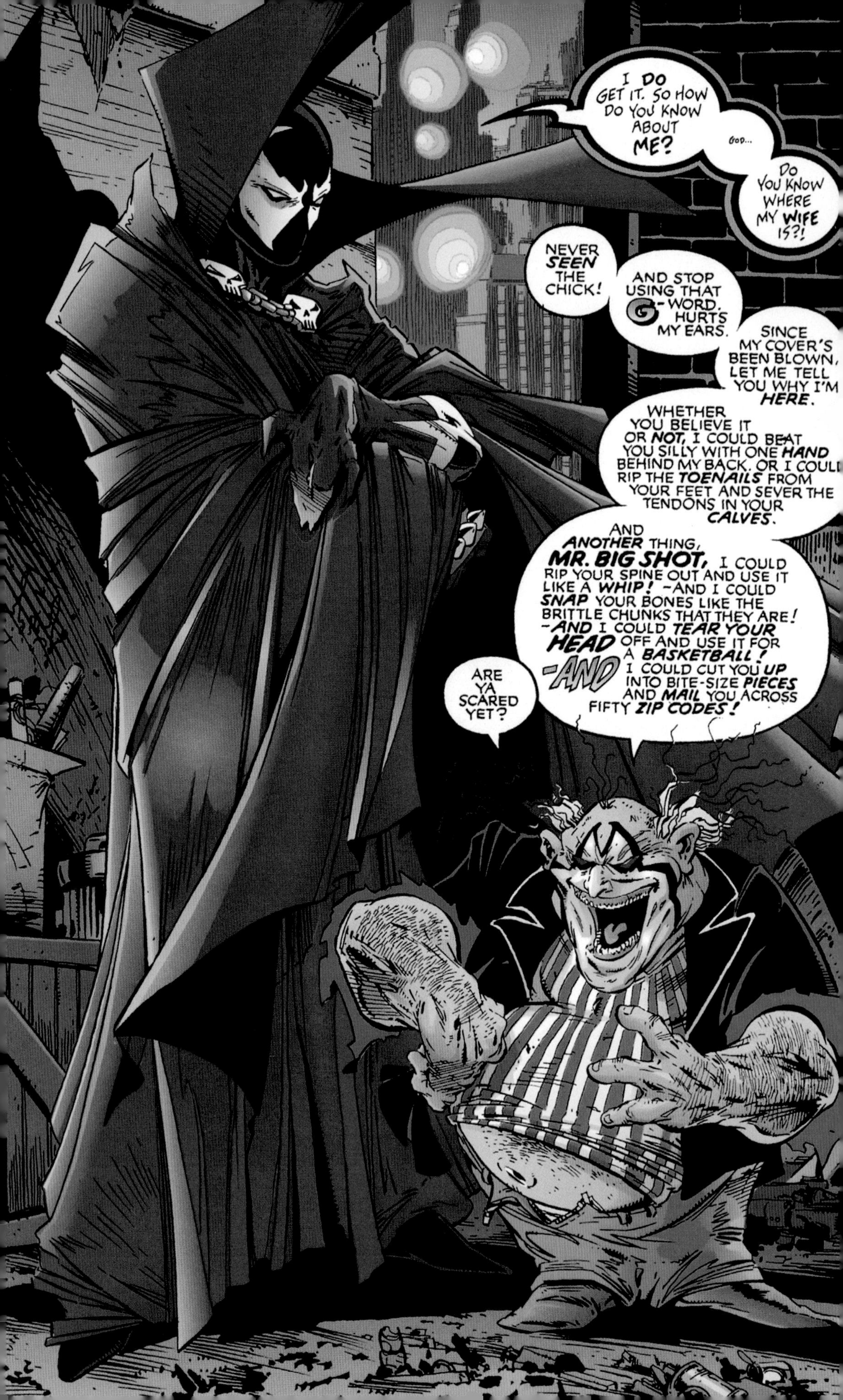

I DO GET IT. SO HOW DO YOU KNOW ABOUT ME?
GOD...
DO YOU KNOW WHERE MY WIFE IS?!
NEVER SEEN THE CHICK!
AND STOP USING THAT G-WORD. HURTS MY EARS.
SINCE MY COVER'S BEEN BLOWN, LET ME TELL YOU WHY I'M HERE.
WHETHER YOU BELIEVE IT OR NOT, I COULD BEAT YOU SILLY WITH ONE HAND BEHIND MY BACK. OR I COULD RIP THE TOENAILS FROM YOUR FEET AND SEVER THE TENDONS IN YOUR CALVES.
AND ANOTHER THING, MR. BIG SHOT, I COULD RIP YOUR SPINE OUT AND USE IT LIKE A WHIP! -AND I COULD SNAP YOUR BONES LIKE THE BRITTLE CHUNKS THAT THEY ARE! -AND I COULD TEAR YOUR HEAD OFF AND USE IT FOR A BASKETBALL! -AND I COULD CUT YOU UP INTO BITE-SIZE PIECES AND MAIL YOU ACROSS FIFTY ZIP CODES!
ARE YA SCARED YET?

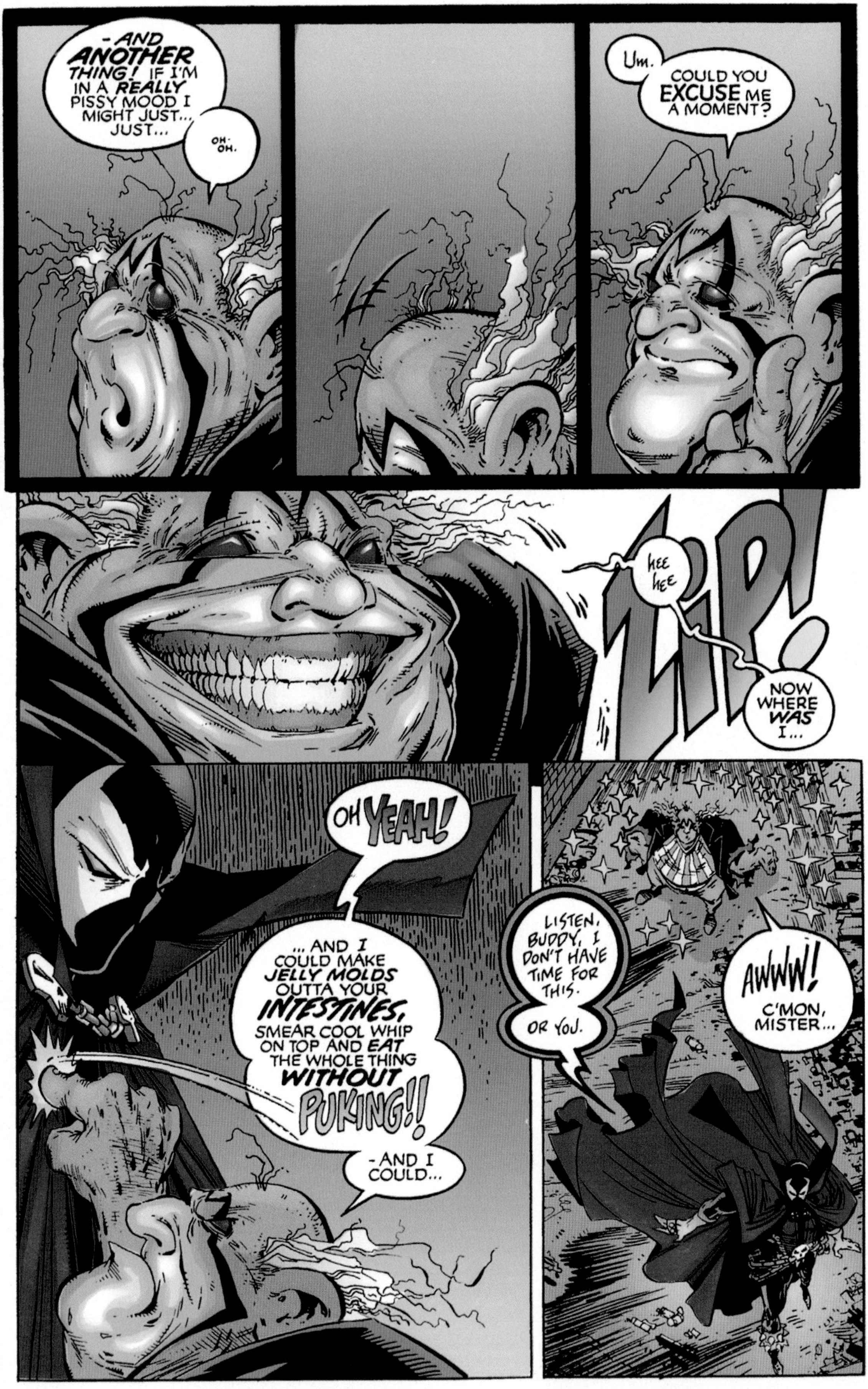
- AND ANOTHER THING! IF I'M IN A REALLY PISSY MOOD I MIGHT JUST... JUST...
OH-OH.
Um.
COULD YOU EXCUSE ME A MOMENT?
ZIP!
hee hee
NOW WHERE WAS I...
OH YEAH!
... AND I COULD MAKE JELLY MOLDS OUTTA YOUR INTESTINES, SMEAR COOL WHIP ON TOP AND EAT THE WHOLE THING WITHOUT PUKING!!
- AND I COULD...
LISTEN, BUDDY, I DON'T HAVE TIME FOR THIS.
OR YOU.
AWWW!
C'MON, MISTER...

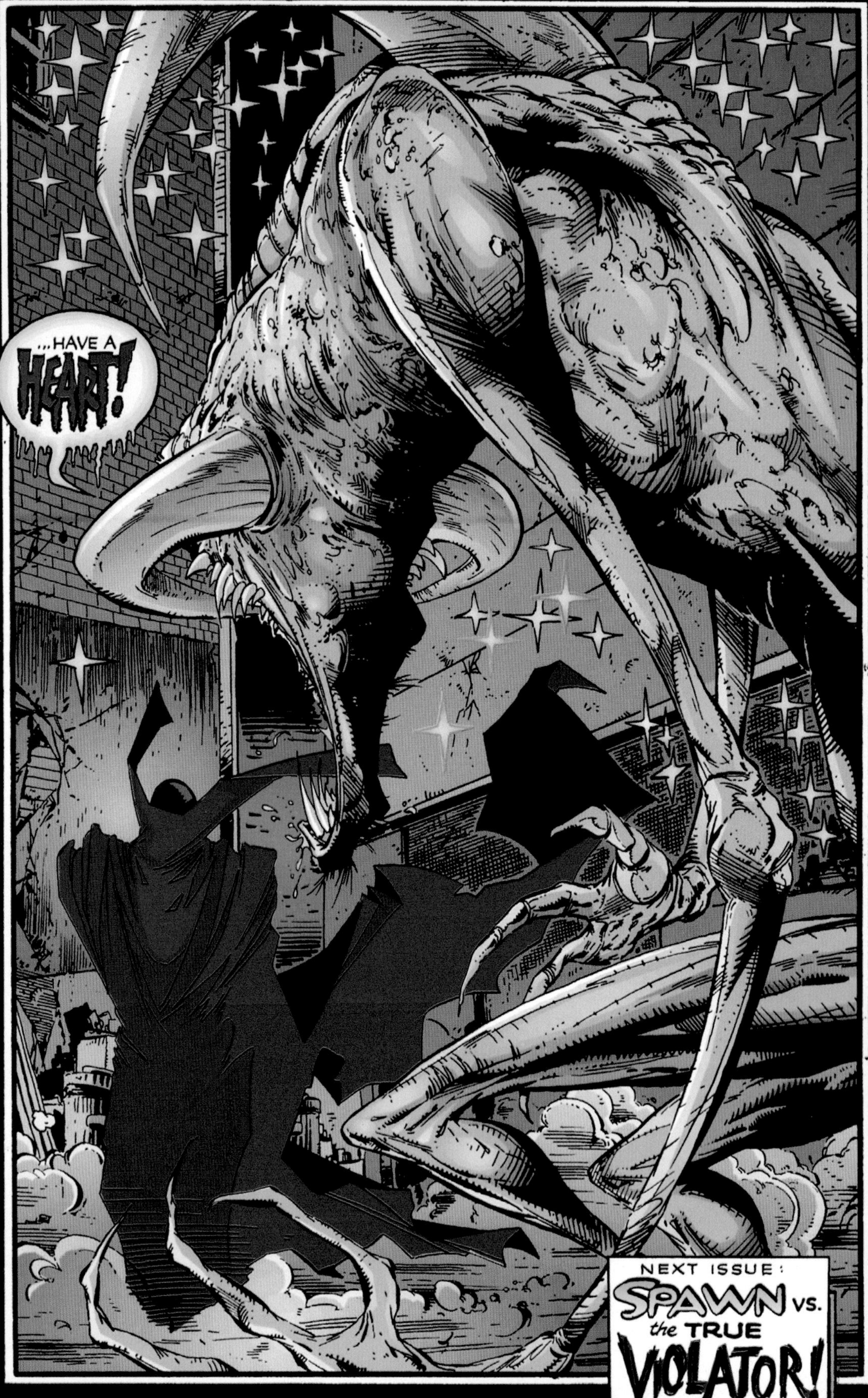
...HAVE A HEART!
NEXT ISSUE: SPAWN VS. the TRUE VIOLATOR!

"I think there is a lot of appeal to characters that have an edge to them. This guy – you push him enough, and he'll kill. He doesn't want to be the hero; he wants to lead a normal life. He has his own needs and he lets his emotions dictate his policy. That would never happen to a guy like Superman – he's too refined for that. I think that Spawn the character can go to places where some of the bigger, "corporate" heroes can't go because they're too commercially successful. This is why Batman has always enamored me, because he's the guy who can go the furthest. But – he stops short of killing the bad guys, even though the bad guys are killers. Spawn can now go there."

-Todd McFarlane
Interview for Millarworld

3 **AUG 1992**

"QUESTIONS"

PART THREE

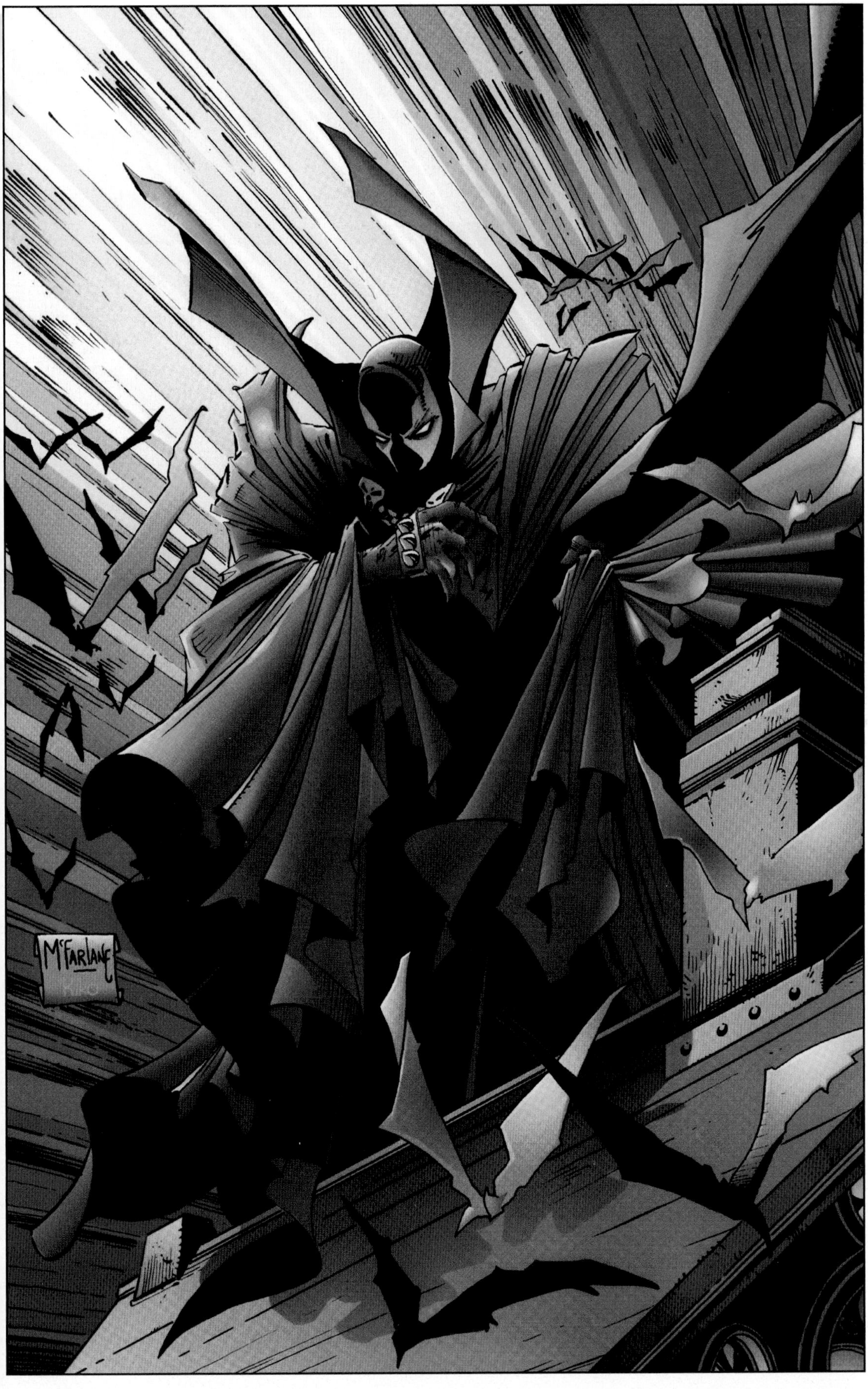
McFarlane

Spawn #3, cover

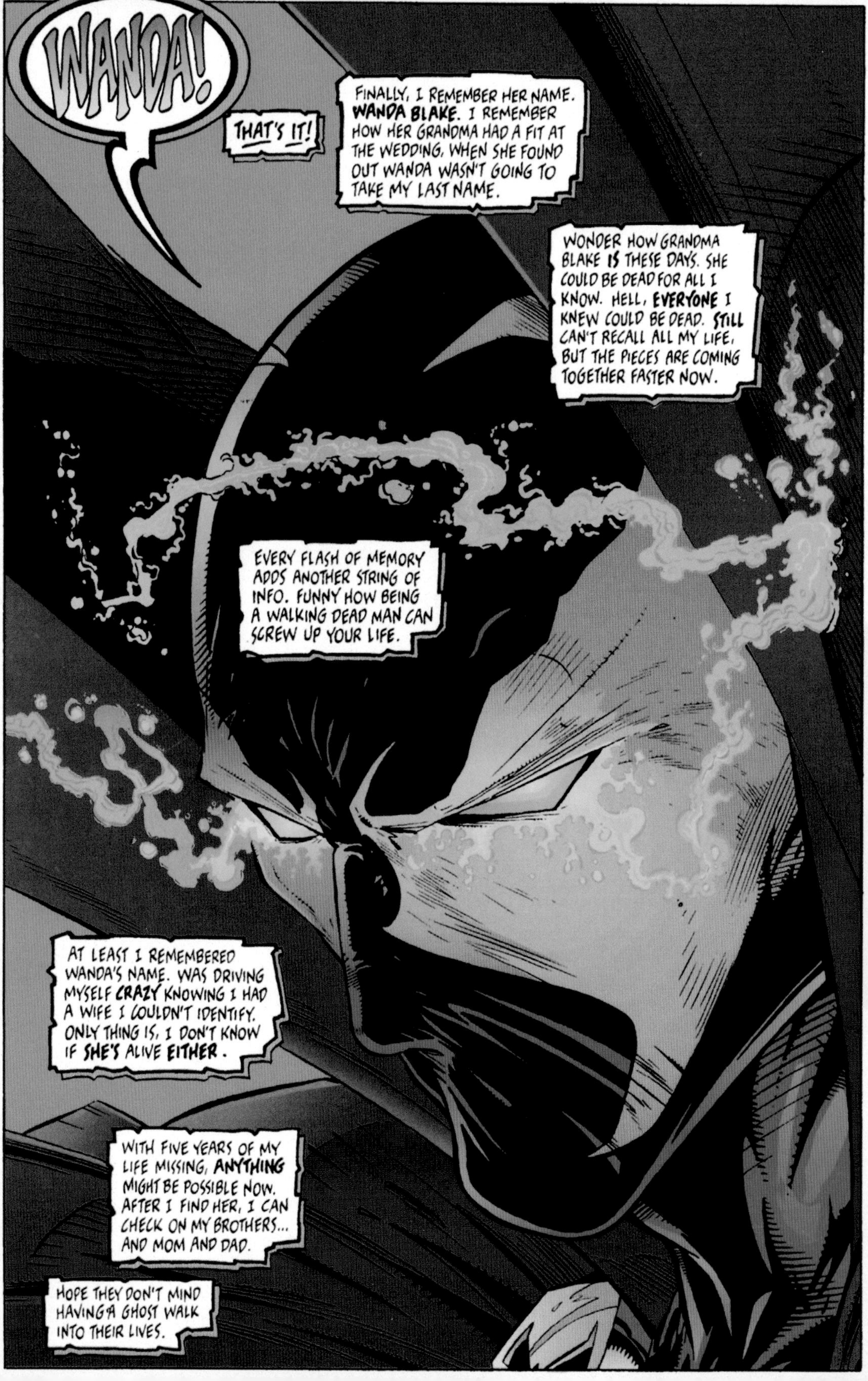
WANDA!
THAT'S IT!
FINALLY, I REMEMBER HER NAME. WANDA BLAKE. I REMEMBER HOW HER GRANDMA HAD A FIT AT THE WEDDING, WHEN SHE FOUND OUT WANDA WASN'T GOING TO TAKE MY LAST NAME.
WONDER HOW GRANDMA BLAKE IS THESE DAYS. SHE COULD BE DEAD FOR ALL I KNOW. HELL, EVERYONE I KNEW COULD BE DEAD. STILL CAN'T RECALL ALL MY LIFE, BUT THE PIECES ARE COMING TOGETHER FASTER NOW.
EVERY FLASH OF MEMORY ADDS ANOTHER STRING OF INFO. FUNNY HOW BEING A WALKING DEAD MAN CAN SCREW UP YOUR LIFE.
AT LEAST I REMEMBERED WANDA'S NAME. WAS DRIVING MYSELF CRAZY KNOWING I HAD A WIFE I COULDN'T IDENTIFY. ONLY THING IS, I DON'T KNOW IF SHE'S ALIVE EITHER.
WITH FIVE YEARS OF MY LIFE MISSING, ANYTHING MIGHT BE POSSIBLE NOW. AFTER I FIND HER, I CAN CHECK ON MY BROTHERS... AND MOM AND DAD.
HOPE THEY DON'T MIND HAVING A GHOST WALK INTO THEIR LIVES.

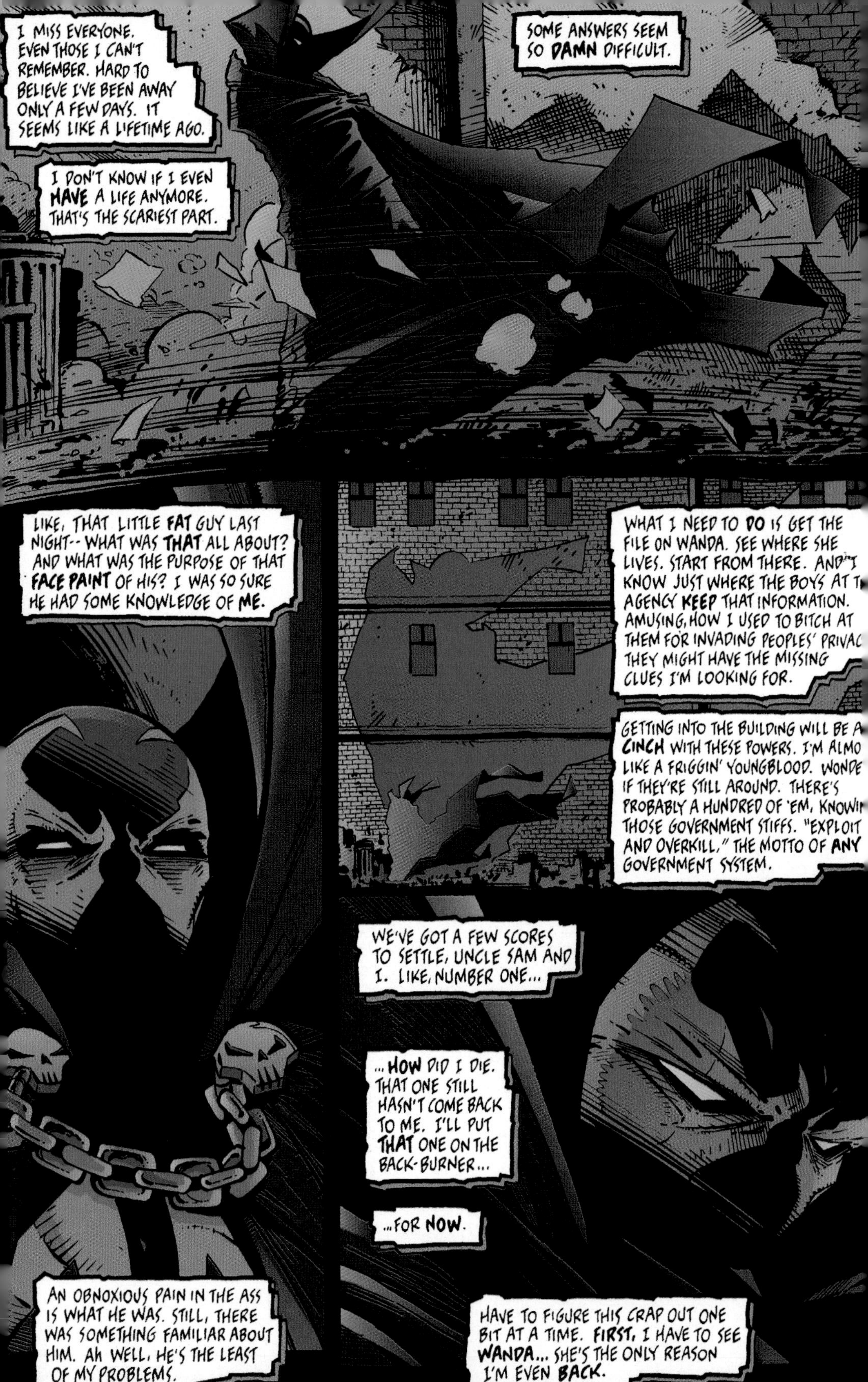
I MISS EVERYONE. EVEN THOSE I CAN'T REMEMBER. HARD TO BELIEVE I'VE BEEN AWAY ONLY A FEW DAYS. IT SEEMS LIKE A LIFETIME AGO.
I DON'T KNOW IF I EVEN HAVE A LIFE ANYMORE. THAT'S THE SCARIEST PART.
SOME ANSWERS SEEM SO DAMN DIFFICULT.
LIKE, THAT LITTLE FAT GUY LAST NIGHT-- WHAT WAS THAT ALL ABOUT? AND WHAT WAS THE PURPOSE OF THAT FACE PAINT OF HIS? I WAS SO SURE HE HAD SOME KNOWLEDGE OF ME.
AN OBNOXIOUS PAIN IN THE ASS IS WHAT HE WAS. STILL, THERE WAS SOMETHING FAMILIAR ABOUT HIM. AH WELL, HE'S THE LEAST OF MY PROBLEMS.
WHAT I NEED TO DO IS GET THE FILE ON WANDA. SEE WHERE SHE LIVES. START FROM THERE. AND I KNOW JUST WHERE THE BOYS AT THE AGENCY KEEP THAT INFORMATION. AMUSING, HOW I USED TO BITCH AT THEM FOR INVADING PEOPLES' PRIVAC THEY MIGHT HAVE THE MISSING CLUES I'M LOOKING FOR.
GETTING INTO THE BUILDING WILL BE A CINCH WITH THESE POWERS. I'M ALMO LIKE A FRIGGIN' YOUNGBLOOD. WONDE IF THEY'RE STILL AROUND. THERE'S PROBABLY A HUNDRED OF 'EM, KNOWI THOSE GOVERNMENT STIFFS. "EXPLOIT AND OVERKILL," THE MOTTO OF ANY GOVERNMENT SYSTEM.
WE'VE GOT A FEW SCORES TO SETTLE, UNCLE SAM AND I. LIKE, NUMBER ONE...
...HOW DID I DIE. THAT ONE STILL HASN'T COME BACK TO ME. I'LL PUT THAT ONE ON THE BACK-BURNER...
...FOR NOW.
HAVE TO FIGURE THIS CRAP OUT ONE BIT AT A TIME. FIRST, I HAVE TO SEE WANDA... SHE'S THE ONLY REASON I'M EVEN BACK.

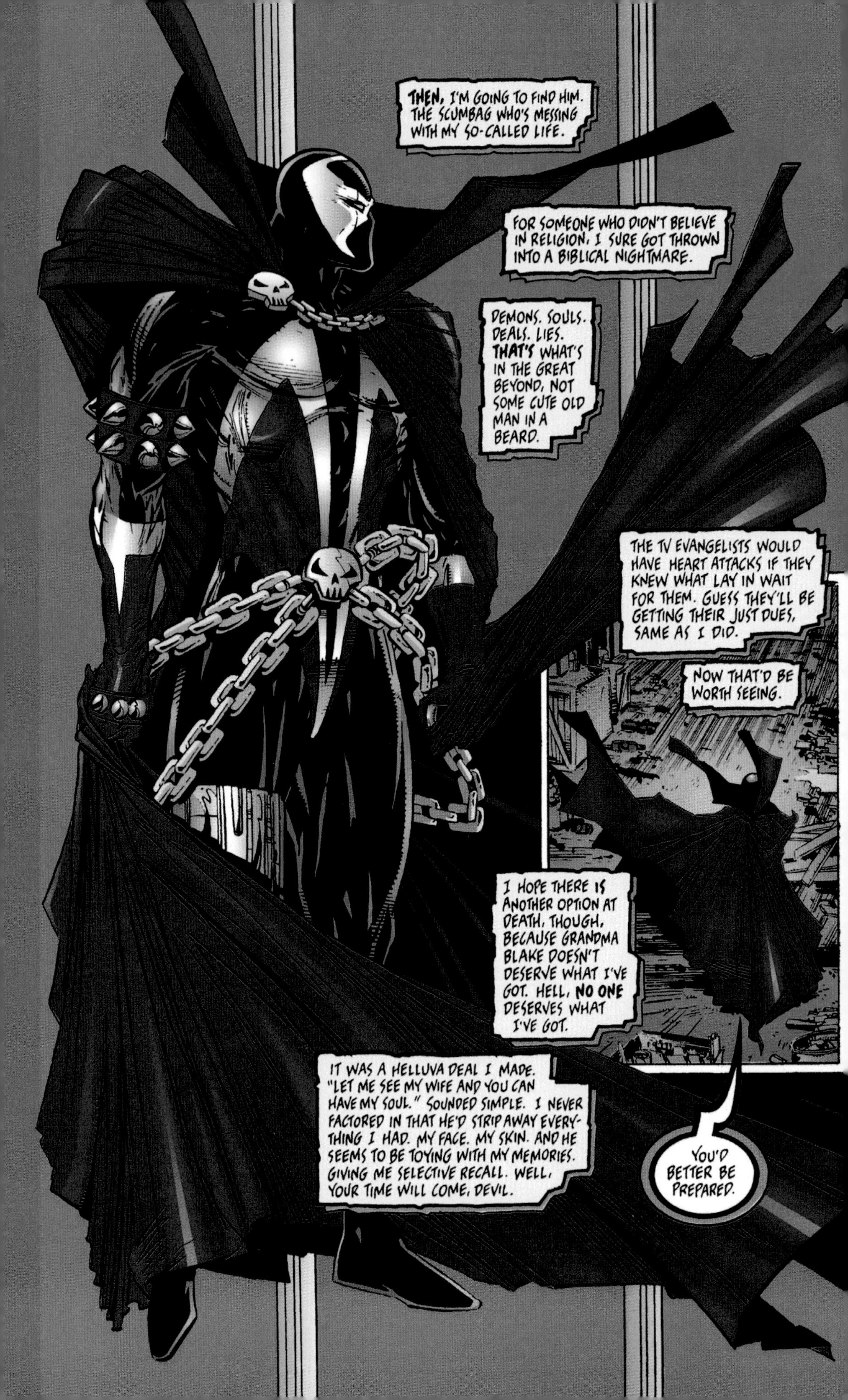
THEN, I'M GOING TO FIND HIM. THE SCUMBAG WHO'S MESSING WITH MY SO-CALLED LIFE.
FOR SOMEONE WHO DIDN'T BELIEVE IN RELIGION, I SURE GOT THROWN INTO A BIBLICAL NIGHTMARE.
DEMONS. SOULS. DEALS. LIES. THAT'S WHAT'S IN THE GREAT BEYOND, NOT SOME CUTE OLD MAN IN A BEARD.
THE TV EVANGELISTS WOULD HAVE HEART ATTACKS IF THEY KNEW WHAT LAY IN WAIT FOR THEM. GUESS THEY'LL BE GETTING THEIR JUST DUES, SAME AS I DID.
NOW THAT'D BE WORTH SEEING.
I HOPE THERE IS ANOTHER OPTION AT DEATH, THOUGH, BECAUSE GRANDMA BLAKE DOESN'T DESERVE WHAT I'VE GOT. HELL, NO ONE DESERVES WHAT I'VE GOT.
IT WAS A HELLUVA DEAL I MADE. "LET ME SEE MY WIFE AND YOU CAN HAVE MY SOUL." SOUNDED SIMPLE. I NEVER FACTORED IN THAT HE'D STRIP AWAY EVERYTHING I HAD. MY FACE. MY SKIN. AND HE SEEMS TO BE TOYING WITH MY MEMORIES. GIVING ME SELECTIVE RECALL. WELL, YOUR TIME WILL COME, DEVIL.
YOU'D BETTER BE PREPARED.

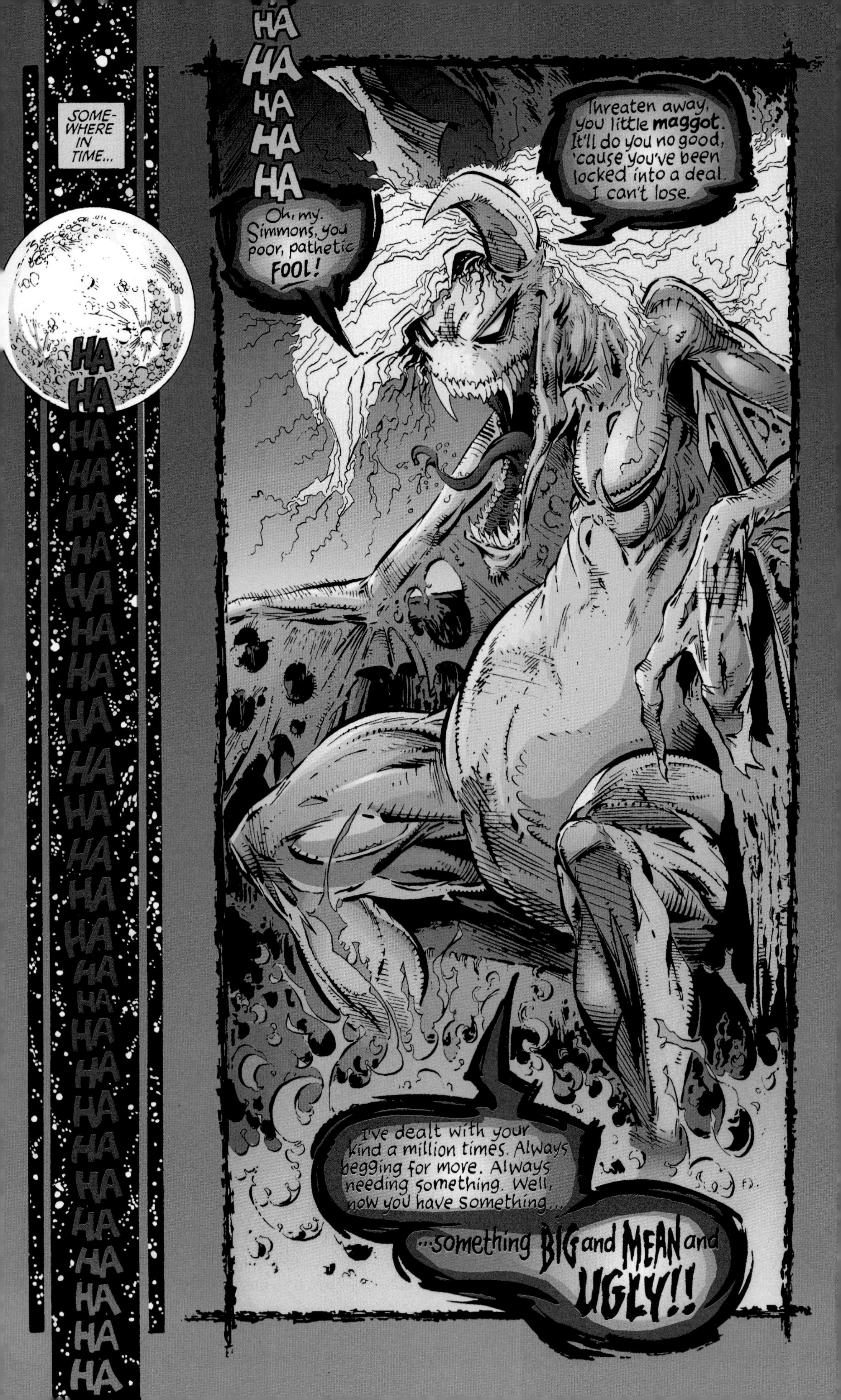

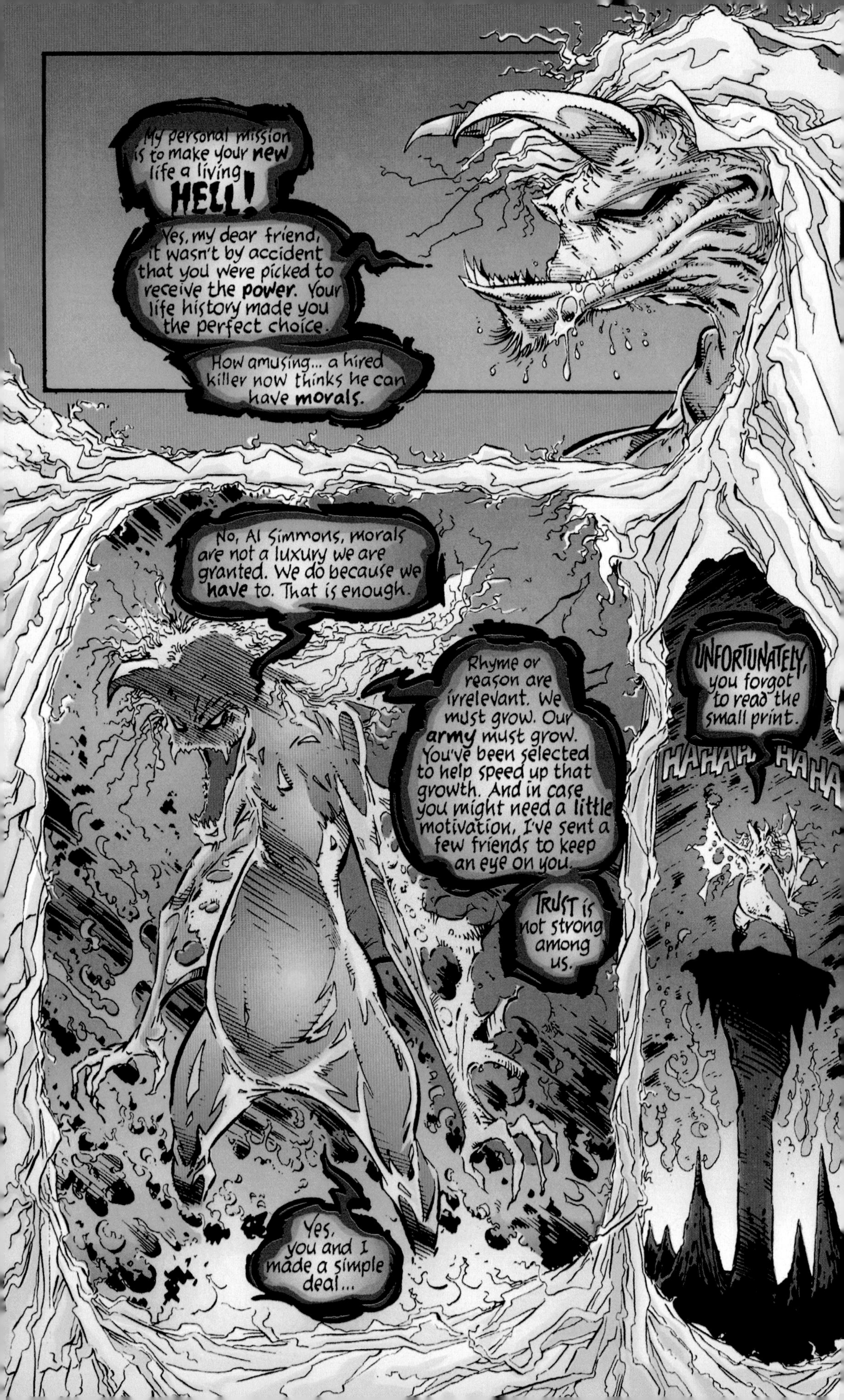

My personal mission is to make your new life a living HELL!
Yes, my dear friend, it wasn't by accident that you were picked to receive the power. Your life history made you the perfect choice.
How amusing... a hired killer now thinks he can have morals.
No, Al Simmons, morals are not a luxury we are granted. We do because we have to. That is enough.
Rhyme or reason are irrelevant. We must grow. Our army must grow. You've been selected to help speed up that growth. And in case you might need a little motivation, I've sent a few friends to keep an eye on you.
TRUST is not strong among us.
Yes, you and I made a simple deal...
UNFORTUNATELY, you forgot to read the small print.
HAHAHA HAHA

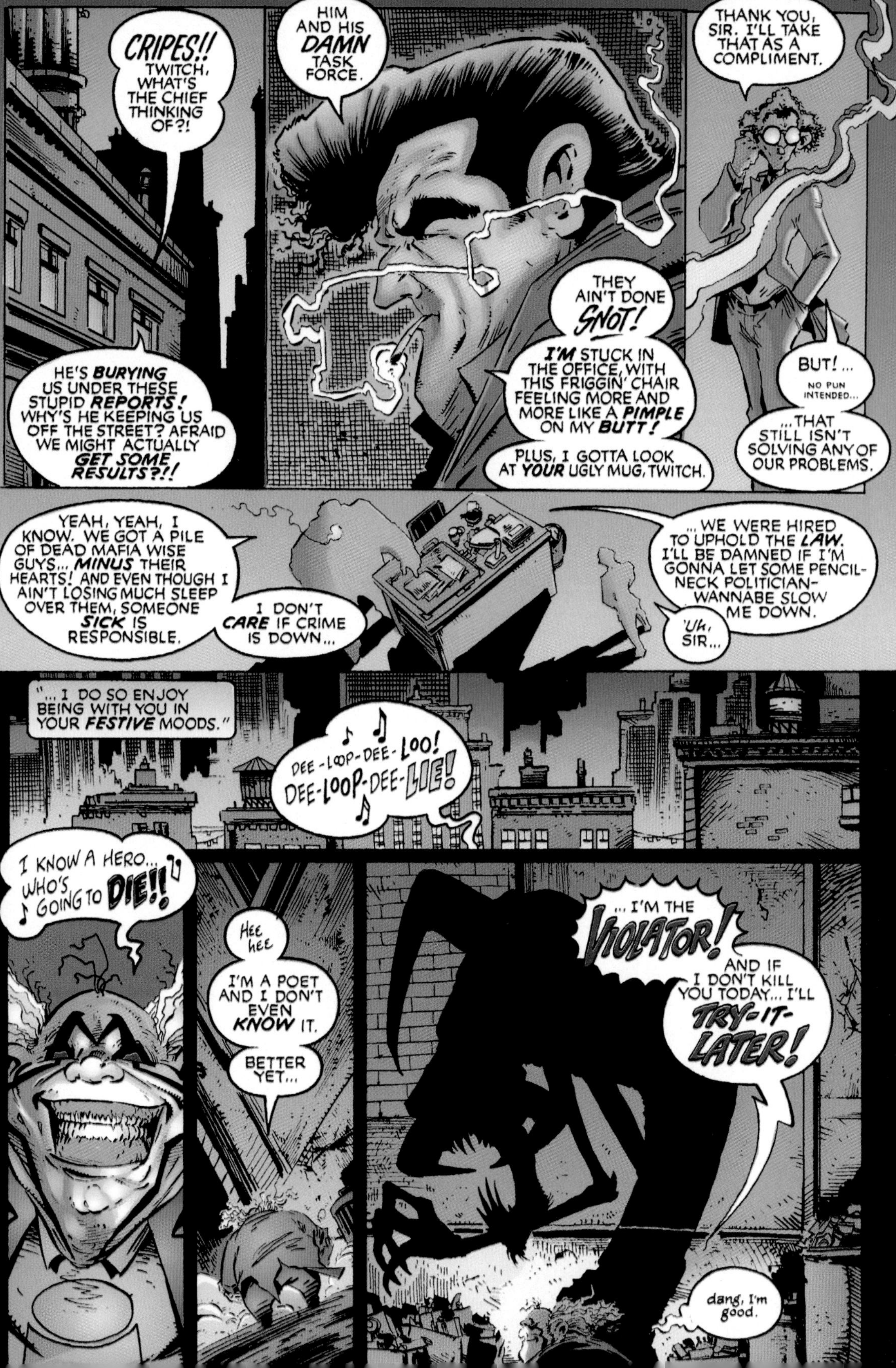
CRIPES!! TWITCH, WHAT'S THE CHIEF THINKING OF?!
HE'S BURYING US UNDER THESE STUPID REPORTS! WHY'S HE KEEPING US OFF THE STREET? AFRAID WE MIGHT ACTUALLY GET SOME RESULTS?!!
HIM AND HIS DAMN TASK FORCE.
THEY AIN'T DONE SNOT!
I'M STUCK IN THE OFFICE, WITH THIS FRIGGIN' CHAIR FEELING MORE AND MORE LIKE A PIMPLE ON MY BUTT!
PLUS, I GOTTA LOOK AT YOUR UGLY MUG, TWITCH.
THANK YOU, SIR. I'LL TAKE THAT AS A COMPLIMENT.
BUT! ...
NO PUN INTENDED...
...THAT STILL ISN'T SOLVING ANY OF OUR PROBLEMS.
YEAH, YEAH, I KNOW. WE GOT A PILE OF DEAD MAFIA WISE GUYS... MINUS THEIR HEARTS! AND EVEN THOUGH I AIN'T LOSING MUCH SLEEP OVER THEM, SOMEONE SICK IS RESPONSIBLE.
I DON'T CARE IF CRIME IS DOWN...
...WE WERE HIRED TO UPHOLD THE LAW. I'LL BE DAMNED IF I'M GONNA LET SOME PENCIL-NECK POLITICIAN-WANNABE SLOW ME DOWN.
'Uh, SIR...
"...I DO SO ENJOY BEING WITH YOU IN YOUR FESTIVE MOODS."
DEE-LOOP-DEE-LOO! DEE-LOOP-DEE-LIE!
I KNOW A HERO... WHO'S GOING TO DIE!!
Hee hee
I'M A POET AND I DON'T EVEN KNOW IT.
BETTER YET...
...I'M THE VIOLATOR!
AND IF I DON'T KILL YOU TODAY... I'LL TRY-IT-LATER!
dang, I'm good.

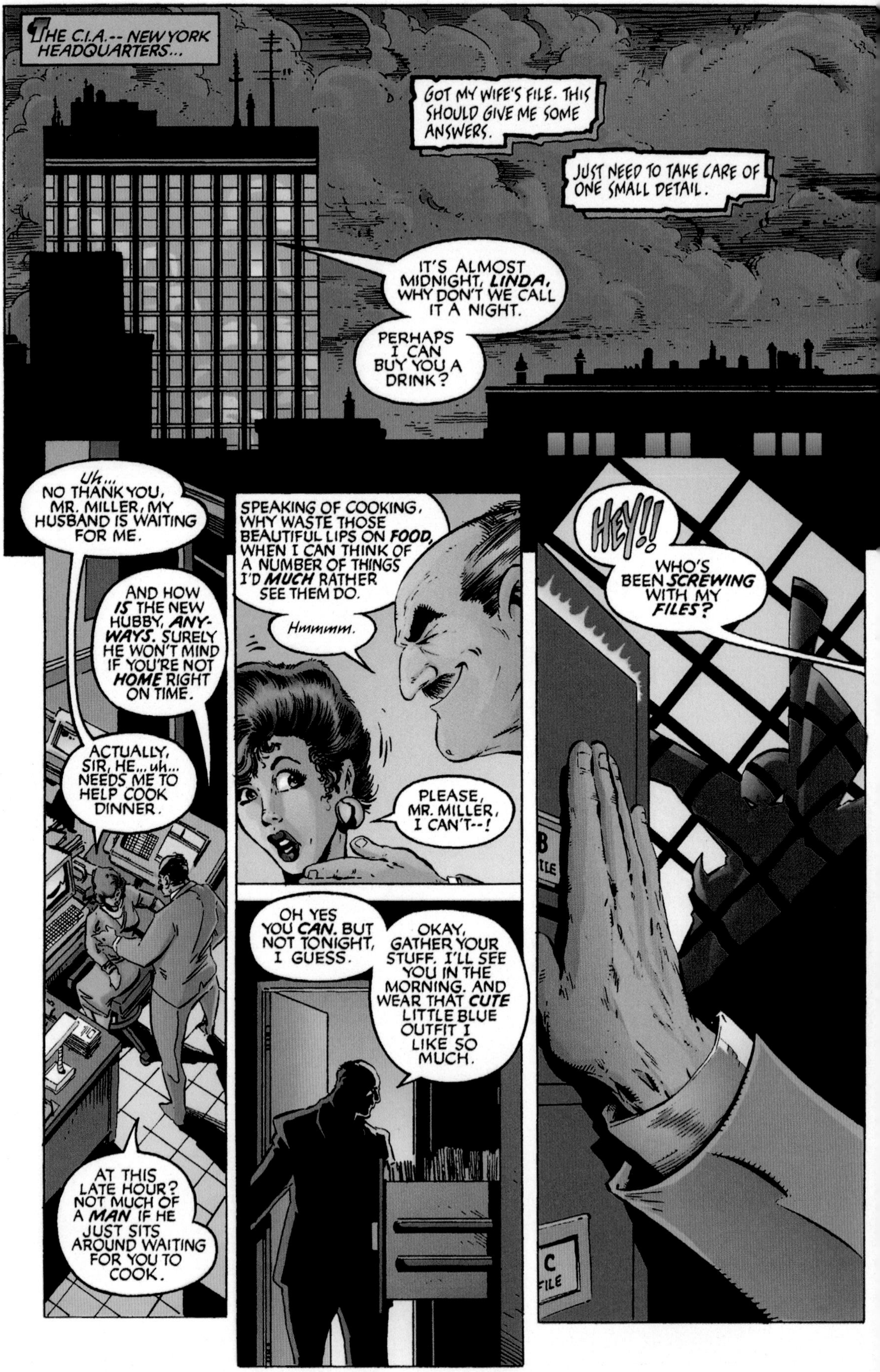
THE C.I.A.-- NEW YORK HEADQUARTERS...
GOT MY WIFE'S FILE. THIS SHOULD GIVE ME SOME ANSWERS.
JUST NEED TO TAKE CARE OF ONE SMALL DETAIL.
IT'S ALMOST MIDNIGHT, LINDA, WHY DON'T WE CALL IT A NIGHT.
PERHAPS I CAN BUY YOU A DRINK?
Uh... NO THANK YOU, MR. MILLER, MY HUSBAND IS WAITING FOR ME.
AND HOW IS THE NEW HUBBY, ANYWAYS. SURELY HE WON'T MIND IF YOU'RE NOT HOME RIGHT ON TIME.
ACTUALLY, SIR, HE... uh... NEEDS ME TO HELP COOK DINNER.
AT THIS LATE HOUR? NOT MUCH OF A MAN IF HE JUST SITS AROUND WAITING FOR YOU TO COOK.
SPEAKING OF COOKING, WHY WASTE THOSE BEAUTIFUL LIPS ON FOOD, WHEN I CAN THINK OF A NUMBER OF THINGS I'D MUCH RATHER SEE THEM DO.
Hmmmm.
PLEASE, MR. MILLER, I CAN'T--!
OH YES YOU CAN. BUT NOT TONIGHT, I GUESS.
OKAY, GATHER YOUR STUFF. I'LL SEE YOU IN THE MORNING. AND WEAR THAT CUTE LITTLE BLUE OUTFIT I LIKE SO MUCH.
HEY!!
WHO'S BEEN SCREWING WITH MY FILES?
C
FILE

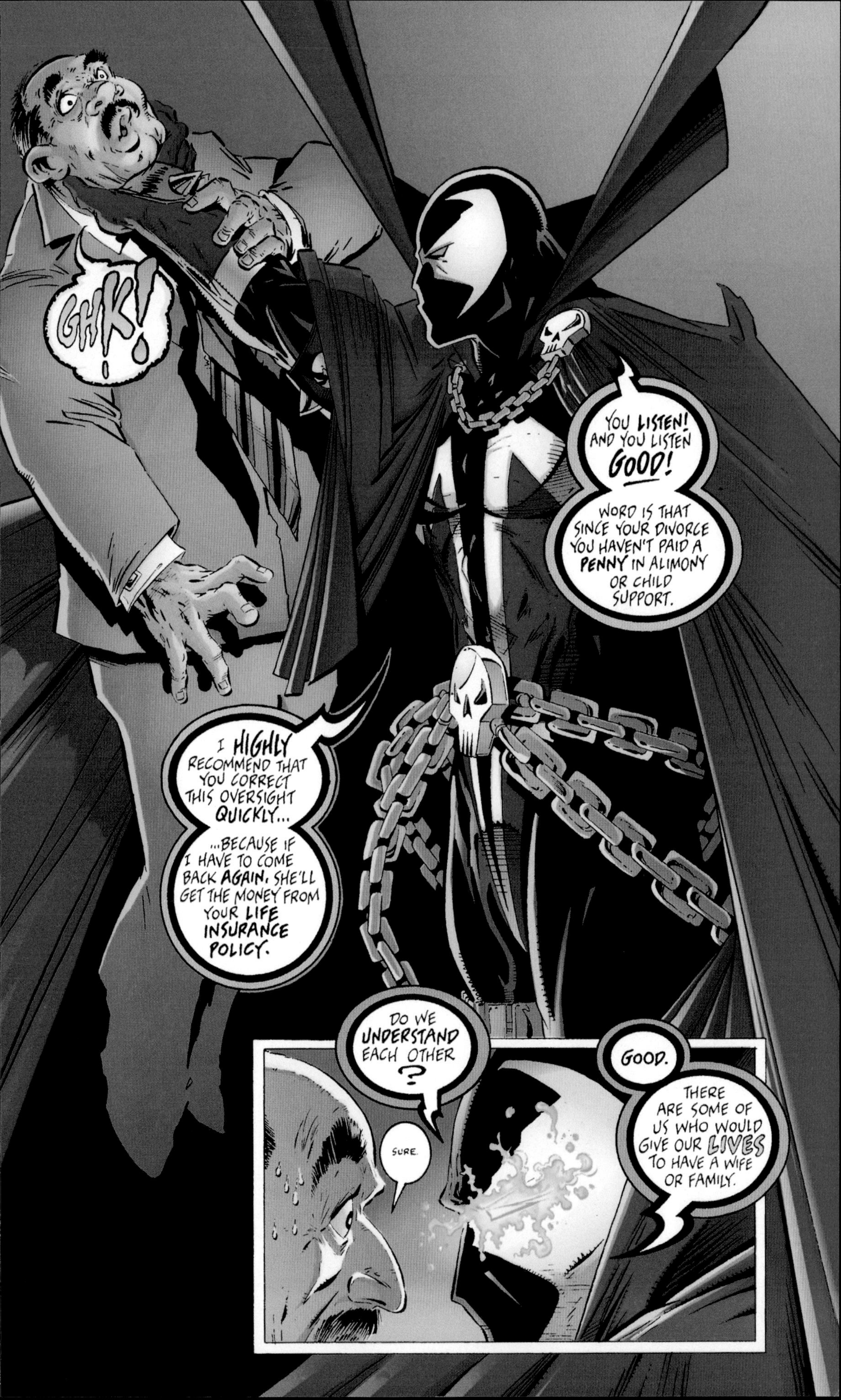
GHK!
YOU LISTEN! AND YOU LISTEN GOOD!
WORD IS THAT SINCE YOUR DIVORCE YOU HAVEN'T PAID A PENNY IN ALIMONY OR CHILD SUPPORT.
I HIGHLY RECOMMEND THAT YOU CORRECT THIS OVERSIGHT QUICKLY...
...BECAUSE IF I HAVE TO COME BACK AGAIN, SHE'LL GET THE MONEY FROM YOUR LIFE INSURANCE POLICY.
DO WE UNDERSTAND EACH OTHER?
SURE.
GOOD.
THERE ARE SOME OF US WHO WOULD GIVE OUR LIVES TO HAVE A WIFE OR FAMILY.

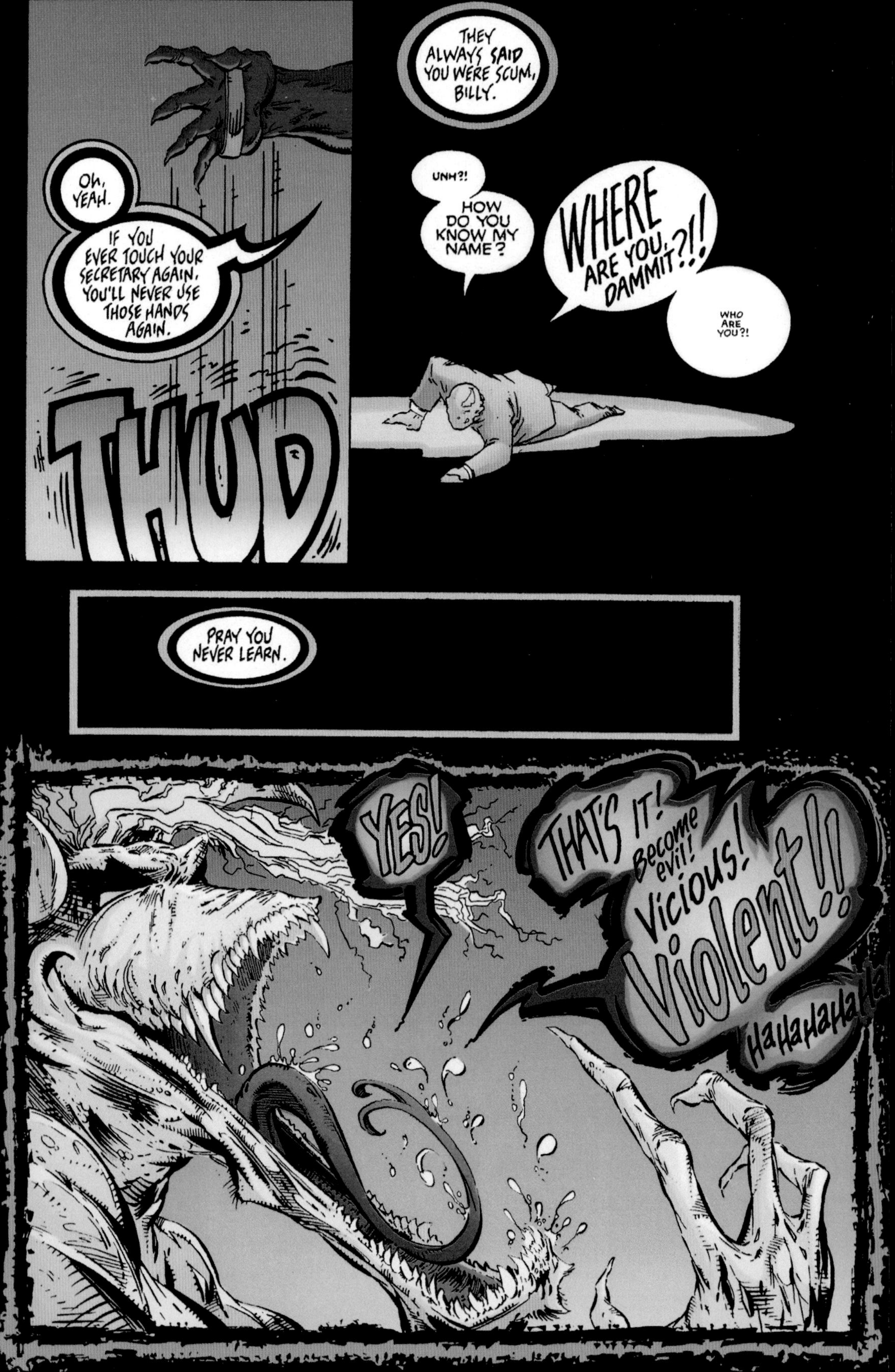
THEY ALWAYS SAID YOU WERE SCUM, BILLY.
UNH?!
HOW DO YOU KNOW MY NAME?
WHERE ARE YOU, DAMMIT?!!
WHO ARE YOU?!
Oh, YEAH.
IF YOU EVER TOUCH YOUR SECRETARY AGAIN, YOU'LL NEVER USE THOSE HANDS AGAIN.
THUD
PRAY YOU NEVER LEARN.
YES!
THAT'S IT! Become evil! Vicious! Violent!!
HaHaHaHaHa

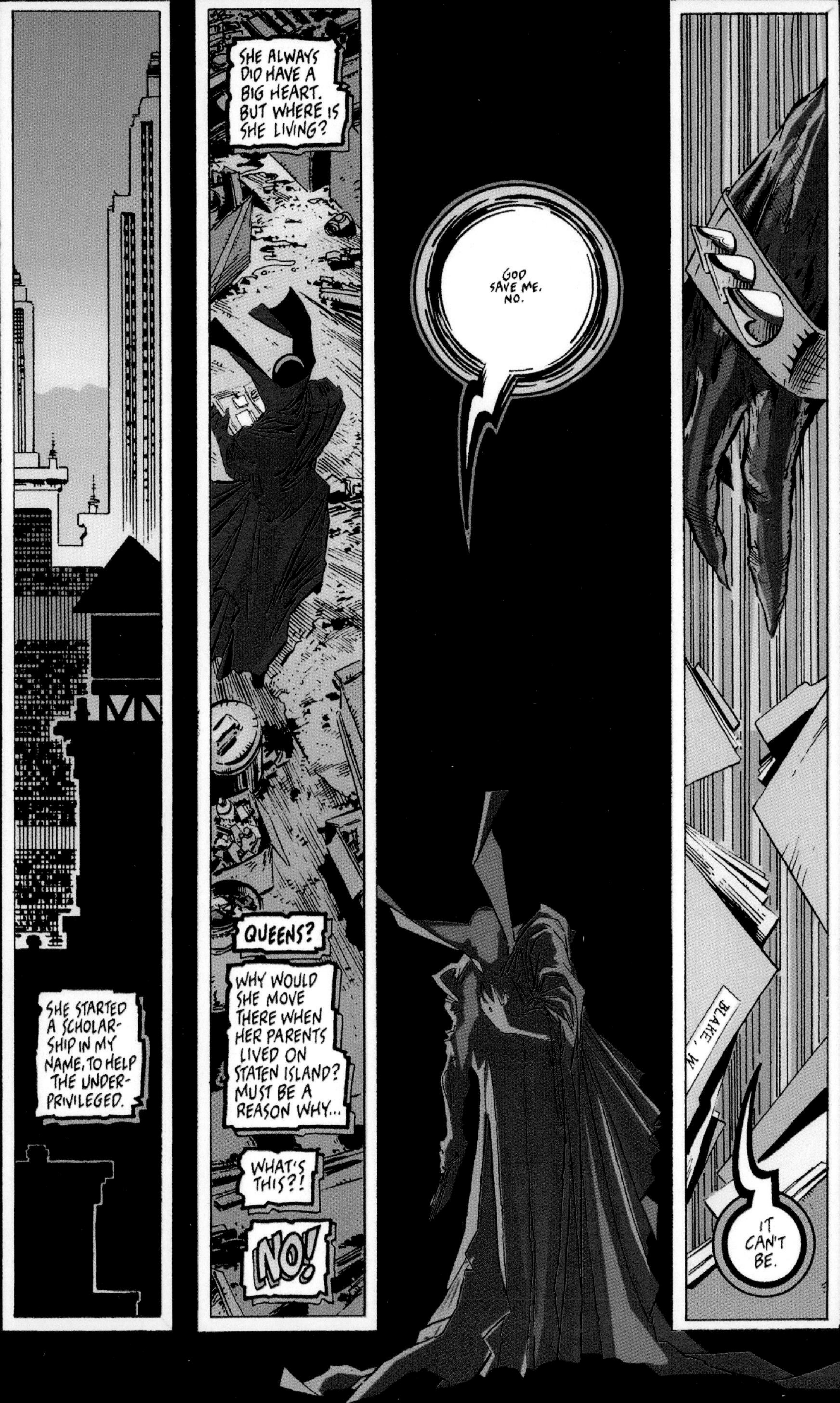

SHE STARTED A SCHOLAR-SHIP IN MY NAME, TO HELP THE UNDER-PRIVILEGED.
SHE ALWAYS DID HAVE A BIG HEART. BUT WHERE IS SHE LIVING?
QUEENS?
WHY WOULD SHE MOVE THERE WHEN HER PARENTS LIVED ON STATEN ISLAND? MUST BE A REASON WHY...
WHAT'S THIS?!
NO!
GOD SAVE ME. NO.
BLAKE, W
IT CAN'T BE.

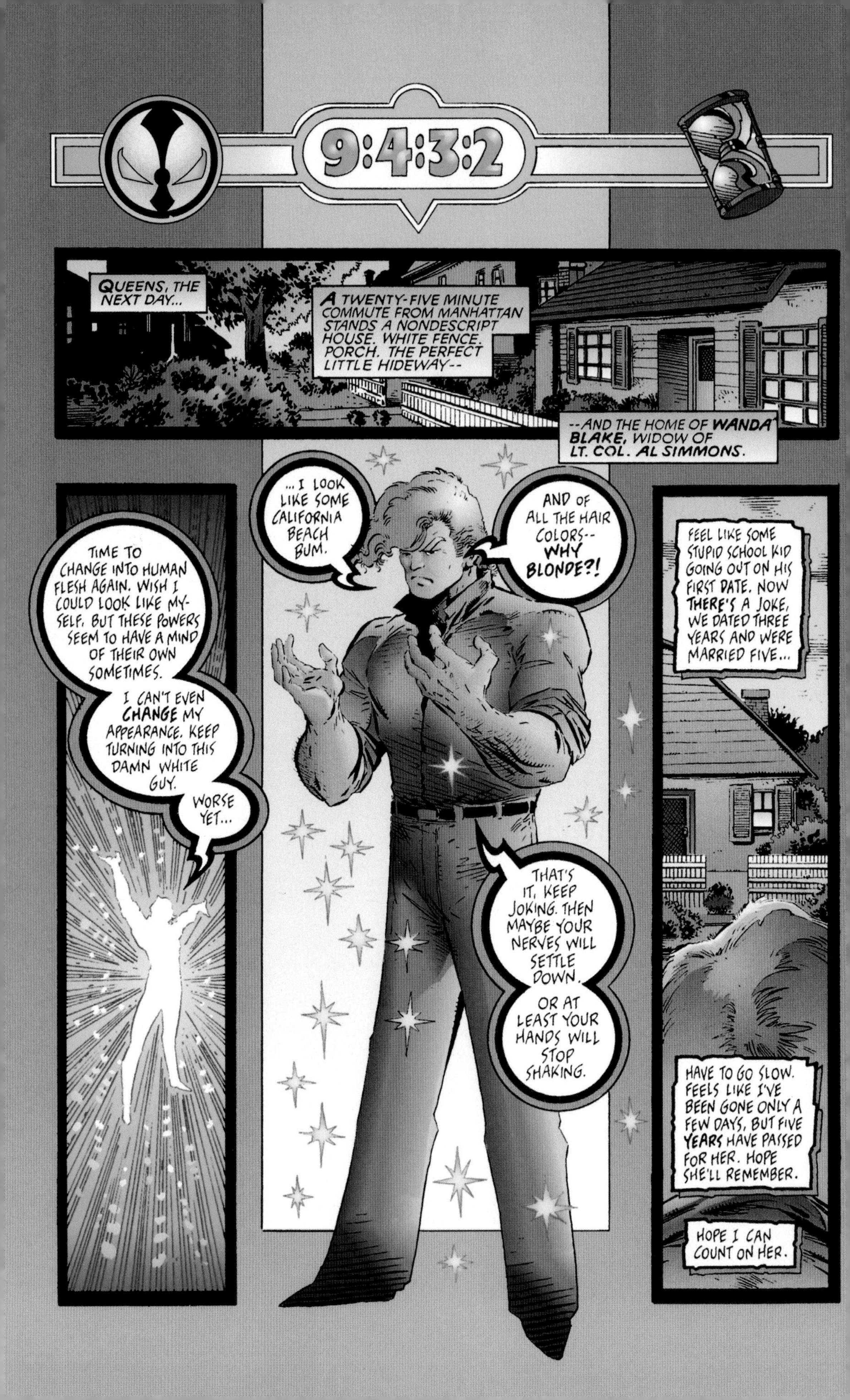
9:4:3:2
QUEENS, THE NEXT DAY...
A TWENTY-FIVE MINUTE COMMUTE FROM MANHATTAN STANDS A NONDESCRIPT HOUSE. WHITE FENCE. PORCH. THE PERFECT LITTLE HIDEWAY--
--AND THE HOME OF WANDA BLAKE, WIDOW OF LT. COL. AL SIMMONS.
TIME TO CHANGE INTO HUMAN FLESH AGAIN. WISH I COULD LOOK LIKE MY-SELF. BUT THESE POWERS SEEM TO HAVE A MIND OF THEIR OWN SOMETIMES.
I CAN'T EVEN CHANGE MY APPEARANCE. KEEP TURNING INTO THIS DAMN WHITE GUY.
WORSE YET...
...I LOOK LIKE SOME CALIFORNIA BEACH BUM.
AND OF ALL THE HAIR COLORS-- WHY BLONDE?!
THAT'S IT, KEEP JOKING. THEN MAYBE YOUR NERVES WILL SETTLE DOWN.
OR AT LEAST YOUR HANDS WILL STOP SHAKING.
FEEL LIKE SOME STUPID SCHOOL KID GOING OUT ON HIS FIRST DATE. NOW THERE'S A JOKE, WE DATED THREE YEARS AND WERE MARRIED FIVE...
HAVE TO GO SLOW. FEELS LIKE I'VE BEEN GONE ONLY A FEW DAYS, BUT FIVE YEARS HAVE PASSED FOR HER. HOPE SHE'LL REMEMBER.
HOPE I CAN COUNT ON HER.

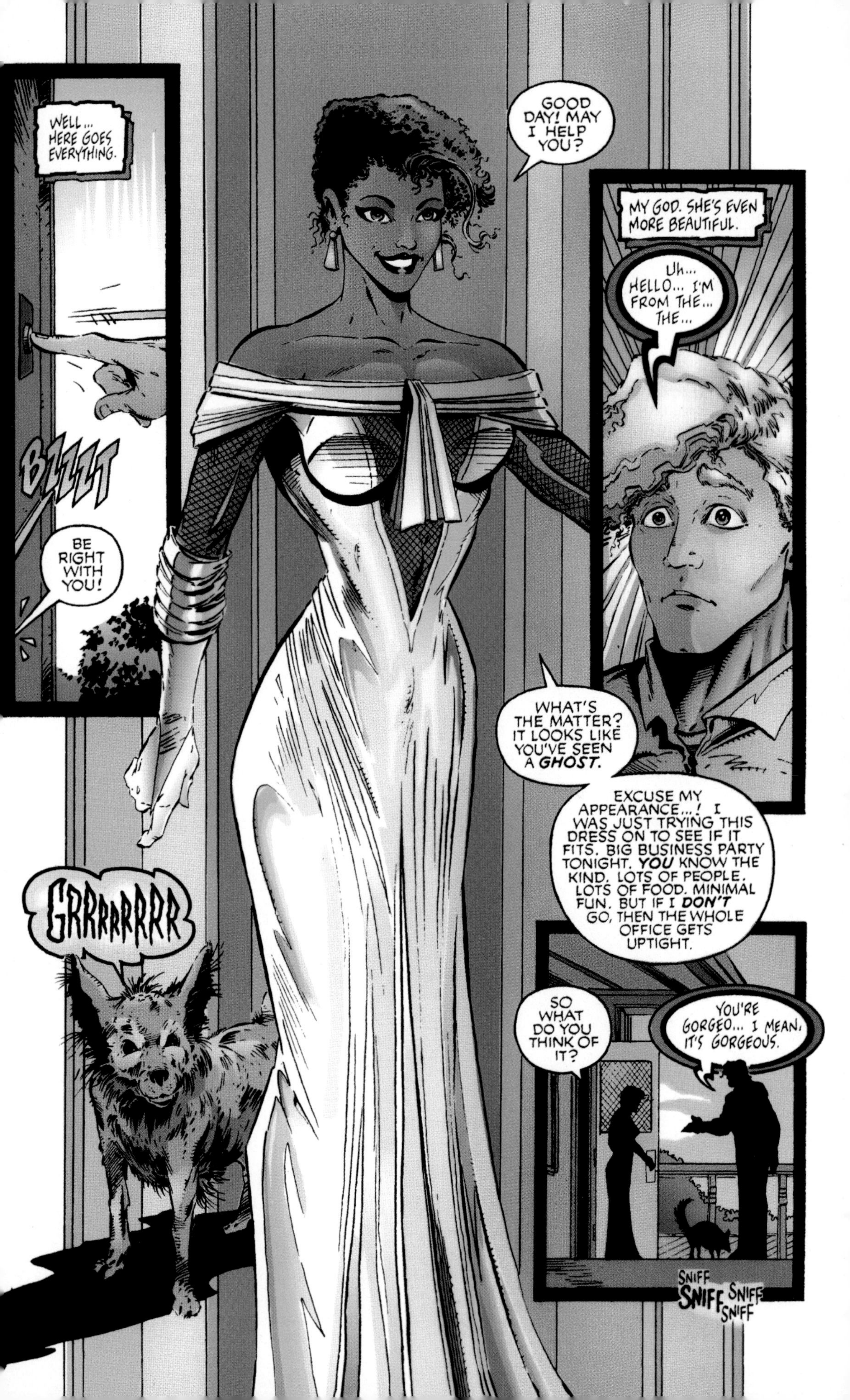
WELL... HERE GOES EVERYTHING.
BZZZT
BE RIGHT WITH YOU!
GOOD DAY! MAY I HELP YOU?
MY GOD. SHE'S EVEN MORE BEAUTIFUL.
Uh... HELLO... I'M FROM THE... THE...
WHAT'S THE MATTER? IT LOOKS LIKE YOU'VE SEEN A GHOST.
EXCUSE MY APPEARANCE...! I WAS JUST TRYING THIS DRESS ON TO SEE IF IT FITS. BIG BUSINESS PARTY TONIGHT. YOU KNOW THE KIND. LOTS OF PEOPLE. LOTS OF FOOD. MINIMAL FUN. BUT IF I DON'T GO, THEN THE WHOLE OFFICE GETS UPTIGHT.
GRRRRRRRR
SO WHAT DO YOU THINK OF IT?
YOU'RE GORGEO... I MEAN, IT'S GORGEOUS.
SNIFF SNIFF SNIFF SNIFF

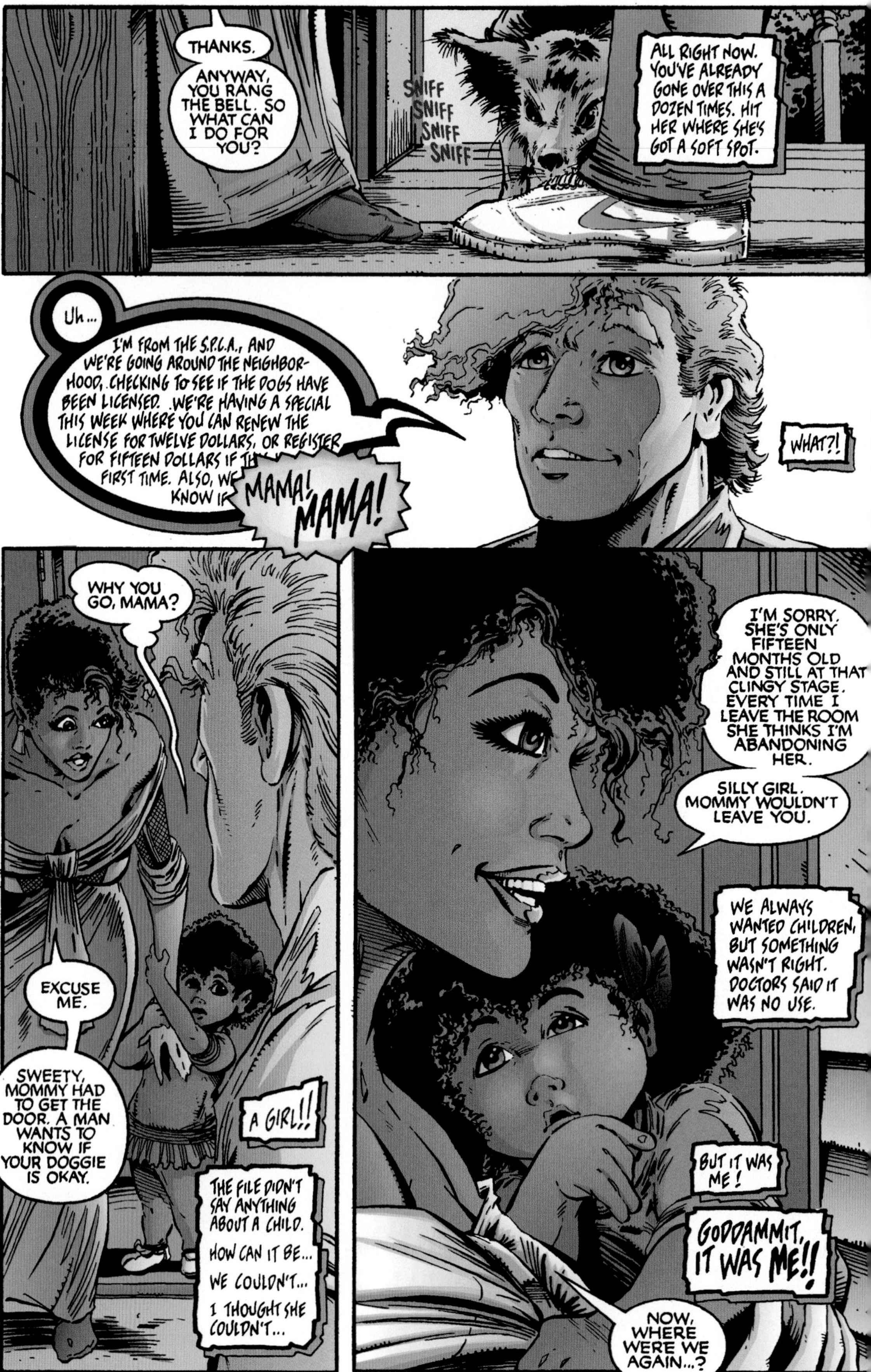
THANKS.
ANYWAY, YOU RANG THE BELL. SO WHAT CAN I DO FOR YOU?
SNIFF SNIFF SNIFF SNIFF
ALL RIGHT NOW. YOU'VE ALREADY GONE OVER THIS A DOZEN TIMES. HIT HER WHERE SHE'S GOT A SOFT SPOT.
Uh...
I'M FROM THE S.P.C.A., AND WE'RE GOING AROUND THE NEIGHBORHOOD, CHECKING TO SEE IF THE DOGS HAVE BEEN LICENSED. WE'RE HAVING A SPECIAL THIS WEEK WHERE YOU CAN RENEW THE LICENSE FOR TWELVE DOLLARS, OR REGISTER FOR FIFTEEN DOLLARS IF TH
FIRST TIME. ALSO, WE
KNOW IF
MAMA! MAMA!
WHAT?!
WHY YOU GO, MAMA?
EXCUSE ME.
SWEETY, MOMMY HAD TO GET THE DOOR. A MAN WANTS TO KNOW IF YOUR DOGGIE IS OKAY.
A GIRL!!
THE FILE DIDN'T SAY ANYTHING ABOUT A CHILD.
HOW CAN IT BE...
WE COULDN'T...
I THOUGHT SHE COULDN'T...
I'M SORRY. SHE'S ONLY FIFTEEN MONTHS OLD AND STILL AT THAT CLINGY STAGE. EVERY TIME I LEAVE THE ROOM SHE THINKS I'M ABANDONING HER.
SILLY GIRL. MOMMY WOULDN'T LEAVE YOU.
WE ALWAYS WANTED CHILDREN, BUT SOMETHING WASN'T RIGHT. DOCTORS SAID IT WAS NO USE.
BUT IT WAS ME!
GODDAMMIT, IT WAS ME!!
NOW, WHERE WERE WE AGAIN...?

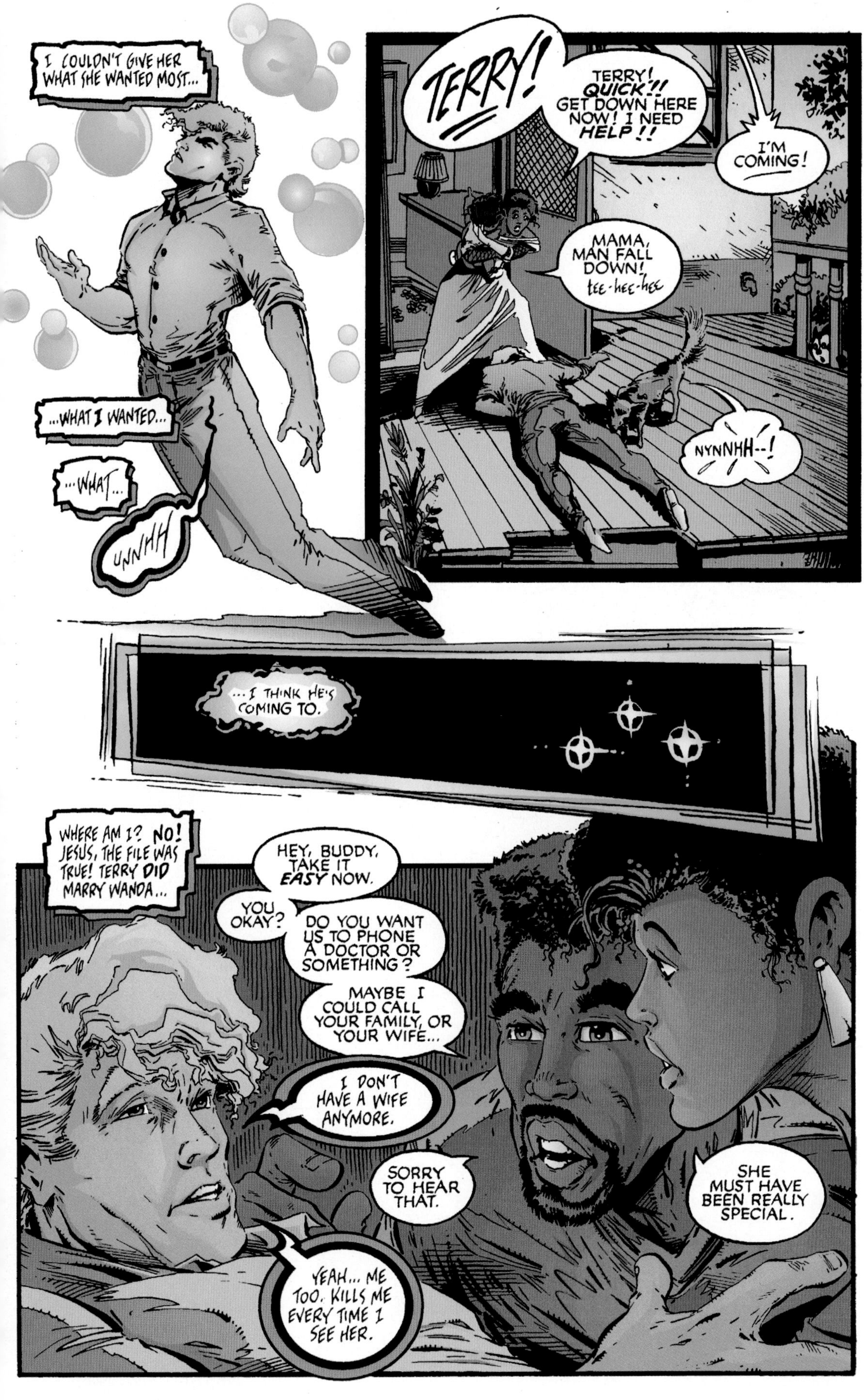
I COULDN'T GIVE HER WHAT SHE WANTED MOST...
...WHAT I WANTED...
...WHAT...
UNNHH
TERRY!
TERRY! QUICK!! GET DOWN HERE NOW! I NEED HELP!!
I'M COMING!
MAMA, MAN FALL DOWN! tee-hee-hee
NYNNHH--!
...I THINK HE'S COMING TO.
WHERE AM I? NO! JESUS, THE FILE WAS TRUE! TERRY DID MARRY WANDA...
HEY, BUDDY, TAKE IT EASY NOW.
YOU OKAY?
DO YOU WANT US TO PHONE A DOCTOR OR SOMETHING?
MAYBE I COULD CALL YOUR FAMILY, OR YOUR WIFE...
I DON'T HAVE A WIFE ANYMORE.
SORRY TO HEAR THAT.
SHE MUST HAVE BEEN REALLY SPECIAL.
YEAH... ME TOO. KILLS ME EVERY TIME I SEE HER.

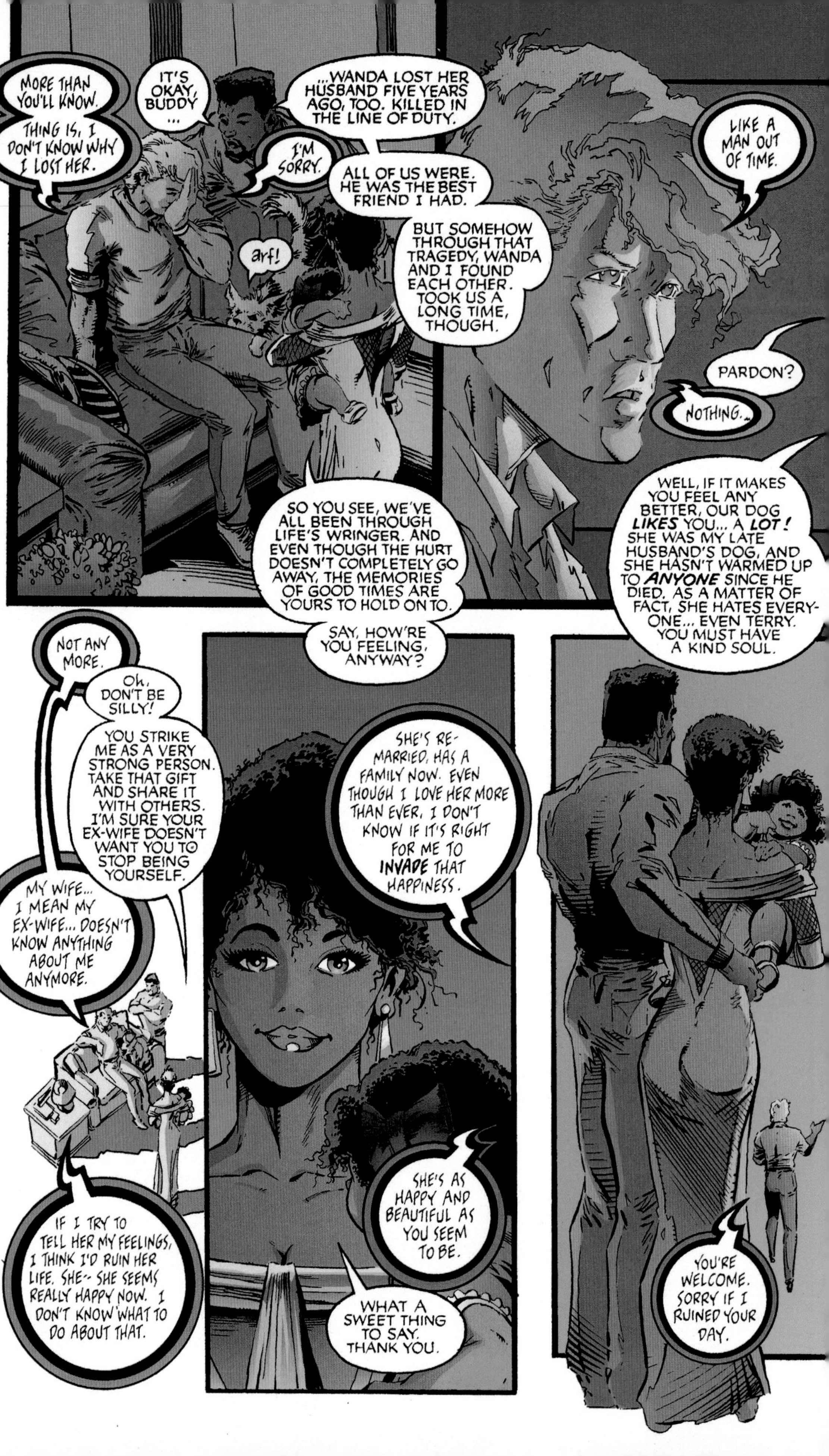
MORE THAN YOU'LL KNOW.
THING IS, I DON'T KNOW WHY I LOST HER.
IT'S OKAY, BUDDY ...
...WANDA LOST HER HUSBAND FIVE YEARS AGO, TOO. KILLED IN THE LINE OF DUTY.
I'M SORRY.
ALL OF US WERE. HE WAS THE BEST FRIEND I HAD.
arf!
BUT SOMEHOW THROUGH THAT TRAGEDY, WANDA AND I FOUND EACH OTHER. TOOK US A LONG TIME, THOUGH.
LIKE A MAN OUT OF TIME.
PARDON?
NOTHING...
SO YOU SEE, WE'VE ALL BEEN THROUGH LIFE'S WRINGER. AND EVEN THOUGH THE HURT DOESN'T COMPLETELY GO AWAY, THE MEMORIES OF GOOD TIMES ARE YOURS TO HOLD ON TO.
SAY, HOW'RE YOU FEELING, ANYWAY?
WELL, IF IT MAKES YOU FEEL ANY BETTER, OUR DOG LIKES YOU... A LOT! SHE WAS MY LATE HUSBAND'S DOG, AND SHE HASN'T WARMED UP TO ANYONE SINCE HE DIED. AS A MATTER OF FACT, SHE HATES EVERY-ONE... EVEN TERRY. YOU MUST HAVE A KIND SOUL.
NOT ANY MORE.
Oh, DON'T BE SILLY!
YOU STRIKE ME AS A VERY STRONG PERSON. TAKE THAT GIFT AND SHARE IT WITH OTHERS. I'M SURE YOUR EX-WIFE DOESN'T WANT YOU TO STOP BEING YOURSELF.
MY WIFE... I MEAN MY EX-WIFE... DOESN'T KNOW ANYTHING ABOUT ME ANYMORE.
IF I TRY TO TELL HER MY FEELINGS, I THINK I'D RUIN HER LIFE. SHE-- SHE SEEMS REALLY HAPPY NOW. I DON'T KNOW WHAT TO DO ABOUT THAT.
SHE'S RE-MARRIED, HAS A FAMILY NOW. EVEN THOUGH I LOVE HER MORE THAN EVER, I DON'T KNOW IF IT'S RIGHT FOR ME TO INVADE THAT HAPPINESS.
SHE'S AS HAPPY AND BEAUTIFUL AS YOU SEEM TO BE.
WHAT A SWEET THING TO SAY. THANK YOU.
YOU'RE WELCOME. SORRY IF I RUINED YOUR DAY.

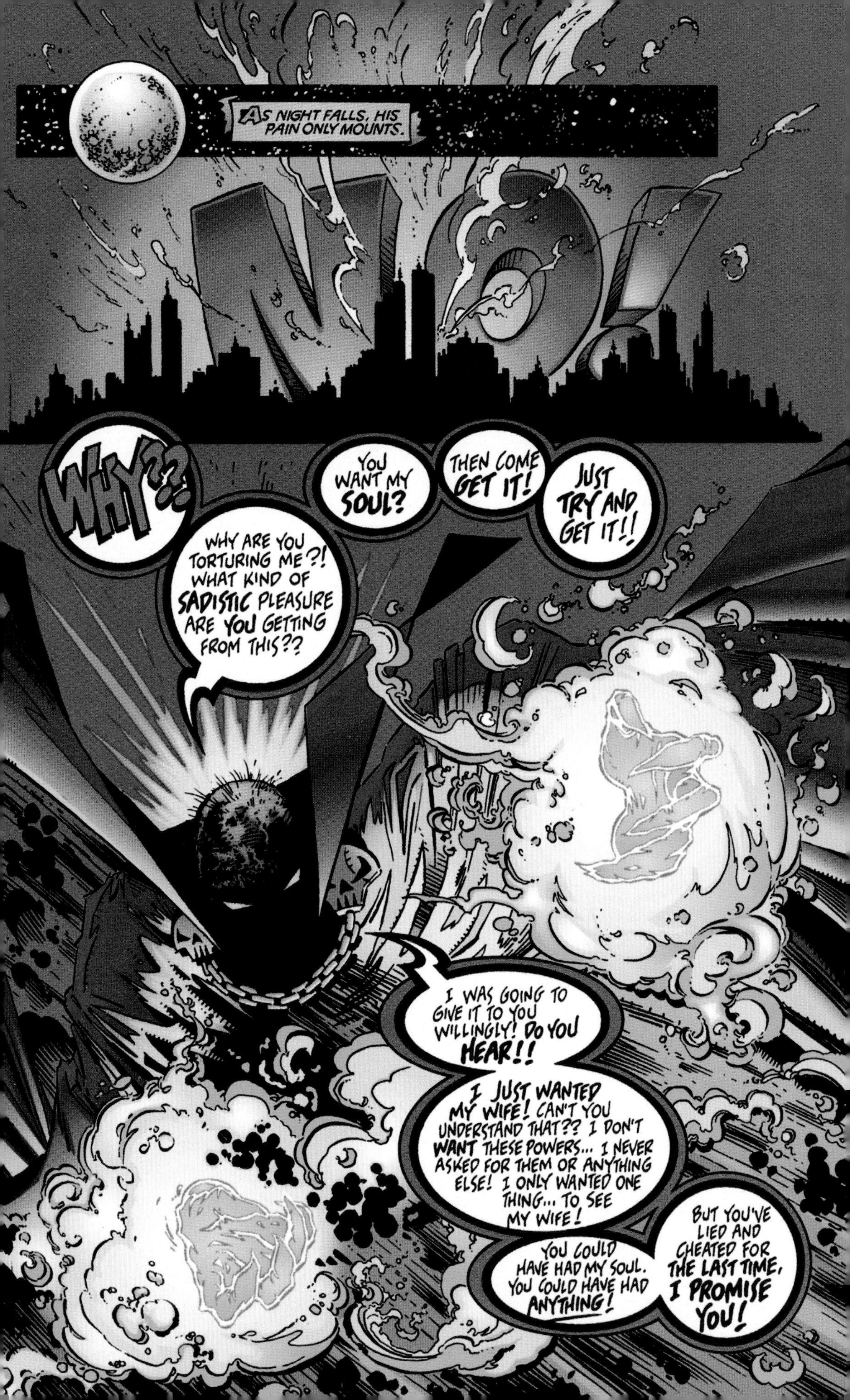

AS NIGHT FALLS, HIS PAIN ONLY MOUNTS.
NO!
WHY??
WHY ARE YOU TORTURING ME?! WHAT KIND OF SADISTIC PLEASURE ARE YOU GETTING FROM THIS??
YOU WANT MY SOUL?
THEN COME GET IT!
JUST TRY AND GET IT!!
I WAS GOING TO GIVE IT TO YOU WILLINGLY! DO YOU HEAR!!
I JUST WANTED MY WIFE! CAN'T YOU UNDERSTAND THAT?? I DON'T WANT THESE POWERS... I NEVER ASKED FOR THEM OR ANYTHING ELSE! I ONLY WANTED ONE THING... TO SEE MY WIFE!
YOU COULD HAVE HAD MY SOUL. YOU COULD HAVE HAD ANYTHING!
BUT YOU'VE LIED AND CHEATED FOR THE LAST TIME, I PROMISE YOU!

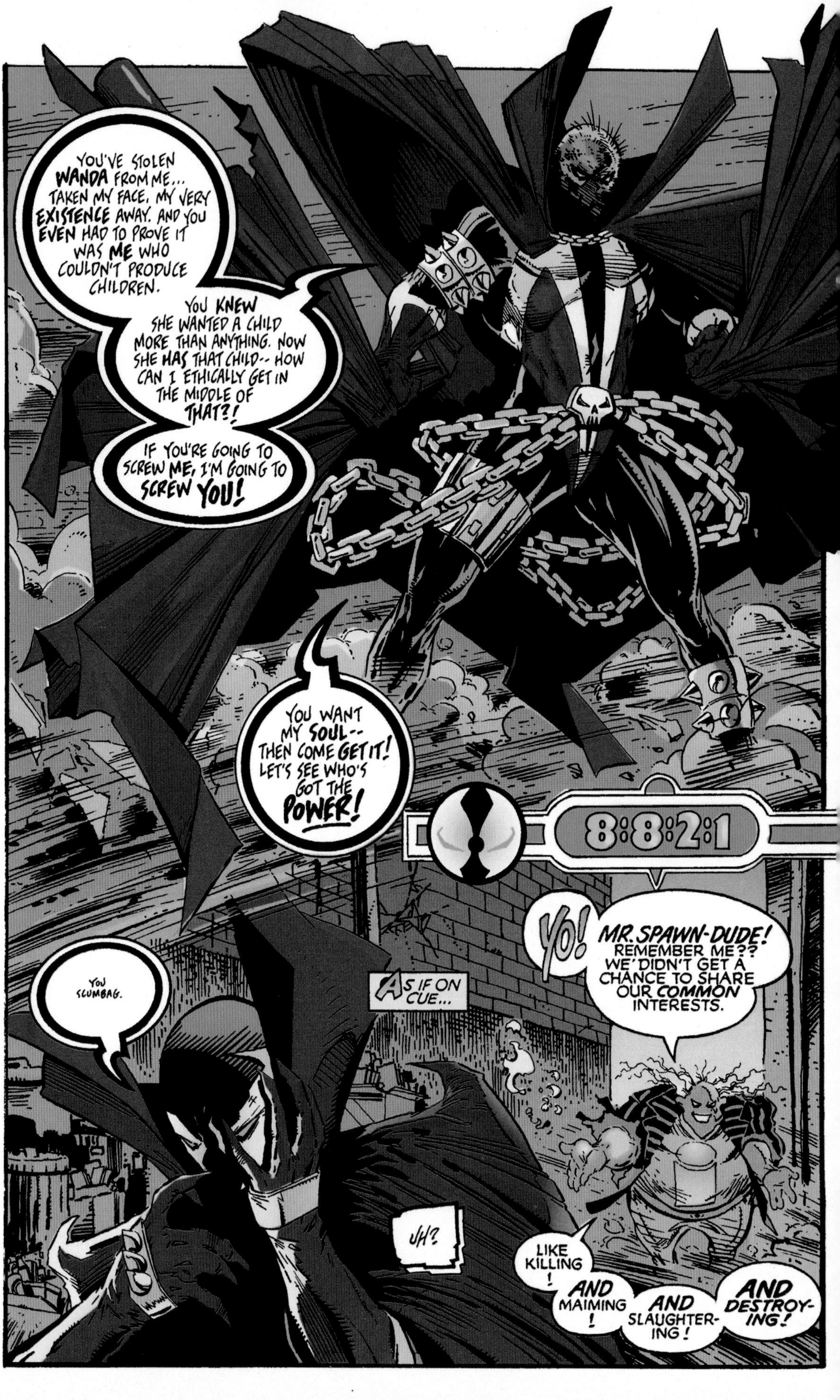
YOU'VE STOLEN WANDA FROM ME... TAKEN MY FACE, MY VERY EXISTENCE AWAY. AND YOU EVEN HAD TO PROVE IT WAS ME WHO COULDN'T PRODUCE CHILDREN.
YOU KNEW SHE WANTED A CHILD MORE THAN ANYTHING. NOW SHE HAS THAT CHILD-- HOW CAN I ETHICALLY GET IN THE MIDDLE OF THAT?!
IF YOU'RE GOING TO SCREW ME, I'M GOING TO SCREW YOU!
YOU WANT MY SOUL-- THEN COME GET IT! LET'S SEE WHO'S GOT THE POWER!
8:8:2:1
YOU SCUMBAG.
AS IF ON CUE...
YO!
MR. SPAWN-DUDE! REMEMBER ME?? WE DIDN'T GET A CHANCE TO SHARE OUR COMMON INTERESTS.
UH?
LIKE KILLING!
AND MAIMING!
AND SLAUGHTER-ING!
AND DESTROY-ING!

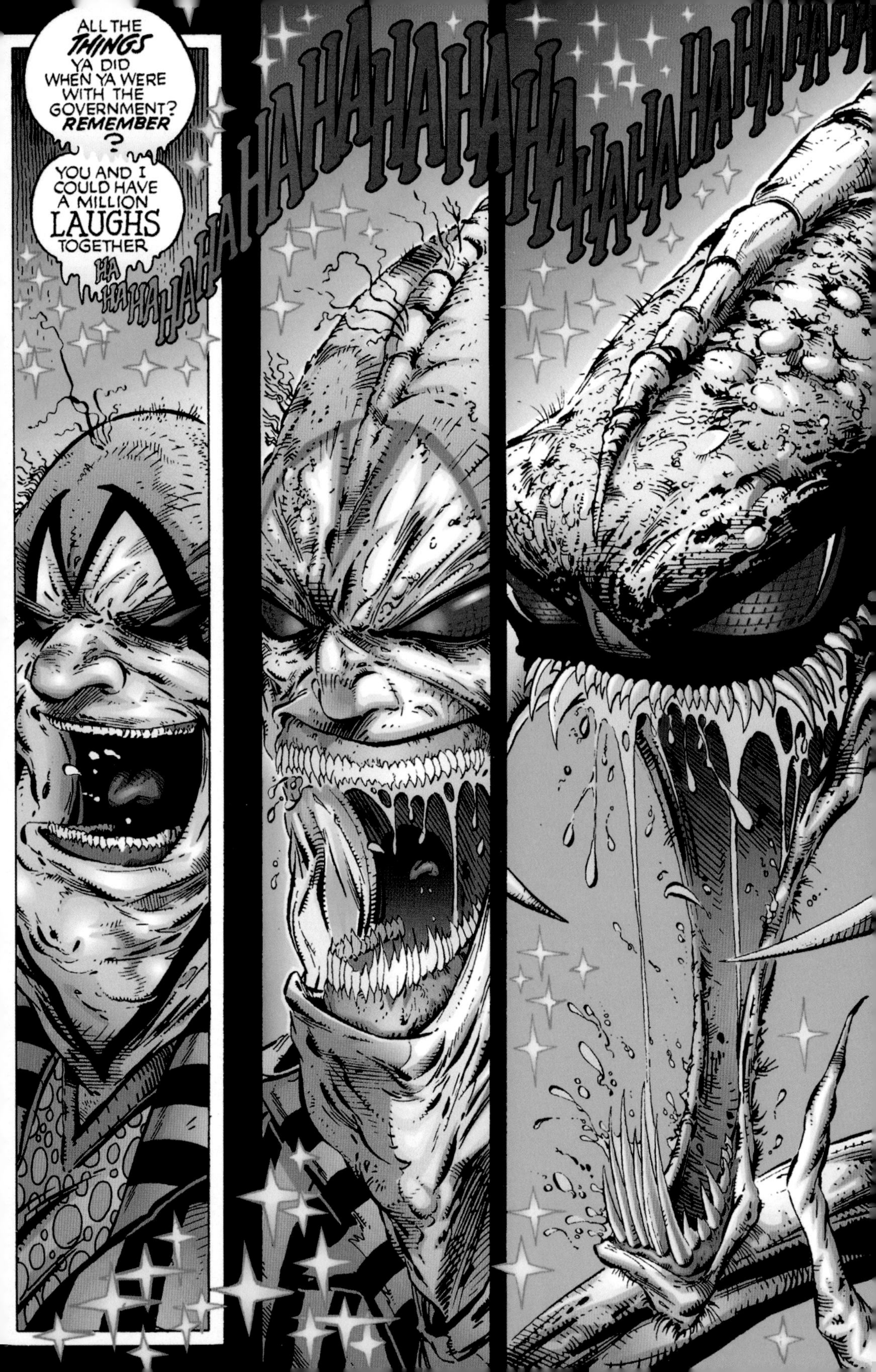

ALL THE THINGS YA DID WHEN YA WERE WITH THE GOVERNMENT? REMEMBER?
YOU AND I COULD HAVE A MILLION LAUGHS TOGETHER
HA HA HA HAHAHAHAHAHAHAHAHAHAHAHAHAHAHAHAHAHAHA

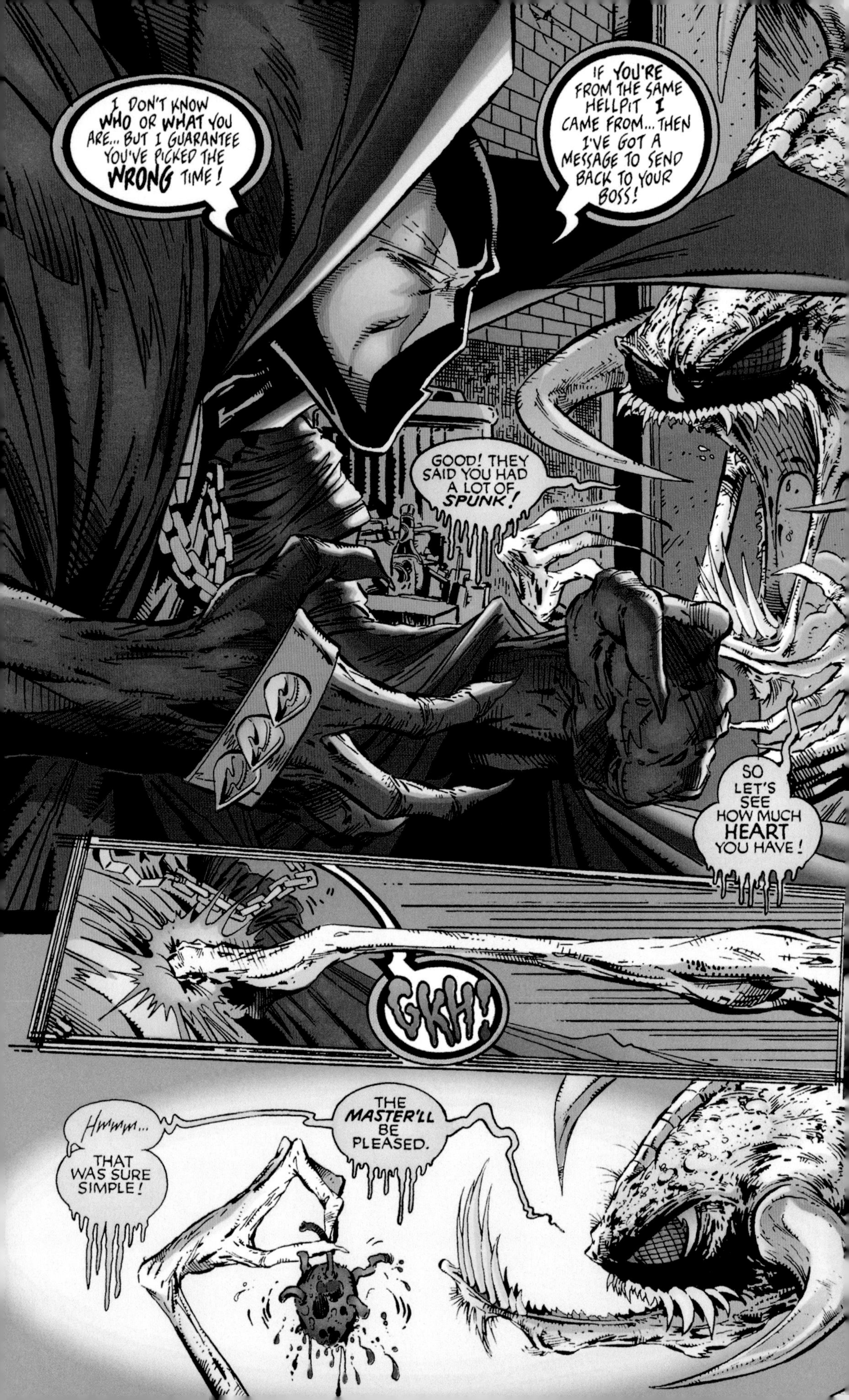
I DON'T KNOW WHO OR WHAT YOU ARE... BUT I GUARANTEE YOU'VE PICKED THE WRONG TIME!
IF YOU'RE FROM THE SAME HELLPIT I CAME FROM... THEN I'VE GOT A MESSAGE TO SEND BACK TO YOUR BOSS!
GOOD! THEY SAID YOU HAD A LOT OF SPUNK!
SO LET'S SEE HOW MUCH HEART YOU HAVE!
GKH!
Hmmm...
THAT WAS SURE SIMPLE!
THE MASTER'LL BE PLEASED.

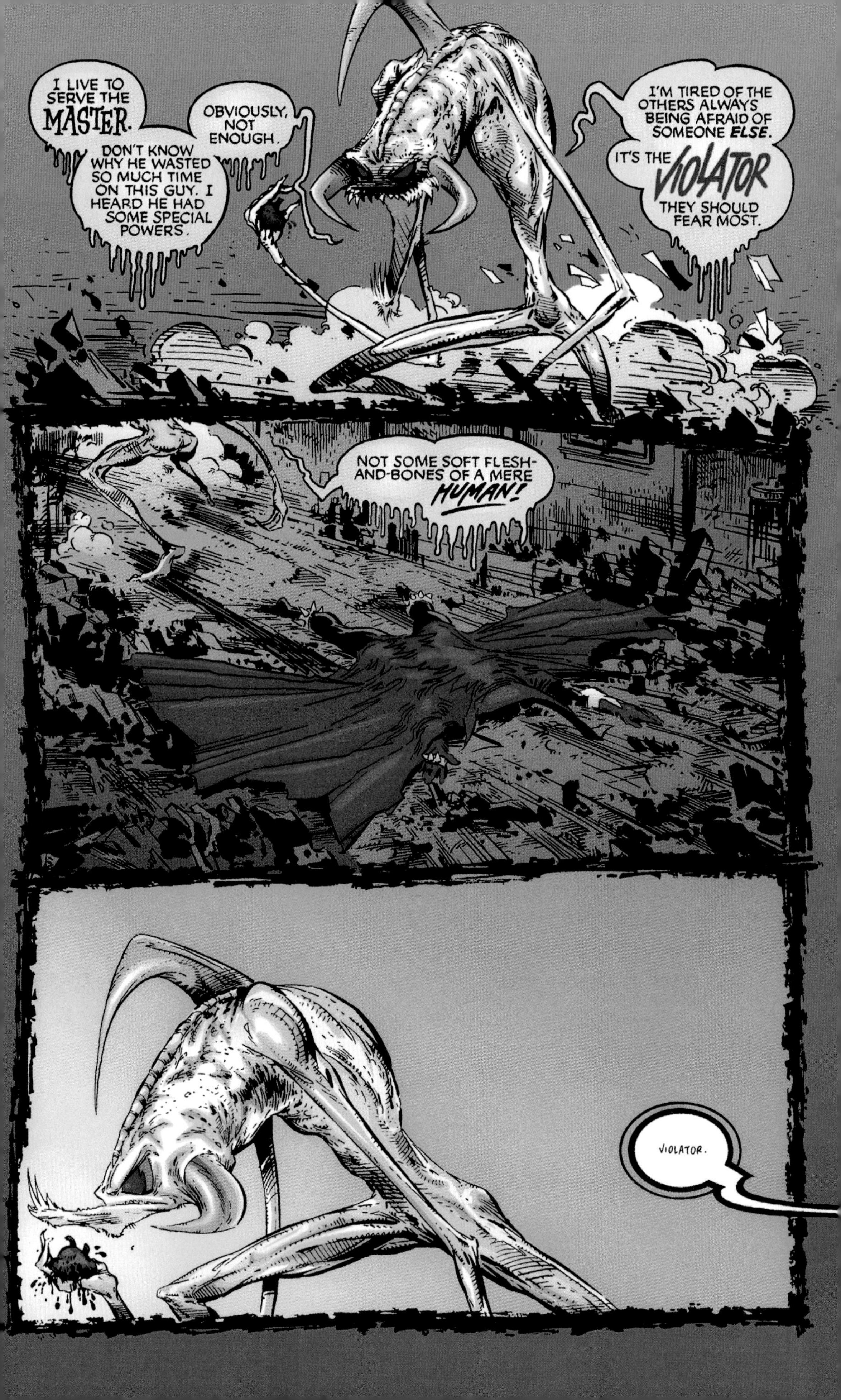

I LIVE TO SERVE THE MASTER.
DON'T KNOW WHY HE WASTED SO MUCH TIME ON THIS GUY. I HEARD HE HAD SOME SPECIAL POWERS.
OBVIOUSLY, NOT ENOUGH.
I'M TIRED OF THE OTHERS ALWAYS BEING AFRAID OF SOMEONE ELSE.
IT'S THE VIOLATOR THEY SHOULD FEAR MOST.
NOT SOME SOFT FLESH-AND-BONES OF A MERE HUMAN!
VIOLATOR.

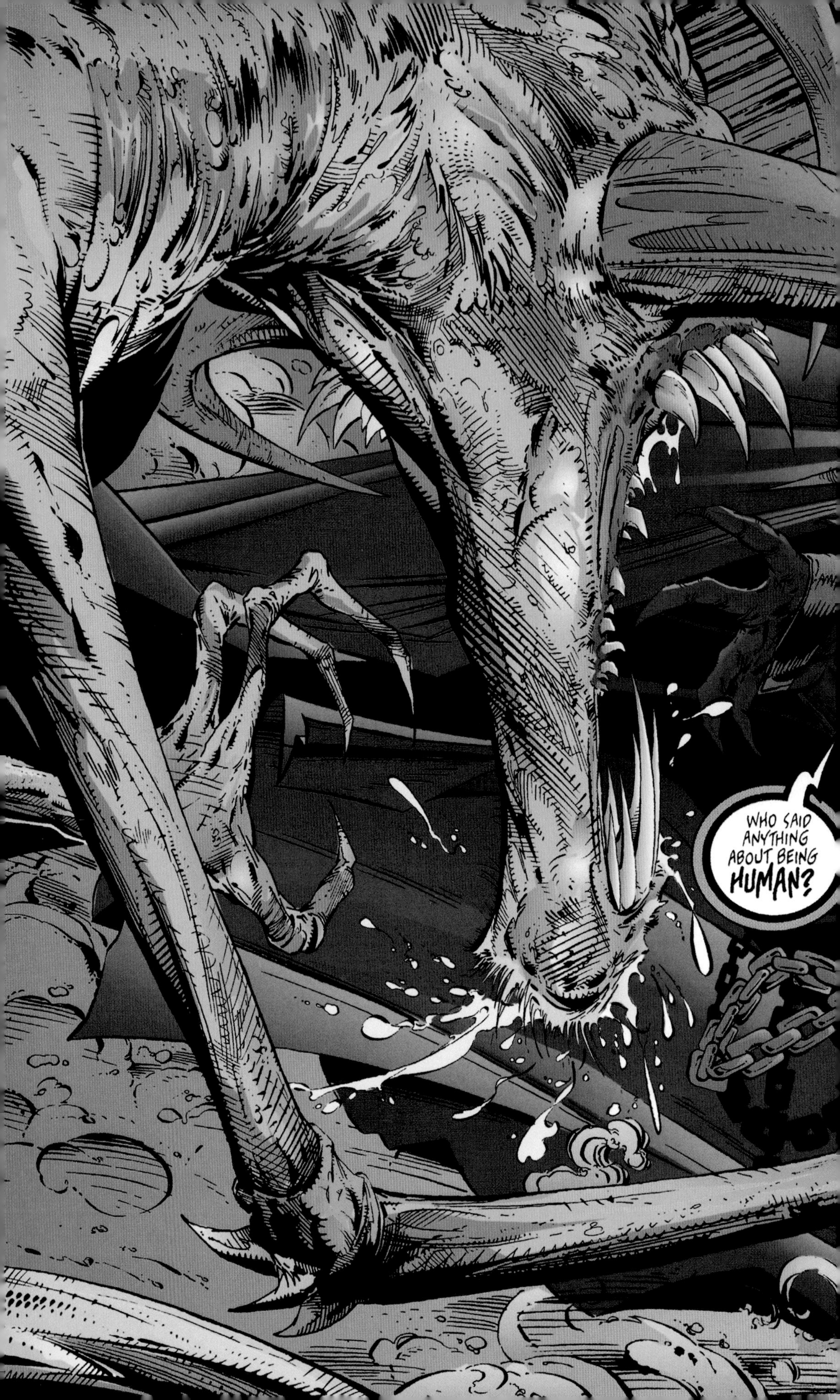
WHO SAID ANYTHING ABOUT BEING HUMAN?

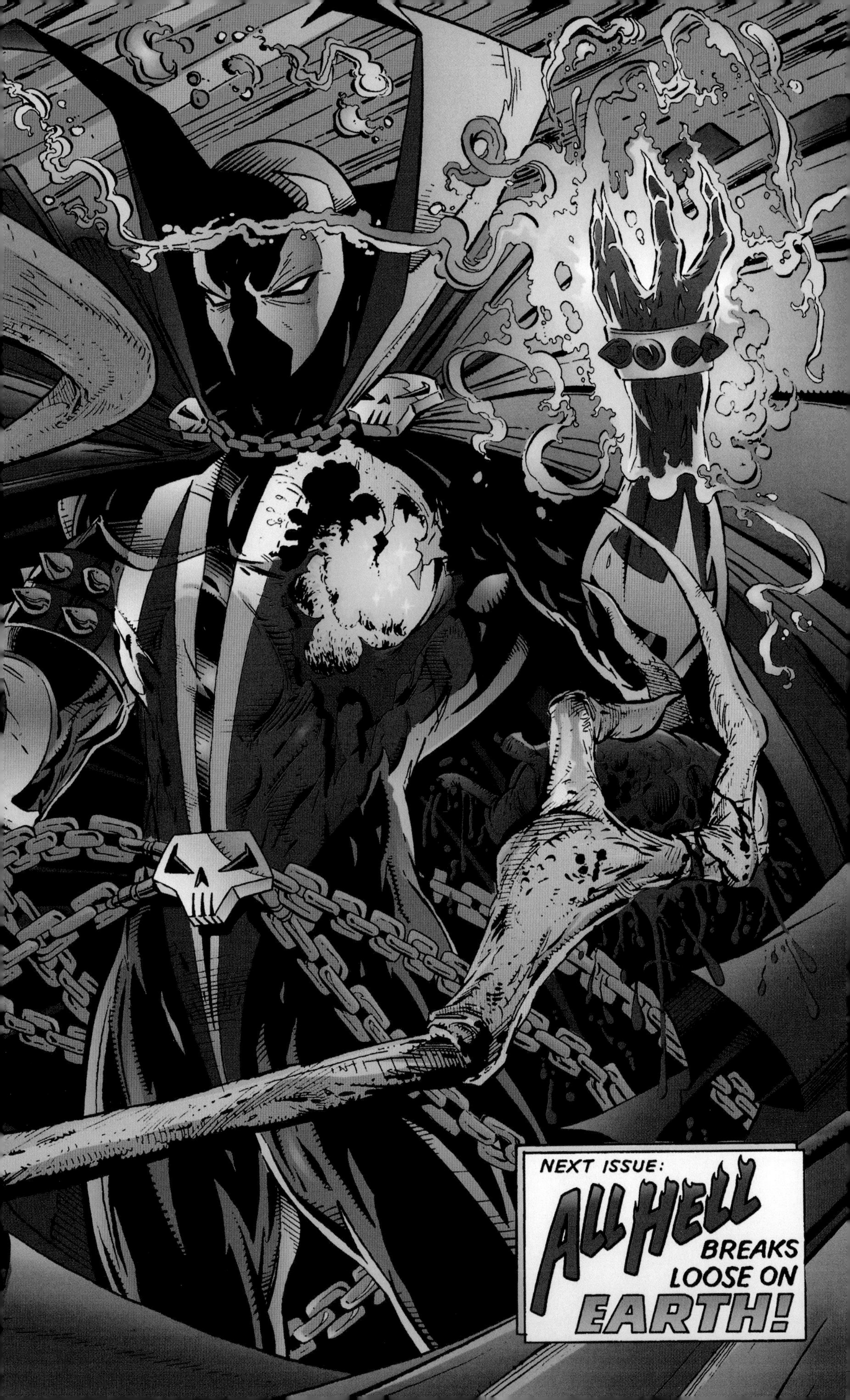
NEXT ISSUE:
ALL HELL BREAKS LOOSE ON EARTH!

"All I am saying is that although there is a great accomplishment in doing what I did, that doesn't necessarily mean I'm patting myself on the back, or that my book is any better than a lot of those that have come in the last 13 years. But very few have been able to keep a book going for 13 years. Even Marvel and DC start and stop a lot of books that don't keep going for 13 years. The sense of pride is just being able to survive in a pool of thousands of other comic books for as long as I have, and to do all that in the same place – Image Comics."

-Todd McFarlane
Interview for Millarworld

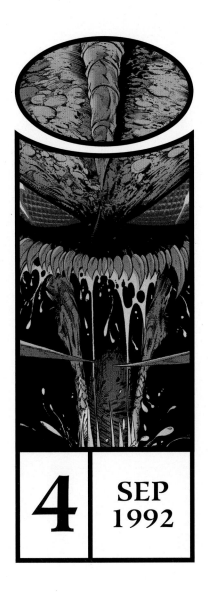

4 | **SEP 1992**

"QUESTIONS"
PART FOUR

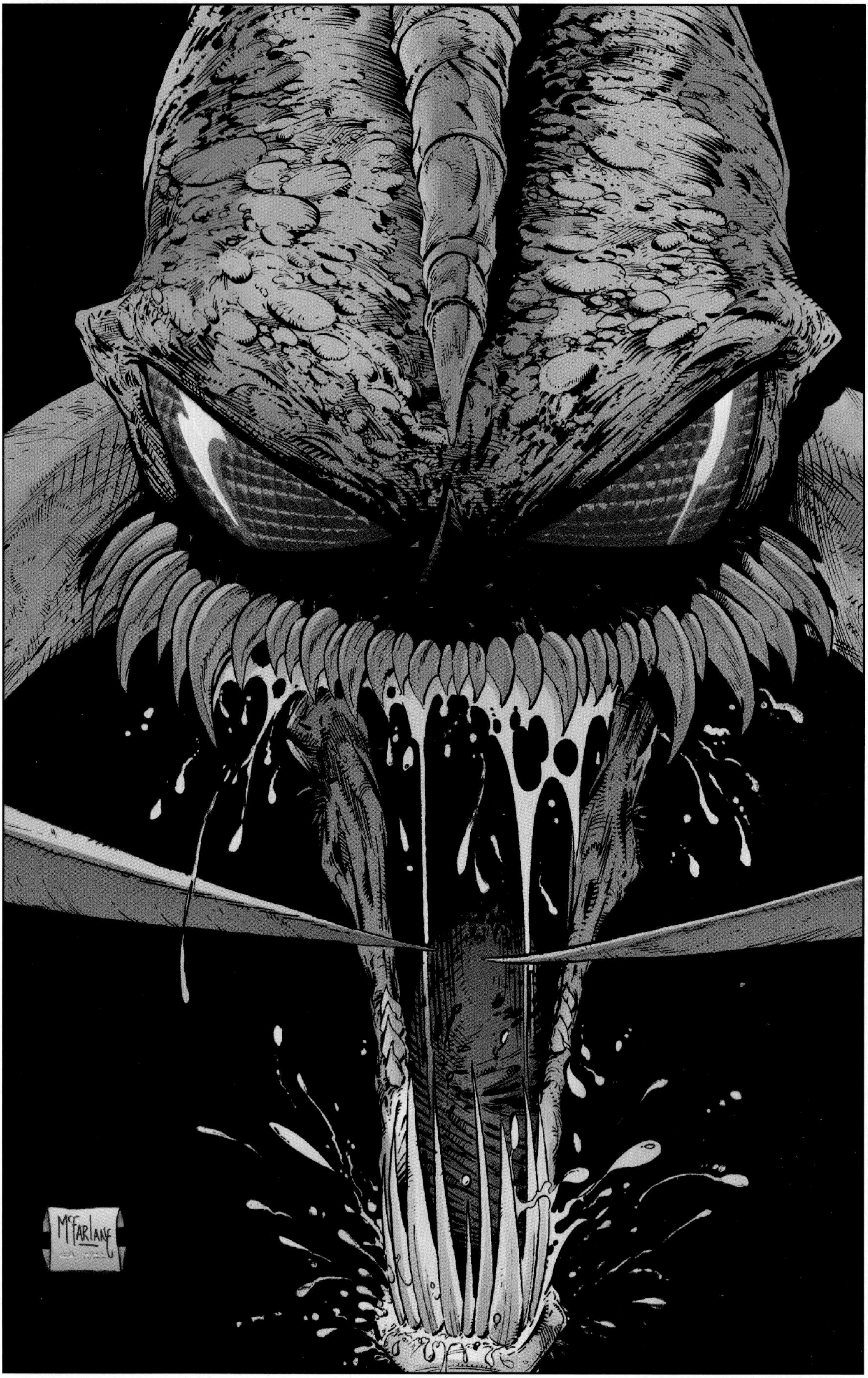
McFARLANE

Spawn #4, cover

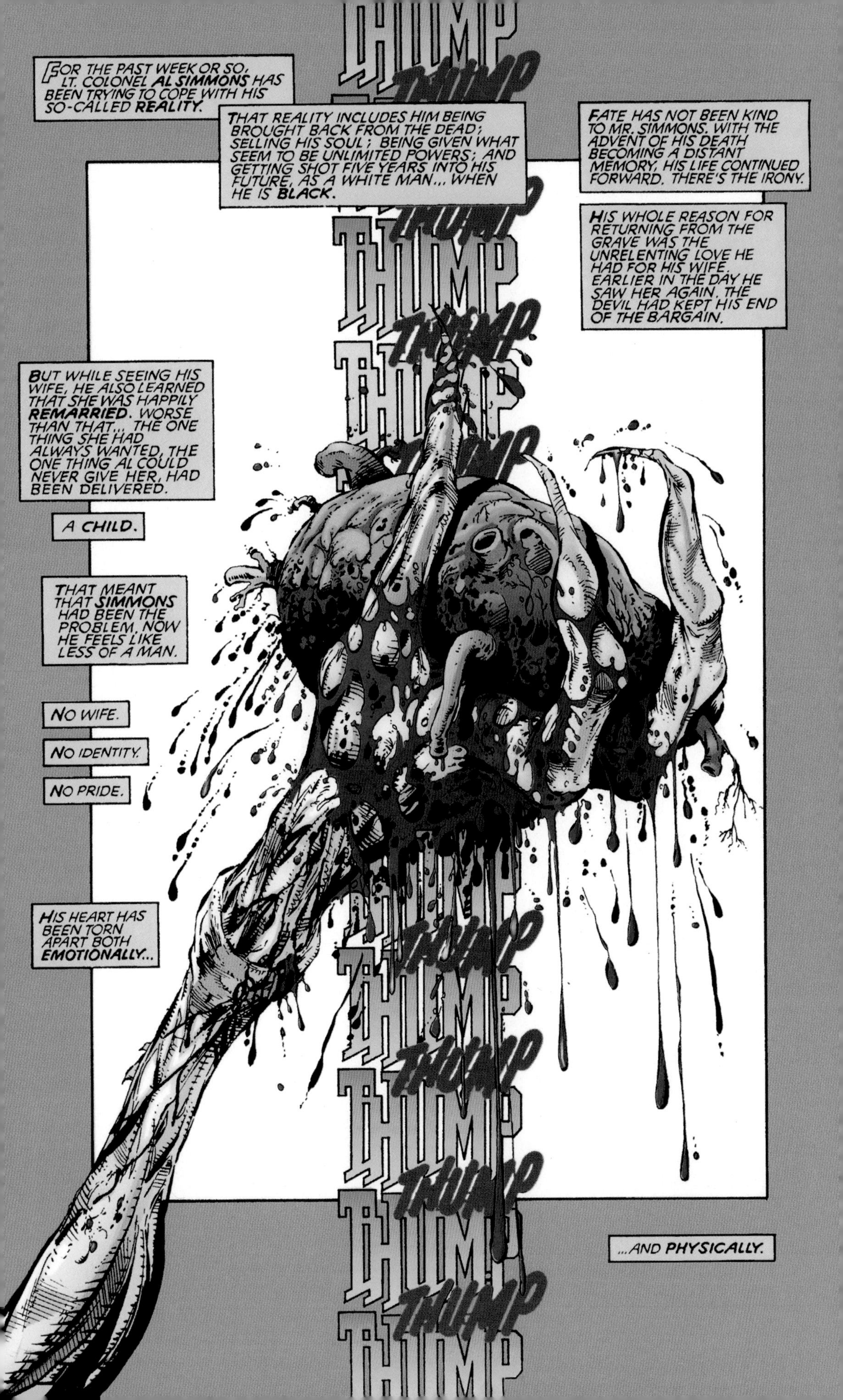
FOR THE PAST WEEK OR SO, LT. COLONEL AL SIMMONS HAS BEEN TRYING TO COPE WITH HIS SO-CALLED REALITY.
THAT REALITY INCLUDES HIM BEING BROUGHT BACK FROM THE DEAD; SELLING HIS SOUL; BEING GIVEN WHAT SEEM TO BE UNLIMITED POWERS; AND GETTING SHOT FIVE YEARS INTO HIS FUTURE, AS A WHITE MAN... WHEN HE IS BLACK.
FATE HAS NOT BEEN KIND TO MR. SIMMONS. WITH THE ADVENT OF HIS DEATH BECOMING A DISTANT MEMORY, HIS LIFE CONTINUED FORWARD. THERE'S THE IRONY.
HIS WHOLE REASON FOR RETURNING FROM THE GRAVE WAS THE UNRELENTING LOVE HE HAD FOR HIS WIFE. EARLIER IN THE DAY HE SAW HER AGAIN. THE DEVIL HAD KEPT HIS END OF THE BARGAIN.
BUT WHILE SEEING HIS WIFE, HE ALSO LEARNED THAT SHE WAS HAPPILY REMARRIED. WORSE THAN THAT... THE ONE THING SHE HAD ALWAYS WANTED, THE ONE THING AL COULD NEVER GIVE HER, HAD BEEN DELIVERED.
A CHILD.
THAT MEANT THAT SIMMONS HAD BEEN THE PROBLEM. NOW HE FEELS LIKE LESS OF A MAN.
NO WIFE.
NO IDENTITY.
NO PRIDE.
HIS HEART HAS BEEN TORN APART BOTH EMOTIONALLY...
...AND PHYSICALLY.
THUMP THUMP THUMP THUMP THUMP THUMP THUMP THUMP

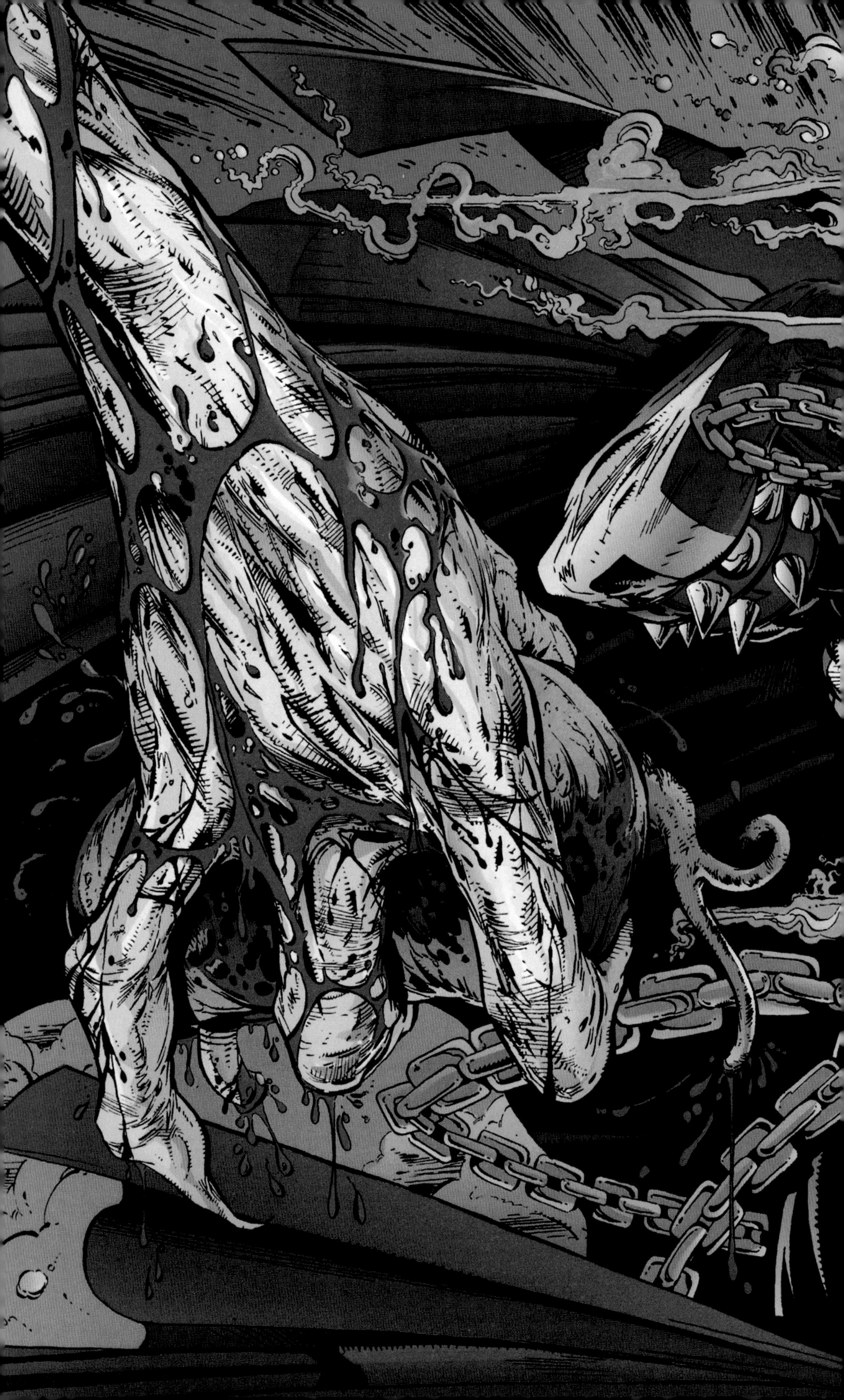

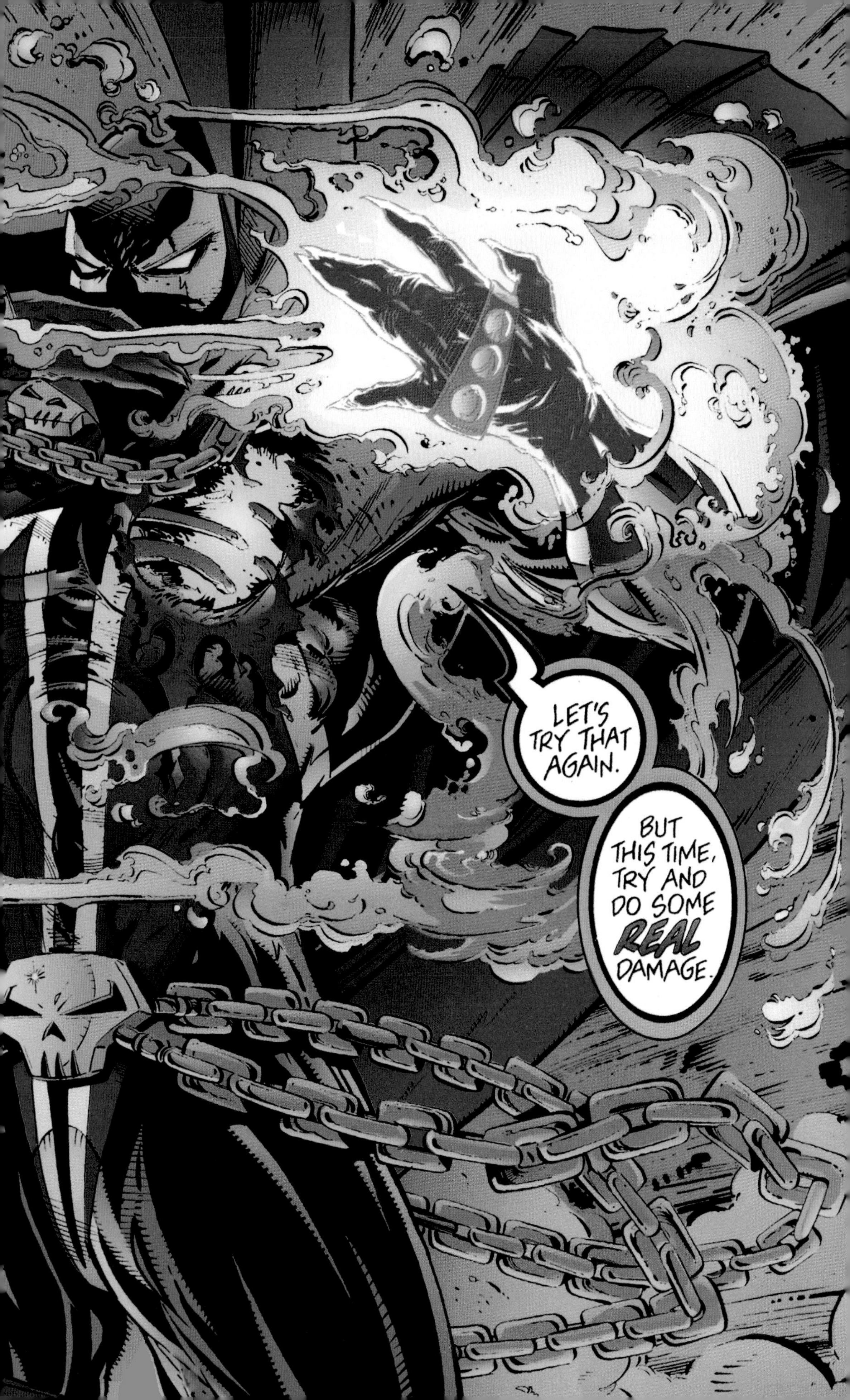

LET'S TRY THAT AGAIN.
BUT THIS TIME, TRY AND DO SOME REAL DAMAGE.

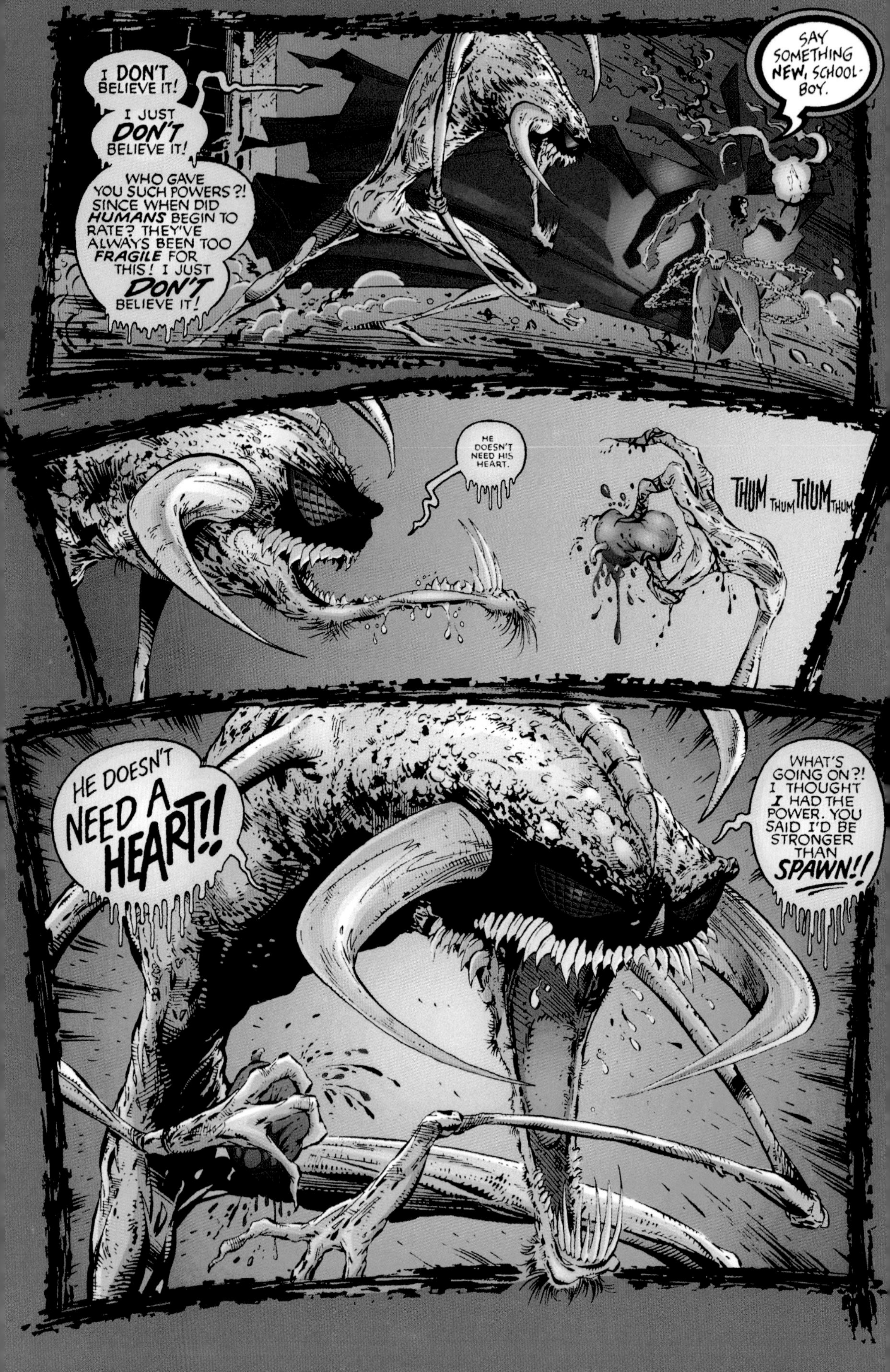
I DON'T BELIEVE IT!
I JUST DON'T BELIEVE IT!
WHO GAVE YOU SUCH POWERS?! SINCE WHEN DID HUMANS BEGIN TO RATE? THEY'VE ALWAYS BEEN TOO FRAGILE FOR THIS! I JUST DON'T BELIEVE IT!
SAY SOMETHING NEW, SCHOOL-BOY.
HE DOESN'T NEED HIS HEART.
THUM THUM THUM THUM
HE DOESN'T NEED A HEART!!
WHAT'S GOING ON?! I THOUGHT I HAD THE POWER. YOU SAID I'D BE STRONGER THAN SPAWN!!

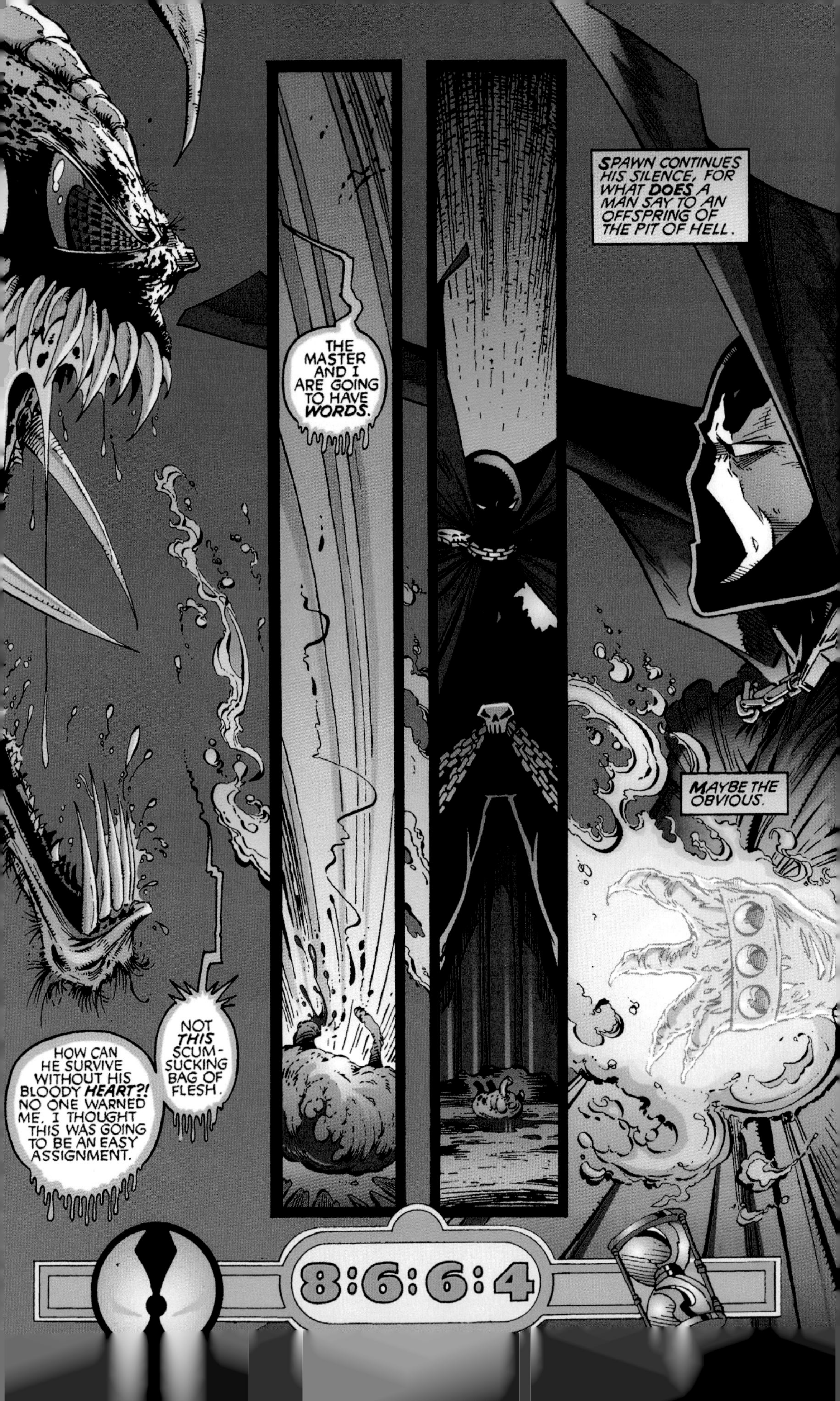
SPAWN CONTINUES HIS SILENCE, FOR WHAT DOES A MAN SAY TO AN OFFSPRING OF THE PIT OF HELL.
THE MASTER AND I ARE GOING TO HAVE WORDS.
MAYBE THE OBVIOUS.
NOT THIS SCUM-SUCKING BAG OF FLESH.
HOW CAN HE SURVIVE WITHOUT HIS BLOODY HEART?! NO ONE WARNED ME. I THOUGHT THIS WAS GOING TO BE AN EASY ASSIGNMENT.
8:6:6:4

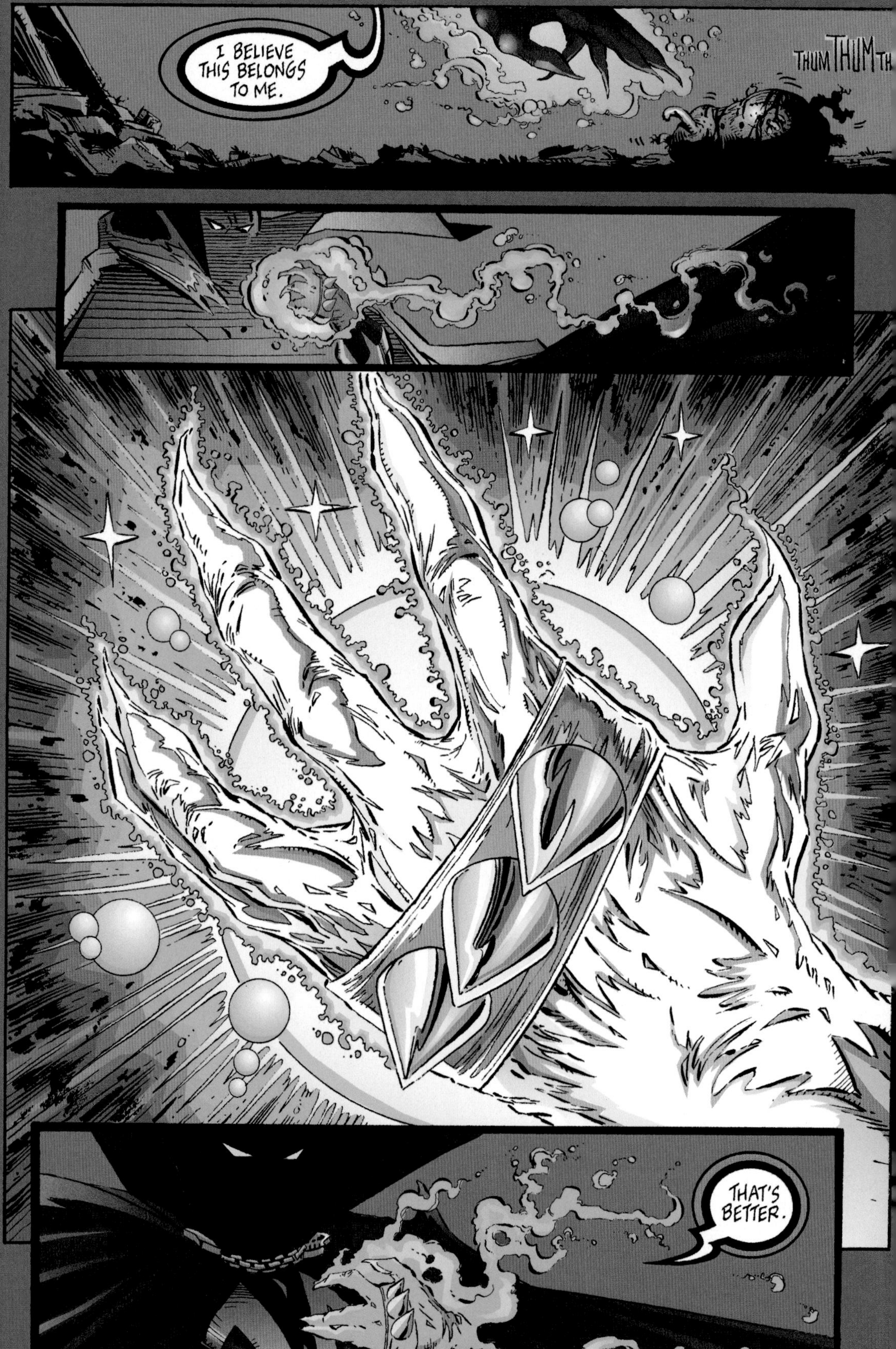
I BELIEVE THIS BELONGS TO ME.
THUM THUM-TH
THAT'S BETTER.

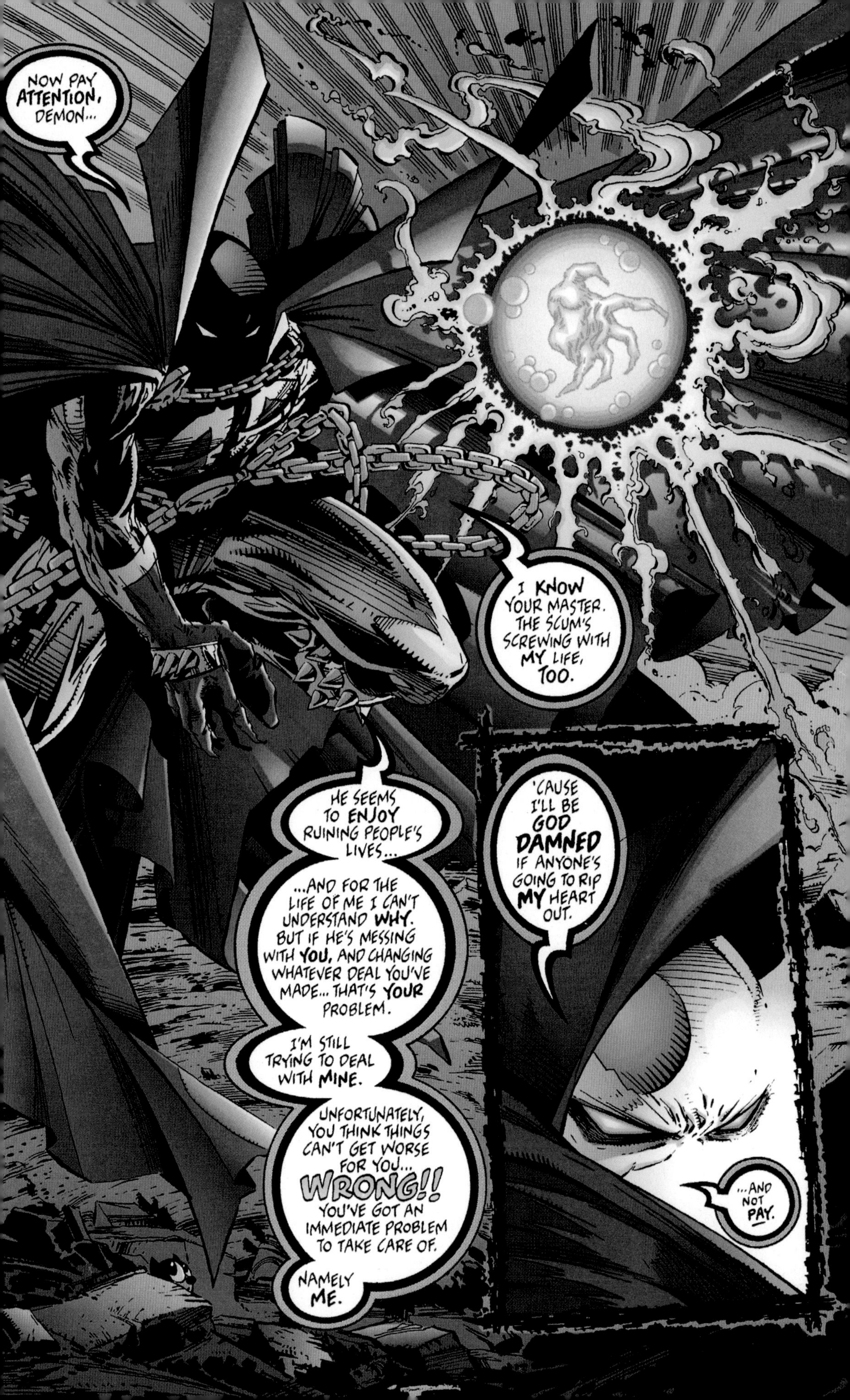

NOW PAY ATTENTION, DEMON...
I KNOW YOUR MASTER. THE SCUM'S SCREWING WITH MY LIFE, TOO.
HE SEEMS TO ENJOY RUINING PEOPLE'S LIVES...
...AND FOR THE LIFE OF ME I CAN'T UNDERSTAND WHY. BUT IF HE'S MESSING WITH YOU, AND CHANGING WHATEVER DEAL YOU'VE MADE... THAT'S YOUR PROBLEM.
I'M STILL TRYING TO DEAL WITH MINE.
UNFORTUNATELY, YOU THINK THINGS CAN'T GET WORSE FOR YOU... WRONG!! YOU'VE GOT AN IMMEDIATE PROBLEM TO TAKE CARE OF.
NAMELY ME.
'CAUSE I'LL BE GOD DAMNED IF ANYONE'S GOING TO RIP MY HEART OUT.
...AND NOT PAY.

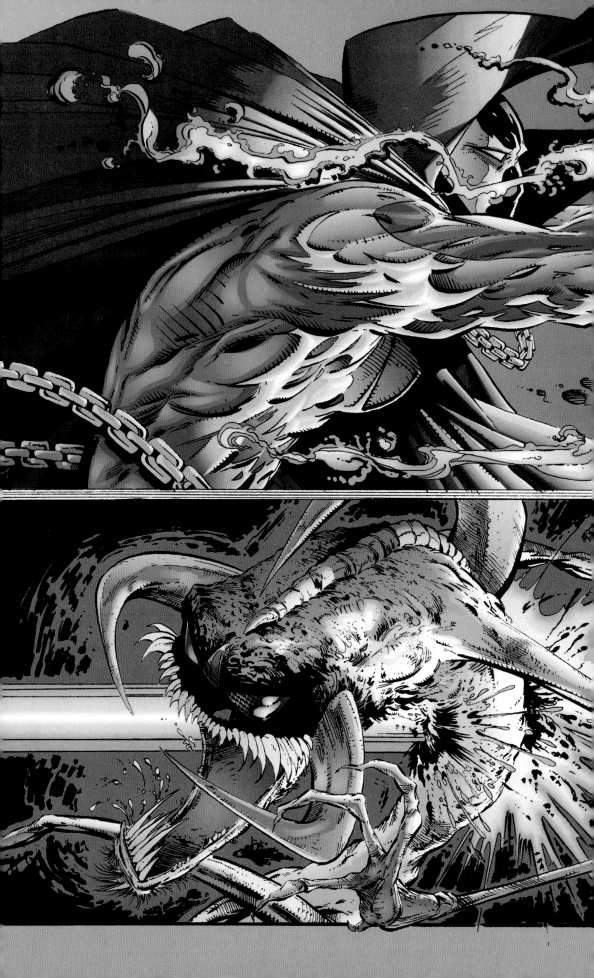

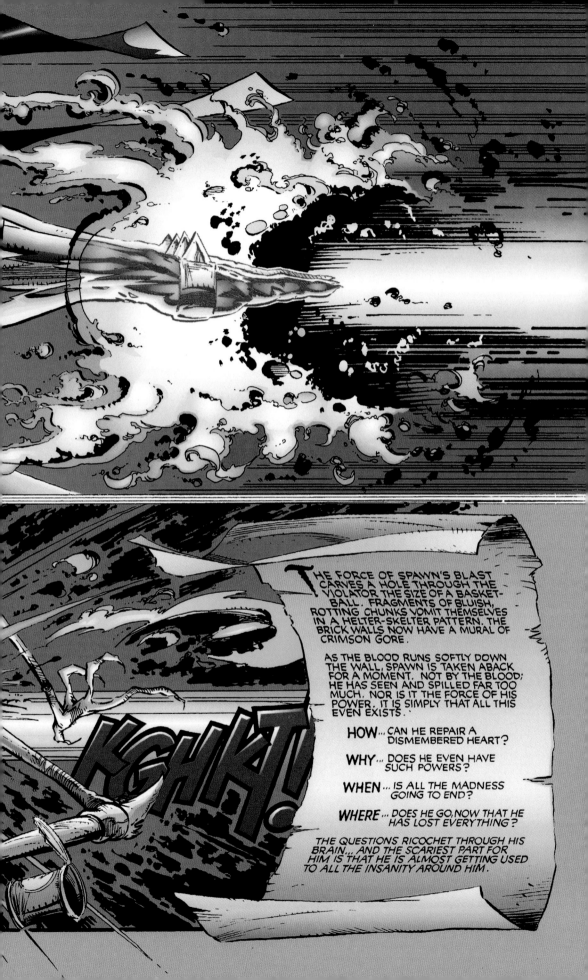

THE FORCE OF SPAWN'S BLAST CARVES A HOLE THROUGH THE VIOLATOR THE SIZE OF A BASKETBALL. FRAGMENTS OF BLUISH, ROTTING CHUNKS VOMIT THEMSELVES IN A HELTER-SKELTER PATTERN. THE BRICK WALLS NOW HAVE A MURAL OF CRIMSON GORE.

AS THE BLOOD RUNS SOFTLY DOWN THE WALL, SPAWN IS TAKEN ABACK FOR A MOMENT. NOT BY THE BLOOD; HE HAS SEEN AND SPILLED FAR TOO MUCH. NOR IS IT THE FORCE OF HIS POWER. IT IS SIMPLY THAT ALL THIS EVEN EXISTS.

HOW... CAN HE REPAIR A DISMEMBERED HEART?

WHY... DOES HE EVEN HAVE SUCH POWERS?

WHEN... IS ALL THE MADNESS GOING TO END?

WHERE... DOES HE GO, NOW THAT HE HAS LOST EVERYTHING?

THE QUESTIONS RICOCHET THROUGH HIS BRAIN... AND THE SCARIEST PART FOR HIM IS THAT HE IS ALMOST GETTING USED TO ALL THE INSANITY AROUND HIM.

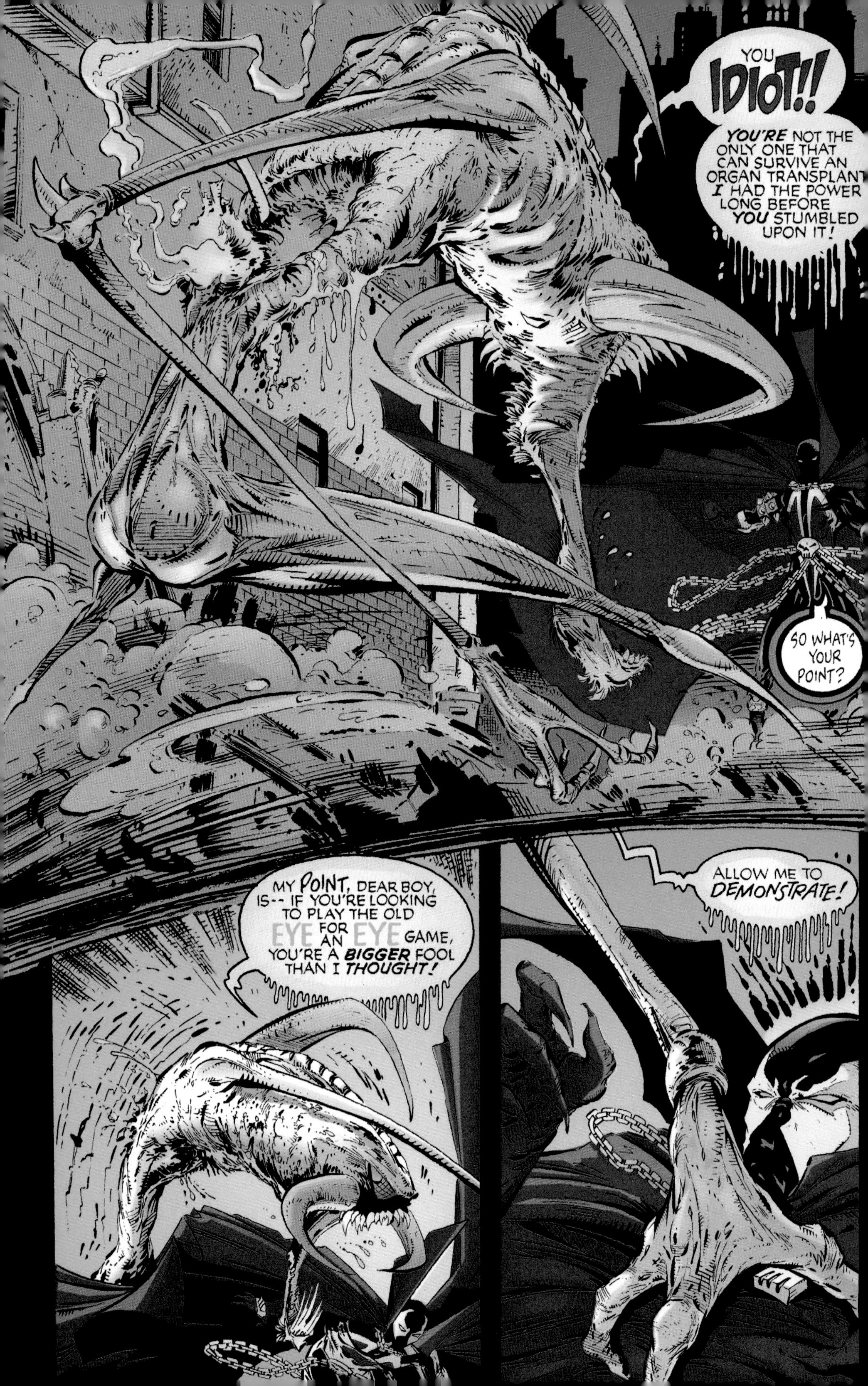
YOU IDIOT!!
YOU'RE NOT THE ONLY ONE THAT CAN SURVIVE AN ORGAN TRANSPLANT. I HAD THE POWER LONG BEFORE YOU STUMBLED UPON IT!
SO WHAT'S YOUR POINT?
MY POINT, DEAR BOY, IS-- IF YOU'RE LOOKING TO PLAY THE OLD EYE FOR AN EYE GAME, YOU'RE A BIGGER FOOL THAN I THOUGHT!
ALLOW ME TO DEMONSTRATE!

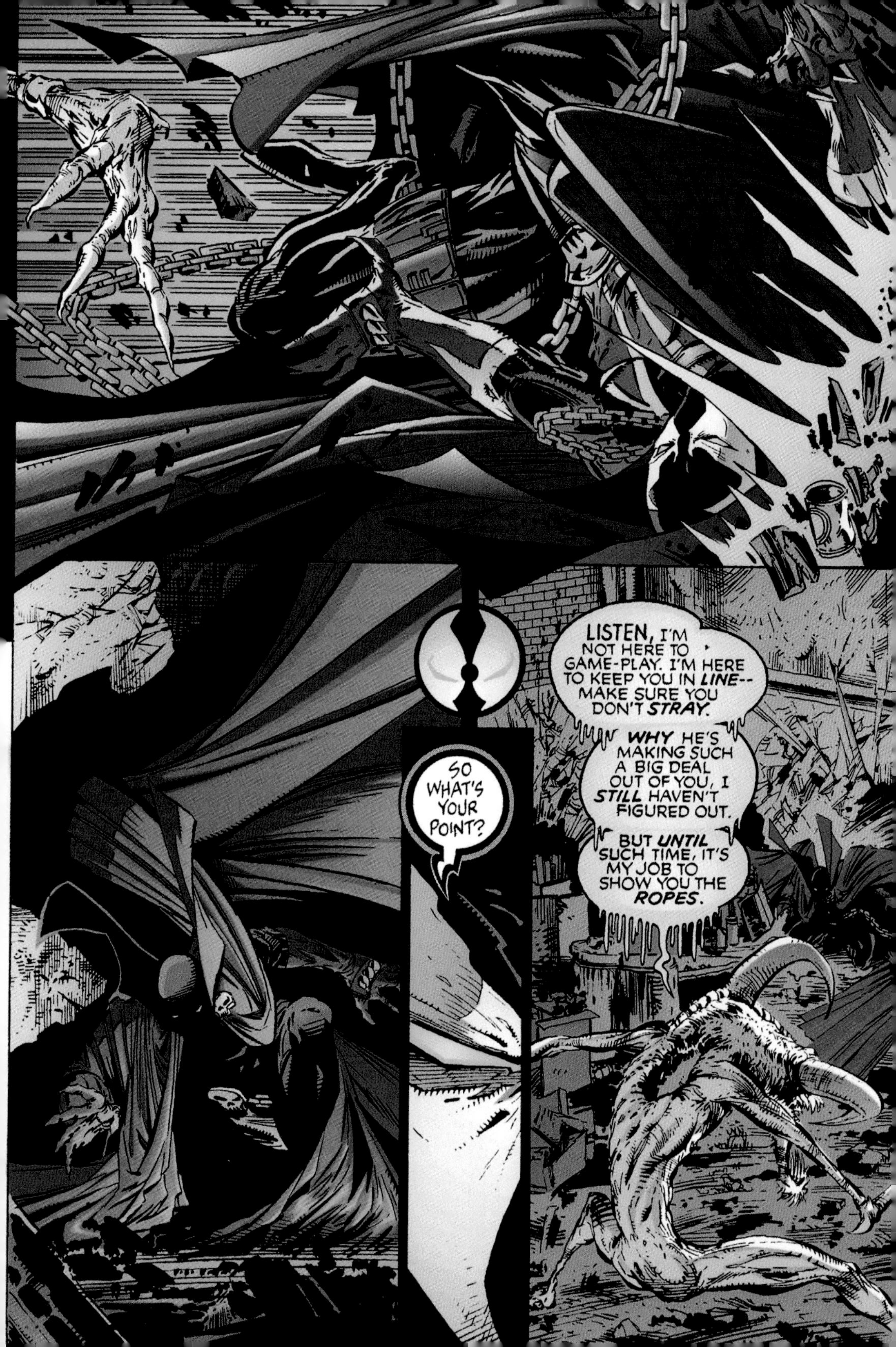
LISTEN, I'M NOT HERE TO GAME-PLAY. I'M HERE TO KEEP YOU IN LINE-- MAKE SURE YOU DON'T STRAY.
SO WHAT'S YOUR POINT?
WHY HE'S MAKING SUCH A BIG DEAL OUT OF YOU, I STILL HAVEN'T FIGURED OUT.
BUT UNTIL SUCH TIME, IT'S MY JOB TO SHOW YOU THE ROPES.

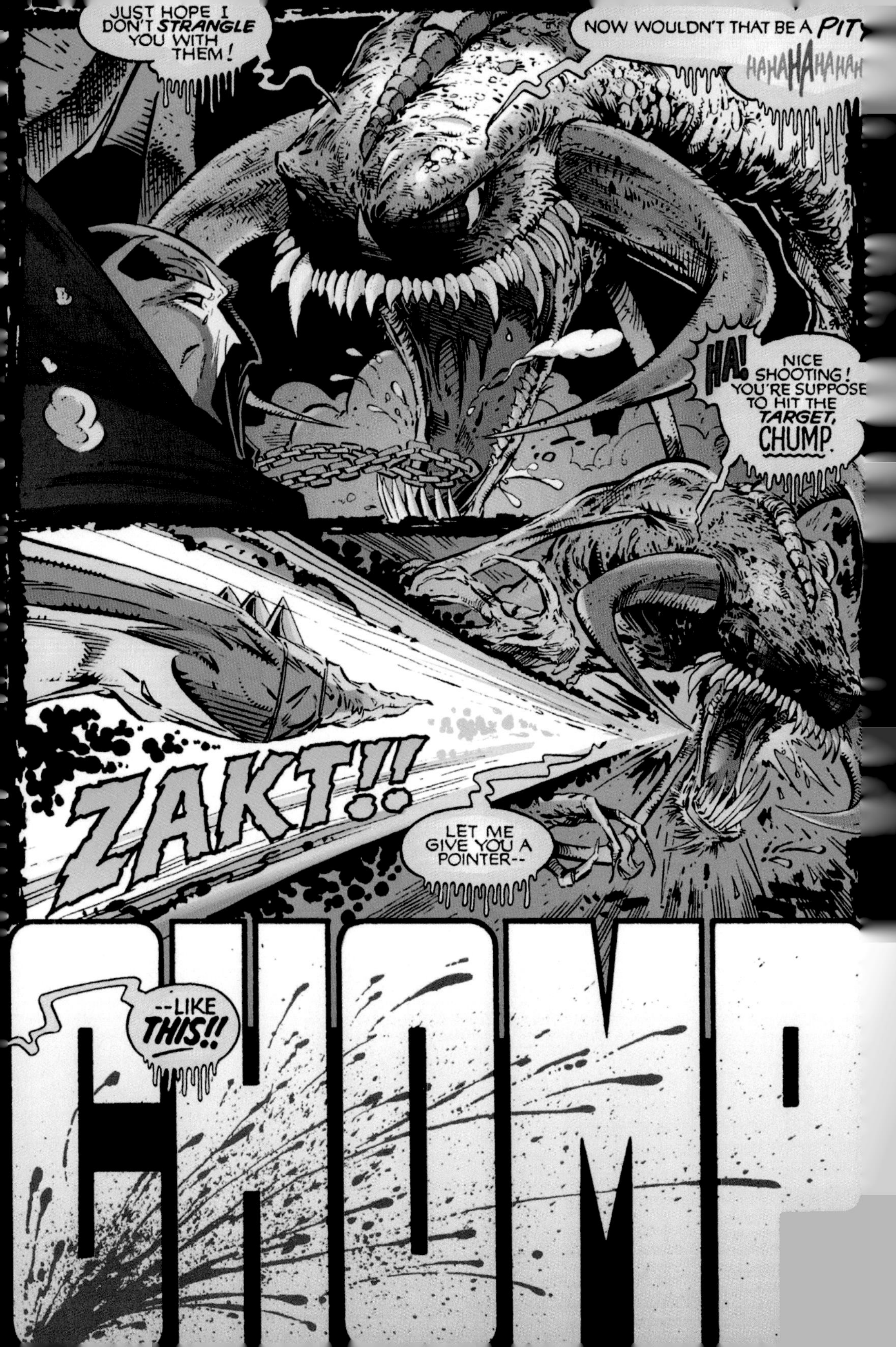
JUST HOPE I DON'T STRANGLE YOU WITH THEM!
NOW WOULDN'T THAT BE A PITY
HAHAHAHAHAHAH
HA! NICE SHOOTING! YOU'RE SUPPOSE TO HIT THE TARGET, CHUMP.
ZAKT!!
LET ME GIVE YOU A POINTER--
CHOMP
--LIKE THIS!!

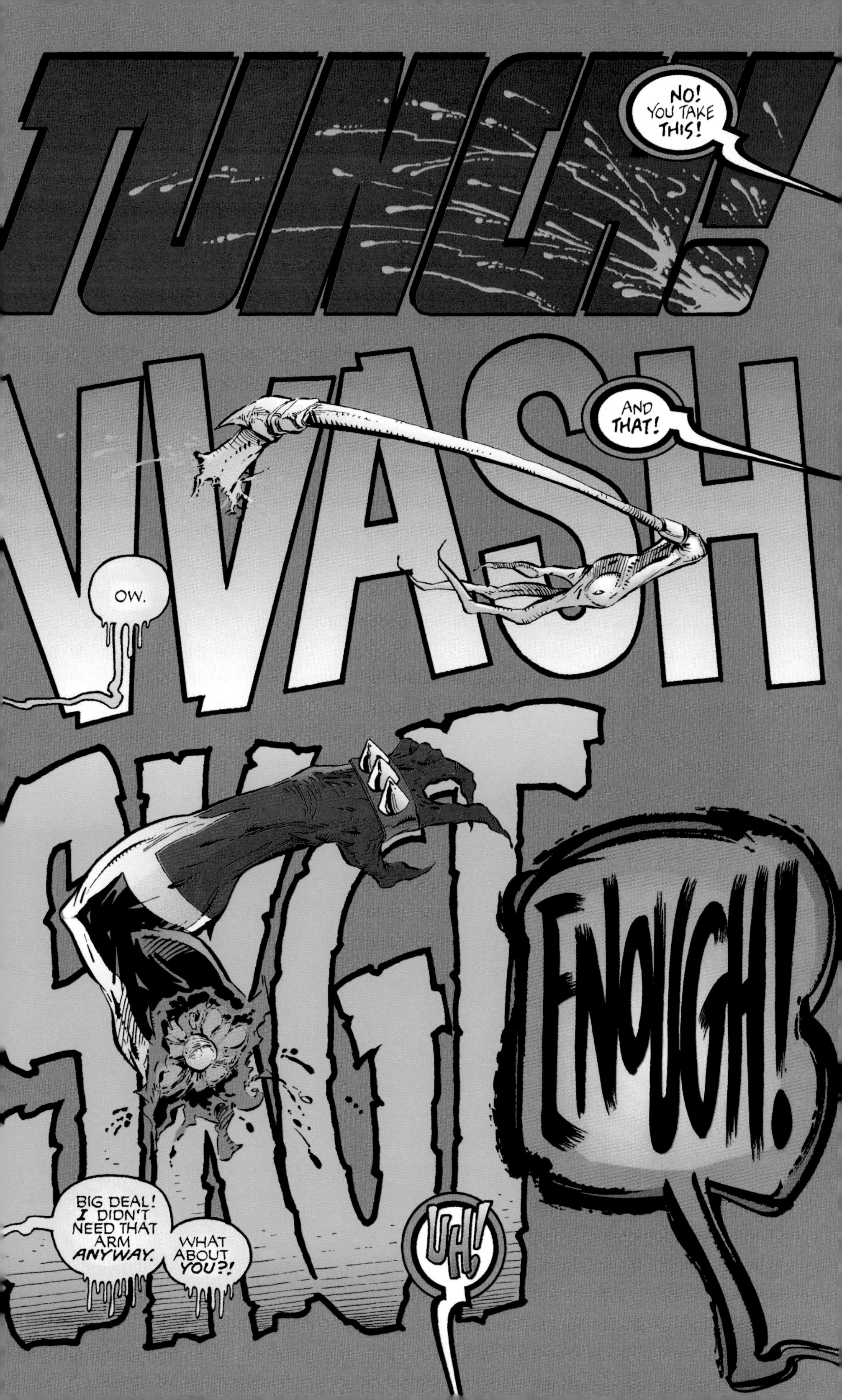
TUNCH!
NO! YOU TAKE THIS!
VVASH
AND THAT!
OW.
SHUNK
ENOUGH!
BIG DEAL! I DIDN'T NEED THAT ARM ANYWAY.
WHAT ABOUT YOU?!
UH!

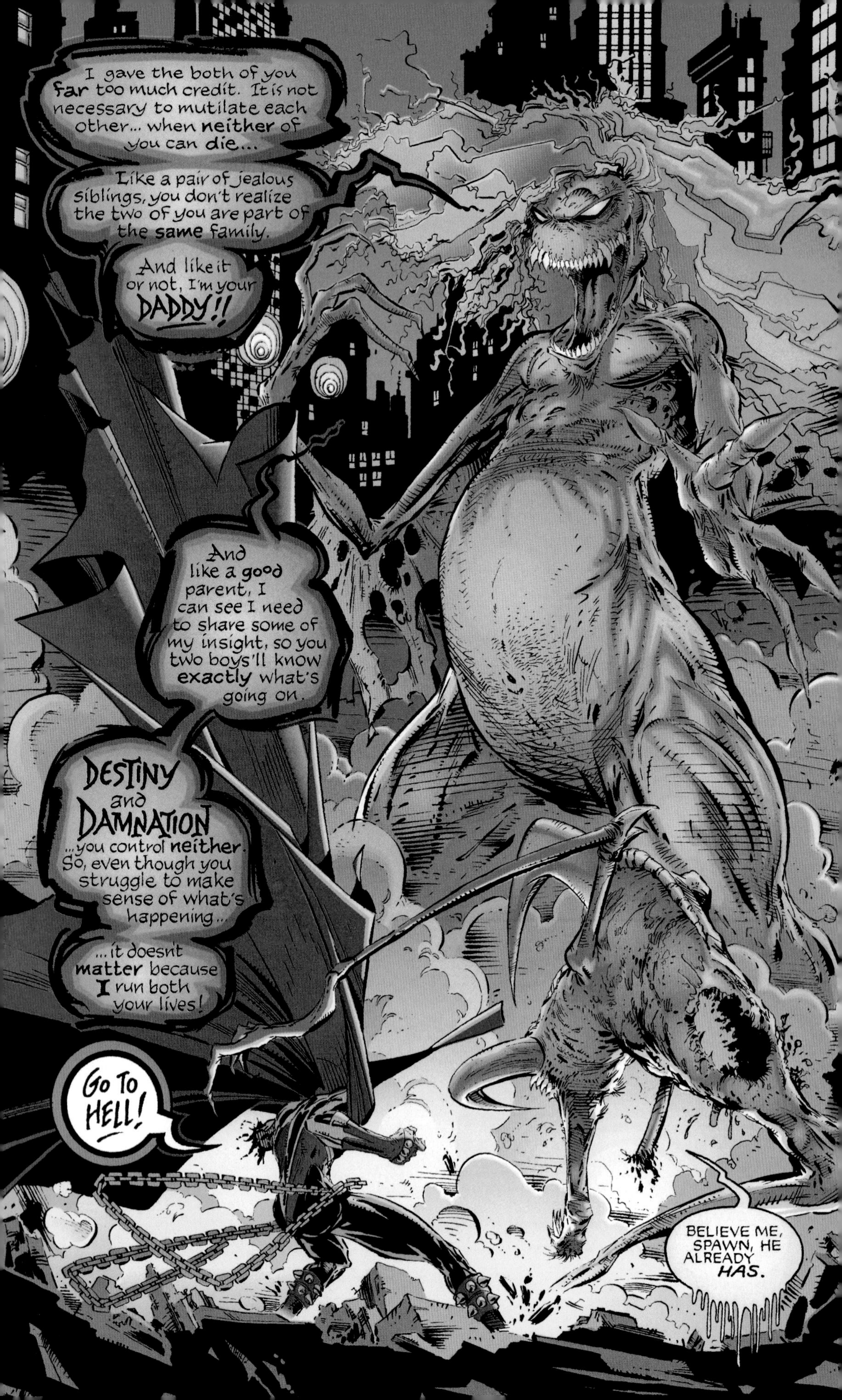

I gave the both of you far too much credit. It is not necessary to mutilate each other... when neither of you can die...
Like a pair of jealous siblings, you don't realize the two of you are part of the same family.
And like it or not, I'm your DADDY!!
And like a good parent, I can see I need to share some of my insight, so you two boys'll know exactly what's going on.
DESTINY and DAMNATION ...you control neither. So, even though you struggle to make sense of what's happening...
...it doesn't matter because I run both your lives!
GO TO HELL!
BELIEVE ME, SPAWN, HE ALREADY HAS.

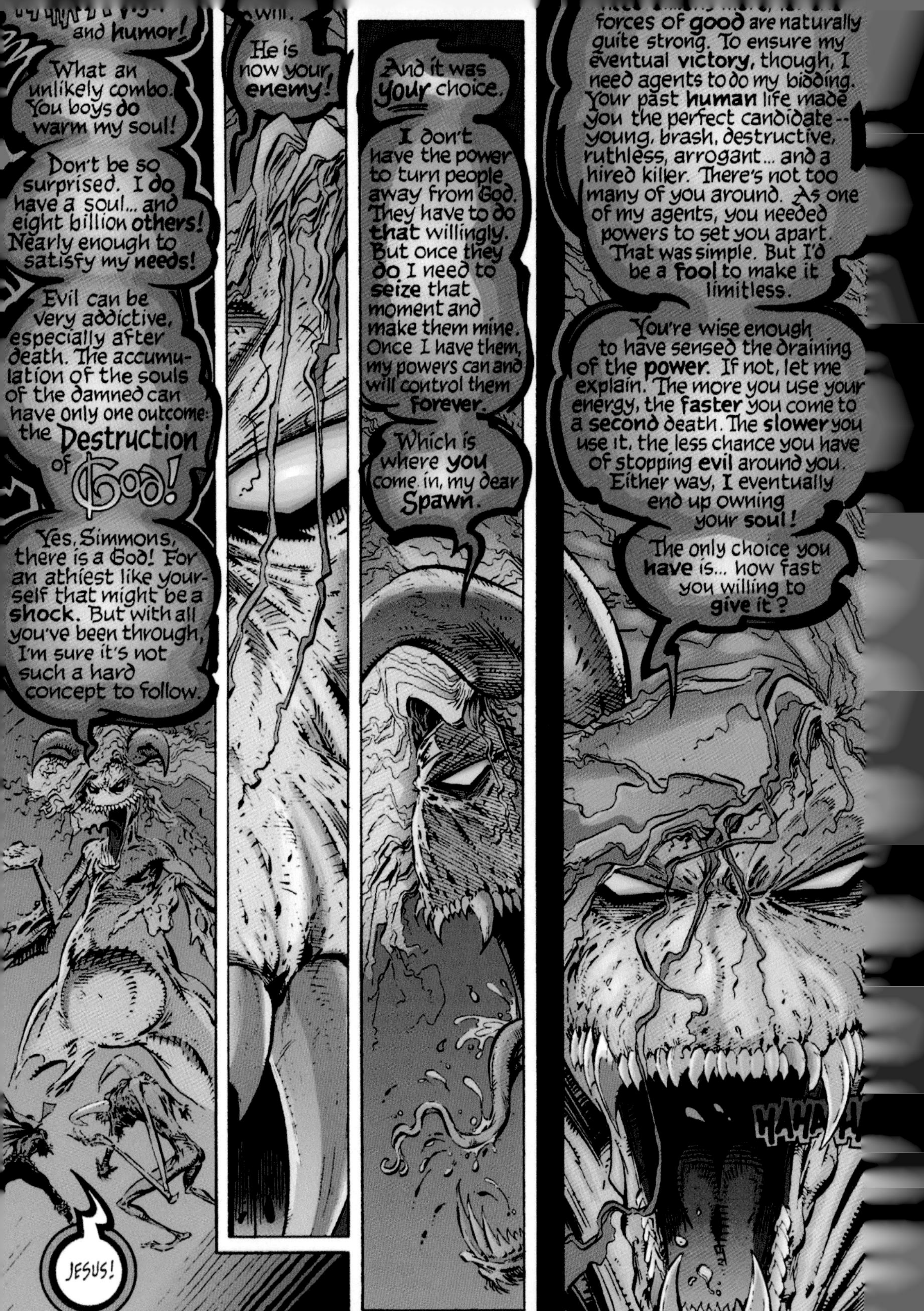
and humor!
What an unlikely combo. You boys do warm my soul!
Don't be so surprised. I do have a soul... and eight billion others! Nearly enough to satisfy my needs!
Evil can be very addictive, especially after death. The accumulation of the souls of the damned can have only one outcome: the Destruction of God!
Yes, Simmons, there is a God! For an athiest like yourself that might be a shock. But with all you've been through, I'm sure it's not such a hard concept to follow.
JESUS!
will.
He is now your enemy!
And it was your choice.
I don't have the power to turn people away from God. They have to do that willingly. But once they do I need to seize that moment and make them mine. Once I have them, my powers can and will control them forever.
Which is where you come in, my dear Spawn.
forces of good are naturally quite strong. To ensure my eventual victory, though, I need agents to do my bidding. Your past human life made you the perfect candidate -- young, brash, destructive, ruthless, arrogant... and a hired killer. There's not too many of you around. As one of my agents, you needed powers to set you apart. That was simple. But I'd be a fool to make it limitless.
You're wise enough to have sensed the draining of the power. If not, let me explain. The more you use your energy, the faster you come to a second death. The slower you use it, the less chance you have of stopping evil around you. Either way, I eventually end up owning your soul!
The only choice you have is... how fast you willing to give it?
HAHAHA

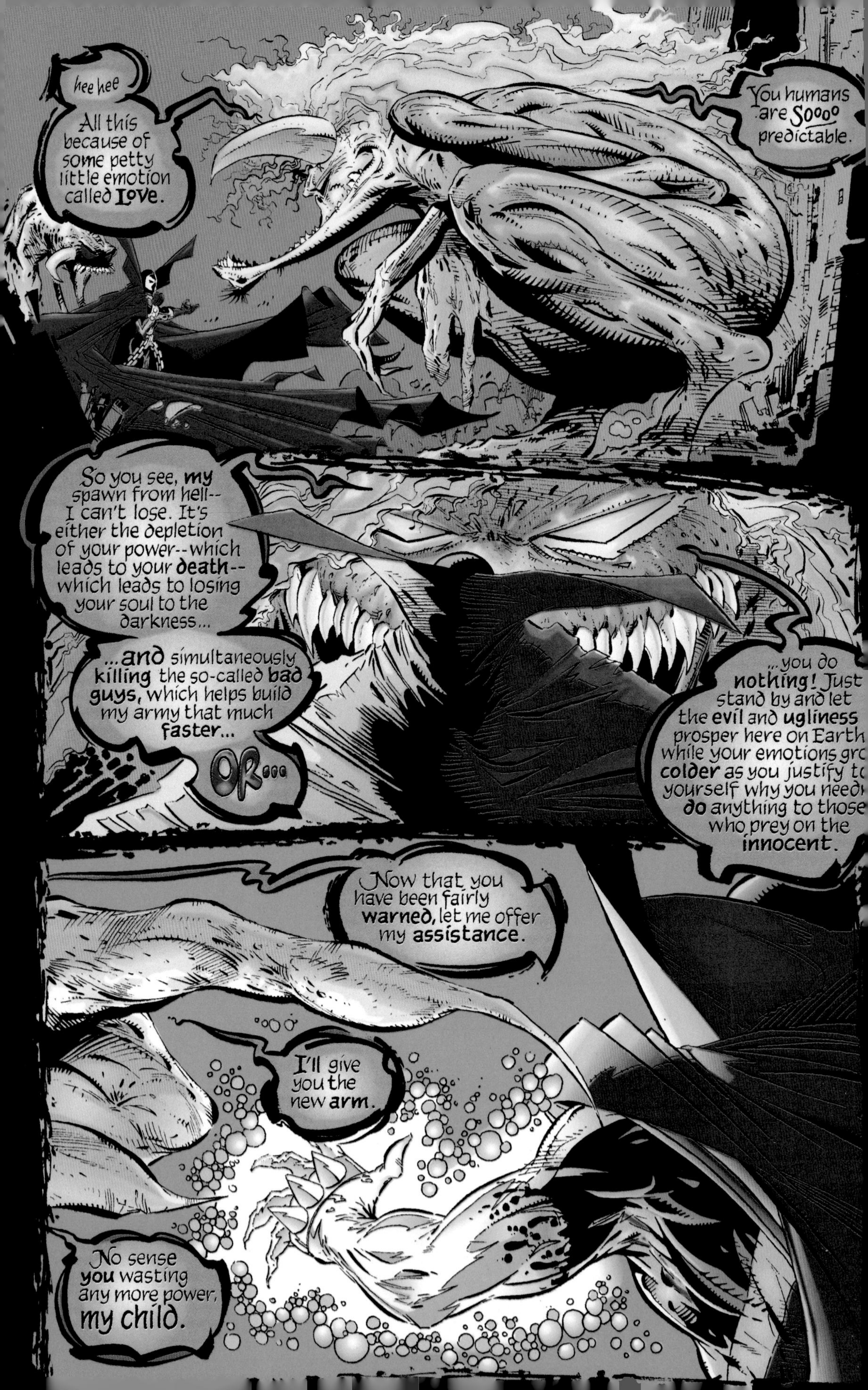

hee hee
All this because of some petty little emotion called Love.
You humans are Soooo predictable.
So you see, my spawn from hell-- I can't lose. It's either the depletion of your power--which leads to your death--which leads to losing your soul to the darkness...
...and simultaneously killing the so-called bad guys, which helps build my army that much faster...
OR...
...you do nothing! Just stand by and let the evil and ugliness prosper here on Earth while your emotions gro colder as you justify t yourself why you need do anything to those who prey on the innocent.
Now that you have been fairly warned, let me offer my assistance.
I'll give you the new arm.
No sense you wasting any more power, my child.

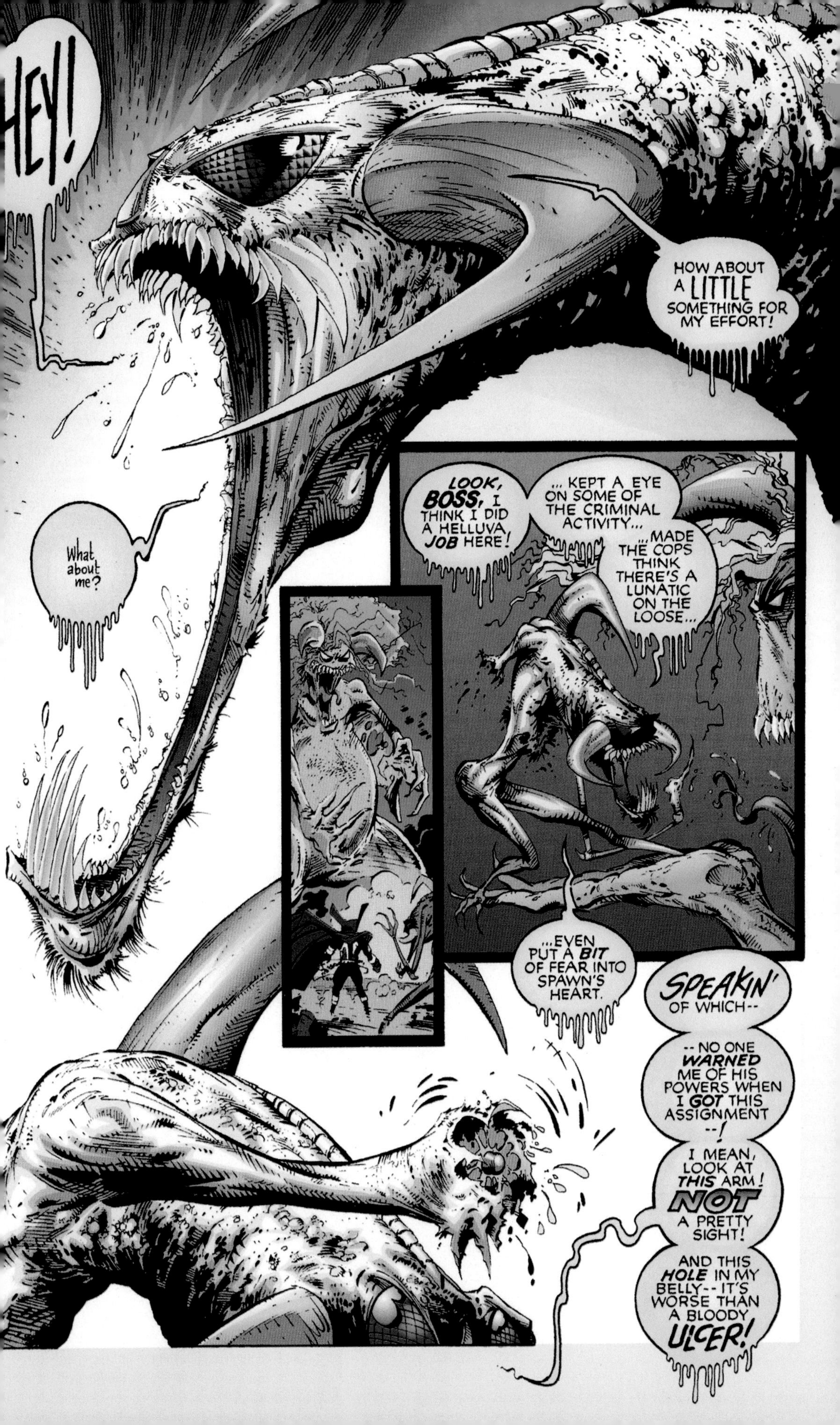
HEY!
HOW ABOUT A LITTLE SOMETHING FOR MY EFFORT!
What about me?
LOOK, BOSS, I THINK I DID A HELLUVA JOB HERE!
...KEPT A EYE ON SOME OF THE CRIMINAL ACTIVITY...
...MADE THE COPS THINK THERE'S A LUNATIC ON THE LOOSE...
...EVEN PUT A BIT OF FEAR INTO SPAWN'S HEART.
SPEAKIN' OF WHICH--
--NO ONE WARNED ME OF HIS POWERS WHEN I GOT THIS ASSIGNMENT--!
I MEAN, LOOK AT THIS ARM! NOT A PRETTY SIGHT!
AND THIS HOLE IN MY BELLY--IT'S WORSE THAN A BLOODY ULCER!

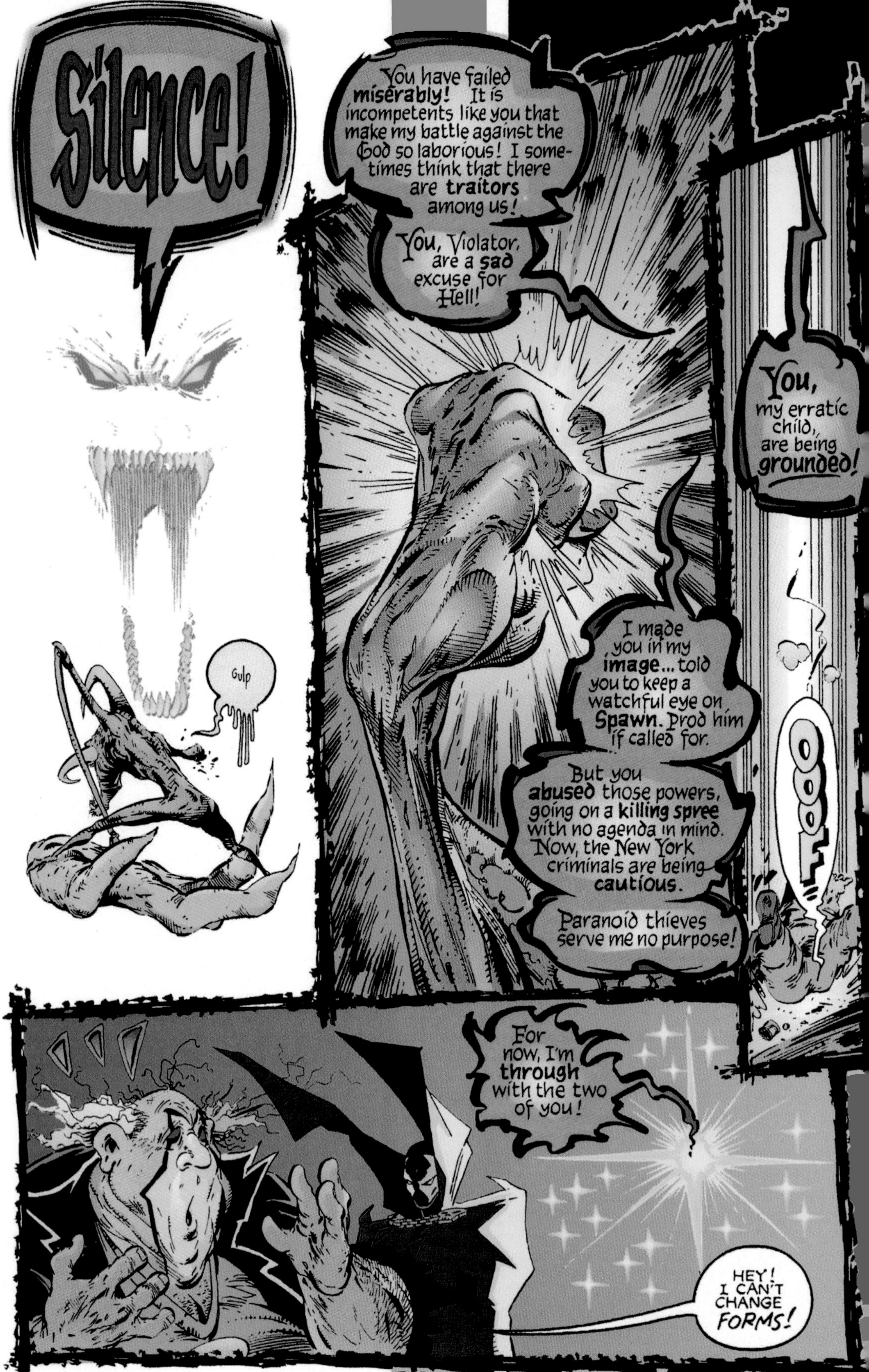
Silence!
You have failed miserably! It is incompetents like you that make my battle against the God so laborious! I sometimes think that there are traitors among us!
You, Violator, are a sad excuse for Hell!
Gulp
You, my erratic child, are being grounded!
I made you in my image... told you to keep a watchful eye on Spawn. Prod him if called for.
But you abused those powers, going on a killing spree with no agenda in mind. Now, the New York criminals are being cautious.
Paranoid thieves serve me no purpose!
OOOF
For now, I'm through with the two of you!
HEY! I CAN'T CHANGE FORMS!

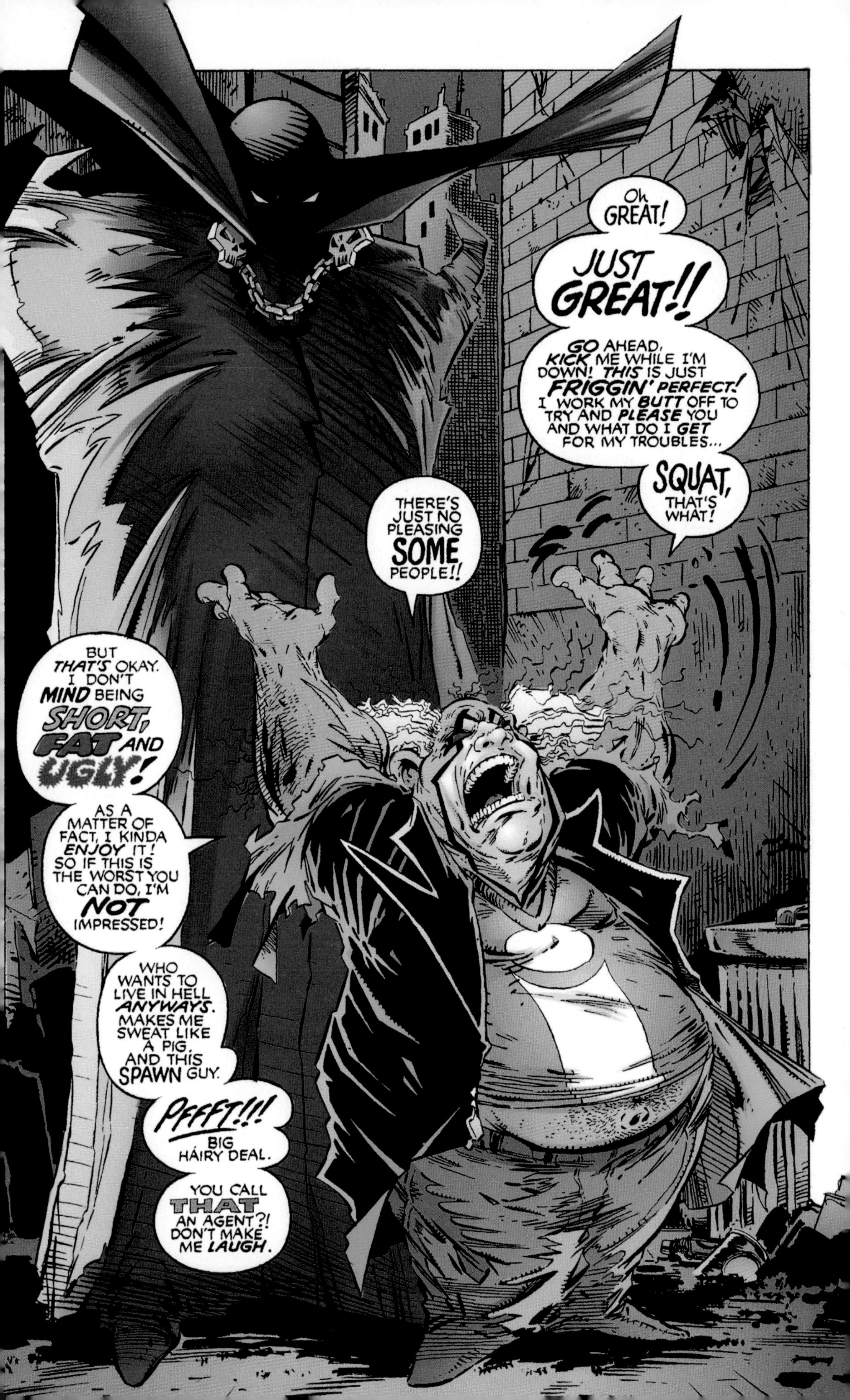

Oh GREAT!
JUST GREAT!!
GO AHEAD, KICK ME WHILE I'M DOWN! THIS IS JUST FRIGGIN' PERFECT! I WORK MY BUTT OFF TO TRY AND PLEASE YOU AND WHAT DO I GET FOR MY TROUBLES...
SQUAT, THAT'S WHAT!
THERE'S JUST NO PLEASING SOME PEOPLE!!
BUT THAT'S OKAY. I DON'T MIND BEING SHORT, FAT AND UGLY!
AS A MATTER OF FACT, I KINDA ENJOY IT! SO IF THIS IS THE WORST YOU CAN DO, I'M NOT IMPRESSED!
WHO WANTS TO LIVE IN HELL ANYWAYS. MAKES ME SWEAT LIKE A PIG. AND THIS SPAWN GUY.
PFFFT!!! BIG HAIRY DEAL.
YOU CALL THAT AN AGENT?! DON'T MAKE ME LAUGH.

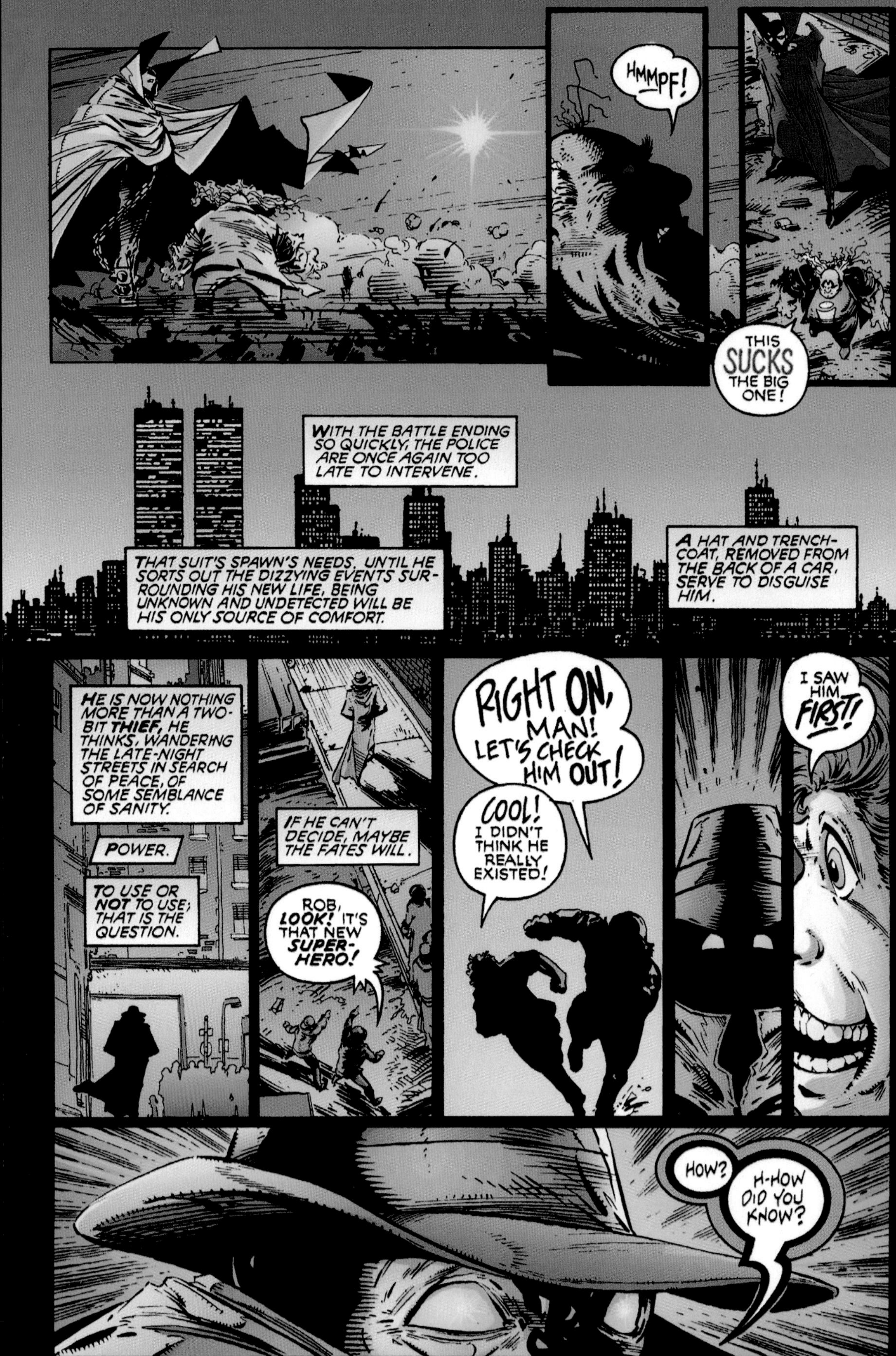
HMMPF!
THIS SUCKS THE BIG ONE!
WITH THE BATTLE ENDING SO QUICKLY, THE POLICE ARE ONCE AGAIN TOO LATE TO INTERVENE.
THAT SUIT'S SPAWN'S NEEDS. UNTIL HE SORTS OUT THE DIZZYING EVENTS SURROUNDING HIS NEW LIFE, BEING UNKNOWN AND UNDETECTED WILL BE HIS ONLY SOURCE OF COMFORT.
A HAT AND TRENCHCOAT, REMOVED FROM THE BACK OF A CAR, SERVE TO DISGUISE HIM.
HE IS NOW NOTHING MORE THAN A TWO-BIT THIEF, HE THINKS, WANDERING THE LATE-NIGHT STREETS IN SEARCH OF PEACE, OF SOME SEMBLANCE OF SANITY.
POWER.
TO USE OR NOT TO USE; THAT IS THE QUESTION.
IF HE CAN'T DECIDE, MAYBE THE FATES WILL.
ROB, LOOK! IT'S THAT NEW SUPER-HERO!
RIGHT ON, MAN! LET'S CHECK HIM OUT!
COOL! I DIDN'T THINK HE REALLY EXISTED!
I SAW HIM FIRST!
HOW?
H-HOW DID YOU KNOW?

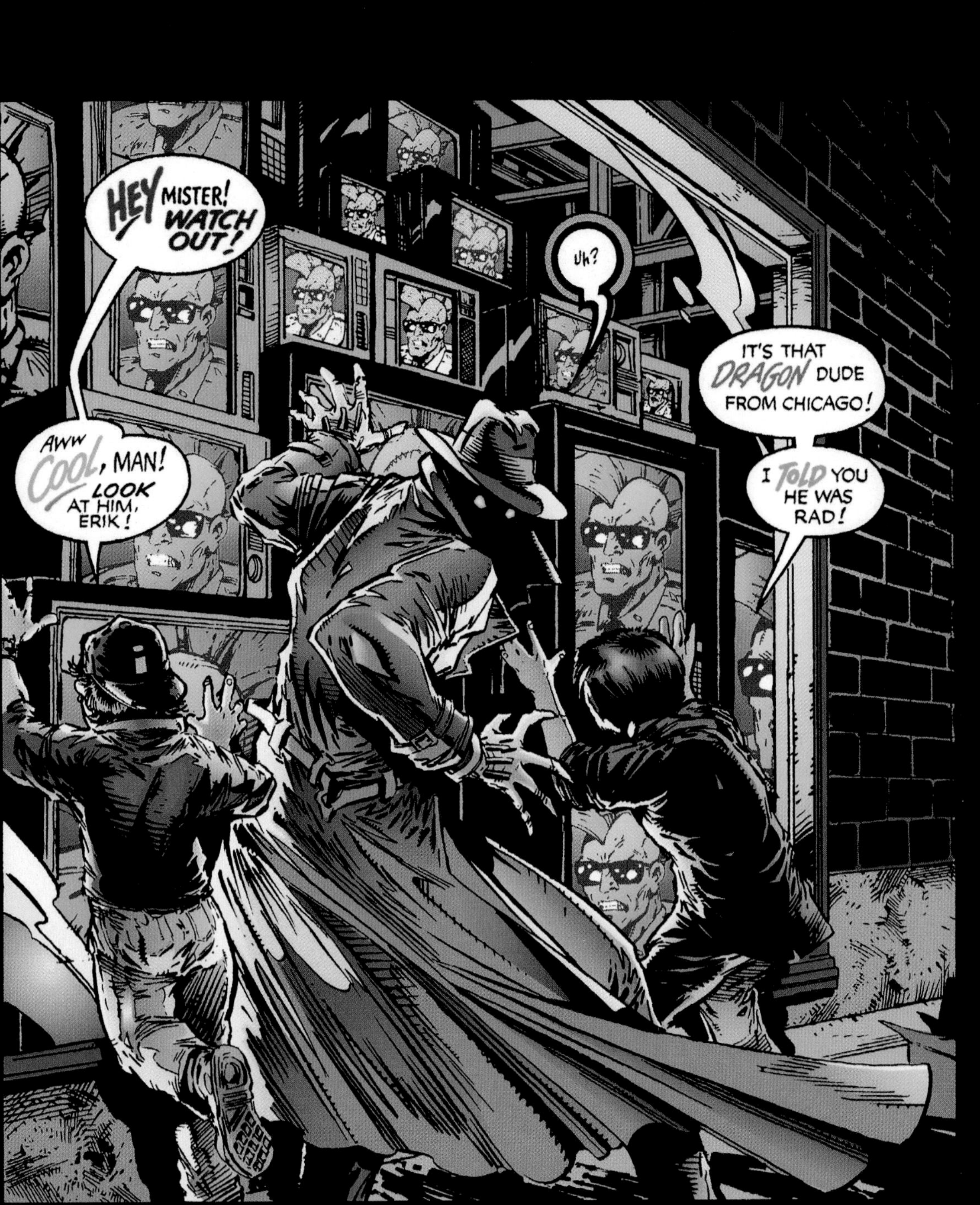
HEY MISTER! WATCH OUT!
Uh?
AWW COOL, MAN! LOOK AT HIM, ERIK!
IT'S THAT DRAGON DUDE FROM CHICAGO!
I TOLD YOU HE WAS RAD!

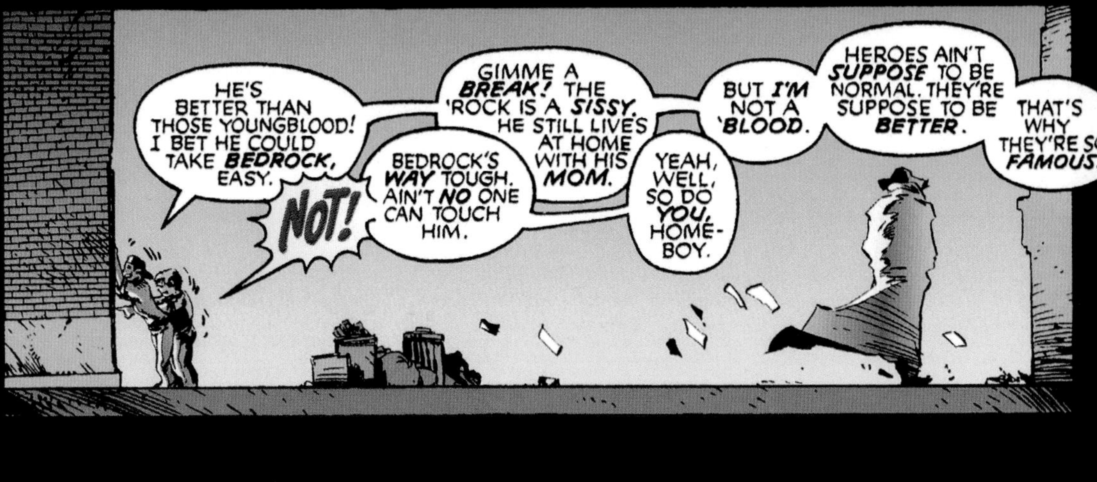
HE'S BETTER THAN THOSE YOUNGBLOOD! I BET HE COULD TAKE BEDROCK, EASY.
NOT!
BEDROCK'S WAY TOUGH. AIN'T NO ONE CAN TOUCH HIM.
GIMME A BREAK! THE 'ROCK IS A SISSY. HE STILL LIVE'S AT HOME WITH HIS MOM.
YEAH, WELL, SO DO YOU, HOME-BOY.
BUT I'M NOT A 'BLOOD.
HEROES AIN'T SUPPOSE TO BE NORMAL. THEY'RE SUPPOSE TO BE BETTER.
THAT'S WHY THEY'RE SO FAMOUS.

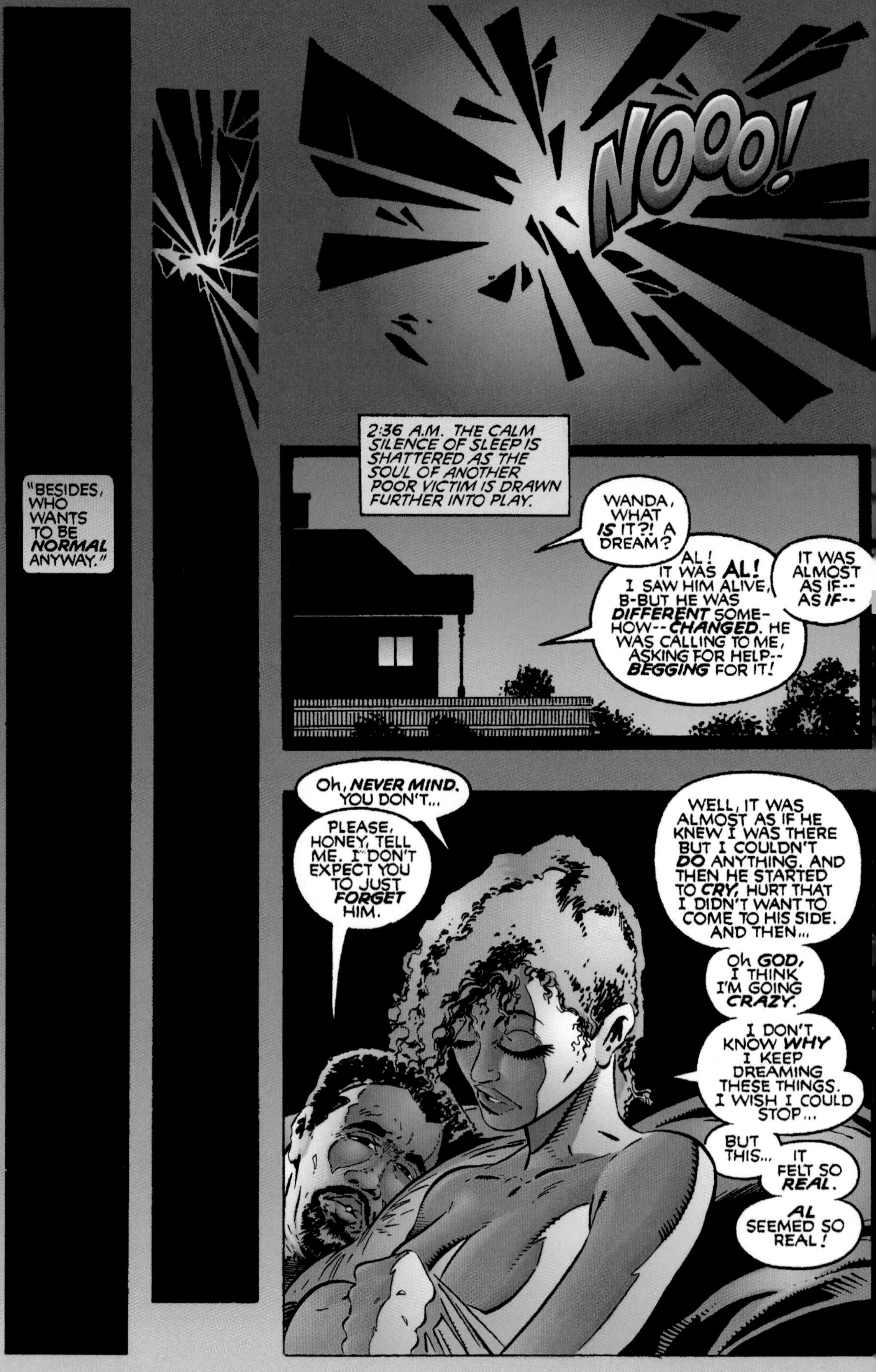
"BESIDES, WHO WANTS TO BE NORMAL ANYWAY."
NOOO!
2:36 A.M. THE CALM SILENCE OF SLEEP IS SHATTERED AS THE SOUL OF ANOTHER POOR VICTIM IS DRAWN FURTHER INTO PLAY.
WANDA, WHAT IS IT?! A DREAM?
AL! IT WAS AL! I SAW HIM ALIVE, B-BUT HE WAS DIFFERENT SOME-HOW--CHANGED. HE WAS CALLING TO ME, ASKING FOR HELP--BEGGING FOR IT!
IT WAS ALMOST AS IF-- AS IF--
Oh, NEVER MIND. YOU DON'T...
PLEASE, HONEY, TELL ME. I DON'T EXPECT YOU TO JUST FORGET HIM.
WELL, IT WAS ALMOST AS IF HE KNEW I WAS THERE BUT I COULDN'T DO ANYTHING. AND THEN HE STARTED TO CRY, HURT THAT I DIDN'T WANT TO COME TO HIS SIDE. AND THEN...
Oh GOD, I THINK I'M GOING CRAZY.
I DON'T KNOW WHY I KEEP DREAMING THESE THINGS. I WISH I COULD STOP...
BUT THIS... IT FELT SO REAL.
AL SEEMED SO REAL!

5 | OCT
1992

"JUSTICE"

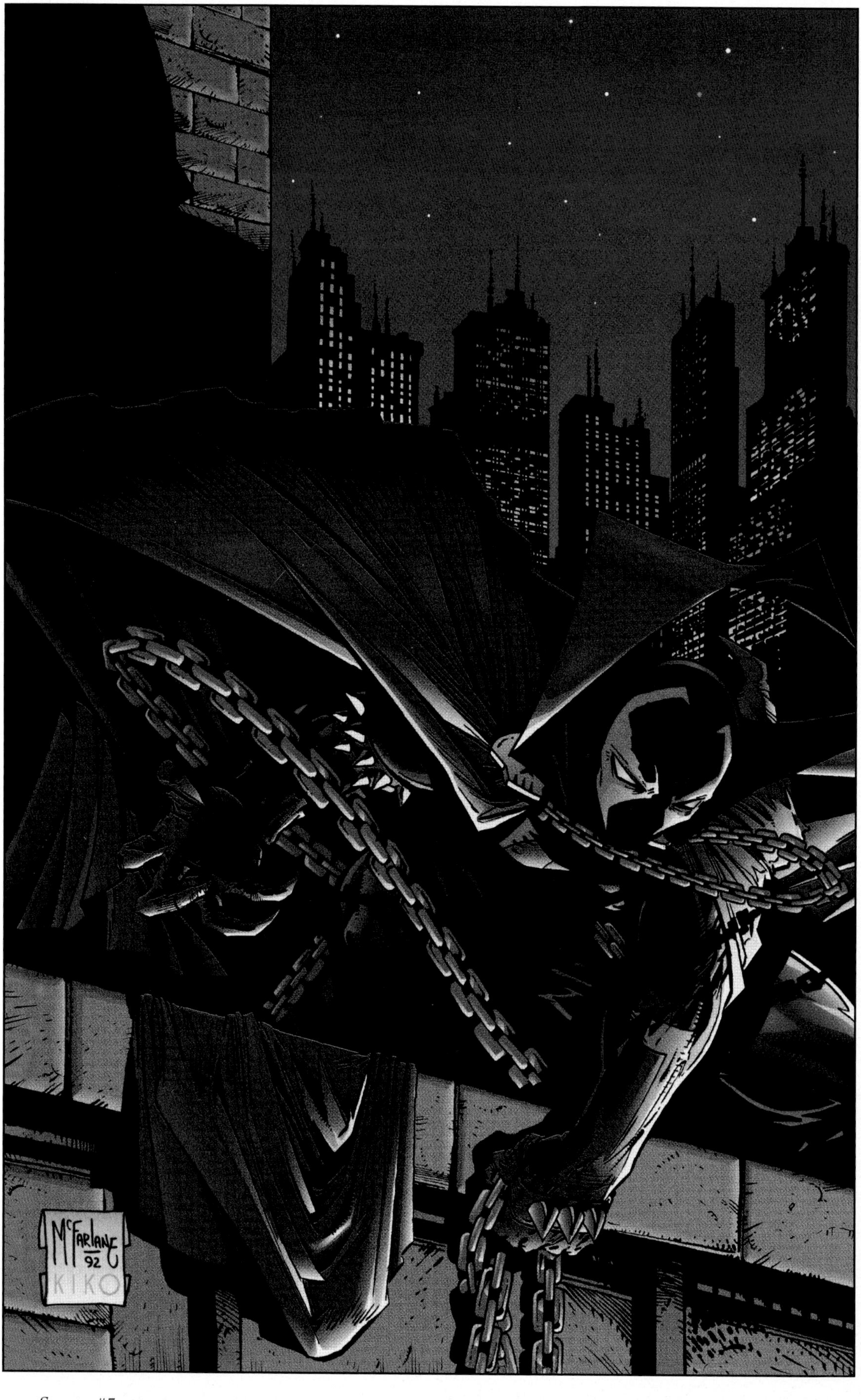
McFarlane
92
KIKO

Spawn #5, cover

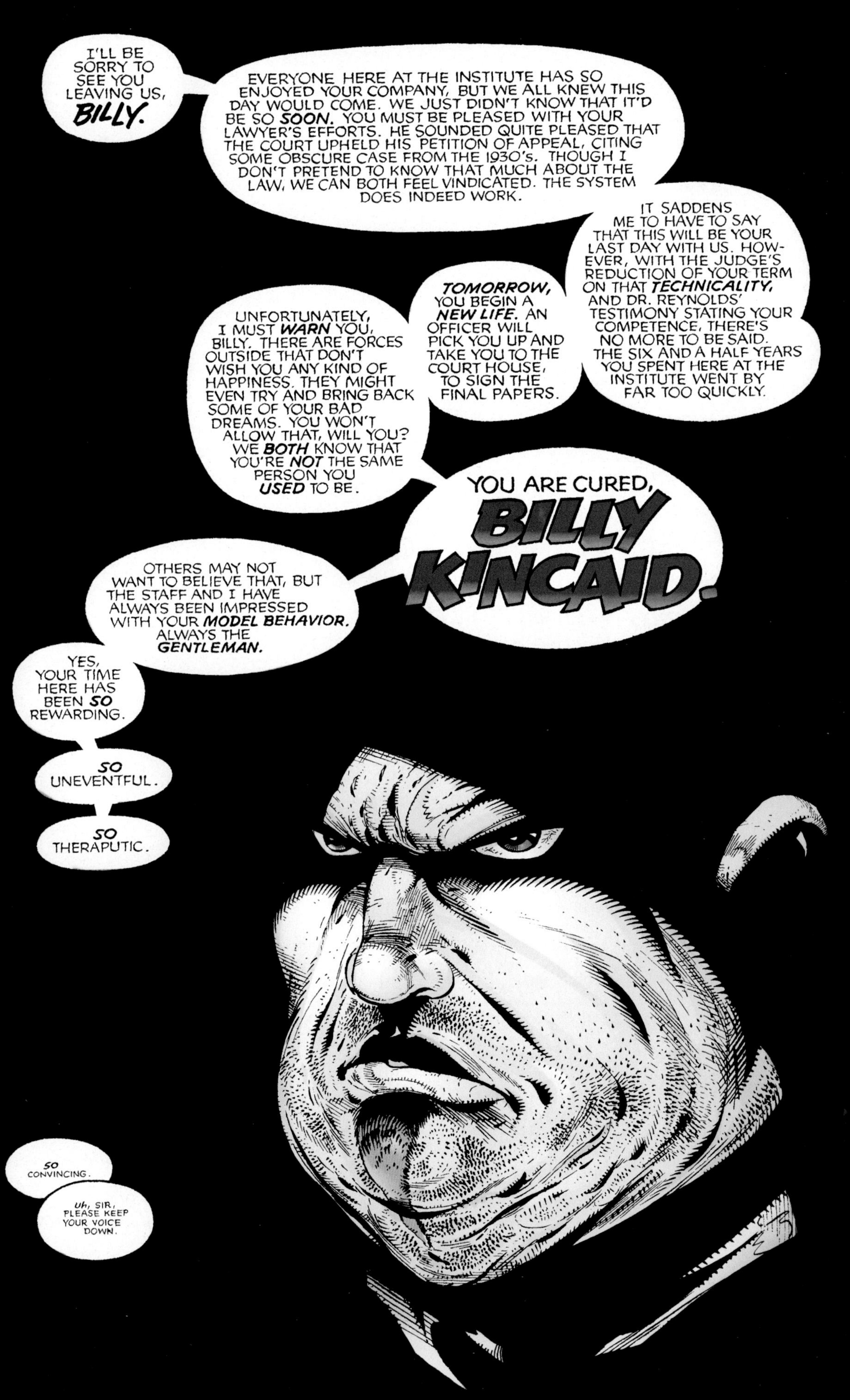
I'LL BE SORRY TO SEE YOU LEAVING US, BILLY.
EVERYONE HERE AT THE INSTITUTE HAS SO ENJOYED YOUR COMPANY, BUT WE ALL KNEW THIS DAY WOULD COME. WE JUST DIDN'T KNOW THAT IT'D BE SO SOON. YOU MUST BE PLEASED WITH YOUR LAWYER'S EFFORTS. HE SOUNDED QUITE PLEASED THAT THE COURT UPHELD HIS PETITION OF APPEAL, CITING SOME OBSCURE CASE FROM THE 1930's. THOUGH I DON'T PRETEND TO KNOW THAT MUCH ABOUT THE LAW, WE CAN BOTH FEEL VINDICATED. THE SYSTEM DOES INDEED WORK.
IT SADDENS ME TO HAVE TO SAY THAT THIS WILL BE YOUR LAST DAY WITH US. HOWEVER, WITH THE JUDGE'S REDUCTION OF YOUR TERM ON THAT TECHNICALITY, AND DR. REYNOLDS' TESTIMONY STATING YOUR COMPETENCE, THERE'S NO MORE TO BE SAID. THE SIX AND A HALF YEARS YOU SPENT HERE AT THE INSTITUTE WENT BY FAR TOO QUICKLY.
TOMORROW, YOU BEGIN A NEW LIFE. AN OFFICER WILL PICK YOU UP AND TAKE YOU TO THE COURT HOUSE, TO SIGN THE FINAL PAPERS.
UNFORTUNATELY, I MUST WARN YOU, BILLY. THERE ARE FORCES OUTSIDE THAT DON'T WISH YOU ANY KIND OF HAPPINESS. THEY MIGHT EVEN TRY AND BRING BACK SOME OF YOUR BAD DREAMS. YOU WON'T ALLOW THAT, WILL YOU? WE BOTH KNOW THAT YOU'RE NOT THE SAME PERSON YOU USED TO BE.
YOU ARE CURED, BILLY KINCAID.
OTHERS MAY NOT WANT TO BELIEVE THAT, BUT THE STAFF AND I HAVE ALWAYS BEEN IMPRESSED WITH YOUR MODEL BEHAVIOR. ALWAYS THE GENTLEMAN.
YES, YOUR TIME HERE HAS BEEN SO REWARDING.
SO UNEVENTFUL.
SO THERAPUTIC.
SO CONVINCING.
Uh, SIR, PLEASE KEEP YOUR VOICE DOWN.

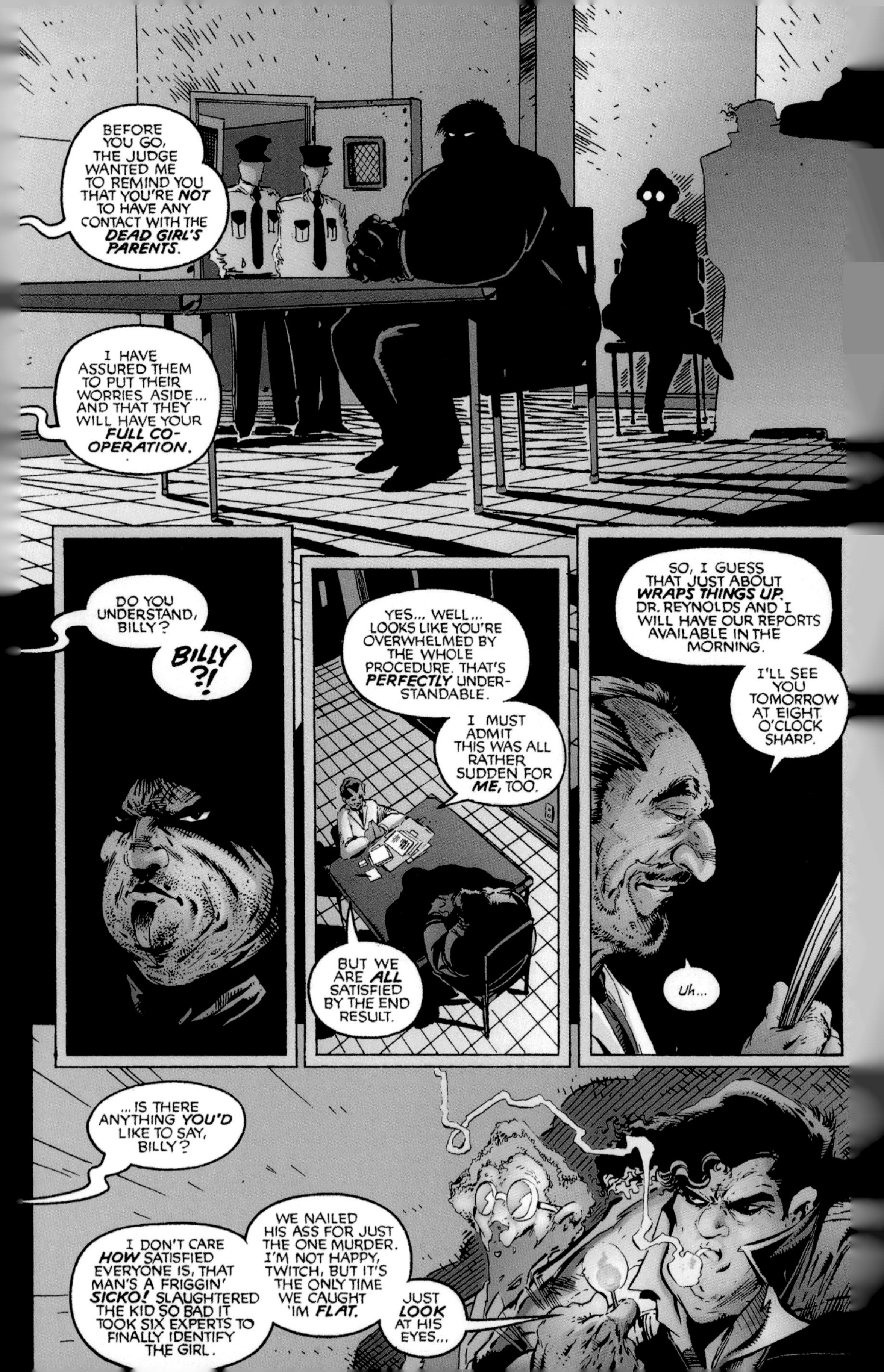
BEFORE YOU GO, THE JUDGE WANTED ME TO REMIND YOU THAT YOU'RE NOT TO HAVE ANY CONTACT WITH THE DEAD GIRL'S PARENTS.
I HAVE ASSURED THEM TO PUT THEIR WORRIES ASIDE... AND THAT THEY WILL HAVE YOUR FULL CO-OPERATION.
DO YOU UNDERSTAND, BILLY?
BILLY ?!
YES... WELL... LOOKS LIKE YOU'RE OVERWHELMED BY THE WHOLE PROCEDURE. THAT'S PERFECTLY UNDER-STANDABLE.
I MUST ADMIT THIS WAS ALL RATHER SUDDEN FOR ME, TOO.
BUT WE ARE ALL SATISFIED BY THE END RESULT.
SO, I GUESS THAT JUST ABOUT WRAPS THINGS UP. DR. REYNOLDS AND I WILL HAVE OUR REPORTS AVAILABLE IN THE MORNING.
I'LL SEE YOU TOMORROW AT EIGHT O'CLOCK SHARP.
Uh...
...IS THERE ANYTHING YOU'D LIKE TO SAY, BILLY?
I DON'T CARE HOW SATISFIED EVERYONE IS, THAT MAN'S A FRIGGIN' SICKO! SLAUGHTERED THE KID SO BAD IT TOOK SIX EXPERTS TO FINALLY IDENTIFY THE GIRL.
WE NAILED HIS ASS FOR JUST THE ONE MURDER. I'M NOT HAPPY, TWITCH, BUT IT'S THE ONLY TIME WE CAUGHT 'IM FLAT.
JUST LOOK AT HIS EYES...

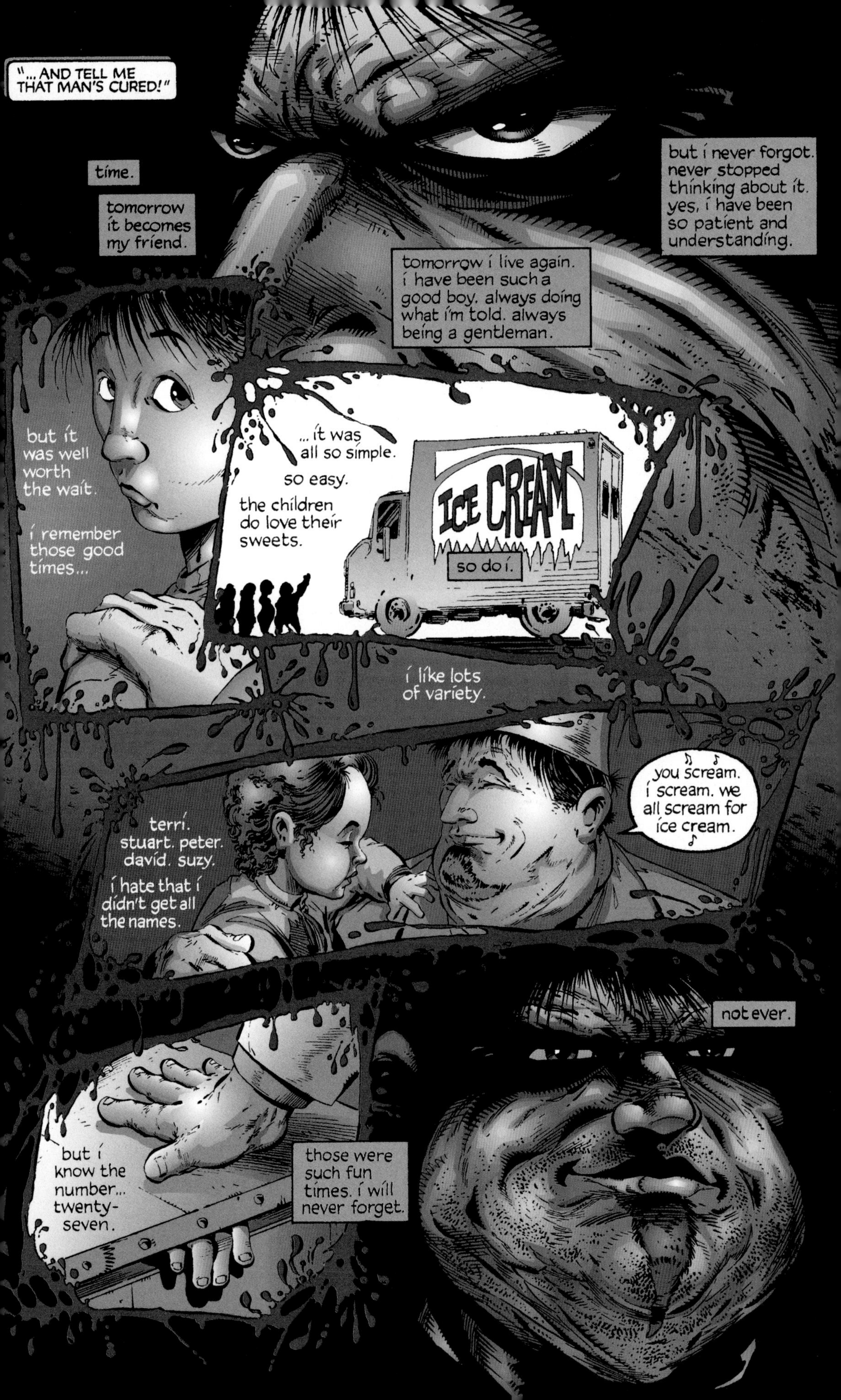
"... AND TELL ME THAT MAN'S CURED!"
time.
tomorrow it becomes my friend.
tomorrow i live again. i have been such a good boy. always doing what i'm told. always being a gentleman.
but i never forgot. never stopped thinking about it. yes, i have been so patient and understanding.
but it was well worth the wait.
i remember those good times...
... it was all so simple.
so easy.
the children do love their sweets.
ICE CREAM
so do i.
i like lots of variety.
terri. stuart. peter. david. suzy.
i hate that i didn't get all the names.
you scream. i scream. we all scream for ice cream.
not ever.
but i know the number... twenty-seven.
those were such fun times. i will never forget.

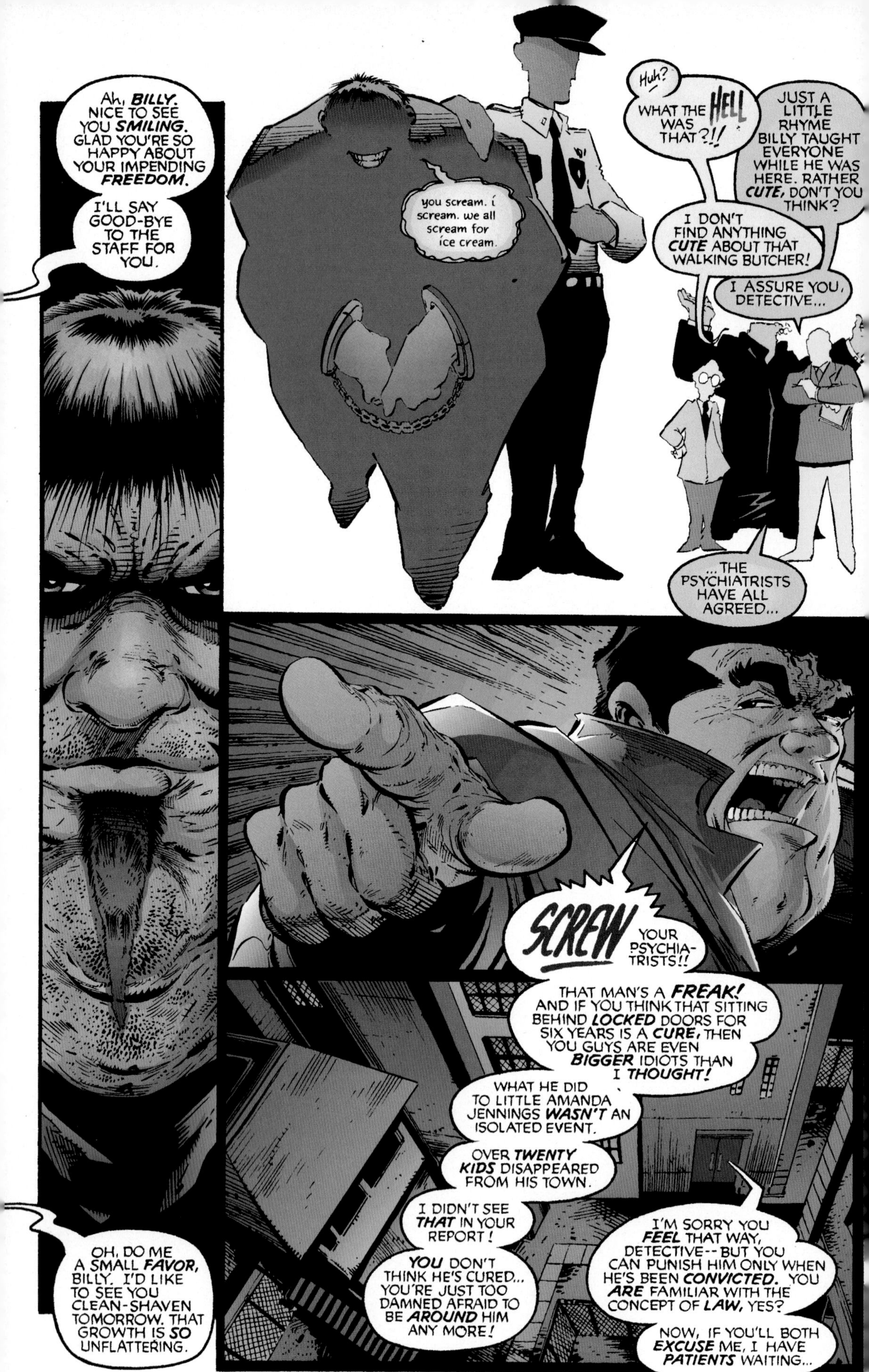

Ah, BILLY. NICE TO SEE YOU SMILING. GLAD YOU'RE SO HAPPY ABOUT YOUR IMPENDING FREEDOM.
I'LL SAY GOOD-BYE TO THE STAFF FOR YOU.
you scream. i scream. we all scream for ice cream.
Huh?
WHAT THE HELL WAS THAT?!!
JUST A LITTLE RHYME BILLY TAUGHT EVERYONE WHILE HE WAS HERE. RATHER CUTE, DON'T YOU THINK?
I DON'T FIND ANYTHING CUTE ABOUT THAT WALKING BUTCHER!
I ASSURE YOU, DETECTIVE...
...THE PSYCHIATRISTS HAVE ALL AGREED...
SCREW YOUR PSYCHIA-TRISTS!!
THAT MAN'S A FREAK! AND IF YOU THINK THAT SITTING BEHIND LOCKED DOORS FOR SIX YEARS IS A CURE, THEN YOU GUYS ARE EVEN BIGGER IDIOTS THAN I THOUGHT!
WHAT HE DID TO LITTLE AMANDA JENNINGS WASN'T AN ISOLATED EVENT.
OVER TWENTY KIDS DISAPPEARED FROM HIS TOWN.
I DIDN'T SEE THAT IN YOUR REPORT!
YOU DON'T THINK HE'S CURED... YOU'RE JUST TOO DAMNED AFRAID TO BE AROUND HIM ANY MORE!
I'M SORRY YOU FEEL THAT WAY, DETECTIVE-- BUT YOU CAN PUNISH HIM ONLY WHEN HE'S BEEN CONVICTED. YOU ARE FAMILIAR WITH THE CONCEPT OF LAW, YES?
NOW, IF YOU'LL BOTH EXCUSE ME, I HAVE PATIENTS WAITING...
OH, DO ME A SMALL FAVOR, BILLY. I'D LIKE TO SEE YOU CLEAN-SHAVEN TOMORROW. THAT GROWTH IS SO UNFLATTERING.

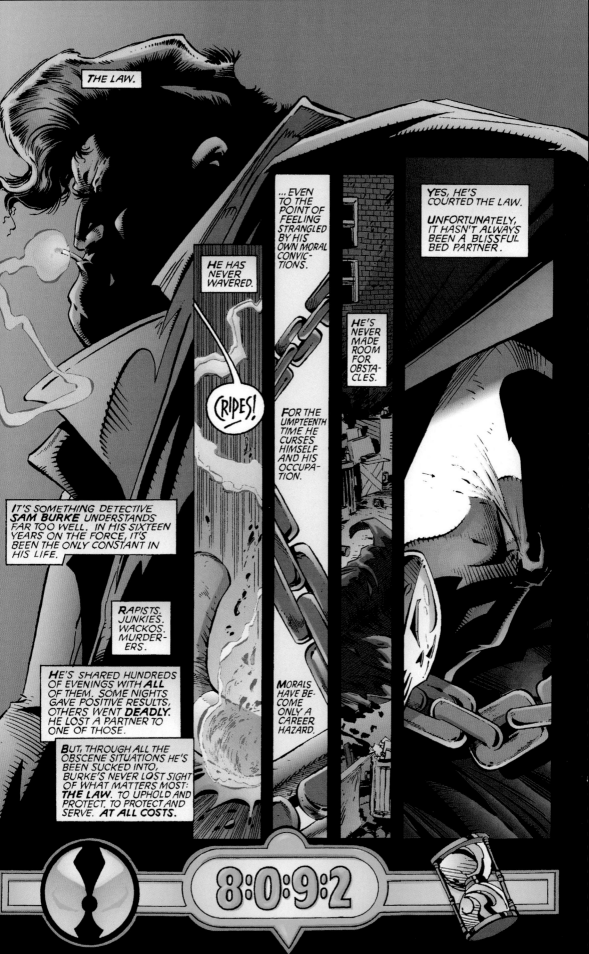

THE LAW.

... EVEN TO THE POINT OF FEELING STRANGLED BY HIS OWN MORAL CONVICTIONS.

HE HAS NEVER WAVERED.

CRIPES!

FOR THE UMPTEENTH TIME HE CURSES HIMSELF AND HIS OCCUPATION.

YES, HE'S COURTED THE LAW.

UNFORTUNATELY, IT HASN'T ALWAYS BEEN A BLISSFUL BED PARTNER.

HE'S NEVER MADE ROOM FOR OBSTACLES.

IT'S SOMETHING DETECTIVE SAM BURKE UNDERSTANDS FAR TOO WELL. IN HIS SIXTEEN YEARS ON THE FORCE, IT'S BEEN THE ONLY CONSTANT IN HIS LIFE.

RAPISTS. JUNKIES. WACKOS. MURDERERS.

MORALS HAVE BECOME ONLY A CAREER HAZARD.

HE'S SHARED HUNDREDS OF EVENINGS WITH ALL OF THEM. SOME NIGHTS GAVE POSITIVE RESULTS, OTHERS WENT DEADLY. HE LOST A PARTNER TO ONE OF THOSE.

BUT, THROUGH ALL THE OBSCENE SITUATIONS HE'S BEEN SUCKED INTO, BURKE'S NEVER LOST SIGHT OF WHAT MATTERS MOST: THE LAW. TO UPHOLD AND PROTECT. TO PROTECT AND SERVE. AT ALL COSTS.

8:0:9:2

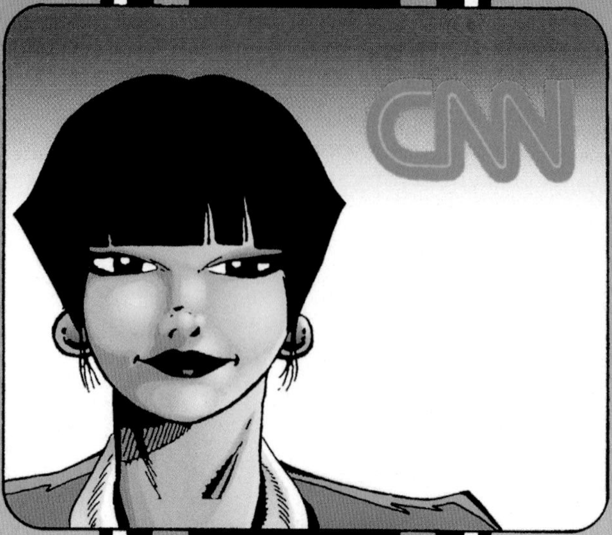
CNN

AND IN NEW YORK, JEFF PITMAN, ATTORNEY FOR CONVICTED CHILD KILLER BILL KINCAID, WAS FINALLY SUCCESSFUL IN HIS ATTEMPTS TO MITIGATE KINCAID'S SENTENCE. THE ORIGINAL TWENTY-TWO YEAR TERM WAS REDUCED TO TEN YEARS. THAT, COMBINED WITH TIME OFF FOR GOOD BEHAVIOR AND TIME SERVED, MAKE BILL KINCAID A FREE MAN TOMORROW.

IT WAS NEARLY EIGHT YEARS AGO THAT A JOGGER IN NEW YORK CITY FOUND AMANDA JENNINGS' BODY UNDER THE GEORGE WASHINGTON BRIDGE. THE EIGHT YEAR OLD GIRL WAS THE DAUGHTER OF FORMER SENATOR PAUL JENNINGS.

JENNINGS' HIGH-PROFILE EXTRA-MARITAL AFFAIR TARNISHED HIS RE-ELECTION BID A YEAR EARLIER. SOME SOURCES FELT THAT HIS MORE TRADITIONALLY-ORIENTED FORMER SUPPORTERS IN LAW ENFORCEMENT GAVE THE MATTER LESS ATTENTION THAN IT WARRANTED.

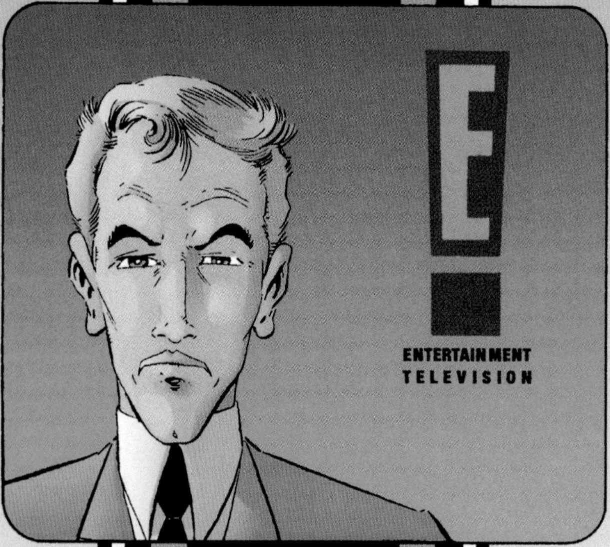
E!
ENTERTAINMENT
TELEVISION

BELIEVE ME, IT WAS ***ONE*** TORRID LOVE AFFAIR. SENATOR JENNINGS AND ***MARLA FLEET*** WERE THE TALK OF THE TOWN DURING HIS RE-ELECTION CAMPAIGN. VOTERS DIDN'T WANT TO HEAR ABOUT BUDGETS OR TAXES. THEY WERE MORE INTERESTED IN THE ***STEAMY DETAILS*** OF HOW SENATOR JENNINGS SWEPT THE FORMER ***MISS UNIVERSE*** OFF HER FEET. MIX IN AN ***EXTREMELY*** VENGEFUL WIFE AND THE MEDIA HAD ITSELF A FEAST FOR ***MONTHS***.

THE STORY THAT MADE THE ROUNDS AT THE TIME-- THAT THE ***FORMER*** SENATOR'S ***RAGING*** HORMONES LED TO LESS OF AN INVESTIGATION OF HIS DAUGHTER'S DEATH-- IS TRULY DISTURBING. THESE WAGS IMPLY THAT WHILE JENNINGS WASN'T MUCH LOVED WHILE ***IN*** OFFICE, THE TAWDRY TRUTH BEHIND HIS DOWNFALL MAY HAVE LED TO INADEQUATE INFORMATION REACHING THE INTERESTED PARTIES.

AS A RESULT, BILLY KINCAID RECEIVED A TWENTY-TWO YEAR STRETCH INSTEAD OF THE LIFE SENTENCE WITHOUT PAROLE THAT THE PUBLIC SO DEARLY WANTED.

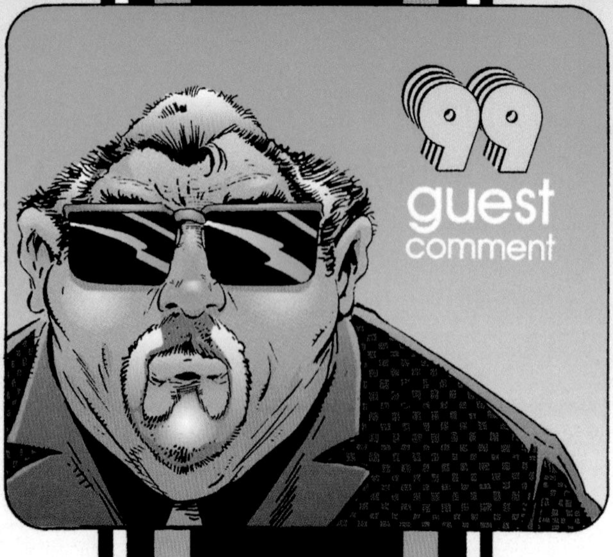
99
guest
comment

SURPRISE! SURPRISE!

KIDDIE KILLER KINCAID, FREE TO WALK THE STREETS OF THE BIG APPLE! WE'VE BEEN FAVORED WITH YET ***ANOTHER*** AWE-INSPIRING RULING AS THE COURTS ALLOW THIS CHILD-MURDERER HIS FREEDOM. AFTER PESTERING THE JUDICIAL SYSTEM WITH HIS ***WHINING*** AND ***APPEALS*** THESE PAST FIVE YEARS, KINCAID'S LAWYER FINALLY GOT WHAT HE WANTED-- ANOTHER ***PSYCHO*** READY TO ROAM CENTRAL PARK. OH JOY! OH RAPTURE! I FEEL SAFER ALREADY.

C'MON, FOLKS! I HATE REPEATING MYSELF BUT I'M NOT SURE ANYONE'S ***LISTENING.*** LOOKIT, THE WAY ***I*** SEE IT, KINCAID'S LAWYER DID US ***ALL*** A FAVOR. FOR THE PAST SIX YEARS, BILLY'S BEEN ***HIDDEN*** FROM US, BUT NOW WE HAVE AN OPEN ***OPPORTUNITY.*** I GUARANTEE THAT HE WAS A LOT ***SAFER*** ON THE ***INSIDE***.

MY ONLY WISH IS THAT SOMEONE BREAKS HIS BACK. ***HELLO!*** ARE YOU LISTENING, ***MR. SHADOWHAWK?***

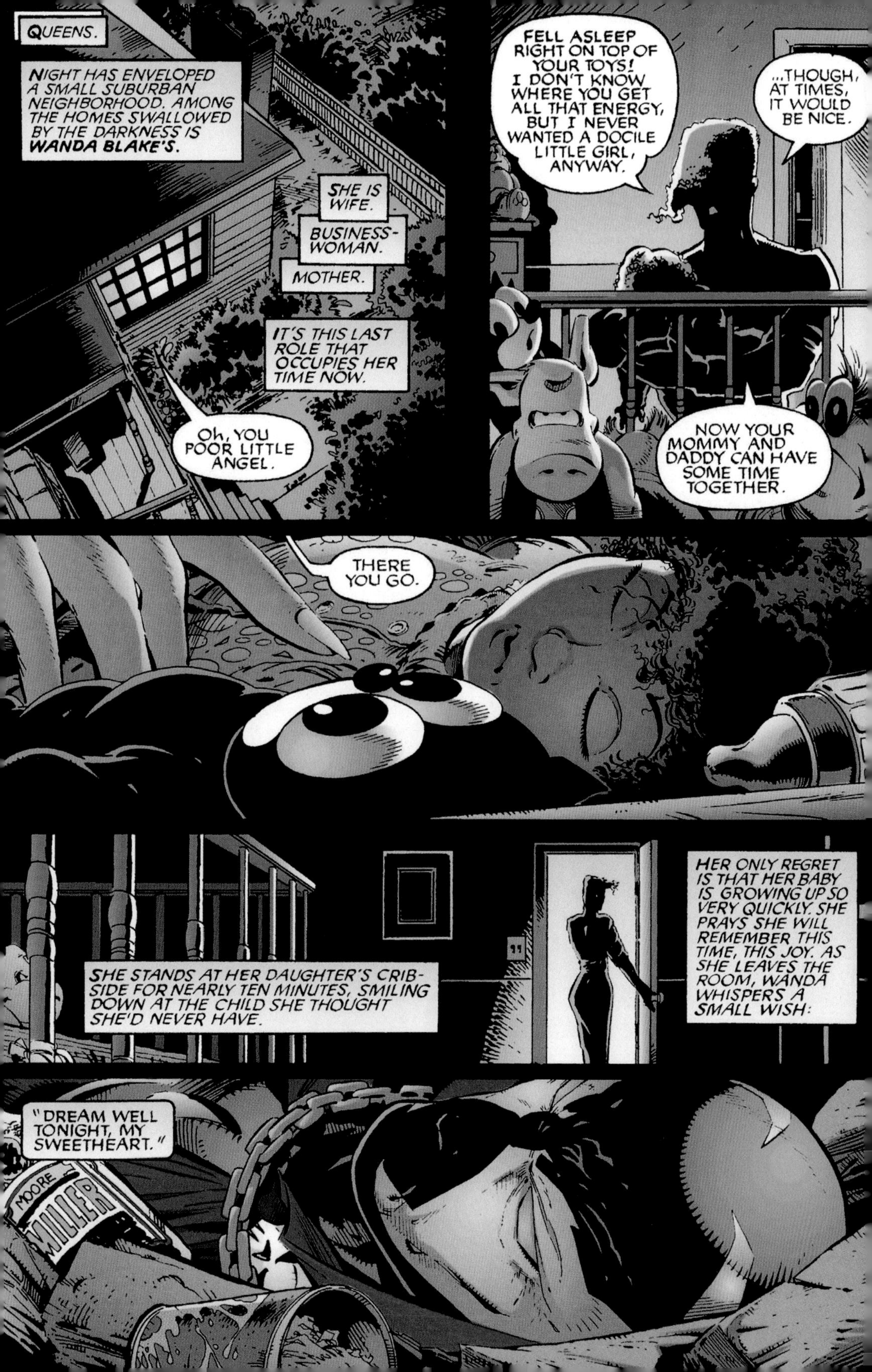
QUEENS.
NIGHT HAS ENVELOPED A SMALL SUBURBAN NEIGHBORHOOD. AMONG THE HOMES SWALLOWED BY THE DARKNESS IS WANDA BLAKE'S.
SHE IS WIFE.
BUSINESS-WOMAN.
MOTHER.
IT'S THIS LAST ROLE THAT OCCUPIES HER TIME NOW.
Oh, YOU POOR LITTLE ANGEL.
FELL ASLEEP RIGHT ON TOP OF YOUR TOYS! I DON'T KNOW WHERE YOU GET ALL THAT ENERGY, BUT I NEVER WANTED A DOCILE LITTLE GIRL, ANYWAY.
...THOUGH, AT TIMES, IT WOULD BE NICE.
NOW YOUR MOMMY AND DADDY CAN HAVE SOME TIME TOGETHER.
THERE YOU GO.
SHE STANDS AT HER DAUGHTER'S CRIB-SIDE FOR NEARLY TEN MINUTES, SMILING DOWN AT THE CHILD SHE THOUGHT SHE'D NEVER HAVE.
HER ONLY REGRET IS THAT HER BABY IS GROWING UP SO VERY QUICKLY. SHE PRAYS SHE WILL REMEMBER THIS TIME, THIS JOY. AS SHE LEAVES THE ROOM, WANDA WHISPERS A SMALL WISH:
"DREAM WELL TONIGHT, MY SWEETHEART."
MOORE
MILLER

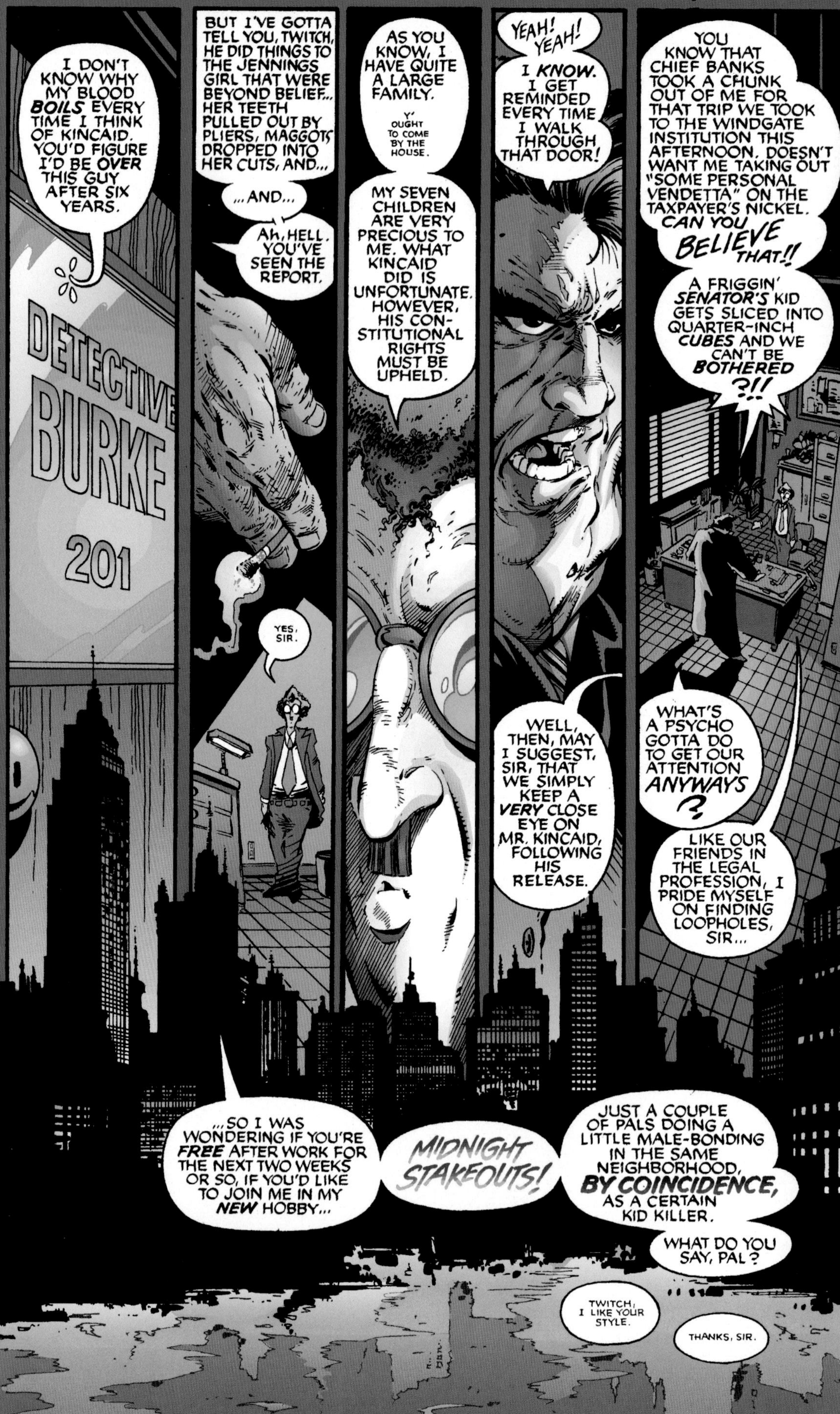
I DON'T KNOW WHY MY BLOOD BOILS EVERY TIME I THINK OF KINCAID. YOU'D FIGURE I'D BE OVER THIS GUY AFTER SIX YEARS.
DETECTIVE BURKE
201
BUT I'VE GOTTA TELL YOU, TWITCH, HE DID THINGS TO THE JENNINGS GIRL THAT WERE BEYOND BELIEF... HER TEETH PULLED OUT BY PLIERS, MAGGOTS DROPPED INTO HER CUTS, AND...
...AND...
Ah, HELL. YOU'VE SEEN THE REPORT.
YES, SIR.
AS YOU KNOW, I HAVE QUITE A LARGE FAMILY.
Y' OUGHT TO COME BY THE HOUSE.
MY SEVEN CHILDREN ARE VERY PRECIOUS TO ME. WHAT KINCAID DID IS UNFORTUNATE. HOWEVER, HIS CONSTITUTIONAL RIGHTS MUST BE UPHELD.
YEAH! YEAH!
I KNOW. I GET REMINDED EVERY TIME I WALK THROUGH THAT DOOR!
WELL, THEN, MAY I SUGGEST, SIR, THAT WE SIMPLY KEEP A VERY CLOSE EYE ON MR. KINCAID, FOLLOWING HIS RELEASE.
YOU KNOW THAT CHIEF BANKS TOOK A CHUNK OUT OF ME FOR THAT TRIP WE TOOK TO THE WINDGATE INSTITUTION THIS AFTERNOON. DOESN'T WANT ME TAKING OUT "SOME PERSONAL VENDETTA" ON THE TAXPAYER'S NICKEL. CAN YOU BELIEVE THAT!!
A FRIGGIN' SENATOR'S KID GETS SLICED INTO QUARTER-INCH CUBES AND WE CAN'T BE BOTHERED ?!!
WHAT'S A PSYCHO GOTTA DO TO GET OUR ATTENTION ANYWAYS ?
LIKE OUR FRIENDS IN THE LEGAL PROFESSION, I PRIDE MYSELF ON FINDING LOOPHOLES, SIR...
...SO I WAS WONDERING IF YOU'RE FREE AFTER WORK FOR THE NEXT TWO WEEKS OR SO, IF YOU'D LIKE TO JOIN ME IN MY NEW HOBBY...
MIDNIGHT STAKEOUTS!
JUST A COUPLE OF PALS DOING A LITTLE MALE-BONDING IN THE SAME NEIGHBORHOOD, BY COINCIDENCE, AS A CERTAIN KID KILLER.
WHAT DO YOU SAY, PAL?
TWITCH, I LIKE YOUR STYLE.
THANKS, SIR.

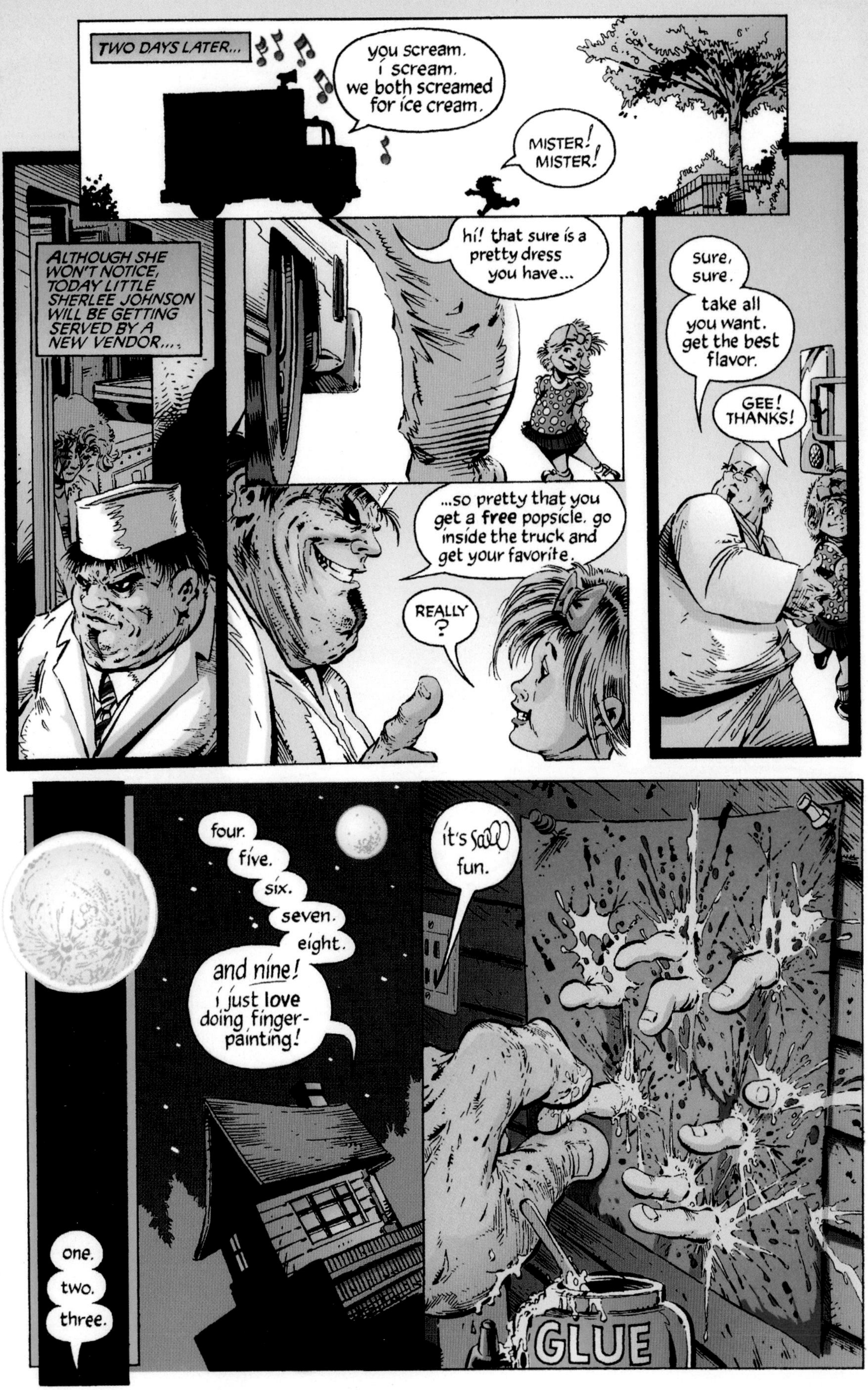
TWO DAYS LATER...
you scream. i scream. we both screamed for ice cream.
MISTER! MISTER!
ALTHOUGH SHE WON'T NOTICE, TODAY LITTLE SHERLEE JOHNSON WILL BE GETTING SERVED BY A NEW VENDOR....
hi! that sure is a pretty dress you have...
...so pretty that you get a free popsicle. go inside the truck and get your favorite.
REALLY?
sure, sure.
take all you want. get the best flavor.
GEE! THANKS!
one.
two.
three.
four.
five.
six.
seven.
eight.
and nine! i just love doing finger-painting!
it's sooo fun.
GLUE

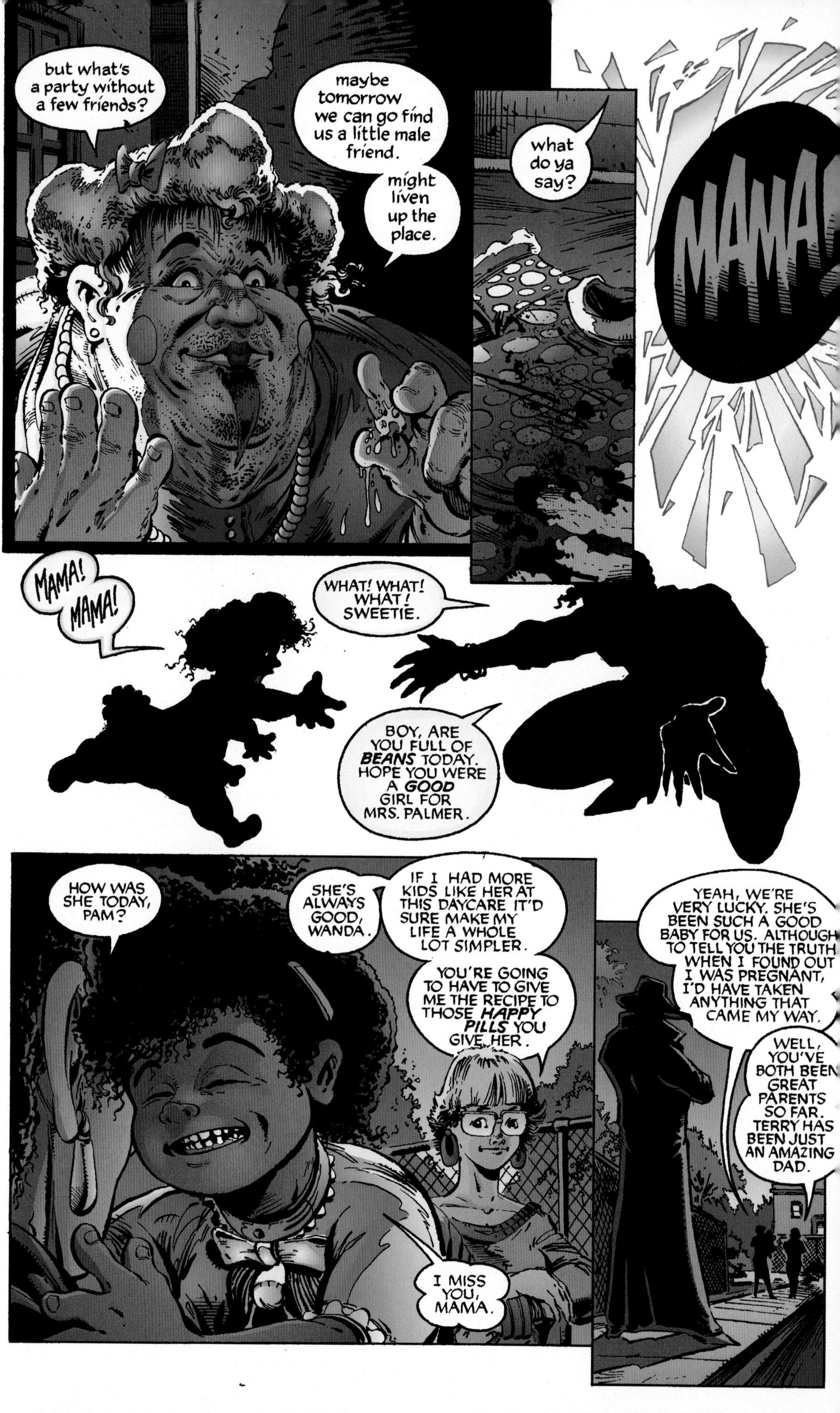

but what's a party without a few friends?
maybe tomorrow we can go find us a little male friend.
might liven up the place.
what do ya say?
MAMA!
MAMA! MAMA!
WHAT! WHAT! WHAT! SWEETIE.
BOY, ARE YOU FULL OF BEANS TODAY. HOPE YOU WERE A GOOD GIRL FOR MRS. PALMER.
HOW WAS SHE TODAY, PAM?
SHE'S ALWAYS GOOD, WANDA.
IF I HAD MORE KIDS LIKE HER AT THIS DAYCARE IT'D SURE MAKE MY LIFE A WHOLE LOT SIMPLER.
YOU'RE GOING TO HAVE TO GIVE ME THE RECIPE TO THOSE HAPPY PILLS YOU GIVE HER.
I MISS YOU, MAMA.
YEAH, WE'RE VERY LUCKY. SHE'S BEEN SUCH A GOOD BABY FOR US. ALTHOUGH TO TELL YOU THE TRUTH WHEN I FOUND OUT I WAS PREGNANT, I'D HAVE TAKEN ANYTHING THAT CAME MY WAY.
WELL, YOU'VE BOTH BEEN GREAT PARENTS SO FAR. TERRY HAS BEEN JUST AN AMAZING DAD.

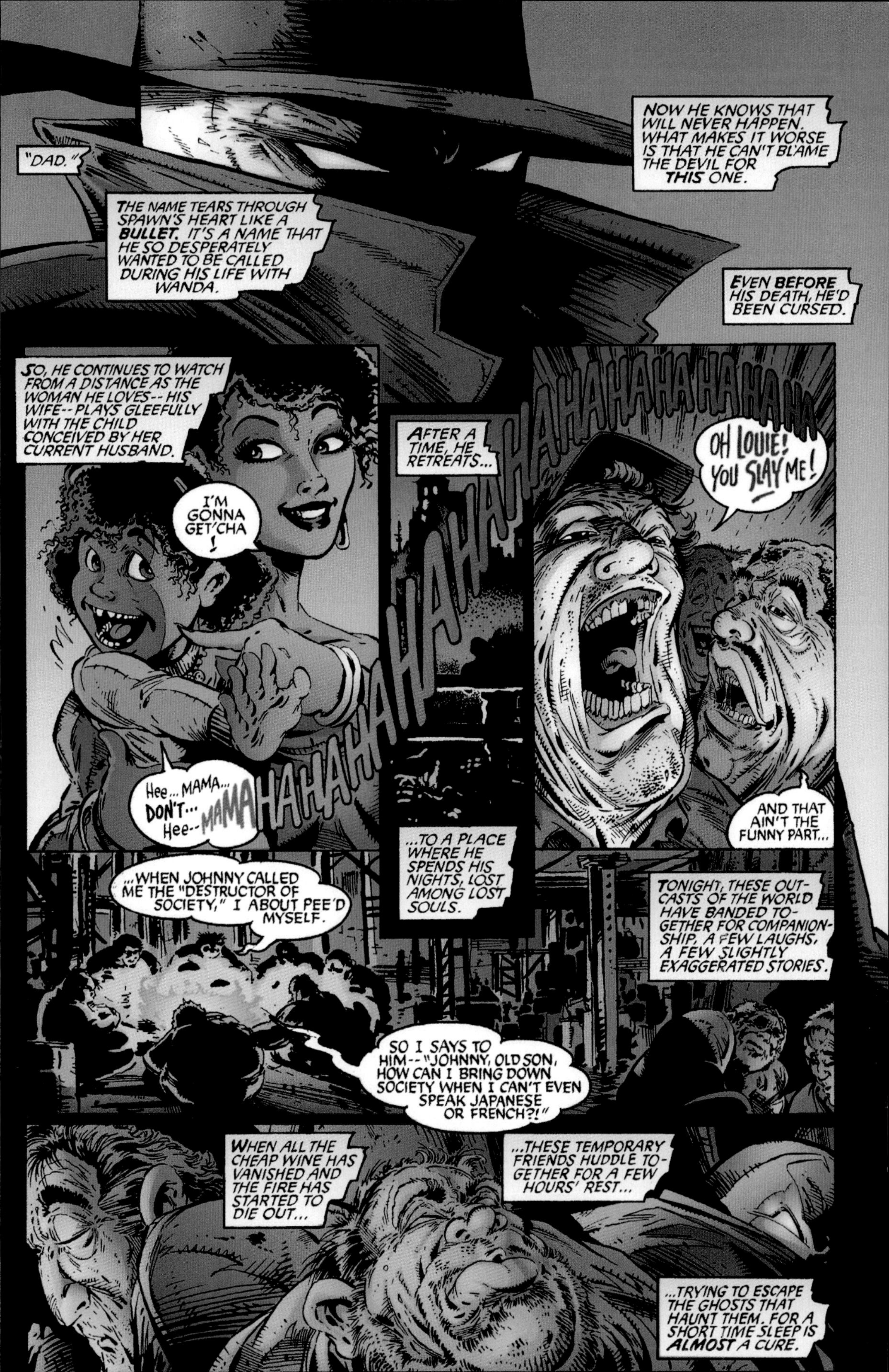
"DAD."
THE NAME TEARS THROUGH SPAWN'S HEART LIKE A BULLET. IT'S A NAME THAT HE SO DESPERATELY WANTED TO BE CALLED DURING HIS LIFE WITH WANDA.
NOW HE KNOWS THAT WILL NEVER HAPPEN. WHAT MAKES IT WORSE IS THAT HE CAN'T BLAME THE DEVIL FOR THIS ONE.
EVEN BEFORE HIS DEATH, HE'D BEEN CURSED.
SO, HE CONTINUES TO WATCH FROM A DISTANCE AS THE WOMAN HE LOVES-- HIS WIFE-- PLAYS GLEEFULLY WITH THE CHILD CONCEIVED BY HER CURRENT HUSBAND.
I'M GONNA GET'CHA!
Hee... MAMA... DON'T... Hee-- MAMA
HAHAHAHAHAHAHAHAHAHAHAHAHAHAHAHA
AFTER A TIME, HE RETREATS...
...TO A PLACE WHERE HE SPENDS HIS NIGHTS, LOST AMONG LOST SOULS.
OH LOUIE! YOU SLAY ME!
AND THAT AIN'T THE FUNNY PART...
...WHEN JOHNNY CALLED ME THE "DESTRUCTOR OF SOCIETY," I ABOUT PEE'D MYSELF.
TONIGHT, THESE OUT-CASTS OF THE WORLD HAVE BANDED TO-GETHER FOR COMPANION-SHIP, A FEW LAUGHS, A FEW SLIGHTLY EXAGGERATED STORIES.
SO I SAYS TO HIM-- "JOHNNY, OLD SON, HOW CAN I BRING DOWN SOCIETY WHEN I CAN'T EVEN SPEAK JAPANESE OR FRENCH?!"
WHEN ALL THE CHEAP WINE HAS VANISHED AND THE FIRE HAS STARTED TO DIE OUT...
...THESE TEMPORARY FRIENDS HUDDLE TO-GETHER FOR A FEW HOURS' REST...
...TRYING TO ESCAPE THE GHOSTS THAT HAUNT THEM. FOR A SHORT TIME SLEEP IS ALMOST A CURE.

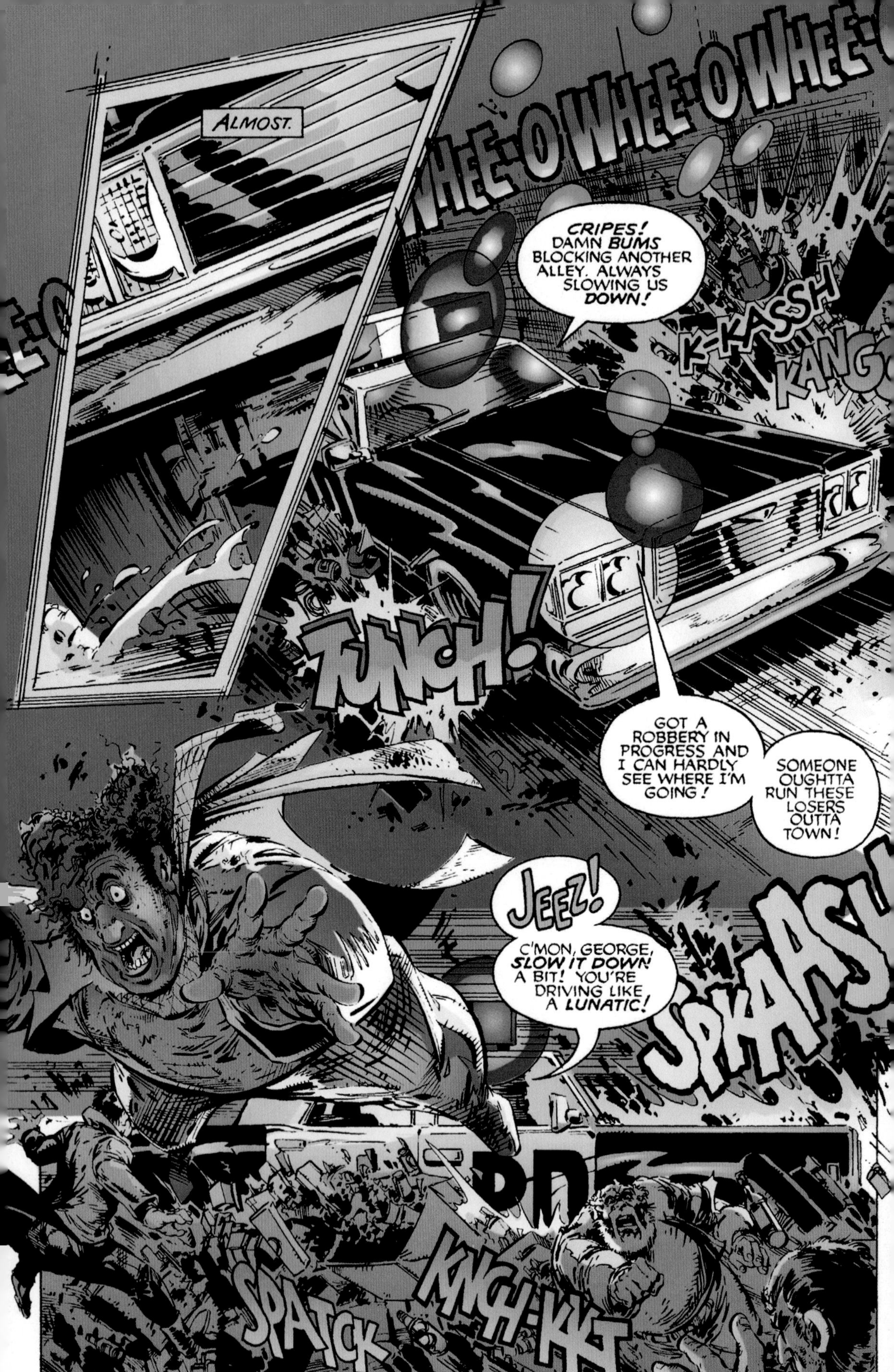

ALMOST.
WHEE-O WHEE-O WHEE-O WHEE-O
CRIPES! DAMN BUMS BLOCKING ANOTHER ALLEY. ALWAYS SLOWING US DOWN!
K-KASSH
KANG
TUNCH!
GOT A ROBBERY IN PROGRESS AND I CAN HARDLY SEE WHERE I'M GOING!
SOMEONE OUGHTTA RUN THESE LOSERS OUTTA TOWN!
JEEZ!
C'MON, GEORGE, SLOW IT DOWN! A BIT! YOU'RE DRIVING LIKE A LUNATIC!
SPKASH
SPATCK
KNCH-KKT

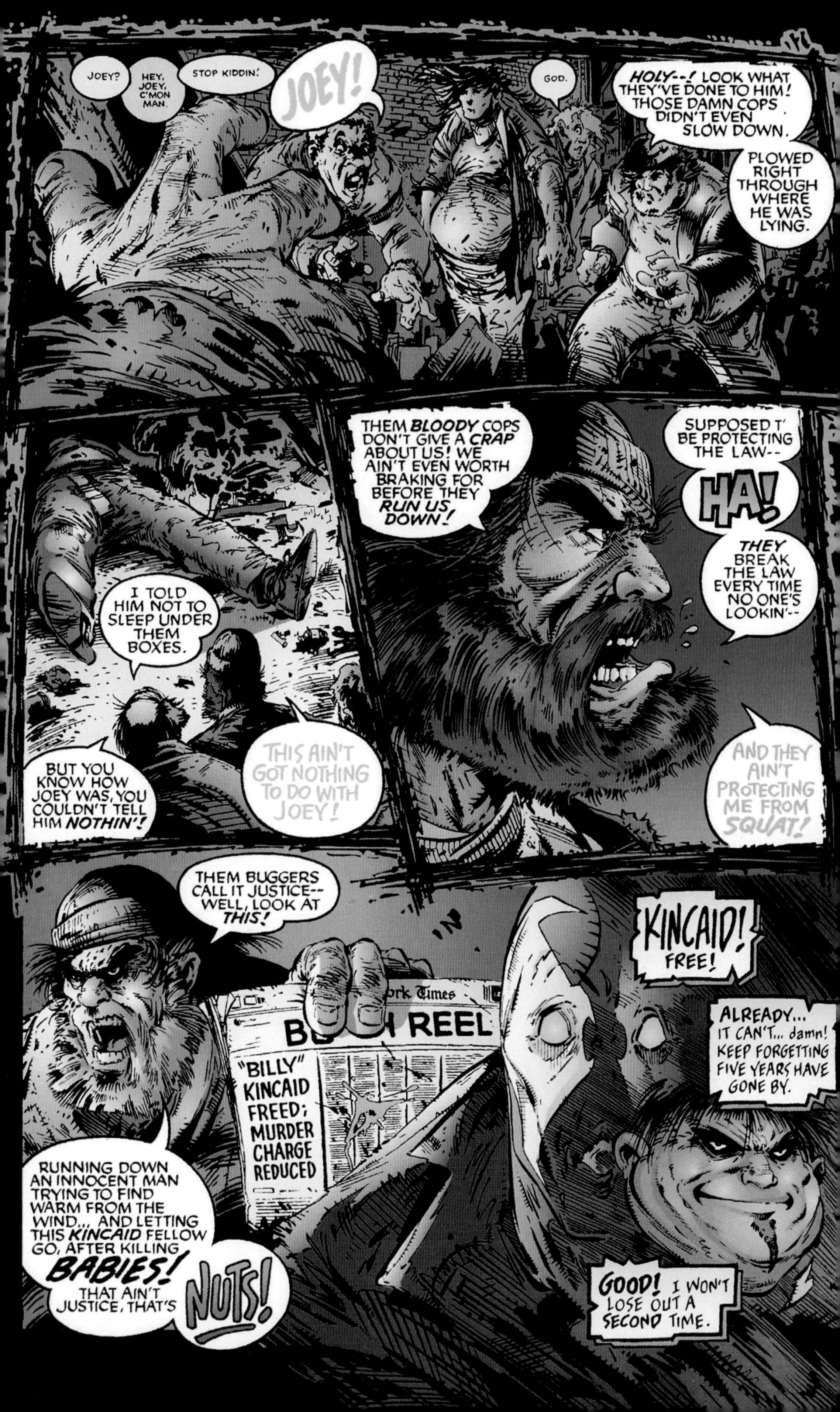

JOEY?
HEY, JOEY, C'MON MAN.
STOP KIDDIN'!
JOEY!
GOD.
HOLY--! LOOK WHAT THEY'VE DONE TO HIM! THOSE DAMN COPS DIDN'T EVEN SLOW DOWN.
PLOWED RIGHT THROUGH WHERE HE WAS LYING.
I TOLD HIM NOT TO SLEEP UNDER THEM BOXES.
BUT YOU KNOW HOW JOEY WAS, YOU COULDN'T TELL HIM NOTHIN'!
THIS AIN'T GOT NOTHING TO DO WITH JOEY!
THEM BLOODY COPS DON'T GIVE A CRAP ABOUT US! WE AIN'T EVEN WORTH BRAKING FOR BEFORE THEY RUN US DOWN!
SUPPOSED T' BE PROTECTING THE LAW--
HA!
THEY BREAK THE LAW EVERY TIME NO ONE'S LOOKIN'--
AND THEY AIN'T PROTECTING ME FROM SQUAT!
THEM BUGGERS CALL IT JUSTICE-- WELL, LOOK AT THIS!
"BILLY" KINCAID FREED; MURDER CHARGE REDUCED
KINCAID! FREE!
ALREADY... IT CAN'T... damn! KEEP FORGETTING FIVE YEARS HAVE GONE BY.
RUNNING DOWN AN INNOCENT MAN TRYING TO FIND WARM FROM THE WIND.., AND LETTING THIS KINCAID FELLOW GO, AFTER KILLING BABIES!
THAT AIN'T JUSTICE, THAT'S NUTS!
GOOD! I WON'T LOSE OUT A SECOND TIME.

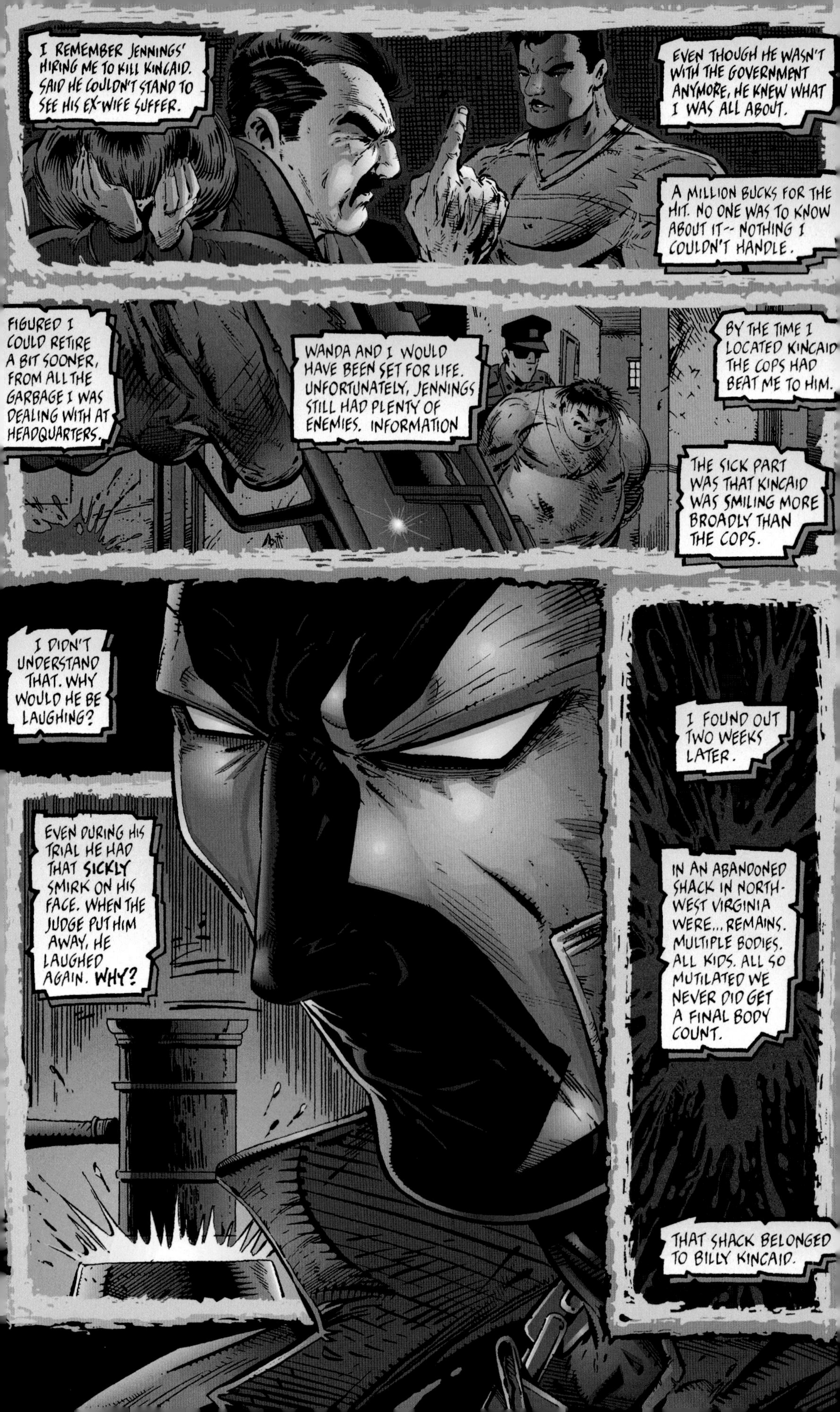
I REMEMBER JENNINGS' HIRING ME TO KILL KINCAID. SAID HE COULDN'T STAND TO SEE HIS EX-WIFE SUFFER.
EVEN THOUGH HE WASN'T WITH THE GOVERNMENT ANYMORE, HE KNEW WHAT I WAS ALL ABOUT.
A MILLION BUCKS FOR THE HIT. NO ONE WAS TO KNOW ABOUT IT-- NOTHING I COULDN'T HANDLE.
FIGURED I COULD RETIRE A BIT SOONER, FROM ALL THE GARBAGE I WAS DEALING WITH AT HEADQUARTERS.
WANDA AND I WOULD HAVE BEEN SET FOR LIFE. UNFORTUNATELY, JENNINGS STILL HAD PLENTY OF ENEMIES. INFORMATION
BY THE TIME I LOCATED KINCAID THE COPS HAD BEAT ME TO HIM.
THE SICK PART WAS THAT KINCAID WAS SMILING MORE BROADLY THAN THE COPS.
I DIDN'T UNDERSTAND THAT. WHY WOULD HE BE LAUGHING?
I FOUND OUT TWO WEEKS LATER.
EVEN DURING HIS TRIAL HE HAD THAT SICKLY SMIRK ON HIS FACE. WHEN THE JUDGE PUT HIM AWAY, HE LAUGHED AGAIN. WHY?
IN AN ABANDONED SHACK IN NORTH-WEST VIRGINIA WERE... REMAINS. MULTIPLE BODIES. ALL KIDS. ALL SO MUTILATED WE NEVER DID GET A FINAL BODY COUNT.
THAT SHACK BELONGED TO BILLY KINCAID.

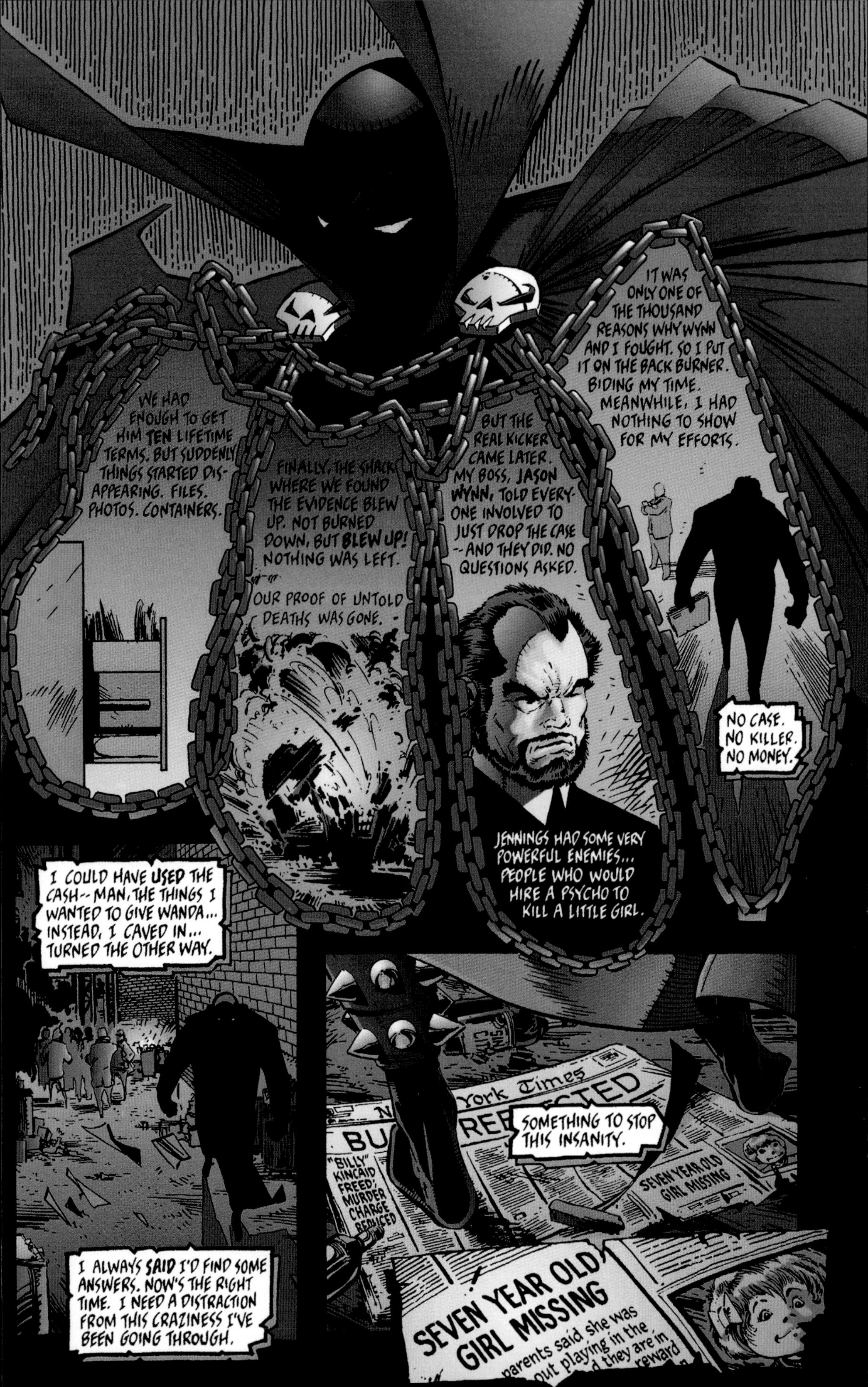
WE HAD ENOUGH TO GET HIM TEN LIFETIME TERMS. BUT SUDDENLY THINGS STARTED DIS-APPEARING. FILES. PHOTOS. CONTAINERS.
FINALLY, THE SHACK WHERE WE FOUND THE EVIDENCE BLEW UP. NOT BURNED DOWN, BUT BLEW UP! NOTHING WAS LEFT.
OUR PROOF OF UNTOLD DEATHS WAS GONE.
BUT THE REAL KICKER CAME LATER. MY BOSS, JASON WYNN, TOLD EVERY-ONE INVOLVED TO JUST DROP THE CASE -- AND THEY DID. NO QUESTIONS ASKED.
JENNINGS HAD SOME VERY POWERFUL ENEMIES... PEOPLE WHO WOULD HIRE A PSYCHO TO KILL A LITTLE GIRL.
IT WAS ONLY ONE OF THE THOUSAND REASONS WHY WYNN AND I FOUGHT. SO I PUT IT ON THE BACK BURNER. BIDING MY TIME. MEANWHILE, I HAD NOTHING TO SHOW FOR MY EFFORTS.
NO CASE. NO KILLER. NO MONEY.
I COULD HAVE USED THE CASH-- MAN, THE THINGS I WANTED TO GIVE WANDA... INSTEAD, I CAVED IN... TURNED THE OTHER WAY.
I ALWAYS SAID I'D FIND SOME ANSWERS. NOW'S THE RIGHT TIME. I NEED A DISTRACTION FROM THIS CRAZINESS I'VE BEEN GOING THROUGH.
SOMETHING TO STOP THIS INSANITY.
York Times
"BILLY" KINCAID FREED; MURDER CHARGE REDUCED
SEVEN YEAR OLD GIRL MISSING
SEVEN YEAR OLD GIRL MISSING
parents said she was out playing in the
they are in
reward

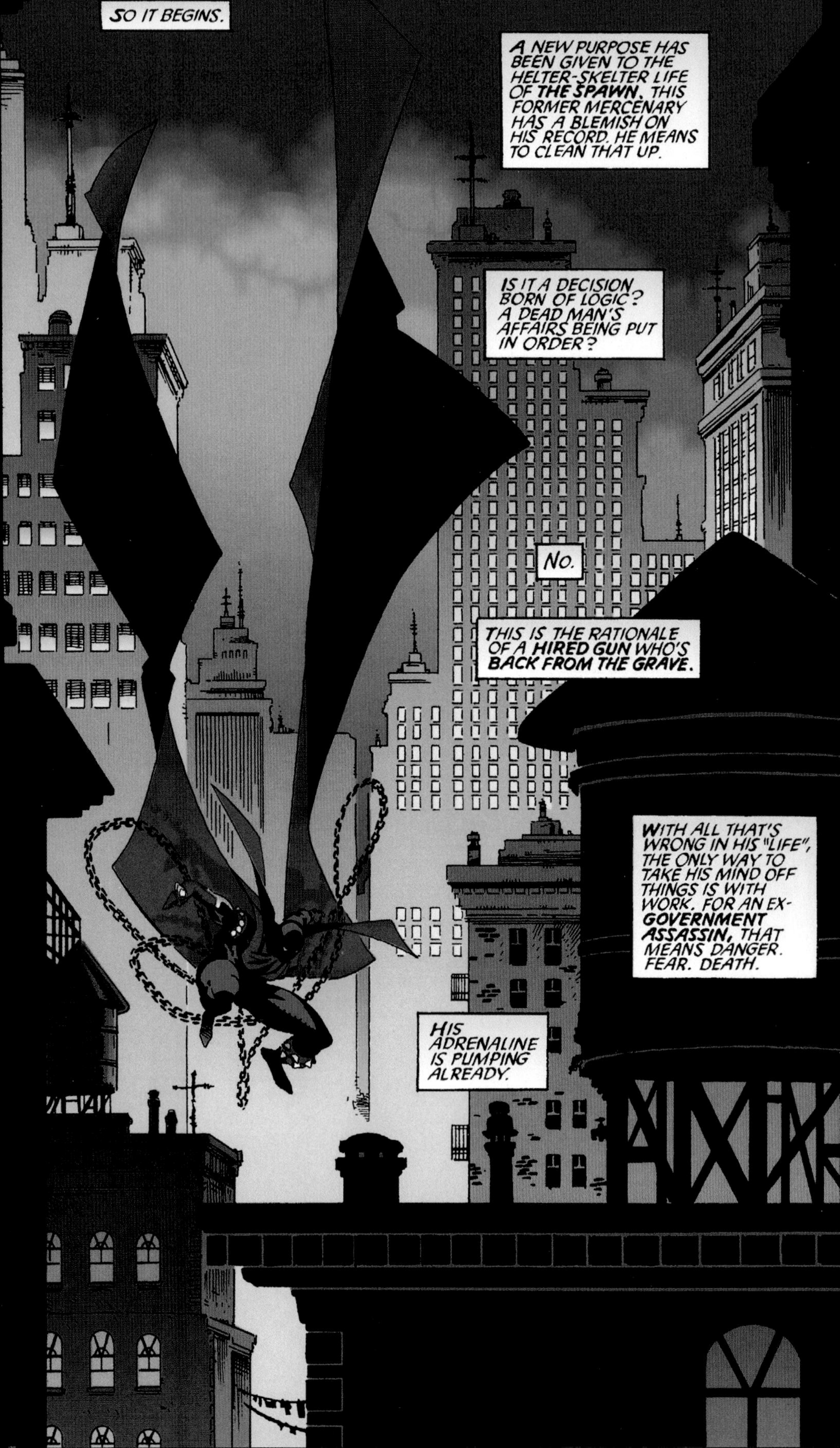
SO IT BEGINS.
A NEW PURPOSE HAS BEEN GIVEN TO THE HELTER-SKELTER LIFE OF THE SPAWN. THIS FORMER MERCENARY HAS A BLEMISH ON HIS RECORD. HE MEANS TO CLEAN THAT UP.
IS IT A DECISION BORN OF LOGIC? A DEAD MAN'S AFFAIRS BEING PUT IN ORDER?
No.
THIS IS THE RATIONALE OF A HIRED GUN WHO'S BACK FROM THE GRAVE.
WITH ALL THAT'S WRONG IN HIS "LIFE", THE ONLY WAY TO TAKE HIS MIND OFF THINGS IS WITH WORK. FOR AN EX-GOVERNMENT ASSASSIN, THAT MEANS DANGER. FEAR. DEATH.
HIS ADRENALINE IS PUMPING ALREADY.

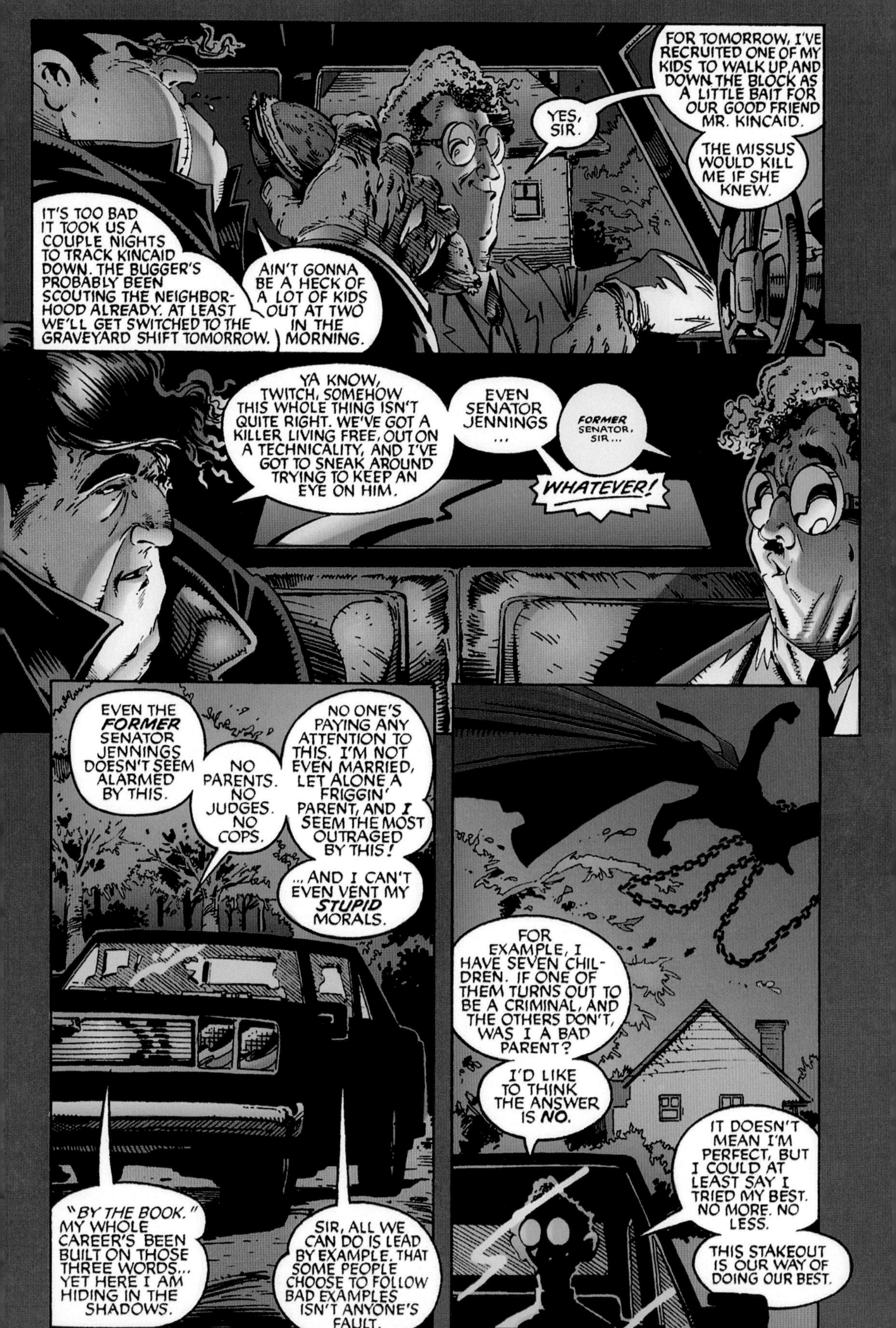

IT'S TOO BAD IT TOOK US A COUPLE NIGHTS TO TRACK KINCAID DOWN. THE BUGGER'S PROBABLY BEEN SCOUTING THE NEIGHBORHOOD ALREADY. AT LEAST WE'LL GET SWITCHED TO THE GRAVEYARD SHIFT TOMORROW.
AIN'T GONNA BE A HECK OF A LOT OF KIDS OUT AT TWO IN THE MORNING.
YES, SIR.
FOR TOMORROW, I'VE RECRUITED ONE OF MY KIDS TO WALK UP AND DOWN THE BLOCK AS A LITTLE BAIT FOR OUR GOOD FRIEND MR. KINCAID.
THE MISSUS WOULD KILL ME IF SHE KNEW.
YA KNOW, TWITCH, SOMEHOW THIS WHOLE THING ISN'T QUITE RIGHT. WE'VE GOT A KILLER LIVING FREE, OUT ON A TECHNICALITY, AND I'VE GOT TO SNEAK AROUND TRYING TO KEEP AN EYE ON HIM.
EVEN SENATOR JENNINGS ...
FORMER SENATOR, SIR...
WHATEVER!
EVEN THE FORMER SENATOR JENNINGS DOESN'T SEEM ALARMED BY THIS.
NO PARENTS. NO JUDGES. NO COPS.
NO ONE'S PAYING ANY ATTENTION TO THIS. I'M NOT EVEN MARRIED, LET ALONE A FRIGGIN' PARENT, AND I SEEM THE MOST OUTRAGED BY THIS!
... AND I CAN'T EVEN VENT MY STUPID MORALS.
"BY THE BOOK." MY WHOLE CAREER'S BEEN BUILT ON THOSE THREE WORDS... YET HERE I AM HIDING IN THE SHADOWS.
SIR, ALL WE CAN DO IS LEAD BY EXAMPLE. THAT SOME PEOPLE CHOOSE TO FOLLOW BAD EXAMPLES ISN'T ANYONE'S FAULT.
FOR EXAMPLE, I HAVE SEVEN CHILDREN. IF ONE OF THEM TURNS OUT TO BE A CRIMINAL, AND THE OTHERS DON'T, WAS I A BAD PARENT?
I'D LIKE TO THINK THE ANSWER IS NO.
IT DOESN'T MEAN I'M PERFECT, BUT I COULD AT LEAST SAY I TRIED MY BEST. NO MORE. NO LESS.
THIS STAKEOUT IS OUR WAY OF DOING OUR BEST.

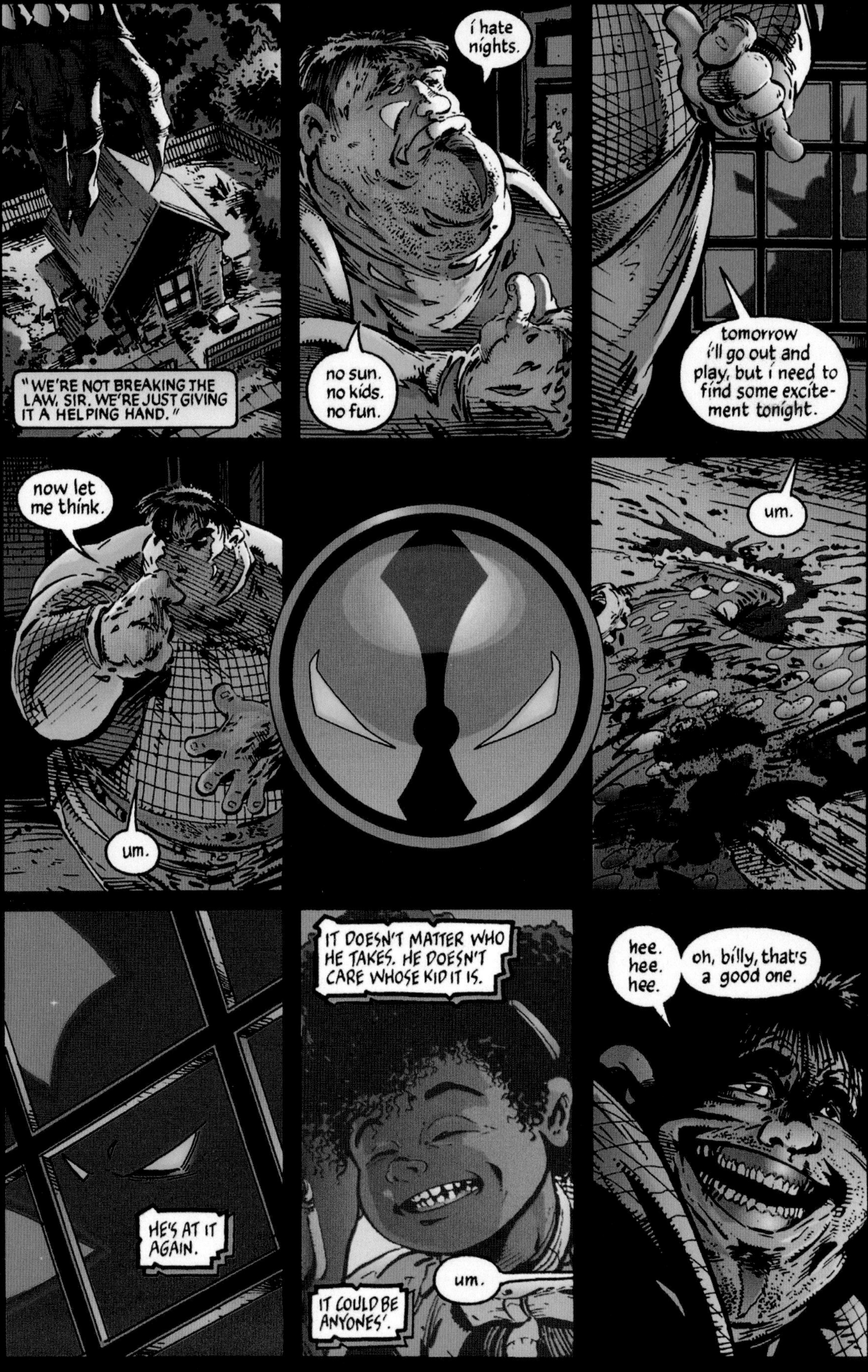
"WE'RE NOT BREAKING THE LAW, SIR. WE'RE JUST GIVING IT A HELPING HAND."
i hate nights.
no sun. no kids. no fun.
tomorrow i'll go out and play, but i need to find some excitement tonight.
now let me think.
um.
um.
HE'S AT IT AGAIN.
IT DOESN'T MATTER WHO HE TAKES. HE DOESN'T CARE WHOSE KID IT IS.
IT COULD BE ANYONES'.
um.
hee. hee. hee.
oh, billy, that's a good one.

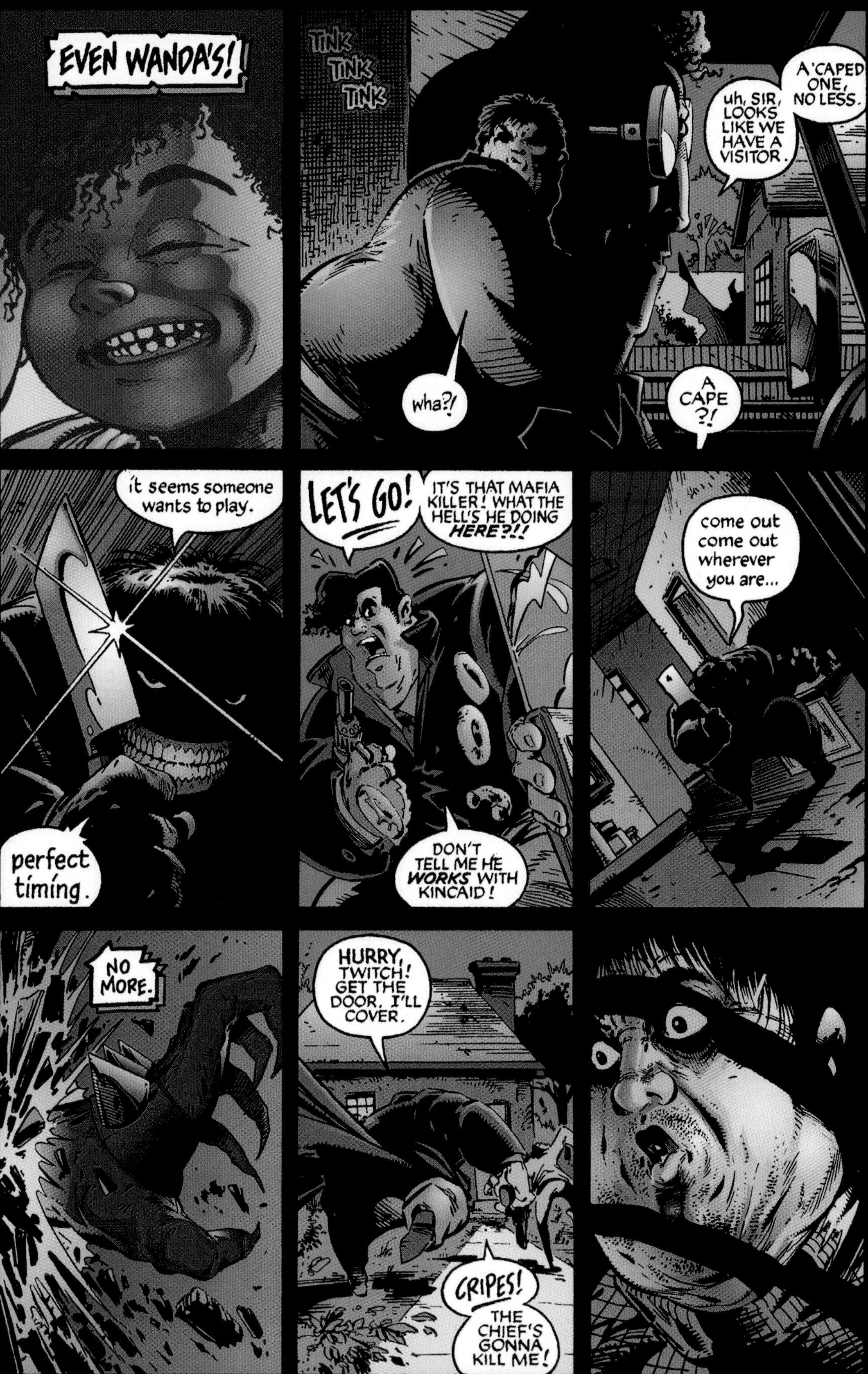
EVEN WANDA'S!
TINK TINK TINK
wha?!
uh, SIR, LOOKS LIKE WE HAVE A VISITOR.
A 'CAPED ONE, NO LESS.
A CAPE ?!
it seems someone wants to play.
perfect timing.
LET'S GO!
IT'S THAT MAFIA KILLER! WHAT THE HELL'S HE DOING HERE?!!
DON'T TELL ME HE WORKS WITH KINCAID!
come out come out wherever you are...
NO MORE.
HURRY, TWITCH! GET THE DOOR. I'LL COVER.
CRIPES!
THE CHIEF'S GONNA KILL ME!

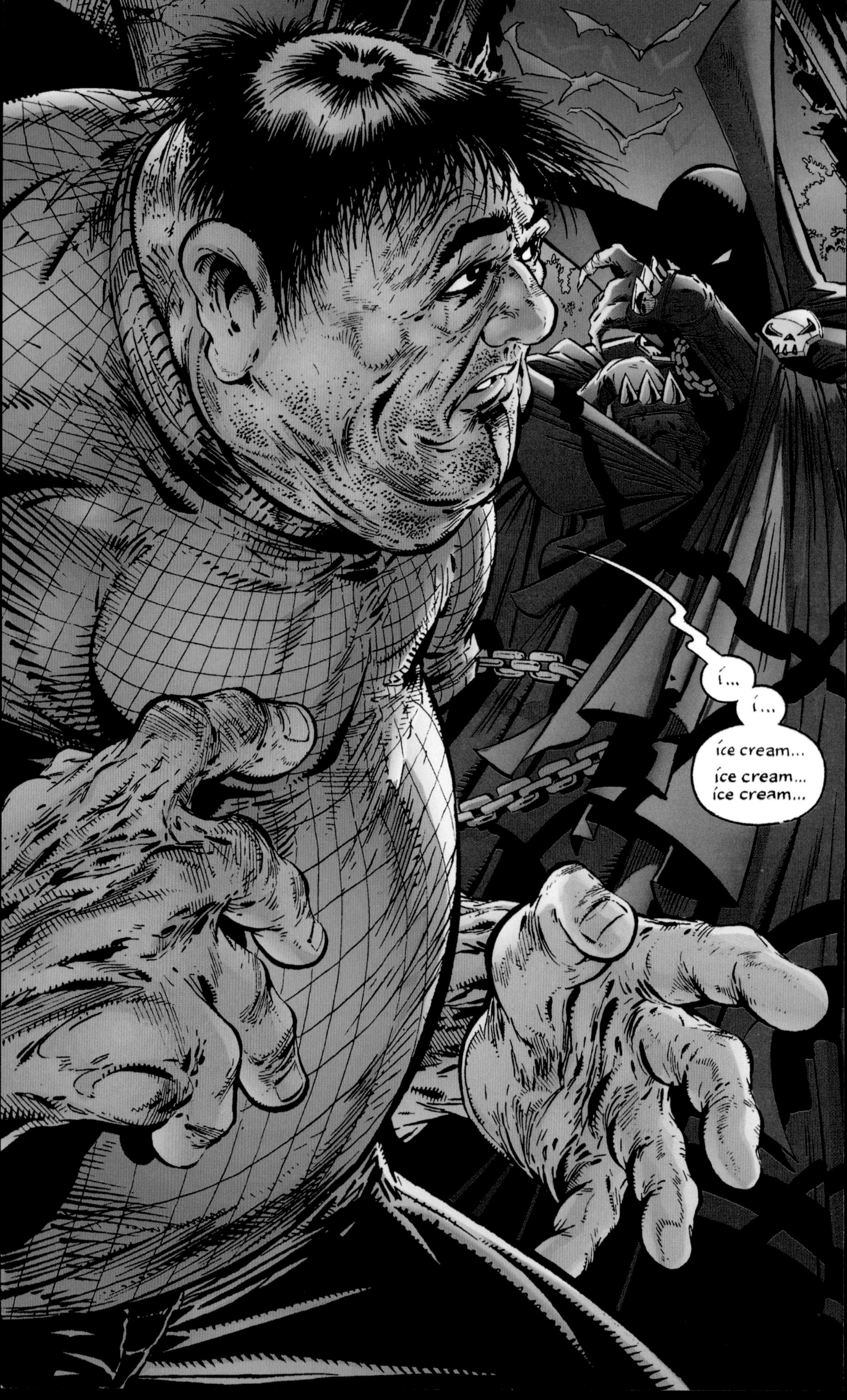

i...
i...
ice cream...
ice cream...
ice cream...

WHAT THE...!

SWEET MOTHER! WHAT'S HAPPENING *HERE?!!*

CHECK THE HOUSE! *NOW!*

A QUICK SEARCH REVEALS EVIDENCE OF ANOTHER CHILD'S DEATH.

DAMMIT! THIS IS *ALL* WRONG.

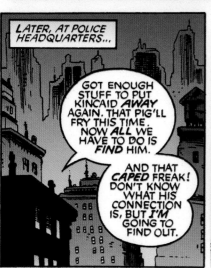

LATER, AT POLICE HEADQUARTERS...

GOT ENOUGH STUFF TO PUT KINCAID *AWAY* AGAIN. THAT PIG'LL FRY THIS TIME. NOW *ALL* WE HAVE TO DO IS *FIND* HIM.

AND THAT *CAPED* FREAK! DON'T KNOW WHAT HIS CONNECTION IS, BUT *I'M* GOING TO FIND OUT.

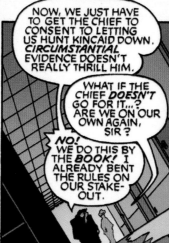

NOW, WE JUST HAVE TO GET THE CHIEF TO CONSENT TO LETTING US HUNT KINCAID DOWN. *CIRCUMSTANTIAL* EVIDENCE DOESN'T REALLY THRILL HIM.

WHAT IF THE CHIEF *DOESN'T* GO FOR IT...? ARE WE ON OUR OWN AGAIN, SIR?

NO! WE DO THIS BY THE *BOOK!* I ALREADY BENT THE RULES ON OUR STAKE-OUT.

I CAN'T MAKE ANY MORE EXCEPTIONS.

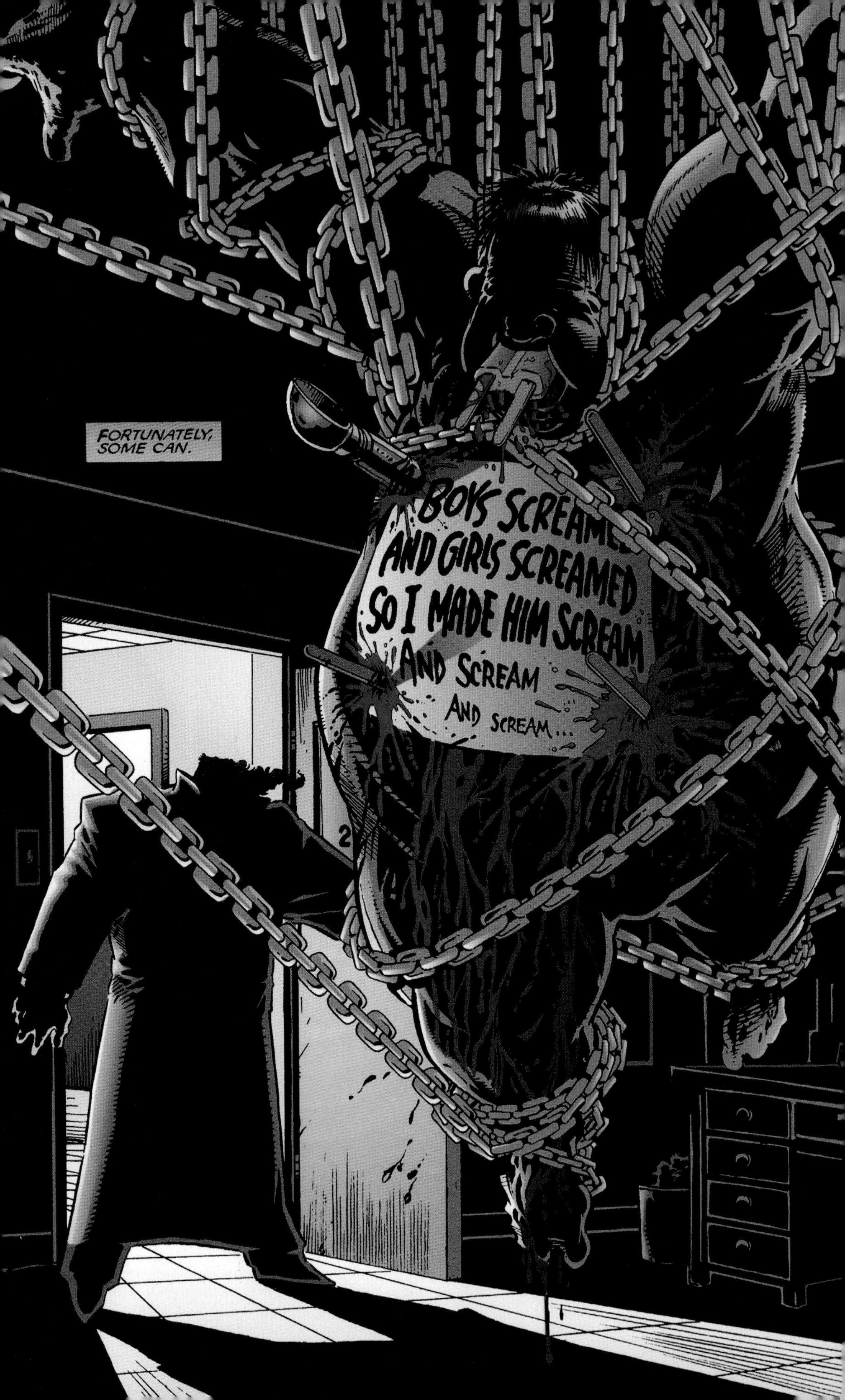
FORTUNATELY, SOME CAN.
BOYS SCREAMED AND GIRLS SCREAMED SO I MADE HIM SCREAM AND SCREAM AND SCREAM...

6 | NOV 1992

"PAYBACK"

PART ONE

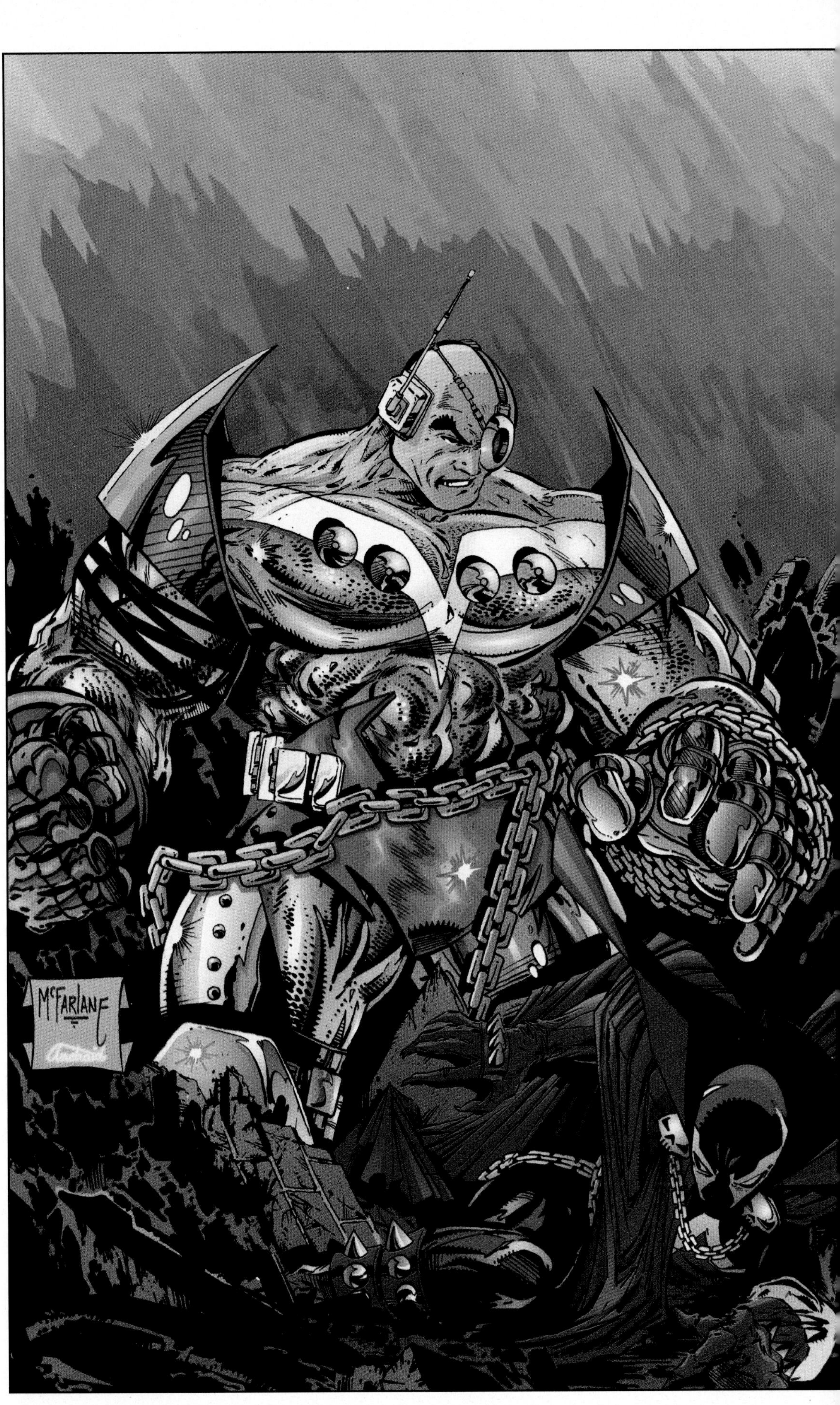
McFARLANE

Spawn #6, cover

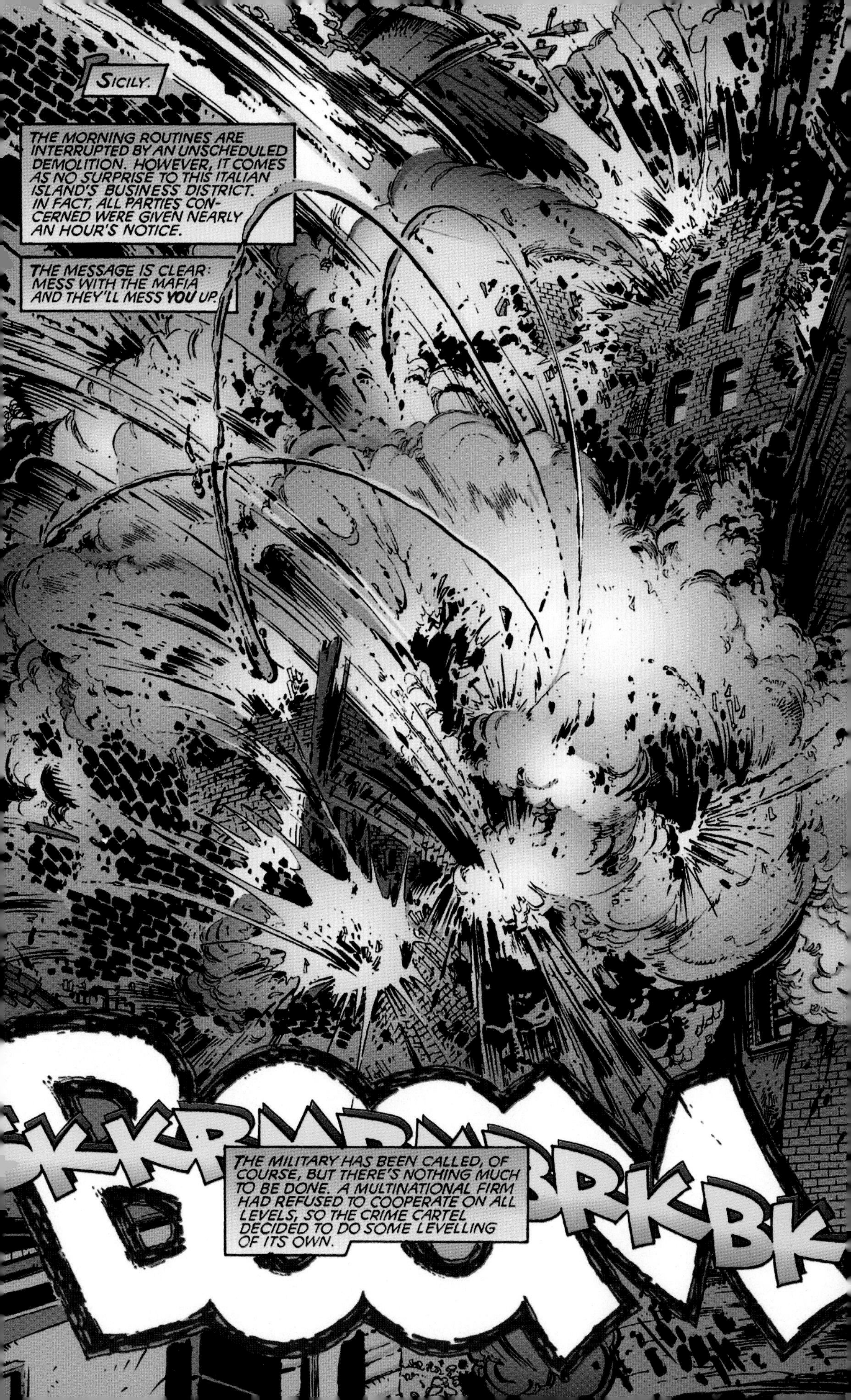
SICILY.
THE MORNING ROUTINES ARE INTERRUPTED BY AN UNSCHEDULED DEMOLITION. HOWEVER, IT COMES AS NO SURPRISE TO THIS ITALIAN ISLAND'S BUSINESS DISTRICT. IN FACT, ALL PARTIES CONCERNED WERE GIVEN NEARLY AN HOUR'S NOTICE.
THE MESSAGE IS CLEAR: MESS WITH THE MAFIA AND THEY'LL MESS YOU UP.
THE MILITARY HAS BEEN CALLED, OF COURSE, BUT THERE'S NOTHING MUCH TO BE DONE. A MULTINATIONAL FIRM HAD REFUSED TO COOPERATE ON ALL LEVELS, SO THE CRIME CARTEL DECIDED TO DO SOME LEVELLING OF ITS OWN.

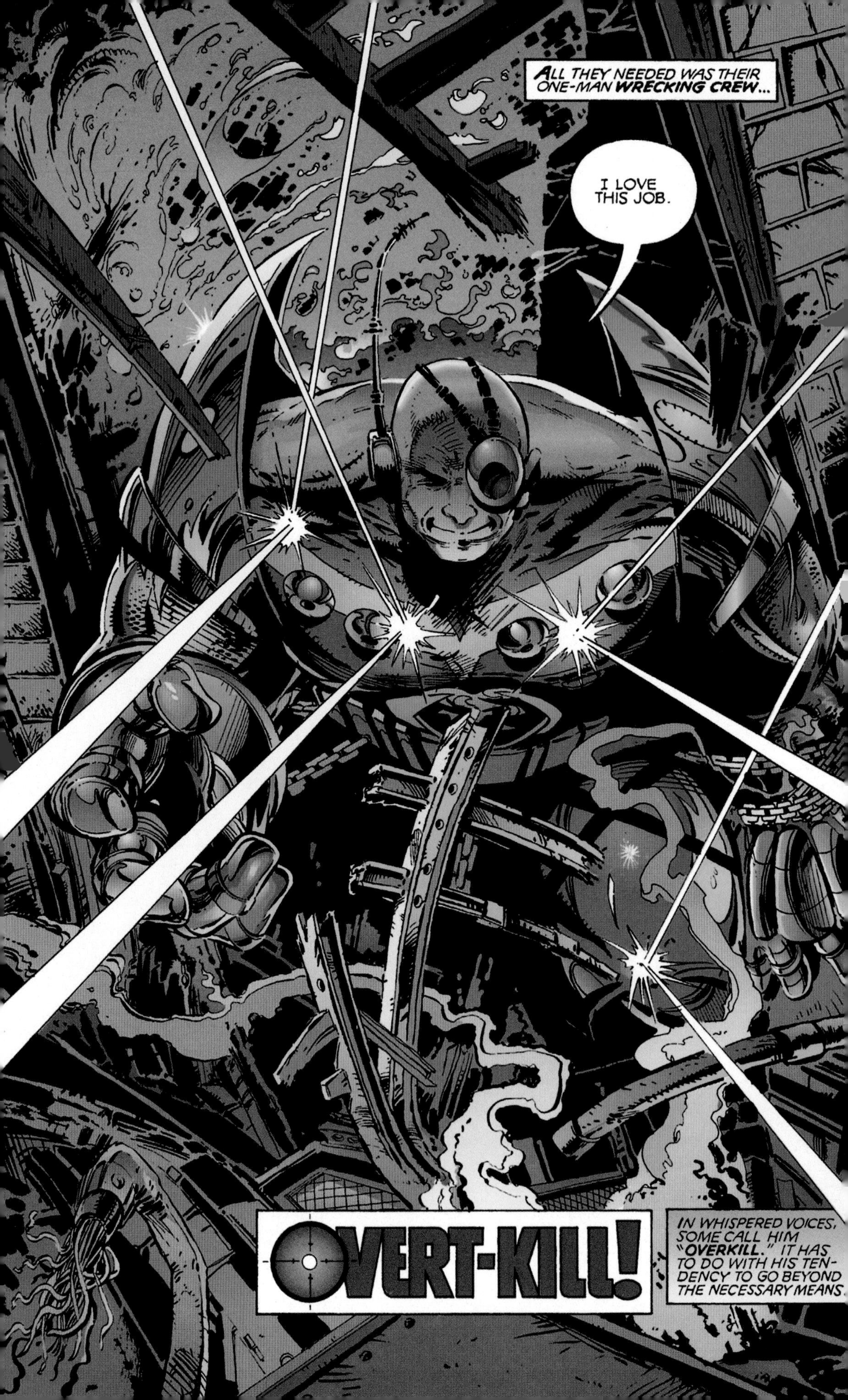
ALL THEY NEEDED WAS THEIR ONE-MAN WRECKING CREW...
I LOVE THIS JOB.
OVERT-KILL!
IN WHISPERED VOICES, SOME CALL HIM "OVERKILL." IT HAS TO DO WITH HIS TENDENCY TO GO BEYOND THE NECESSARY MEANS.

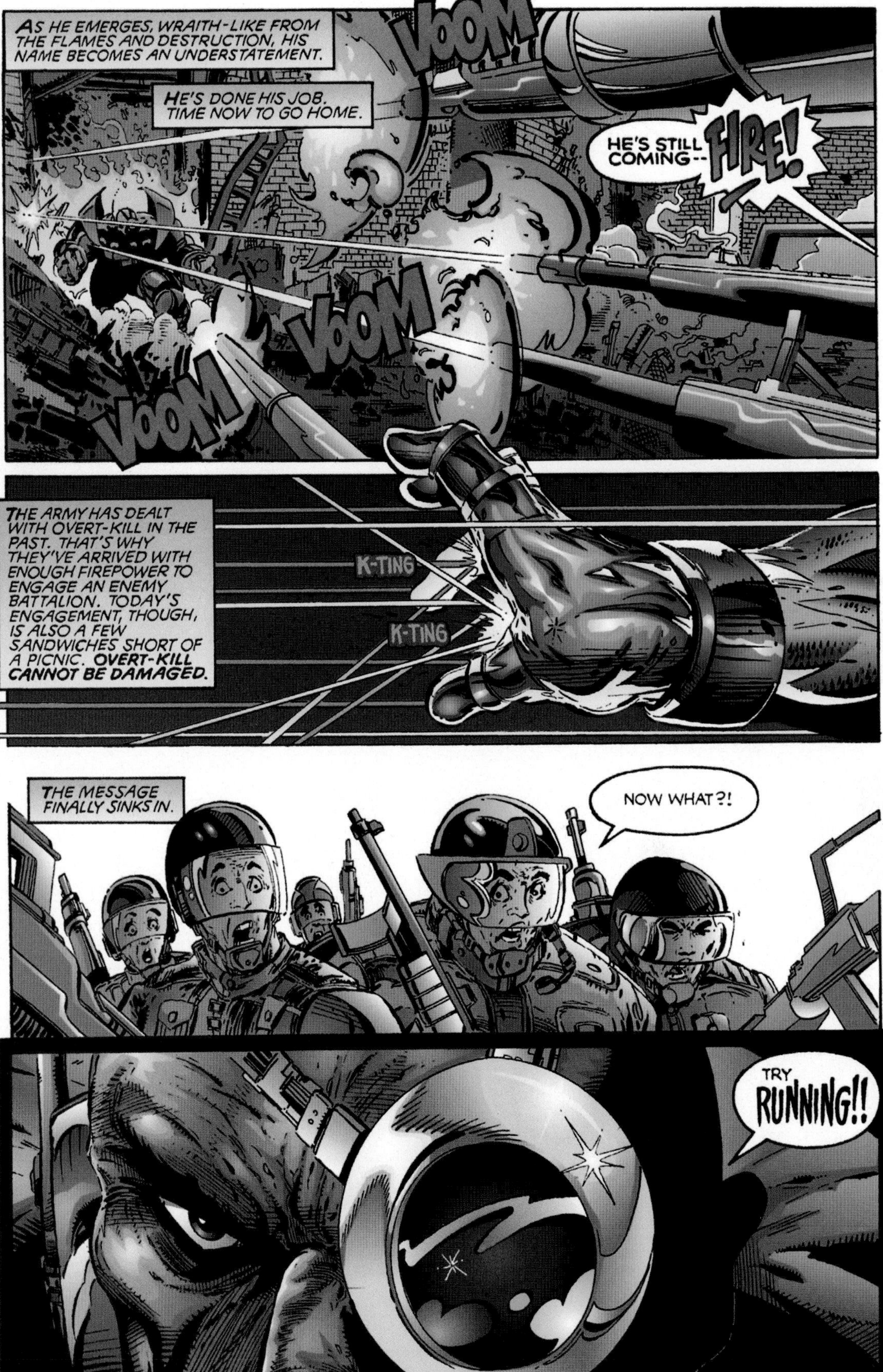

AS HE EMERGES, WRAITH-LIKE FROM THE FLAMES AND DESTRUCTION, HIS NAME BECOMES AN UNDERSTATEMENT.
VOOM
HE'S DONE HIS JOB. TIME NOW TO GO HOME.
HE'S STILL COMING-- FIRE!
VOOM
VOOM
THE ARMY HAS DEALT WITH OVERT-KILL IN THE PAST. THAT'S WHY THEY'VE ARRIVED WITH ENOUGH FIREPOWER TO ENGAGE AN ENEMY BATTALION. TODAY'S ENGAGEMENT, THOUGH, IS ALSO A FEW SANDWICHES SHORT OF A PICNIC. OVERT-KILL CANNOT BE DAMAGED.
K-TING
K-TING
THE MESSAGE FINALLY SINKS IN.
NOW WHAT?!
TRY RUNNING!!

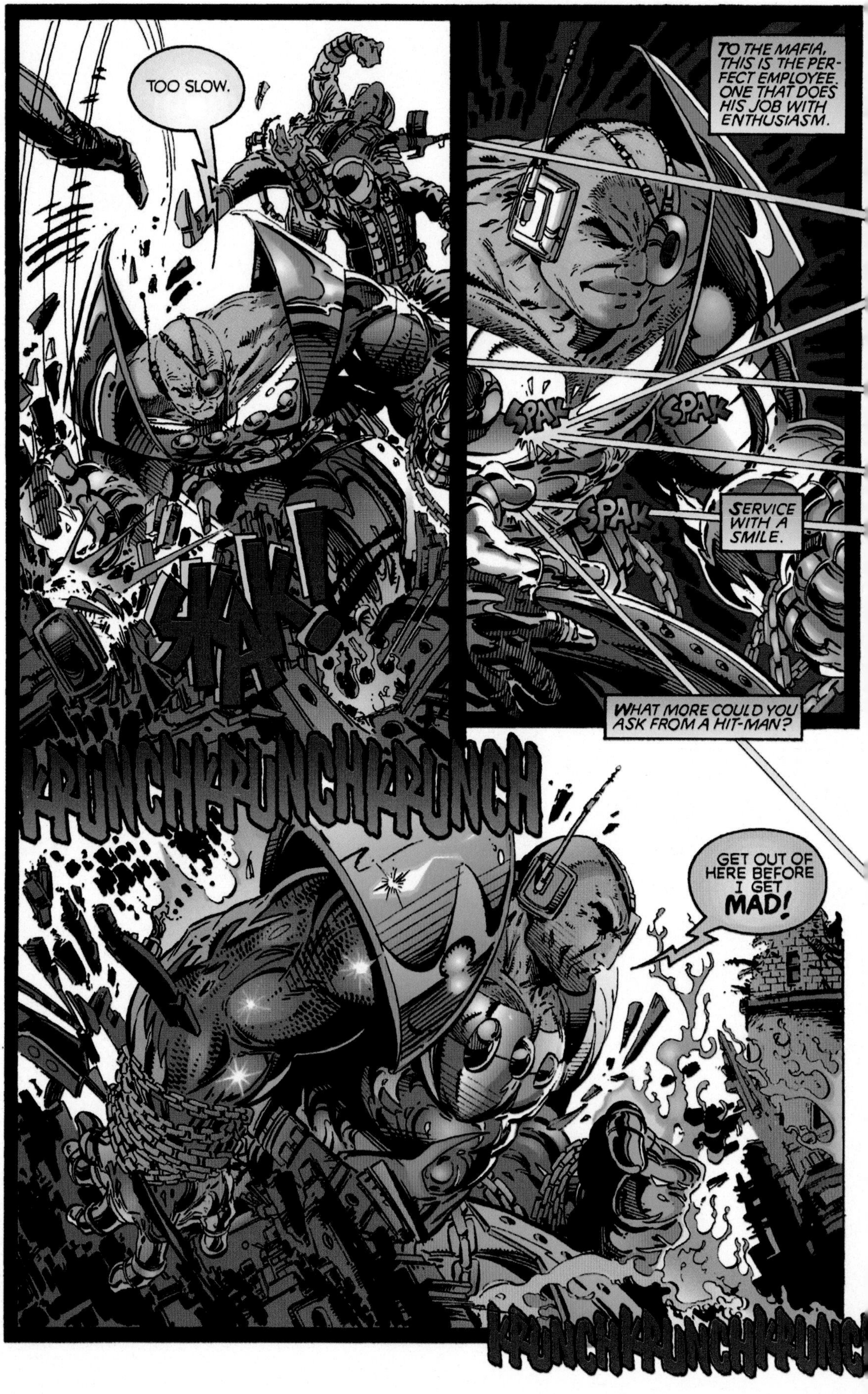
TOO SLOW.
SKAK!
TO THE MAFIA, THIS IS THE PERFECT EMPLOYEE. ONE THAT DOES HIS JOB WITH ENTHUSIASM.
SPAK
SPAK
SPAK
SERVICE WITH A SMILE.
WHAT MORE COULD YOU ASK FROM A HIT-MAN?
KRUNCH KRUNCH KRUNCH
GET OUT OF HERE BEFORE I GET MAD!
KRUNCH KRUNCH KRUNCH

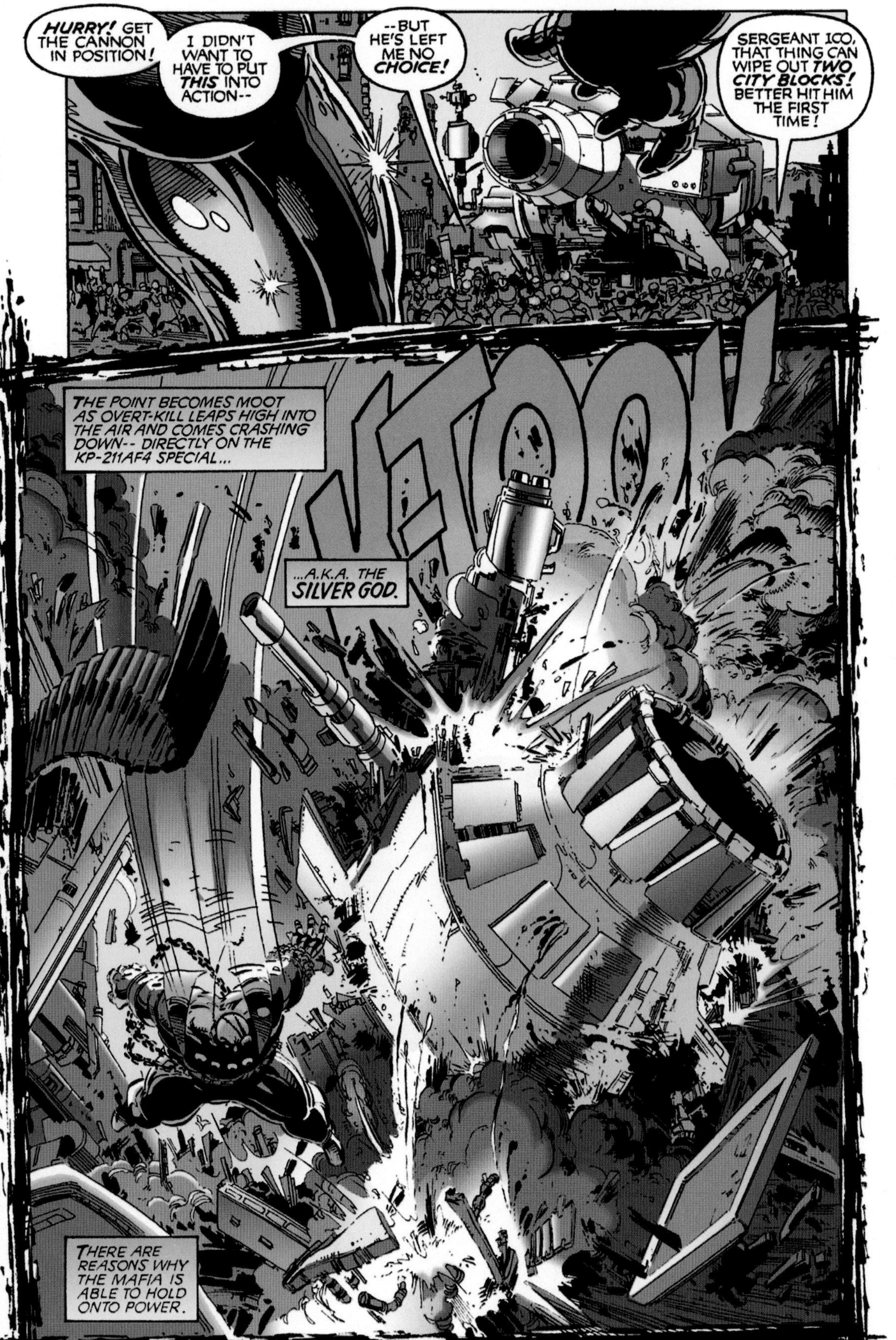
HURRY! GET THE CANNON IN POSITION!
I DIDN'T WANT TO HAVE TO PUT THIS INTO ACTION--
--BUT HE'S LEFT ME NO CHOICE!
SERGEANT ICO, THAT THING CAN WIPE OUT TWO CITY BLOCKS! BETTER HIT HIM THE FIRST TIME!
THE POINT BECOMES MOOT AS OVERT-KILL LEAPS HIGH INTO THE AIR AND COMES CRASHING DOWN-- DIRECTLY ON THE KP-211AF4 SPECIAL...
...A.K.A. THE SILVER GOD.
THERE ARE REASONS WHY THE MAFIA IS ABLE TO HOLD ONTO POWER.

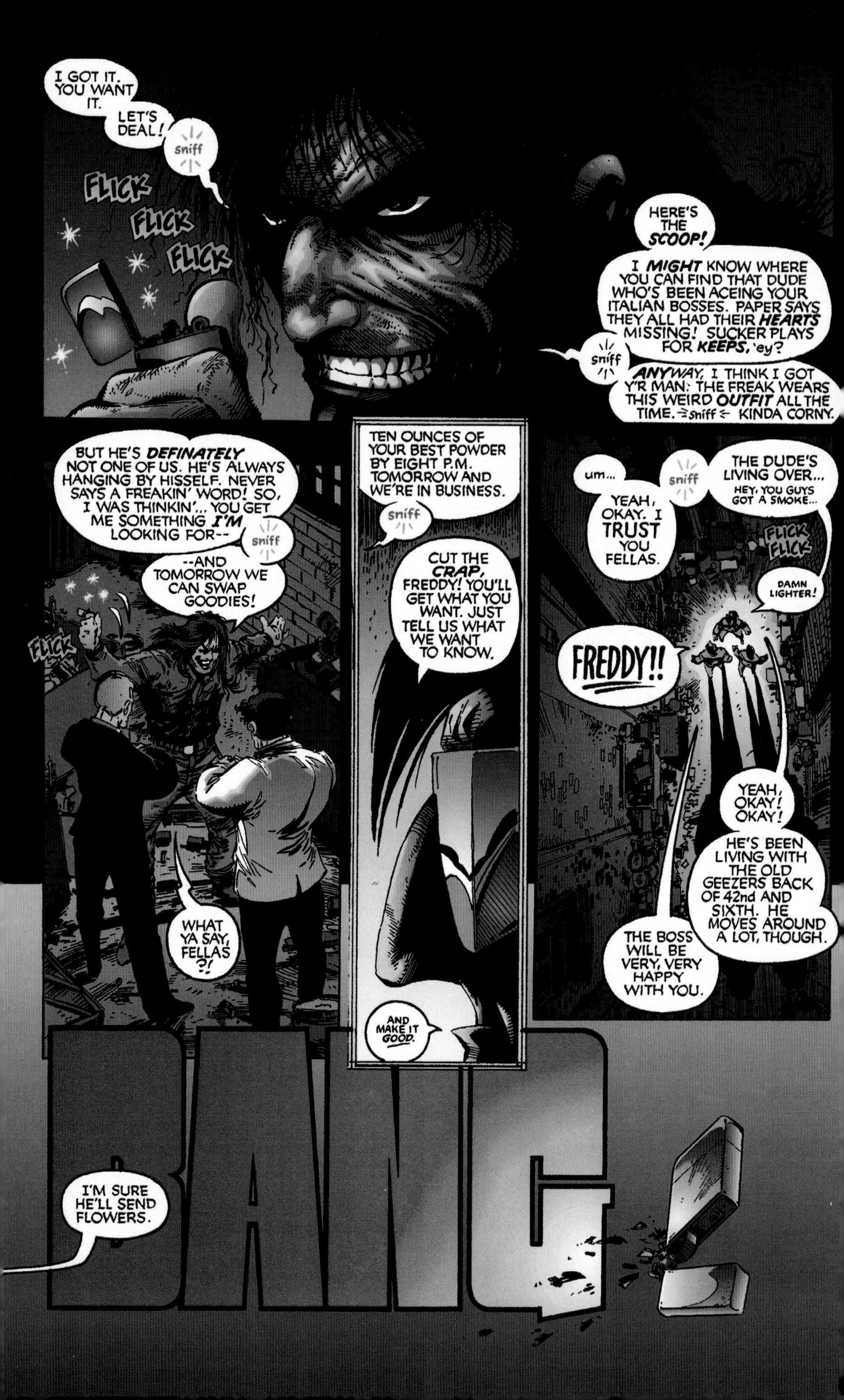

I GOT IT. YOU WANT IT.
LET'S DEAL!
sniff
FLICK
FLICK
FLICK
HERE'S THE SCOOP!
I MIGHT KNOW WHERE YOU CAN FIND THAT DUDE WHO'S BEEN ACEING YOUR ITALIAN BOSSES. PAPER SAYS THEY ALL HAD THEIR HEARTS MISSING! SUCKER PLAYS FOR KEEPS, 'ey?
sniff
ANYWAY, I THINK I GOT Y'R MAN: THE FREAK WEARS THIS WEIRD OUTFIT ALL THE TIME. sniff KINDA CORNY.
BUT HE'S DEFINATELY NOT ONE OF US. HE'S ALWAYS HANGING BY HISSELF. NEVER SAYS A FREAKIN' WORD! SO, I WAS THINKIN'... YOU GET ME SOMETHING I'M LOOKING FOR--
sniff
--AND TOMORROW WE CAN SWAP GOODIES!
FLICK
WHAT YA SAY, FELLAS?!
TEN OUNCES OF YOUR BEST POWDER BY EIGHT P.M. TOMORROW AND WE'RE IN BUSINESS.
sniff
CUT THE CRAP, FREDDY! YOU'LL GET WHAT YOU WANT. JUST TELL US WHAT WE WANT TO KNOW.
AND MAKE IT GOOD.
um...
sniff
YEAH, OKAY. I TRUST YOU FELLAS.
THE DUDE'S LIVING OVER...
HEY, YOU GUYS GOT A SMOKE...
FLICK FLICK
DAMN LIGHTER!
FREDDY!!
YEAH, OKAY! OKAY!
HE'S BEEN LIVING WITH THE OLD GEEZERS BACK OF 42nd AND SIXTH. HE MOVES AROUND A LOT, THOUGH.
THE BOSS WILL BE VERY, VERY HAPPY WITH YOU.
BANG!
I'M SURE HE'LL SEND FLOWERS.

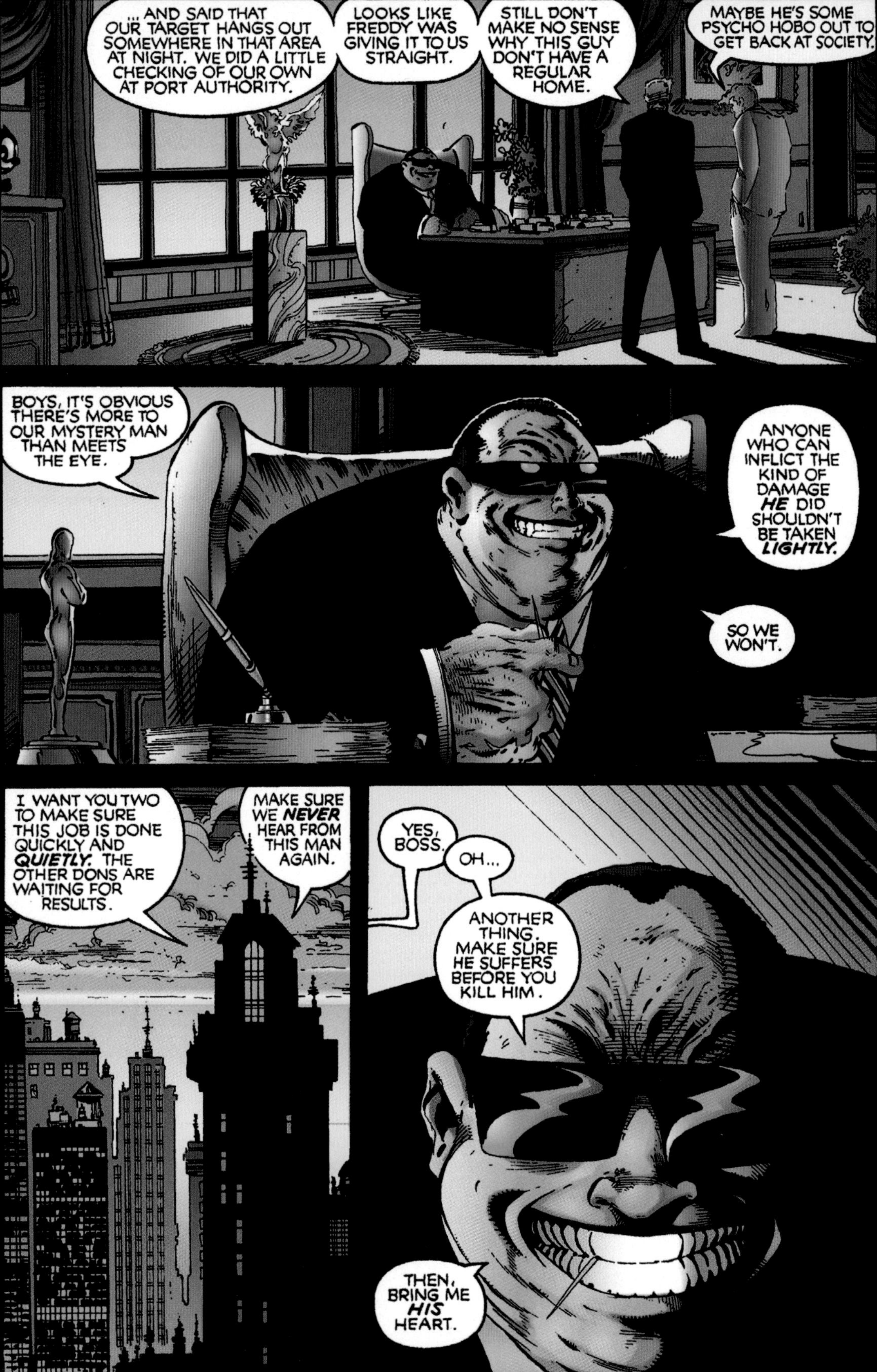
...AND SAID THAT OUR TARGET HANGS OUT SOMEWHERE IN THAT AREA AT NIGHT. WE DID A LITTLE CHECKING OF OUR OWN AT PORT AUTHORITY.
LOOKS LIKE FREDDY WAS GIVING IT TO US STRAIGHT.
STILL DON'T MAKE NO SENSE WHY THIS GUY DON'T HAVE A REGULAR HOME.
MAYBE HE'S SOME PSYCHO HOBO OUT TO GET BACK AT SOCIETY.
BOYS, IT'S OBVIOUS THERE'S MORE TO OUR MYSTERY MAN THAN MEETS THE EYE.
ANYONE WHO CAN INFLICT THE KIND OF DAMAGE *HE* DID SHOULDN'T BE TAKEN *LIGHTLY.*
SO WE WON'T.
I WANT YOU TWO TO MAKE SURE THIS JOB IS DONE QUICKLY AND *QUIETLY.* THE OTHER DONS ARE WAITING FOR RESULTS.
MAKE SURE WE *NEVER* HEAR FROM THIS MAN AGAIN.
YES, BOSS.
OH...
ANOTHER THING. MAKE SURE HE SUFFERS BEFORE YOU KILL HIM.
THEN, BRING ME *HIS* HEART.

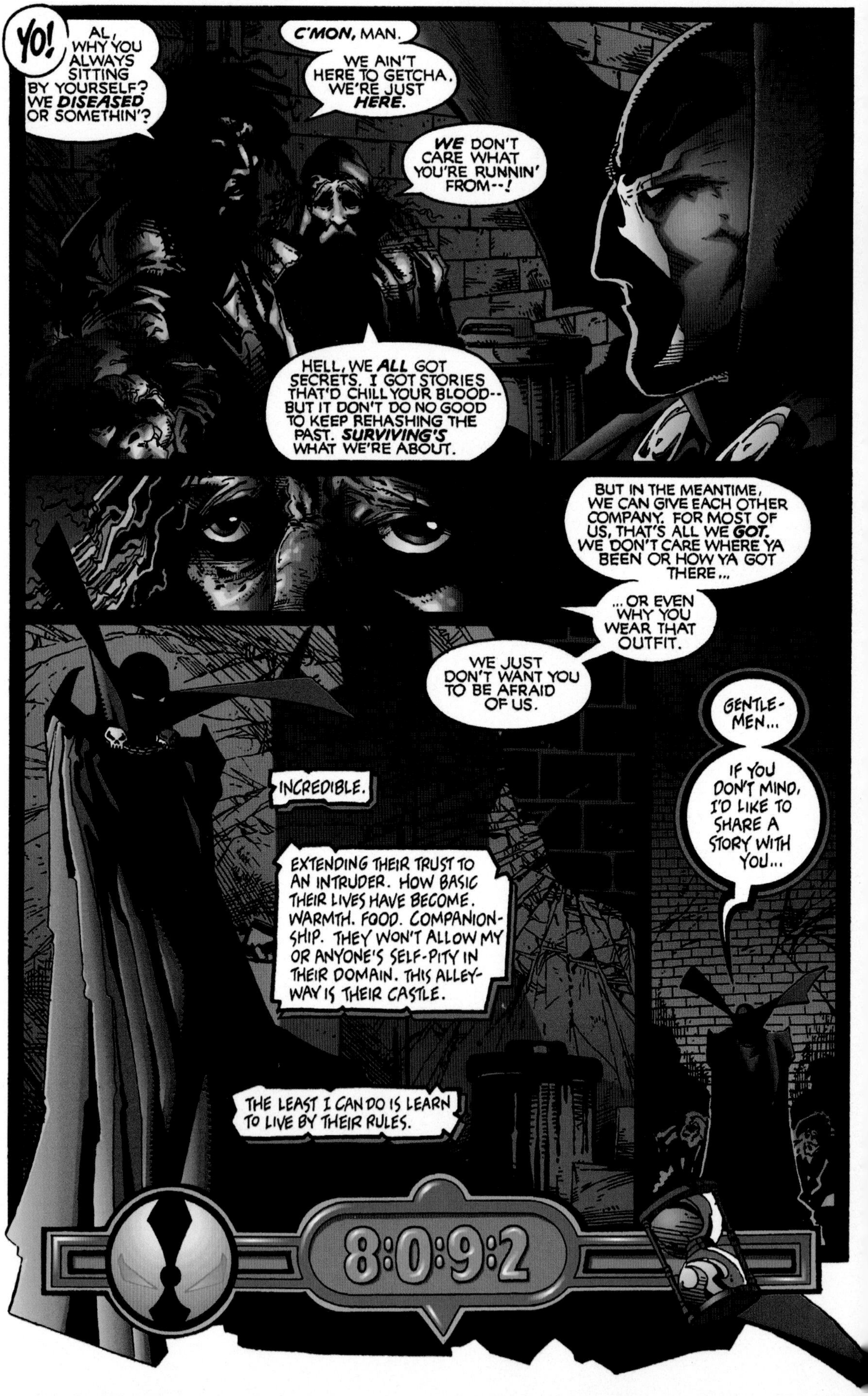
YO!
AL, WHY YOU ALWAYS SITTING BY YOURSELF? WE DISEASED OR SOMETHIN'?
C'MON, MAN.
WE AIN'T HERE TO GETCHA. WE'RE JUST HERE.
WE DON'T CARE WHAT YOU'RE RUNNIN' FROM--!
HELL, WE ALL GOT SECRETS. I GOT STORIES THAT'D CHILL YOUR BLOOD-- BUT IT DON'T DO NO GOOD TO KEEP REHASHING THE PAST. SURVIVING'S WHAT WE'RE ABOUT.
BUT IN THE MEANTIME, WE CAN GIVE EACH OTHER COMPANY. FOR MOST OF US, THAT'S ALL WE GOT. WE DON'T CARE WHERE YA BEEN OR HOW YA GOT THERE...
...OR EVEN WHY YOU WEAR THAT OUTFIT.
WE JUST DON'T WANT YOU TO BE AFRAID OF US.
INCREDIBLE.
EXTENDING THEIR TRUST TO AN INTRUDER. HOW BASIC THEIR LIVES HAVE BECOME. WARMTH. FOOD. COMPANIONSHIP. THEY WON'T ALLOW MY OR ANYONE'S SELF-PITY IN THEIR DOMAIN. THIS ALLEYWAY IS THEIR CASTLE.
THE LEAST I CAN DO IS LEARN TO LIVE BY THEIR RULES.
GENTLEMEN...
IF YOU DON'T MIND, I'D LIKE TO SHARE A STORY WITH YOU...
8:0:9:2

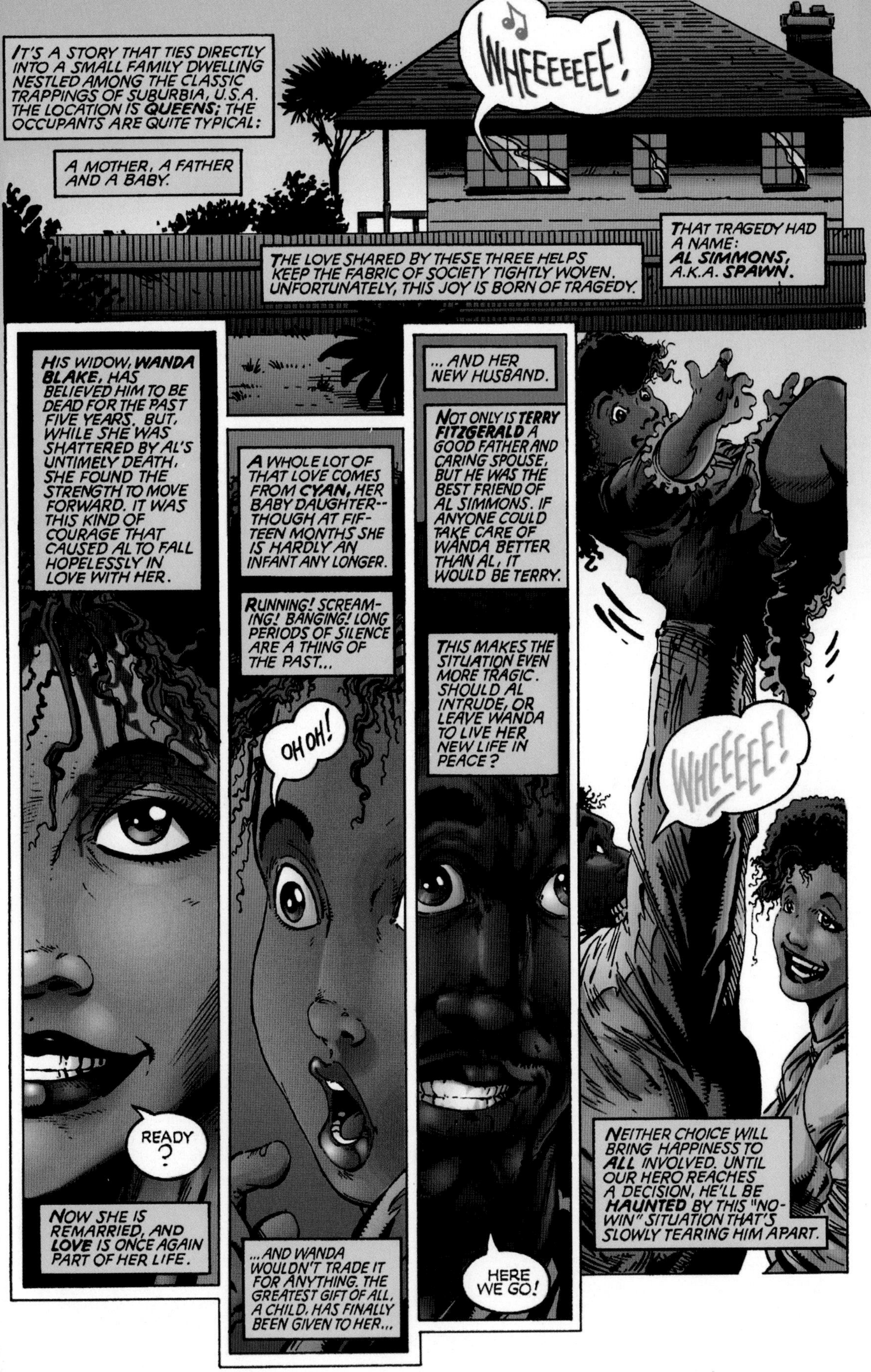

IT'S A STORY THAT TIES DIRECTLY INTO A SMALL FAMILY DWELLING NESTLED AMONG THE CLASSIC TRAPPINGS OF SUBURBIA, U.S.A. THE LOCATION IS QUEENS; THE OCCUPANTS ARE QUITE TYPICAL:
A MOTHER, A FATHER AND A BABY.
WHEEEEEEE!
THE LOVE SHARED BY THESE THREE HELPS KEEP THE FABRIC OF SOCIETY TIGHTLY WOVEN. UNFORTUNATELY, THIS JOY IS BORN OF TRAGEDY.
THAT TRAGEDY HAD A NAME: AL SIMMONS, A.K.A. SPAWN.
HIS WIDOW, WANDA BLAKE, HAS BELIEVED HIM TO BE DEAD FOR THE PAST FIVE YEARS. BUT, WHILE SHE WAS SHATTERED BY AL'S UNTIMELY DEATH, SHE FOUND THE STRENGTH TO MOVE FORWARD. IT WAS THIS KIND OF COURAGE THAT CAUSED AL TO FALL HOPELESSLY IN LOVE WITH HER.
READY?
NOW SHE IS REMARRIED, AND LOVE IS ONCE AGAIN PART OF HER LIFE.
A WHOLE LOT OF THAT LOVE COMES FROM CYAN, HER BABY DAUGHTER-- THOUGH AT FIFTEEN MONTHS SHE IS HARDLY AN INFANT ANY LONGER.
RUNNING! SCREAMING! BANGING! LONG PERIODS OF SILENCE ARE A THING OF THE PAST...
OH OH!
...AND WANDA WOULDN'T TRADE IT FOR ANYTHING. THE GREATEST GIFT OF ALL, A CHILD, HAS FINALLY BEEN GIVEN TO HER...
...AND HER NEW HUSBAND.
NOT ONLY IS TERRY FITZGERALD A GOOD FATHER AND CARING SPOUSE, BUT HE WAS THE BEST FRIEND OF AL SIMMONS. IF ANYONE COULD TAKE CARE OF WANDA BETTER THAN AL, IT WOULD BE TERRY.
THIS MAKES THE SITUATION EVEN MORE TRAGIC. SHOULD AL INTRUDE, OR LEAVE WANDA TO LIVE HER NEW LIFE IN PEACE?
HERE WE GO!
WHEEEEE!
NEITHER CHOICE WILL BRING HAPPINESS TO ALL INVOLVED. UNTIL OUR HERO REACHES A DECISION, HE'LL BE HAUNTED BY THIS "NO-WIN" SITUATION THAT'S SLOWLY TEARING HIM APART.

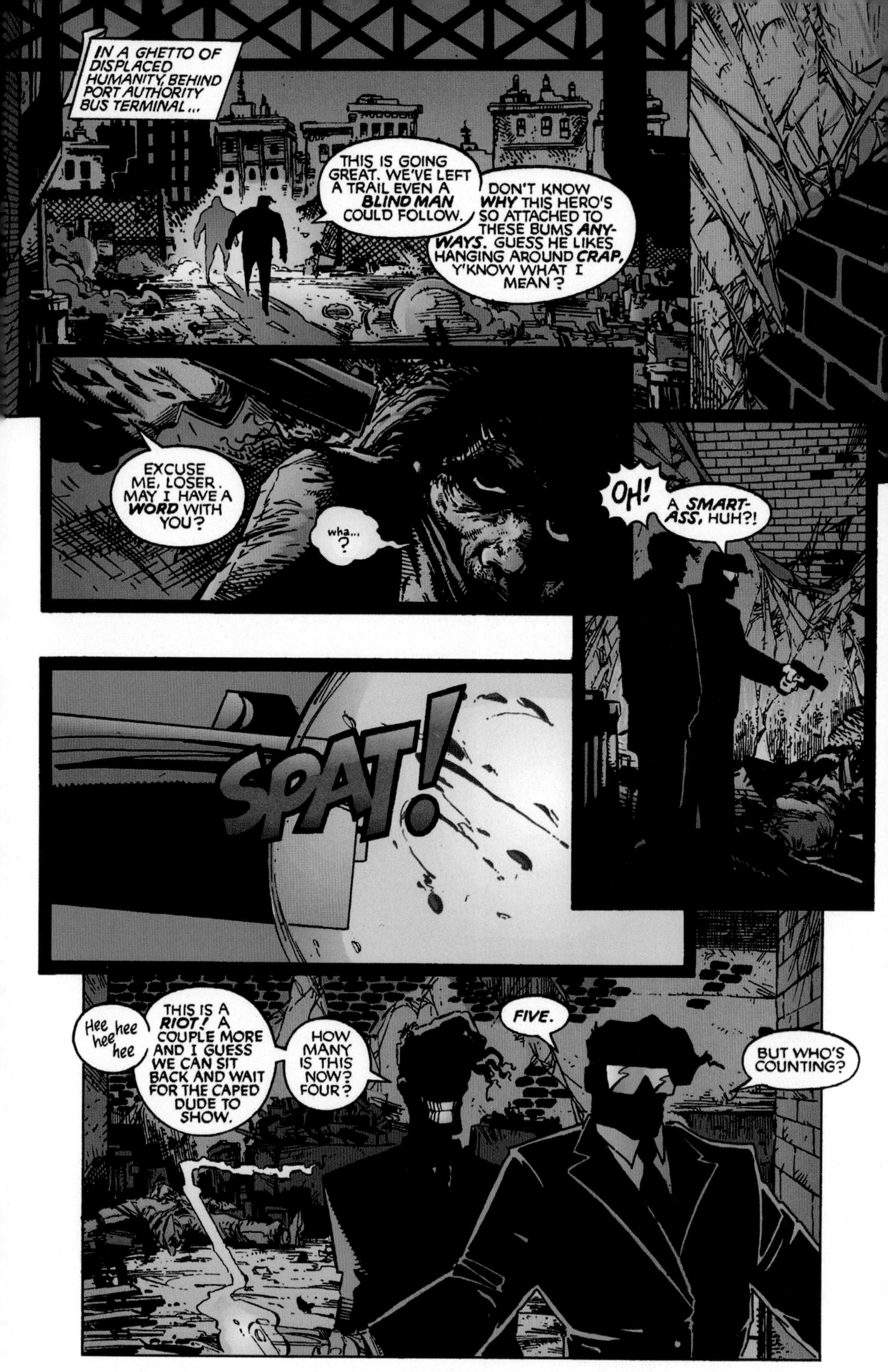
IN A GHETTO OF DISPLACED HUMANITY, BEHIND PORT AUTHORITY BUS TERMINAL...
THIS IS GOING GREAT. WE'VE LEFT A TRAIL EVEN A BLIND MAN COULD FOLLOW.
DON'T KNOW WHY THIS HERO'S SO ATTACHED TO THESE BUMS ANYWAYS. GUESS HE LIKES HANGING AROUND CRAP, Y'KNOW WHAT I MEAN?
EXCUSE ME, LOSER. MAY I HAVE A WORD WITH YOU?
wha...?
OH!
A SMART-ASS, HUH?!
SPAT!
Hee hee hee hee
THIS IS A RIOT! A COUPLE MORE AND I GUESS WE CAN SIT BACK AND WAIT FOR THE CAPED DUDE TO SHOW.
HOW MANY IS THIS NOW? FOUR?
FIVE.
BUT WHO'S COUNTING?

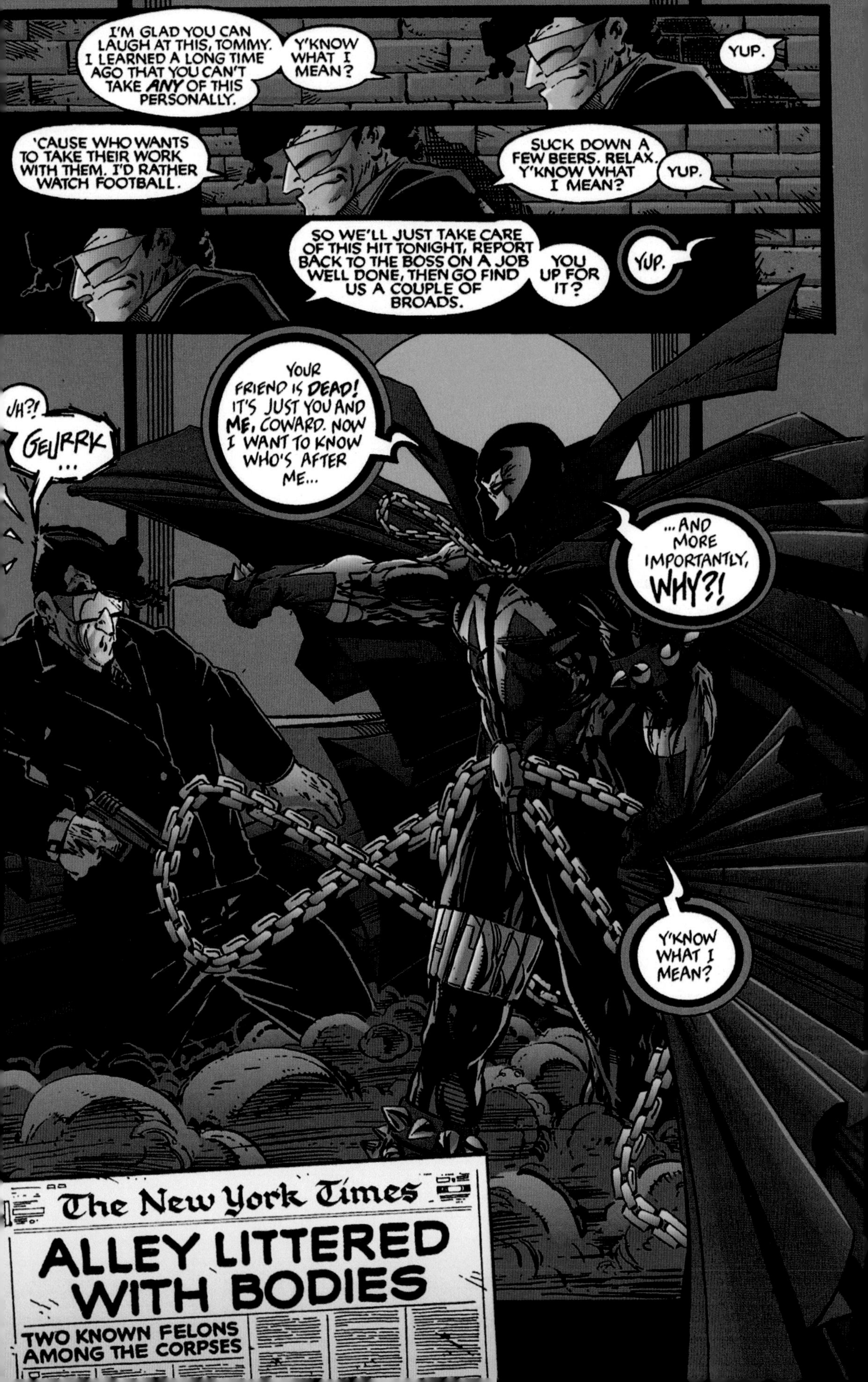

I'M GLAD YOU CAN LAUGH AT THIS, TOMMY. I LEARNED A LONG TIME AGO THAT YOU CAN'T TAKE ANY OF THIS PERSONALLY.
Y'KNOW WHAT I MEAN?
YUP.
'CAUSE WHO WANTS TO TAKE THEIR WORK WITH THEM. I'D RATHER WATCH FOOTBALL.
SUCK DOWN A FEW BEERS. RELAX. Y'KNOW WHAT I MEAN?
YUP.
SO WE'LL JUST TAKE CARE OF THIS HIT TONIGHT, REPORT BACK TO THE BOSS ON A JOB WELL DONE, THEN GO FIND US A COUPLE OF BROADS.
YOU UP FOR IT?
YUP.
UH?!
GEURRK ...
YOUR FRIEND IS DEAD! IT'S JUST YOU AND ME, COWARD. NOW I WANT TO KNOW WHO'S AFTER ME...
...AND MORE IMPORTANTLY, WHY?!
Y'KNOW WHAT I MEAN?
The New York Times
ALLEY LITTERED WITH BODIES
TWO KNOWN FELONS AMONG THE CORPSES

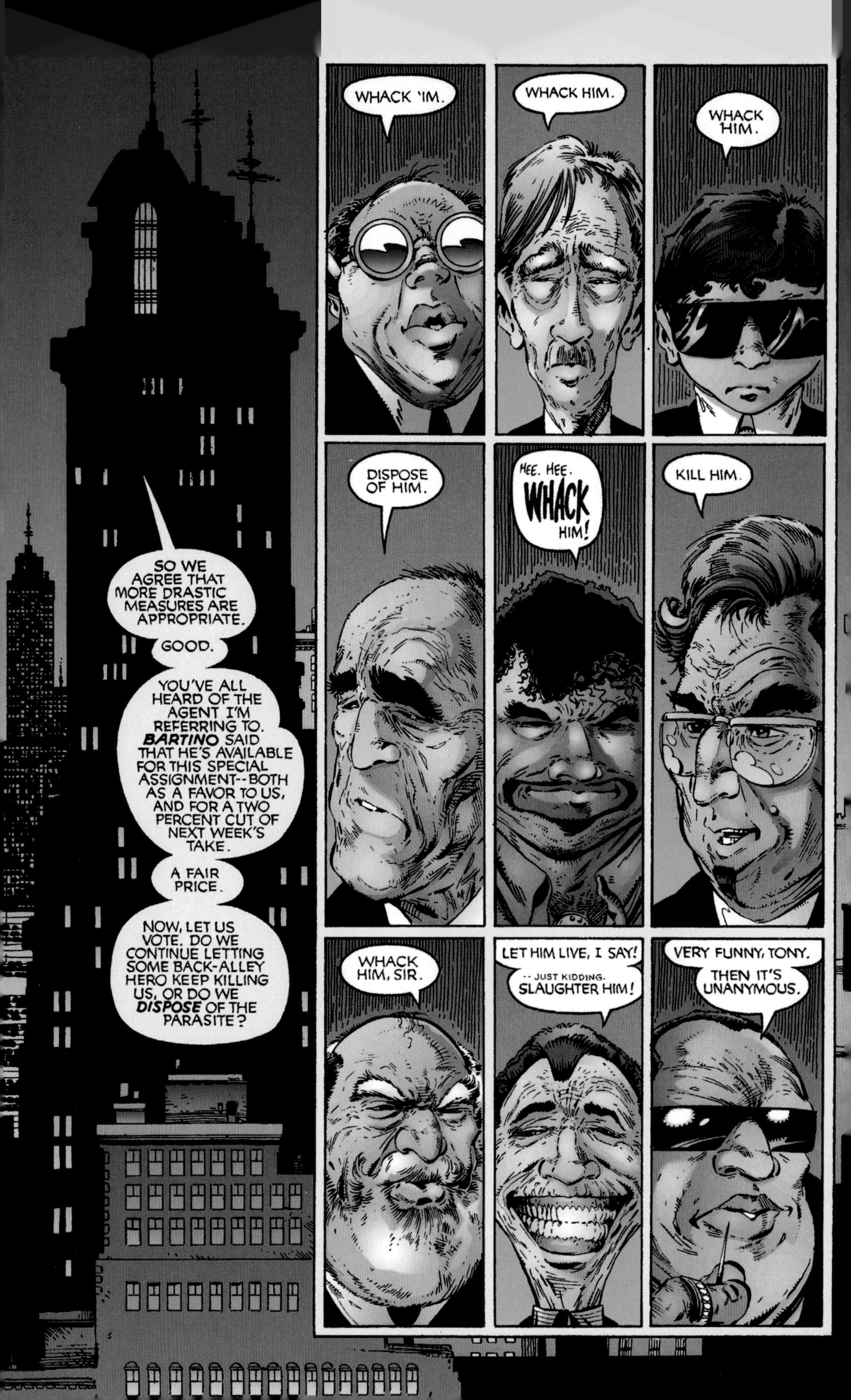
SO WE AGREE THAT MORE DRASTIC MEASURES ARE APPROPRIATE.
GOOD.
YOU'VE ALL HEARD OF THE AGENT I'M REFERRING TO. BARTINO SAID THAT HE'S AVAILABLE FOR THIS SPECIAL ASSIGNMENT-- BOTH AS A FAVOR TO US, AND FOR A TWO PERCENT CUT OF NEXT WEEK'S TAKE.
A FAIR PRICE.
NOW, LET US VOTE. DO WE CONTINUE LETTING SOME BACK-ALLEY HERO KEEP KILLING US, OR DO WE DISPOSE OF THE PARASITE?
WHACK 'IM.
WHACK HIM.
WHACK HIM.
DISPOSE OF HIM.
HEE. HEE. WHACK HIM!
KILL HIM.
WHACK HIM, SIR.
LET HIM LIVE, I SAY!
-- JUST KIDDING. SLAUGHTER HIM!
VERY FUNNY, TONY.
THEN IT'S UNANYMOUS.

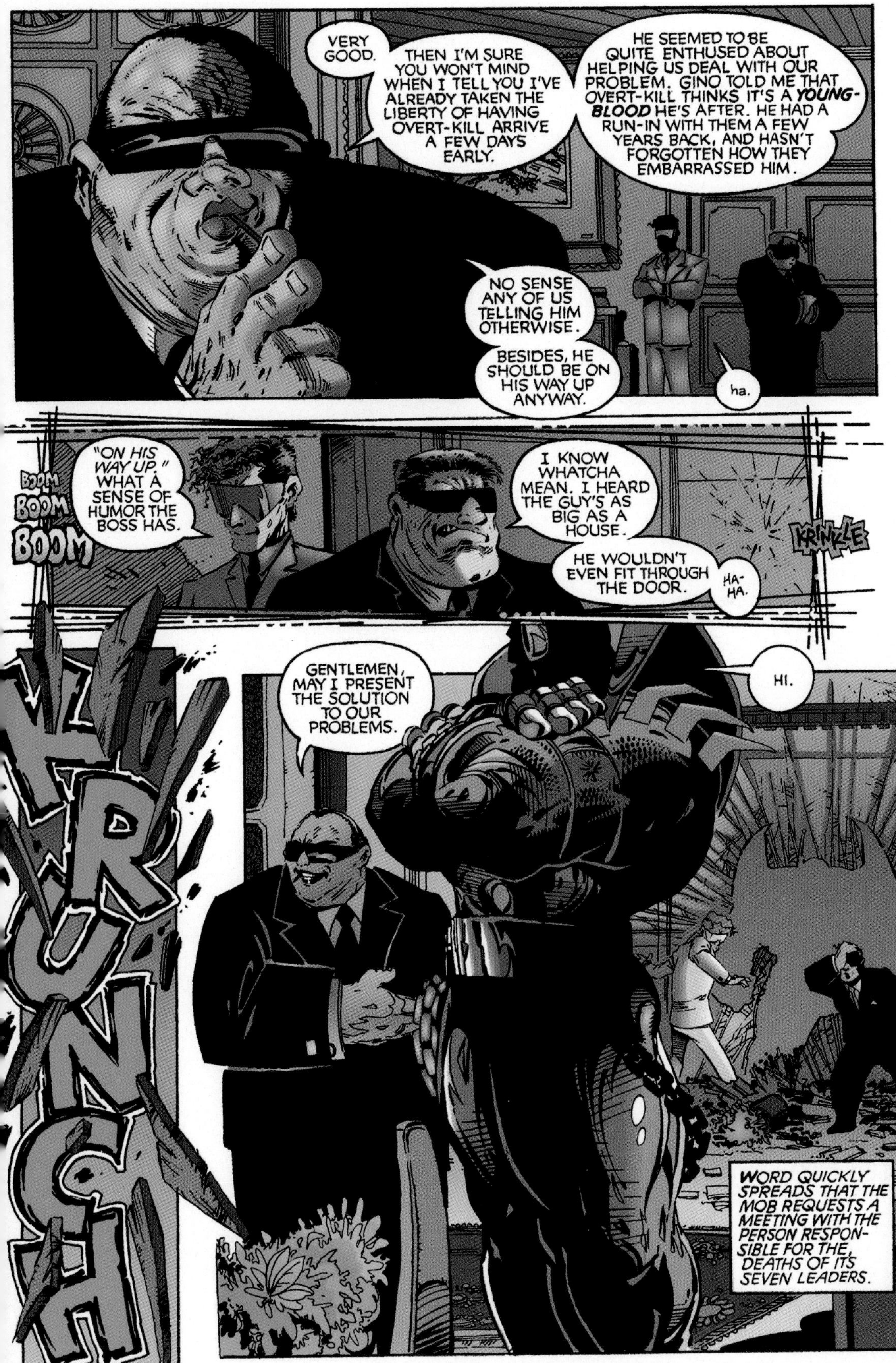
VERY GOOD.
THEN I'M SURE YOU WON'T MIND WHEN I TELL YOU I'VE ALREADY TAKEN THE LIBERTY OF HAVING OVERT-KILL ARRIVE A FEW DAYS EARLY.
HE SEEMED TO BE QUITE ENTHUSED ABOUT HELPING US DEAL WITH OUR PROBLEM. GINO TOLD ME THAT OVERT-KILL THINKS IT'S A YOUNGBLOOD HE'S AFTER. HE HAD A RUN-IN WITH THEM A FEW YEARS BACK, AND HASN'T FORGOTTEN HOW THEY EMBARRASSED HIM.
NO SENSE ANY OF US TELLING HIM OTHERWISE.
BESIDES, HE SHOULD BE ON HIS WAY UP ANYWAY.
ha.
BOOM BOOM BOOM
"ON HIS WAY UP." WHAT A SENSE OF HUMOR THE BOSS HAS.
I KNOW WHATCHA MEAN. I HEARD THE GUY'S AS BIG AS A HOUSE.
HE WOULDN'T EVEN FIT THROUGH THE DOOR.
HA-HA.
KRINKLE
KRUNCH
GENTLEMEN, MAY I PRESENT THE SOLUTION TO OUR PROBLEMS.
HI.
WORD QUICKLY SPREADS THAT THE MOB REQUESTS A MEETING WITH THE PERSON RESPONSIBLE FOR THE DEATHS OF ITS SEVEN LEADERS.

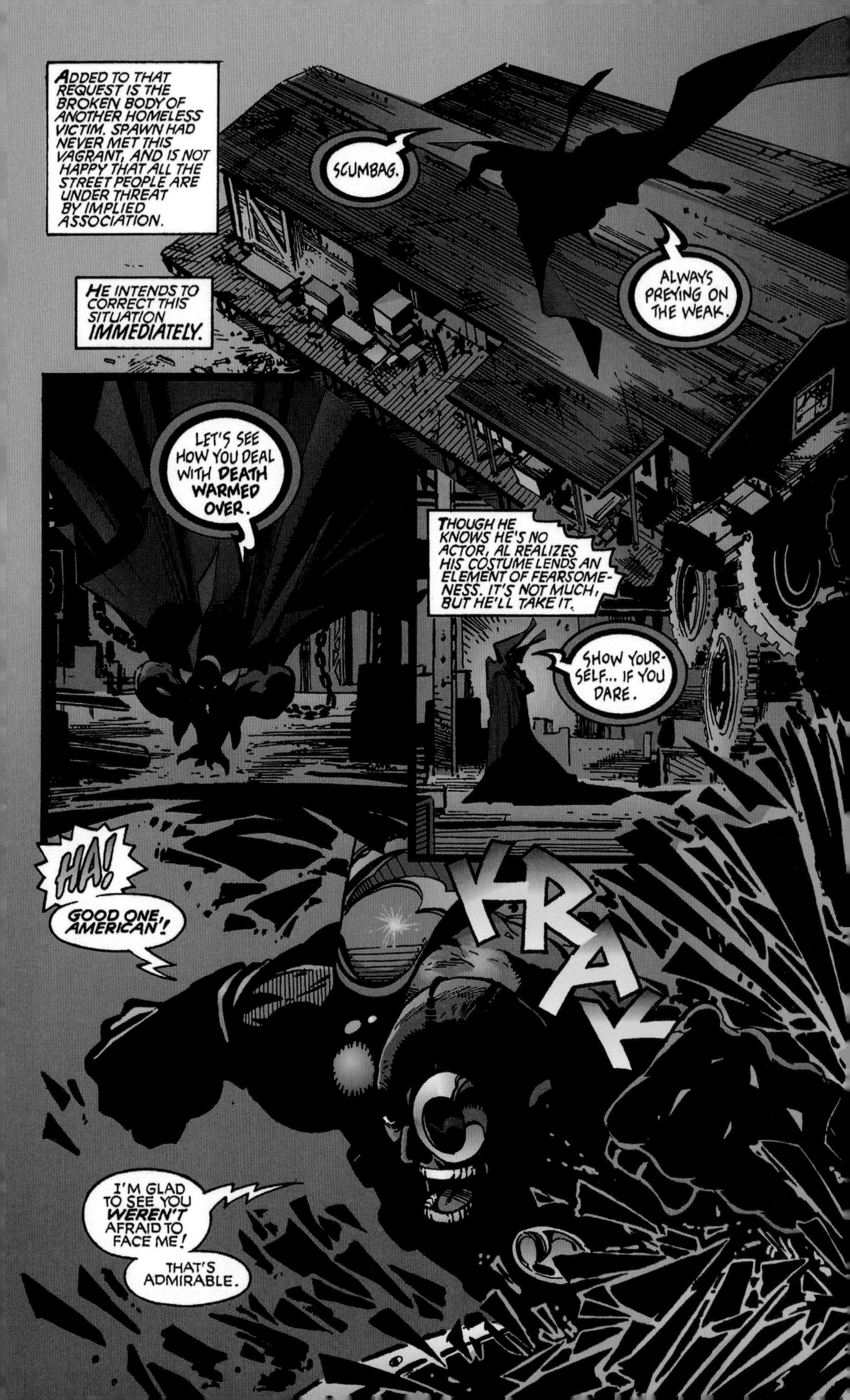
ADDED TO THAT REQUEST IS THE BROKEN BODY OF ANOTHER HOMELESS VICTIM. SPAWN HAD NEVER MET THIS VAGRANT, AND IS NOT HAPPY THAT ALL THE STREET PEOPLE ARE UNDER THREAT BY IMPLIED ASSOCIATION.
SCUMBAG.
ALWAYS PREYING ON THE WEAK.
HE INTENDS TO CORRECT THIS SITUATION IMMEDIATELY.
LET'S SEE HOW YOU DEAL WITH DEATH WARMED OVER.
THOUGH HE KNOWS HE'S NO ACTOR, AL REALIZES HIS COSTUME LENDS AN ELEMENT OF FEARSOME-NESS. IT'S NOT MUCH, BUT HE'LL TAKE IT.
SHOW YOUR-SELF... IF YOU DARE.
HA!
GOOD ONE, AMERICAN!
KRAK
I'M GLAD TO SEE YOU WEREN'T AFRAID TO FACE ME!
THAT'S ADMIRABLE.

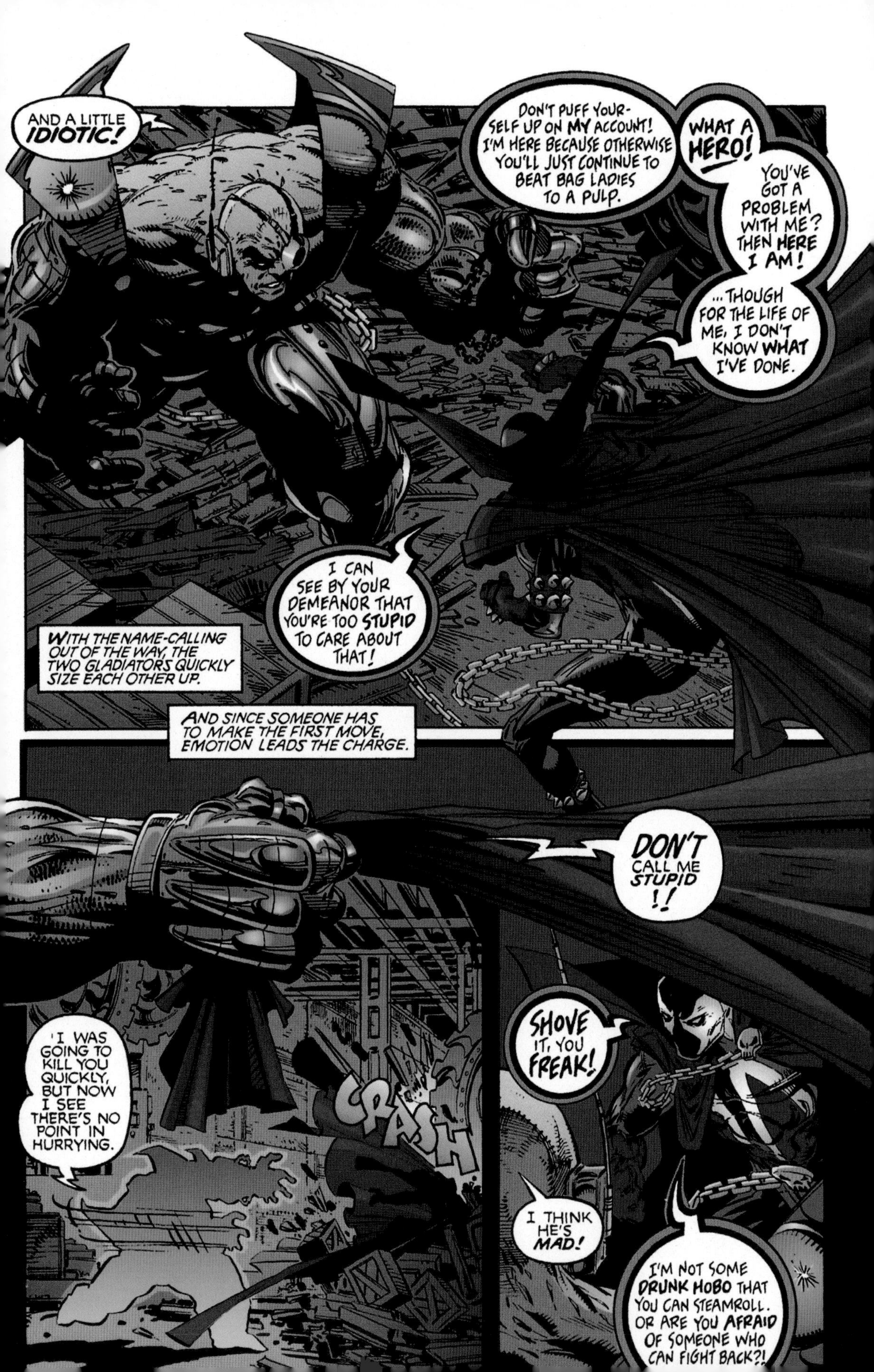
AND A LITTLE IDIOTIC!
DON'T PUFF YOURSELF UP ON MY ACCOUNT! I'M HERE BECAUSE OTHERWISE YOU'LL JUST CONTINUE TO BEAT BAG LADIES TO A PULP.
WHAT A HERO!
YOU'VE GOT A PROBLEM WITH ME? THEN HERE I AM!
...THOUGH FOR THE LIFE OF ME, I DON'T KNOW WHAT I'VE DONE.
I CAN SEE BY YOUR DEMEANOR THAT YOU'RE TOO STUPID TO CARE ABOUT THAT!
WITH THE NAME-CALLING OUT OF THE WAY, THE TWO GLADIATORS QUICKLY SIZE EACH OTHER UP.
AND SINCE SOMEONE HAS TO MAKE THE FIRST MOVE, EMOTION LEADS THE CHARGE.
DON'T CALL ME STUPID!!
I WAS GOING TO KILL YOU QUICKLY, BUT NOW I SEE THERE'S NO POINT IN HURRYING.
CRASH
SHOVE IT, YOU FREAK!
I THINK HE'S MAD!
I'M NOT SOME DRUNK HOBO THAT YOU CAN STEAMROLL. OR ARE YOU AFRAID OF SOMEONE WHO CAN FIGHT BACK?!

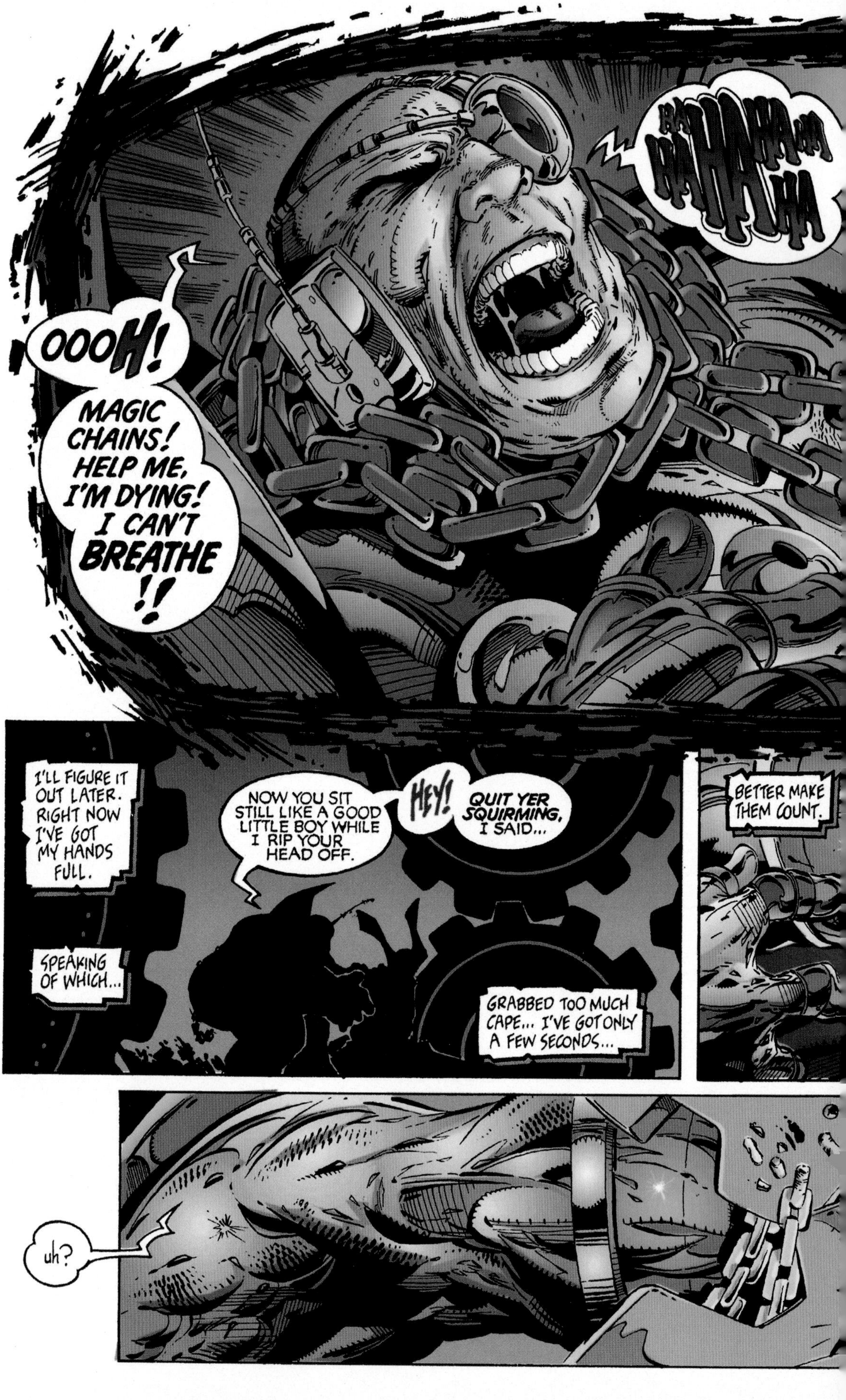
HAHAHAHAHA HAHAHAHA
OOOH!
MAGIC CHAINS! HELP ME, I'M DYING! I CAN'T BREATHE!!
I'LL FIGURE IT OUT LATER. RIGHT NOW I'VE GOT MY HANDS FULL.
NOW YOU SIT STILL LIKE A GOOD LITTLE BOY WHILE I RIP YOUR HEAD OFF.
HEY!
QUIT YER SQUIRMING, I SAID...
SPEAKING OF WHICH...
GRABBED TOO MUCH CAPE... I'VE GOT ONLY A FEW SECONDS...
BETTER MAKE THEM COUNT.
uh?

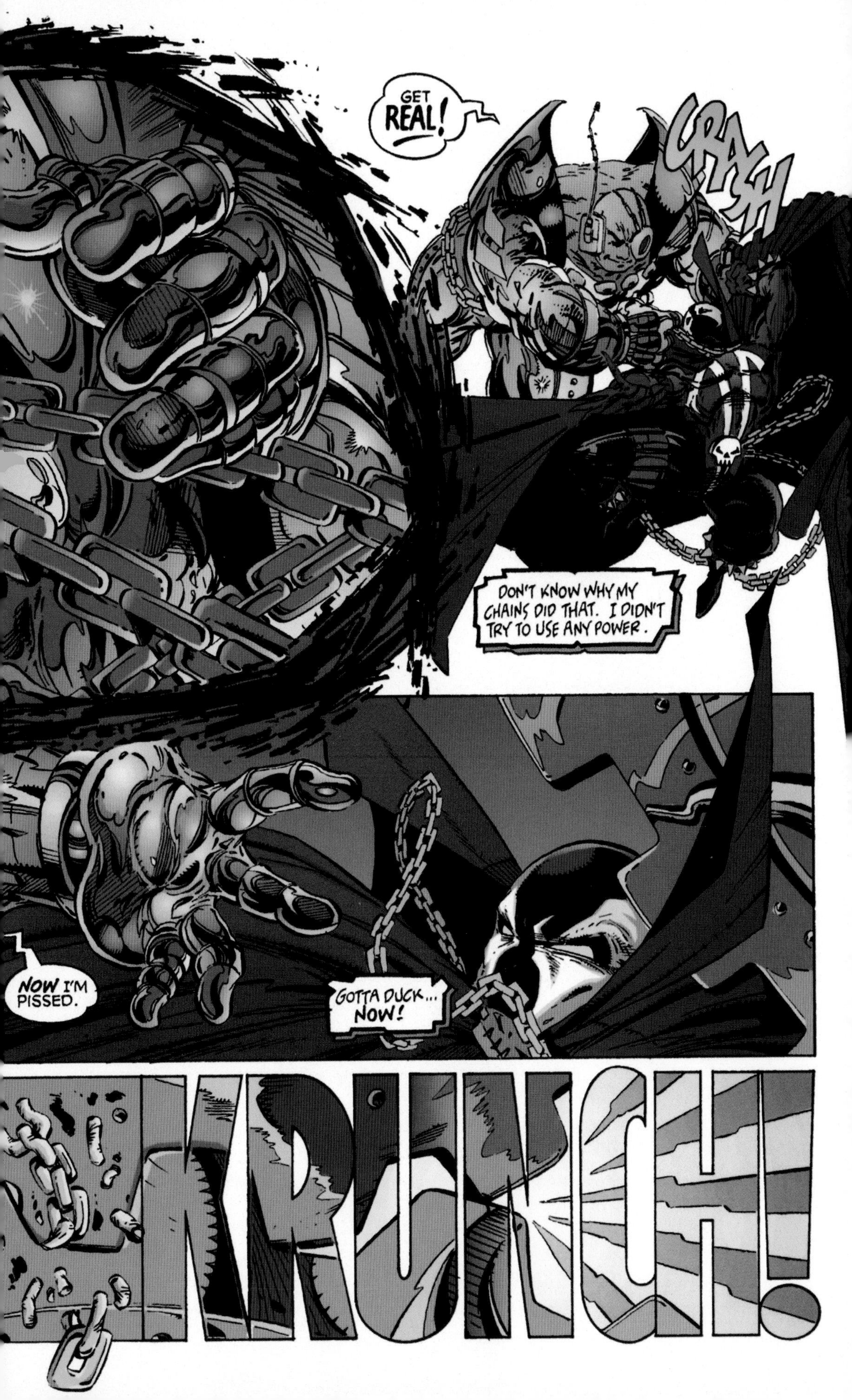
GET REAL!
CRASH
DON'T KNOW WHY MY CHAINS DID THAT. I DIDN'T TRY TO USE ANY POWER.
NOW I'M PISSED.
GOTTA DUCK... NOW!
KRUNCH!

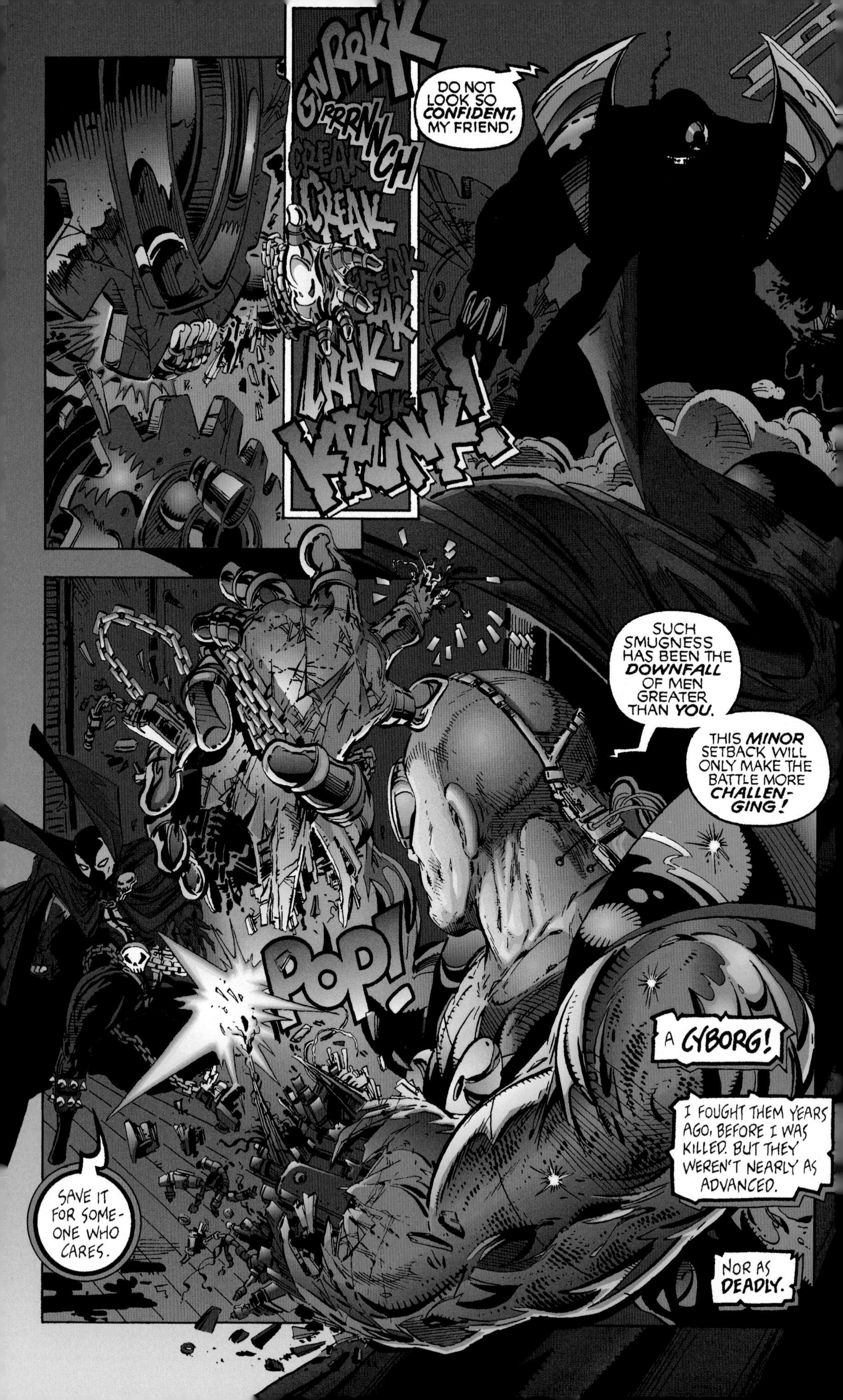
GWRRKK
RRRRNNCH
CREAK
CREAK
DO NOT LOOK SO CONFIDENT, MY FRIEND.
KRUNK!
SUCH SMUGNESS HAS BEEN THE DOWNFALL OF MEN GREATER THAN YOU.
THIS MINOR SETBACK WILL ONLY MAKE THE BATTLE MORE CHALLEN-GING!
POP!
A CYBORG!
I FOUGHT THEM YEARS AGO, BEFORE I WAS KILLED. BUT THEY WEREN'T NEARLY AS ADVANCED.
SAVE IT FOR SOME-ONE WHO CARES.
NOR AS DEADLY.

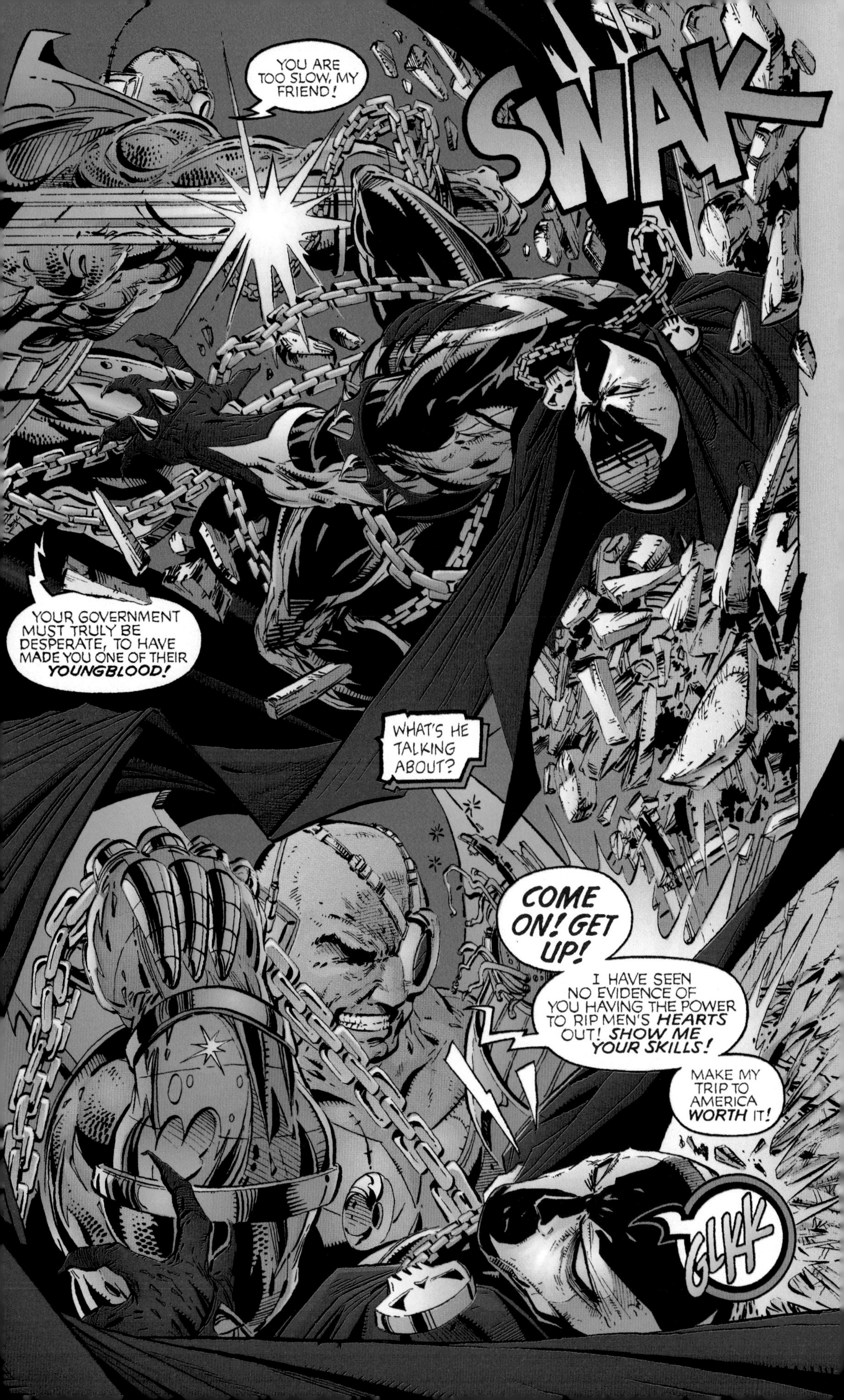

YOU ARE TOO SLOW, MY FRIEND!
SWAK
YOUR GOVERNMENT MUST TRULY BE DESPERATE, TO HAVE MADE YOU ONE OF THEIR YOUNGBLOOD!
WHAT'S HE TALKING ABOUT?
COME ON! GET UP!
I HAVE SEEN NO EVIDENCE OF YOU HAVING THE POWER TO RIP MEN'S HEARTS OUT! SHOW ME YOUR SKILLS!
MAKE MY TRIP TO AMERICA WORTH IT!
GLKK

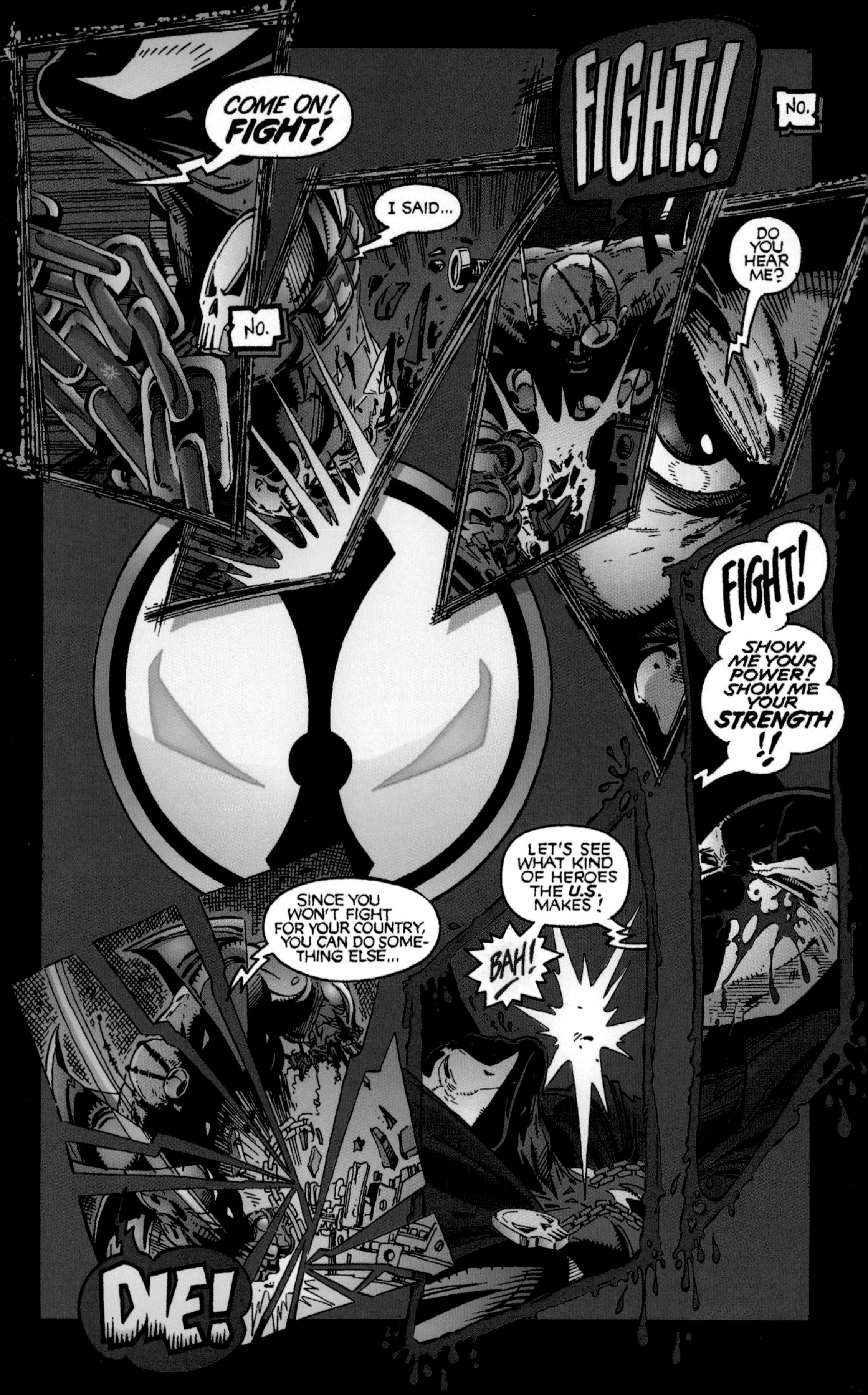
COME ON! FIGHT!
FIGHT!!
NO.
I SAID...
NO.
DO YOU HEAR ME?
FIGHT!
SHOW ME YOUR POWER! SHOW ME YOUR STRENGTH !!
LET'S SEE WHAT KIND OF HEROES THE U.S. MAKES!
SINCE YOU WON'T FIGHT FOR YOUR COUNTRY, YOU CAN DO SOMETHING ELSE...
BAH!
DIE!

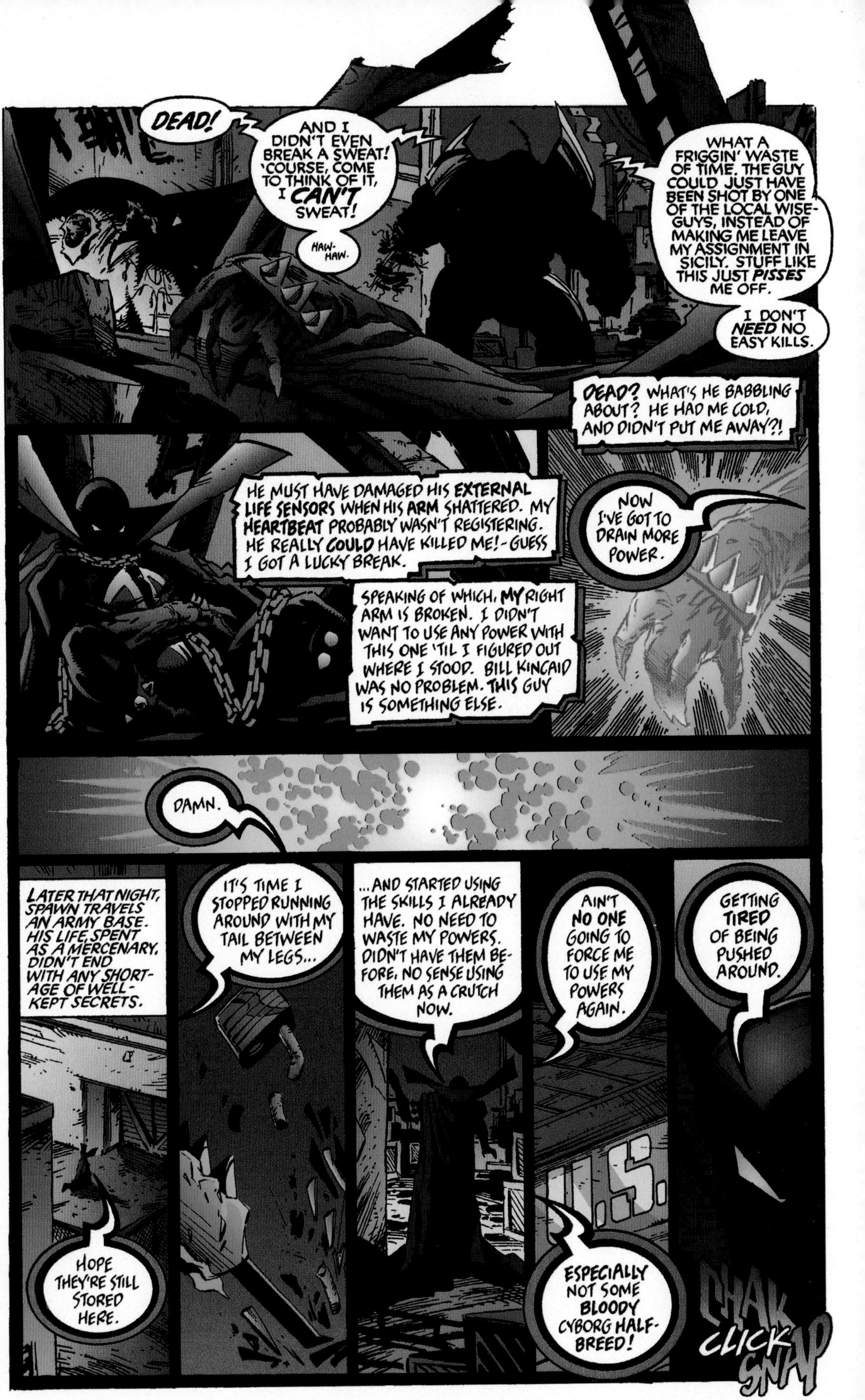
DEAD!
AND I DIDN'T EVEN BREAK A SWEAT! 'COURSE, COME TO THINK OF IT, I CAN'T SWEAT!
HAW-HAW.
WHAT A FRIGGIN' WASTE OF TIME. THE GUY COULD JUST HAVE BEEN SHOT BY ONE OF THE LOCAL WISE-GUYS, INSTEAD OF MAKING ME LEAVE MY ASSIGNMENT IN SICILY. STUFF LIKE THIS JUST PISSES ME OFF.
I DON'T NEED NO EASY KILLS.
DEAD? WHAT'S HE BABBLING ABOUT? HE HAD ME COLD, AND DIDN'T PUT ME AWAY?!
HE MUST HAVE DAMAGED HIS EXTERNAL LIFE SENSORS WHEN HIS ARM SHATTERED. MY HEARTBEAT PROBABLY WASN'T REGISTERING. HE REALLY COULD HAVE KILLED ME! - GUESS I GOT A LUCKY BREAK.
SPEAKING OF WHICH, MY RIGHT ARM IS BROKEN. I DIDN'T WANT TO USE ANY POWER WITH THIS ONE 'TIL I FIGURED OUT WHERE I STOOD. BILL KINCAID WAS NO PROBLEM. THIS GUY IS SOMETHING ELSE.
NOW I'VE GOT TO DRAIN MORE POWER.
DAMN.
LATER THAT NIGHT, SPAWN TRAVELS AN ARMY BASE. HIS LIFE, SPENT AS A MERCENARY, DIDN'T END WITH ANY SHORTAGE OF WELL-KEPT SECRETS.
HOPE THEY'RE STILL STORED HERE.
IT'S TIME I STOPPED RUNNING AROUND WITH MY TAIL BETWEEN MY LEGS...
...AND STARTED USING THE SKILLS I ALREADY HAVE. NO NEED TO WASTE MY POWERS. DIDN'T HAVE THEM BEFORE, NO SENSE USING THEM AS A CRUTCH NOW.
AIN'T NO ONE GOING TO FORCE ME TO USE MY POWERS AGAIN.
ESPECIALLY NOT SOME BLOODY CYBORG HALF-BREED!
GETTING TIRED OF BEING PUSHED AROUND.
CHAK
CLICK
SNAP

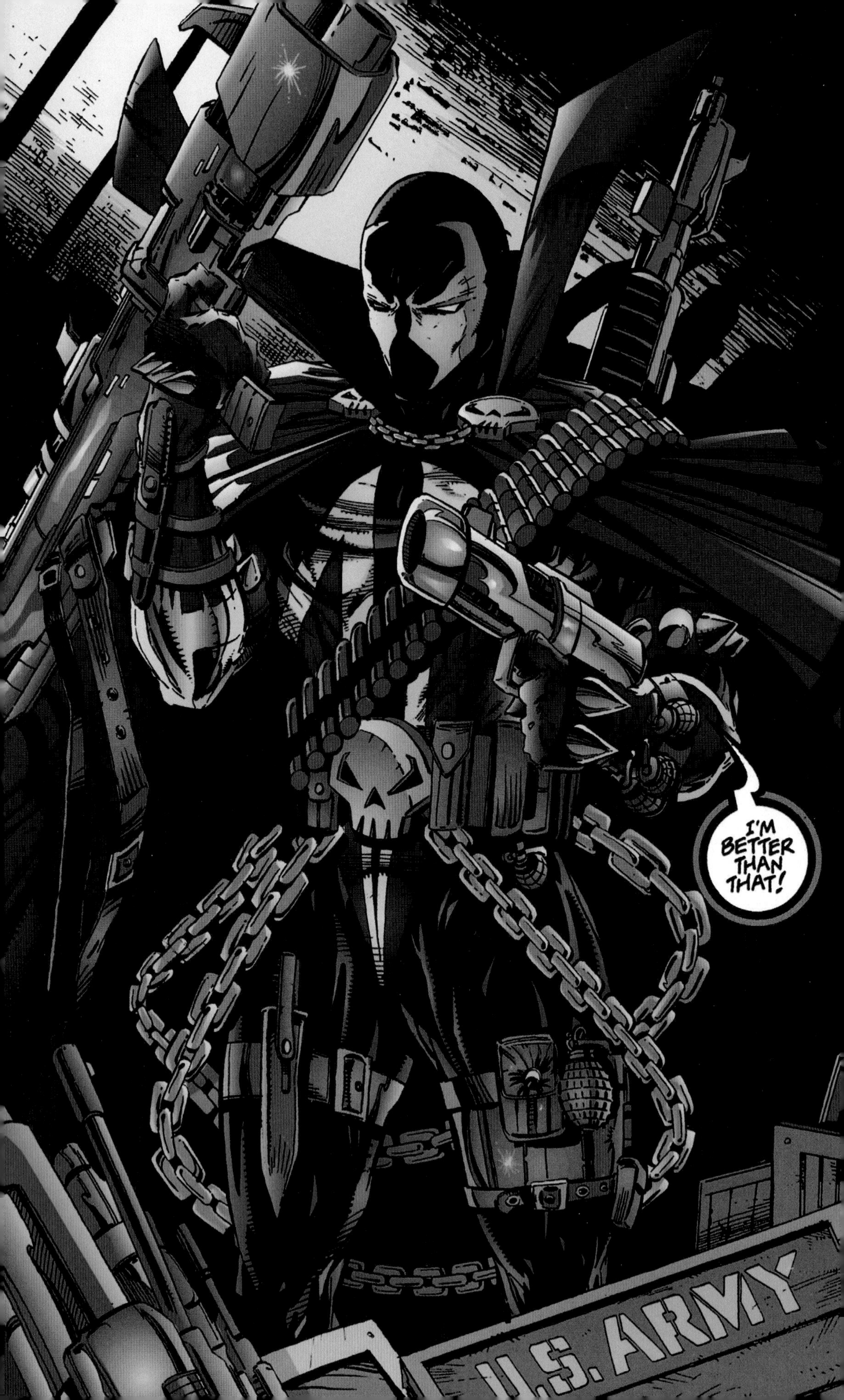
I'M BETTER THAN THAT!
U.S. ARMY

SKETCHBOOK

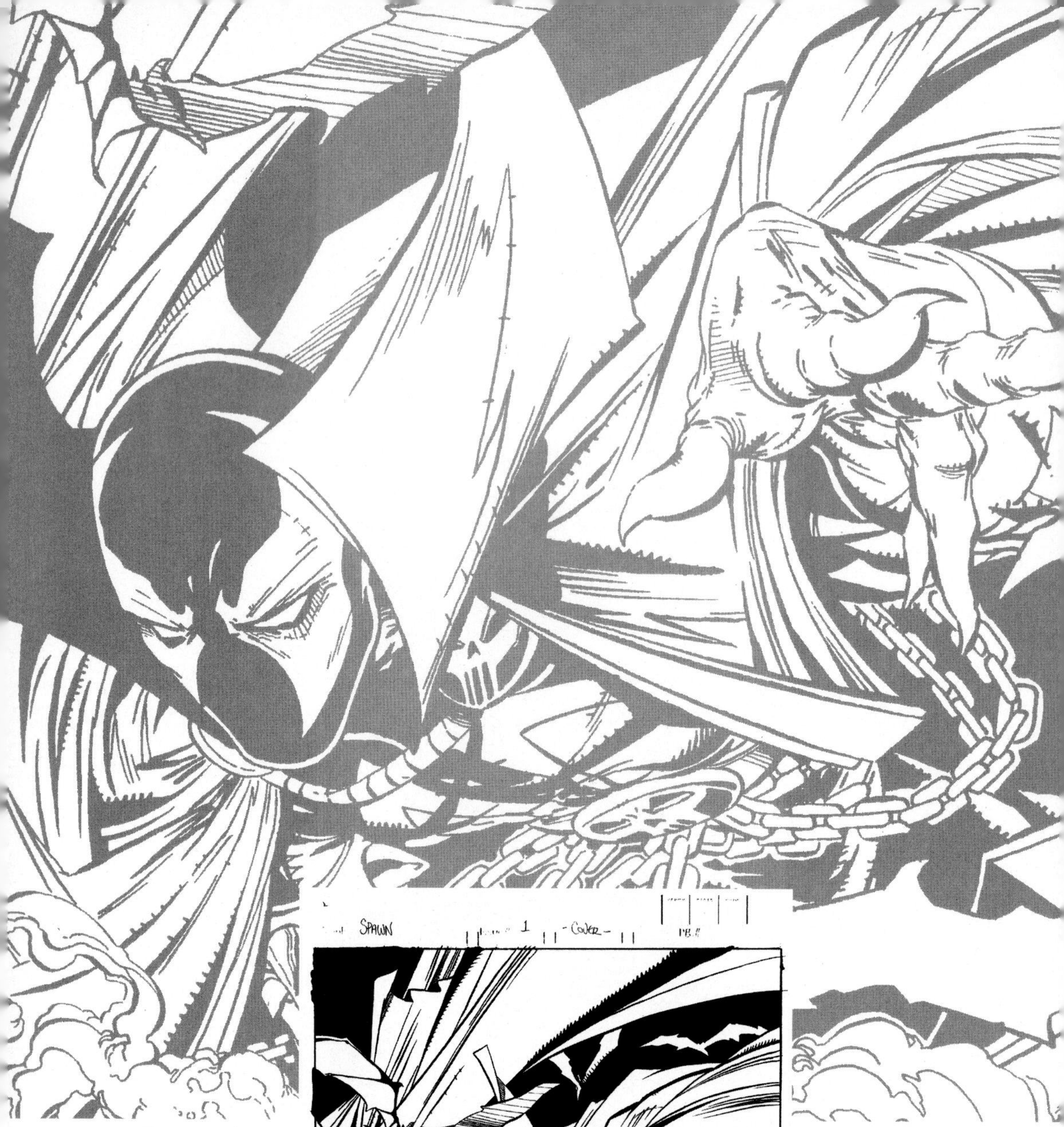

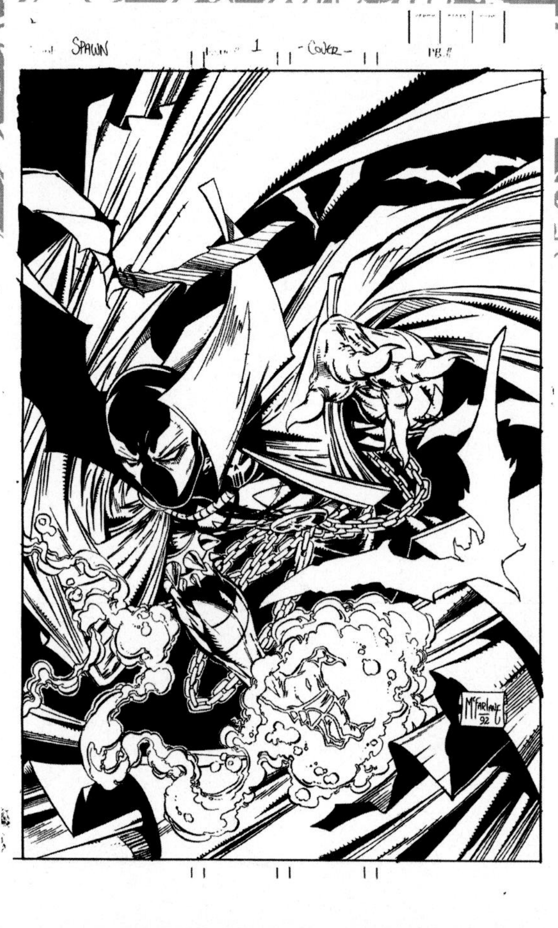
SPAWN
1
-COVER-
McFARLANE 92

Spawn #1 cover, inks

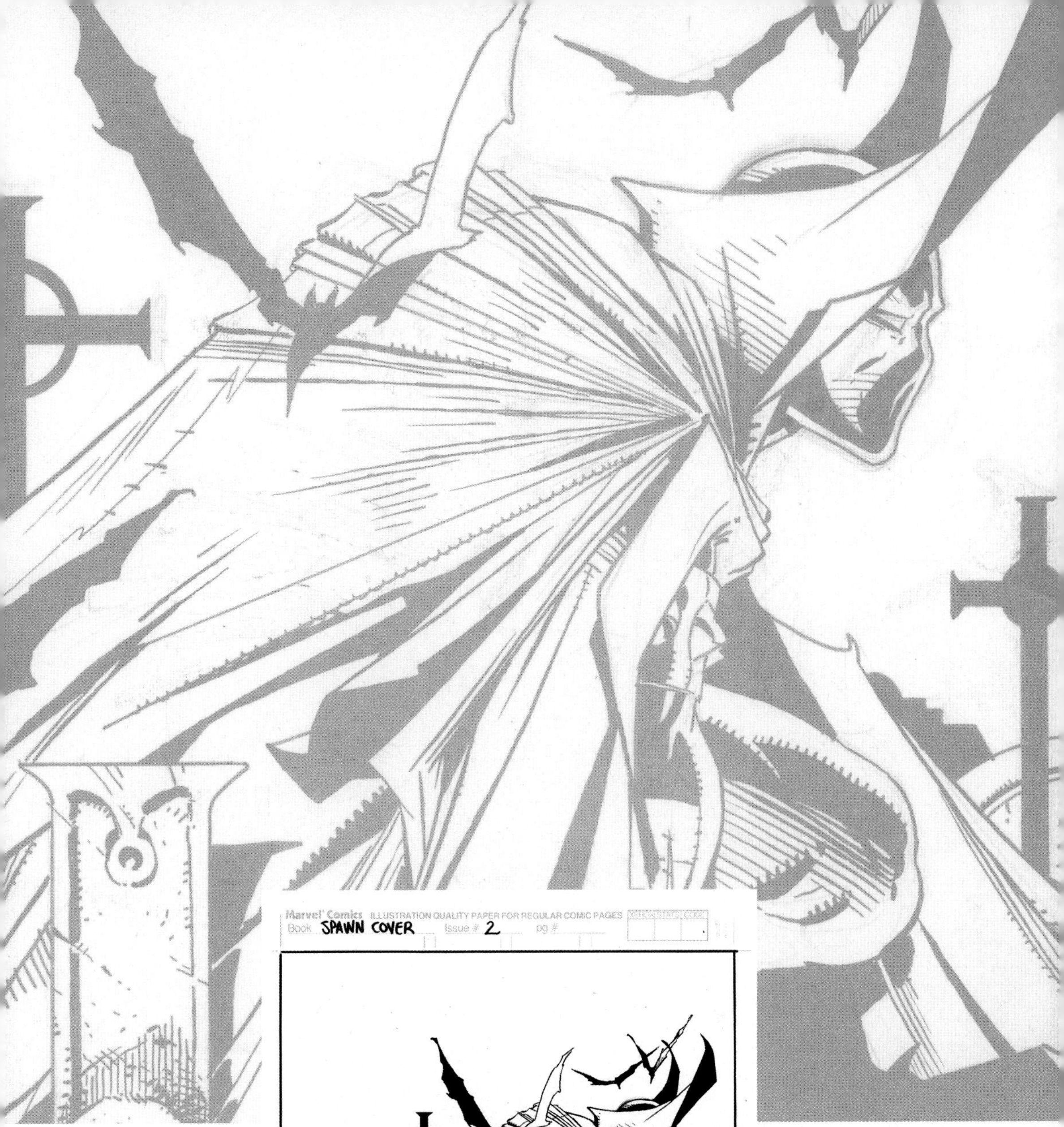

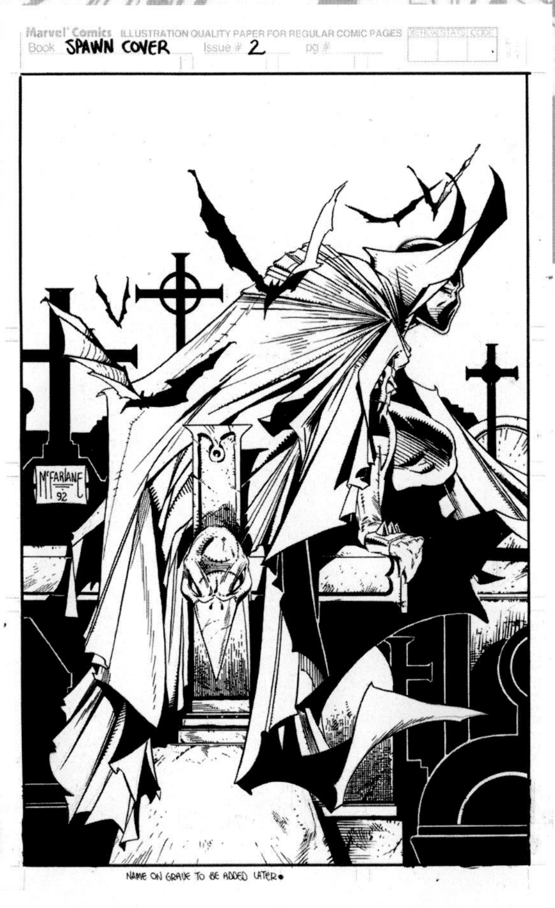
Marvel Comics ILLUSTRATION QUALITY PAPER FOR REGULAR COMIC PAGES
Book SPAWN COVER Issue # 2 pg #
McFARLANE 92
NAME ON GRAVE TO BE ADDED LATER.

Spawn #2 cover, inks

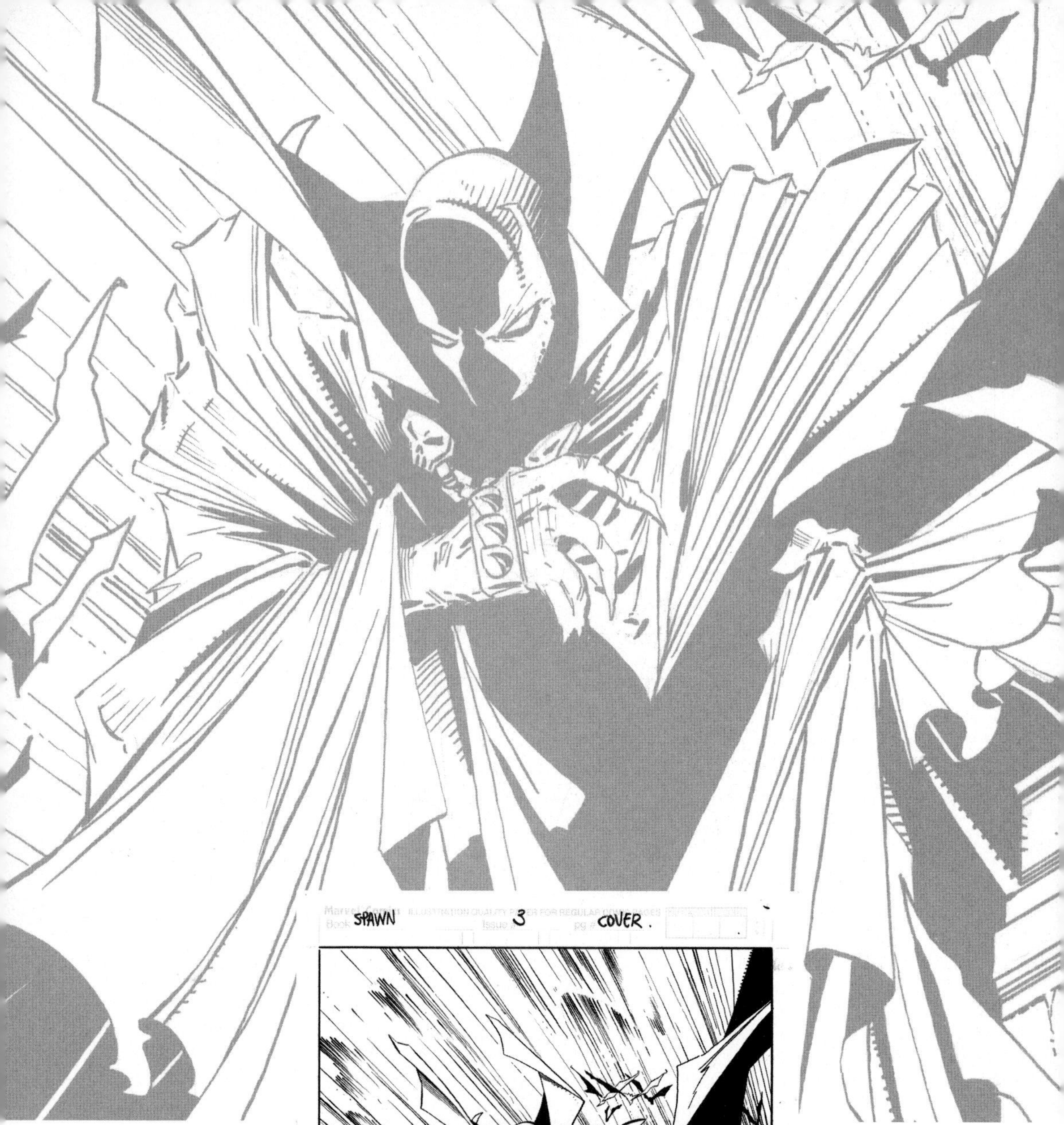

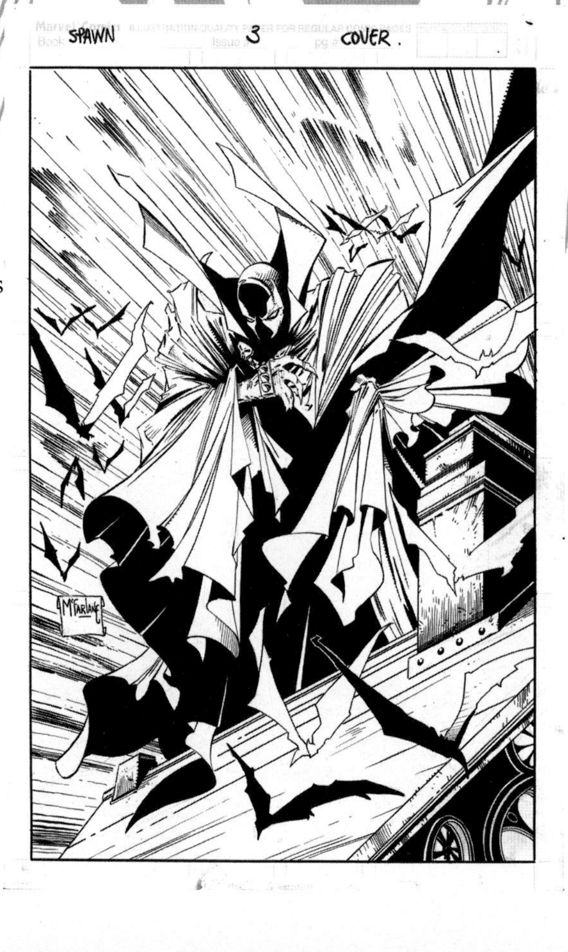
SPAWN
3
COVER.

Spawn #3 cover, inks

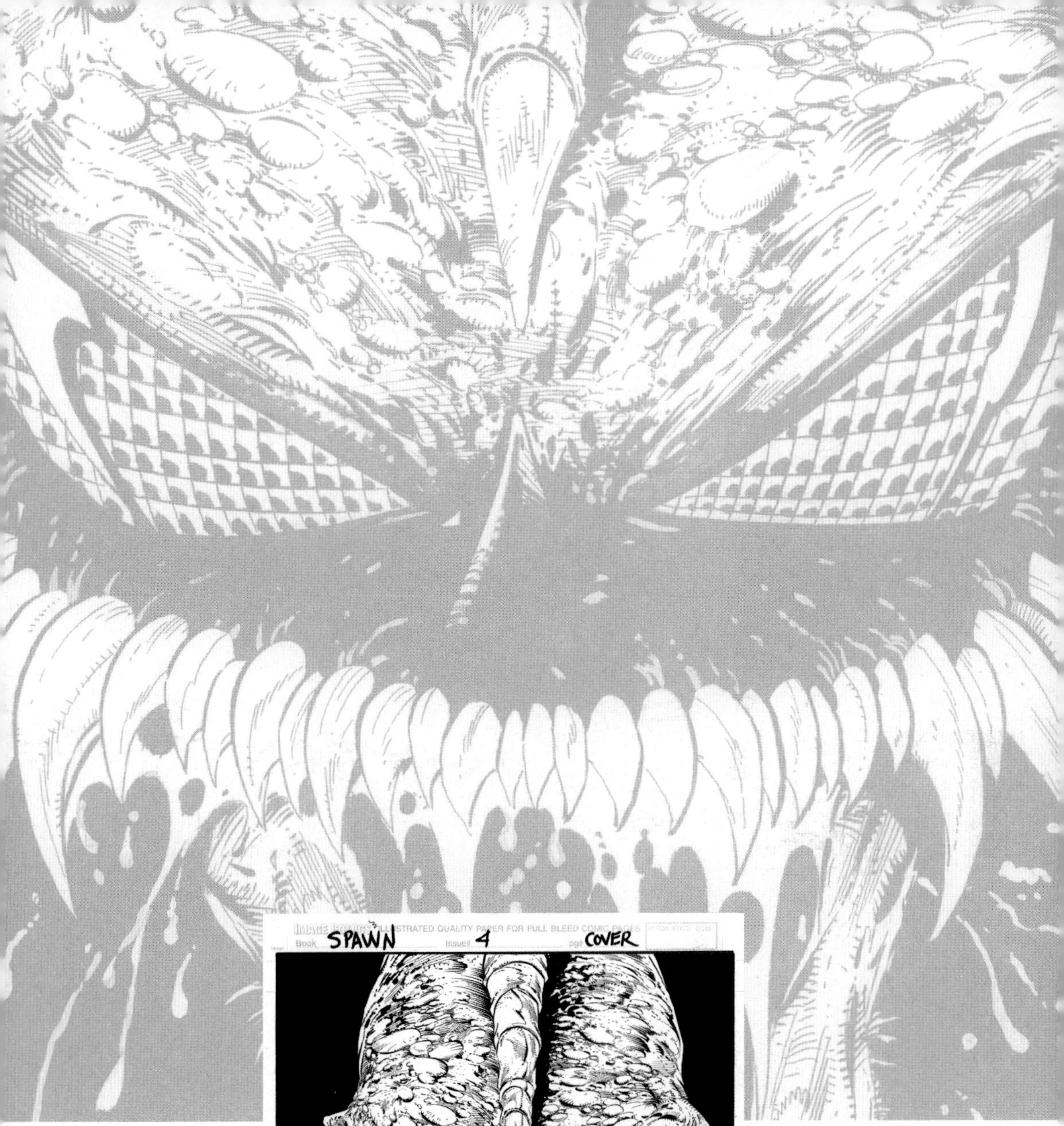

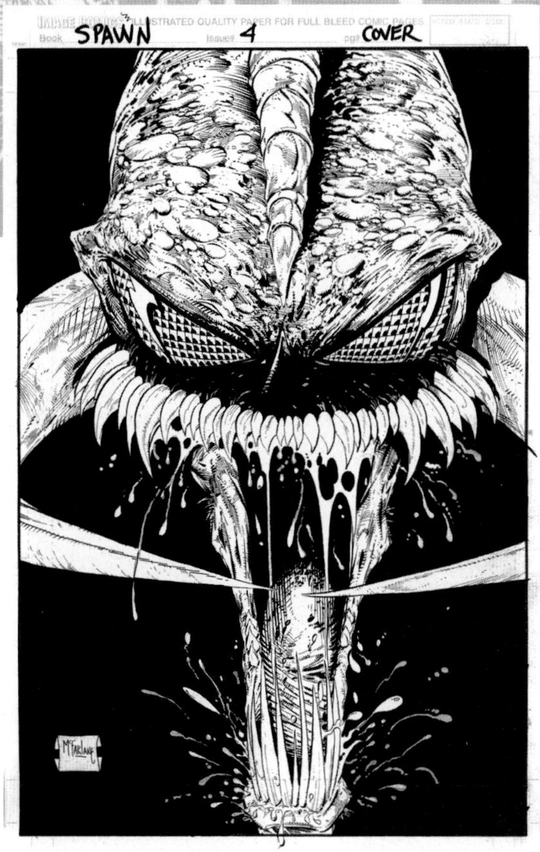

Book SPAWN
Issue 4
COVER

Spawn #4 cover, inks

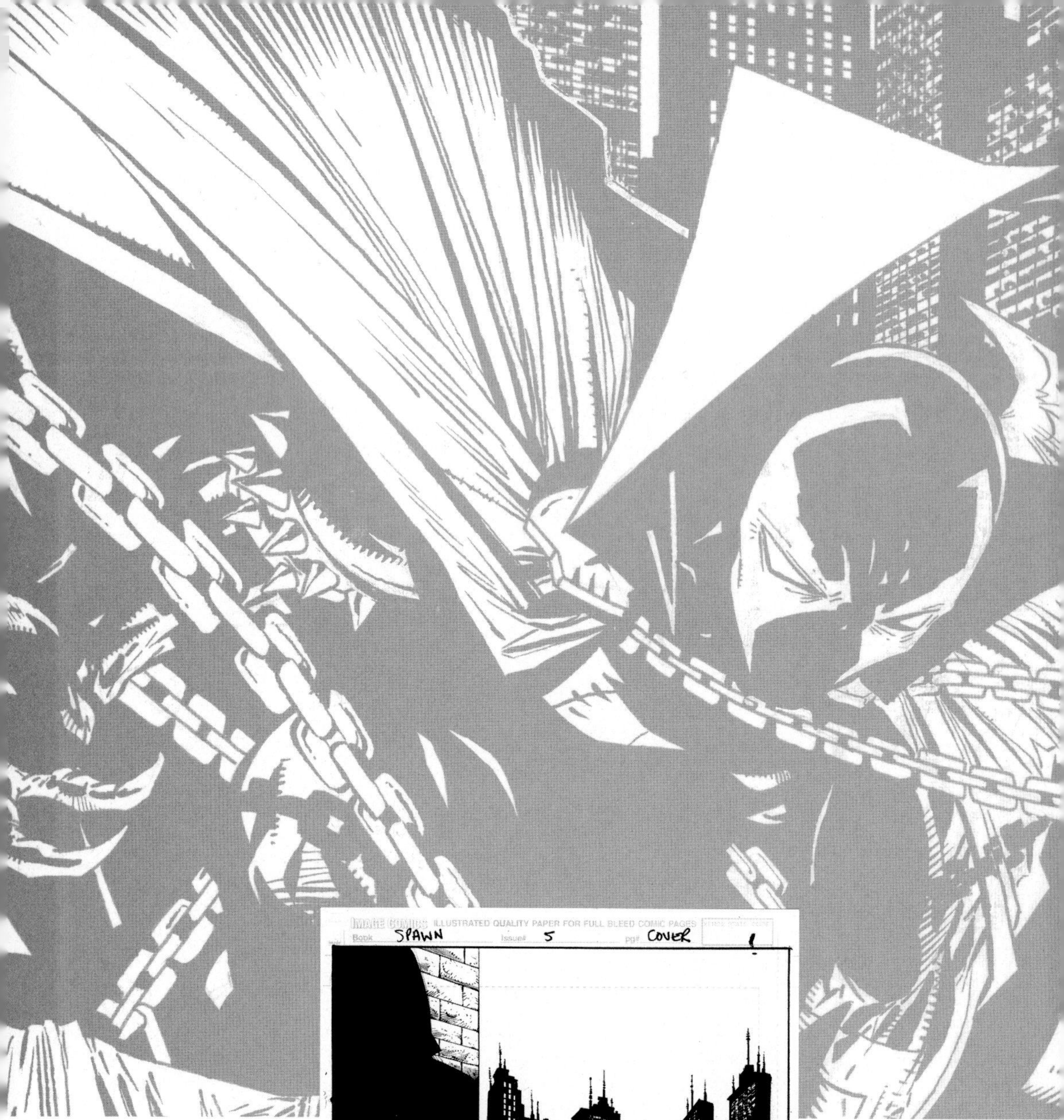

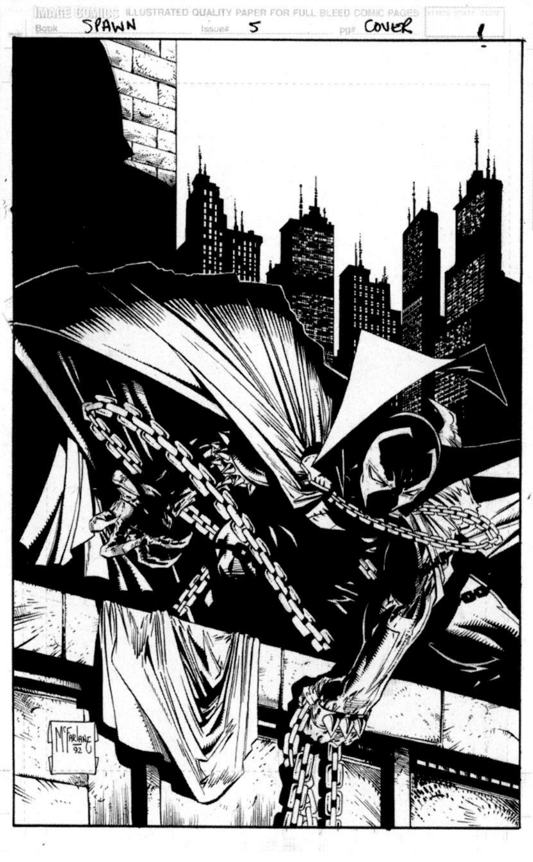
IMAGE COMICS ILLUSTRATED QUALITY PAPER FOR FULL BLEED COMIC PAGES
Book SPAWN
Issue# 5
pg# COVER

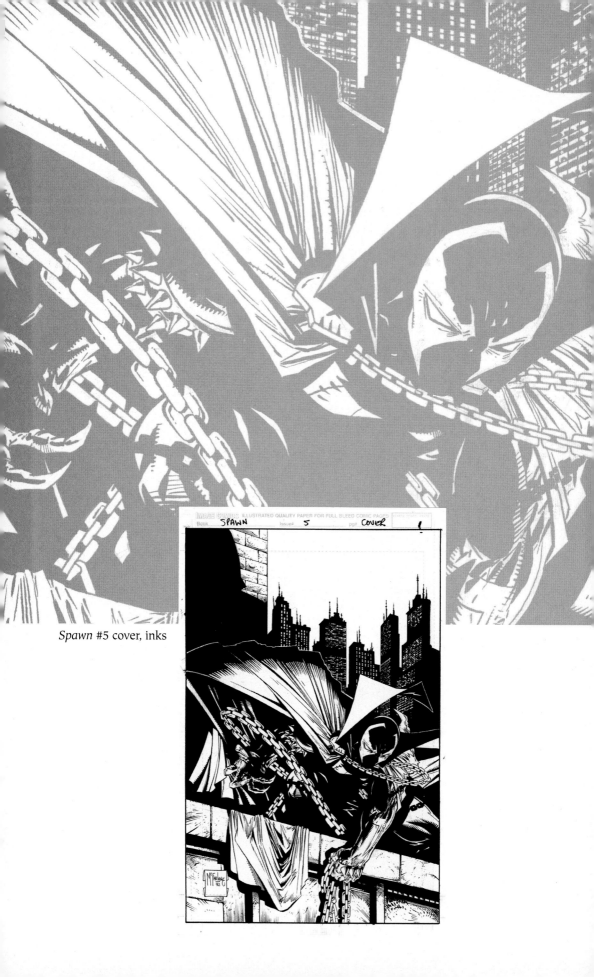

Spawn #5 cover, inks

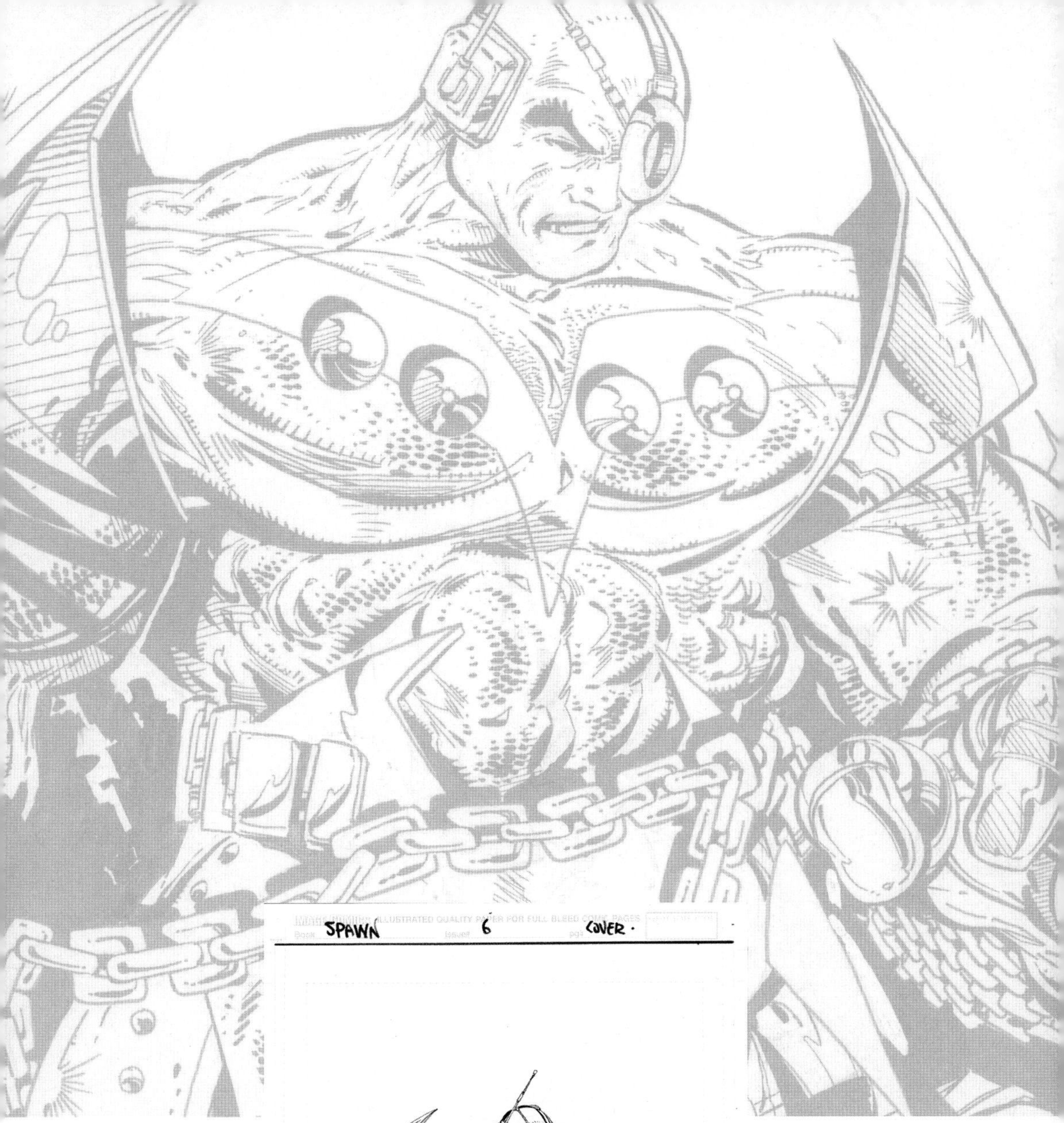

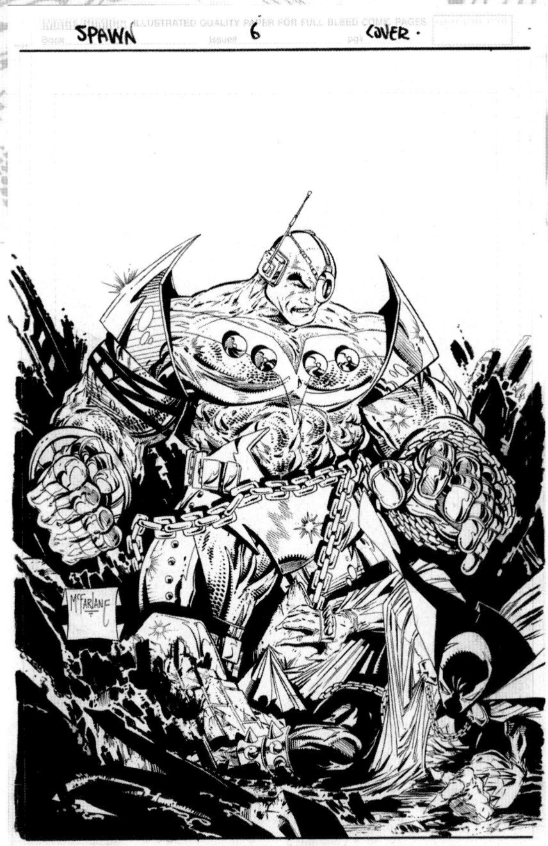
ILLUSTRATED QUALITY PAPER FOR FULL BLEED COMIC PAGES
SPAWN
6
COVER.
McFARLANE

Spawn #6 cover, inks

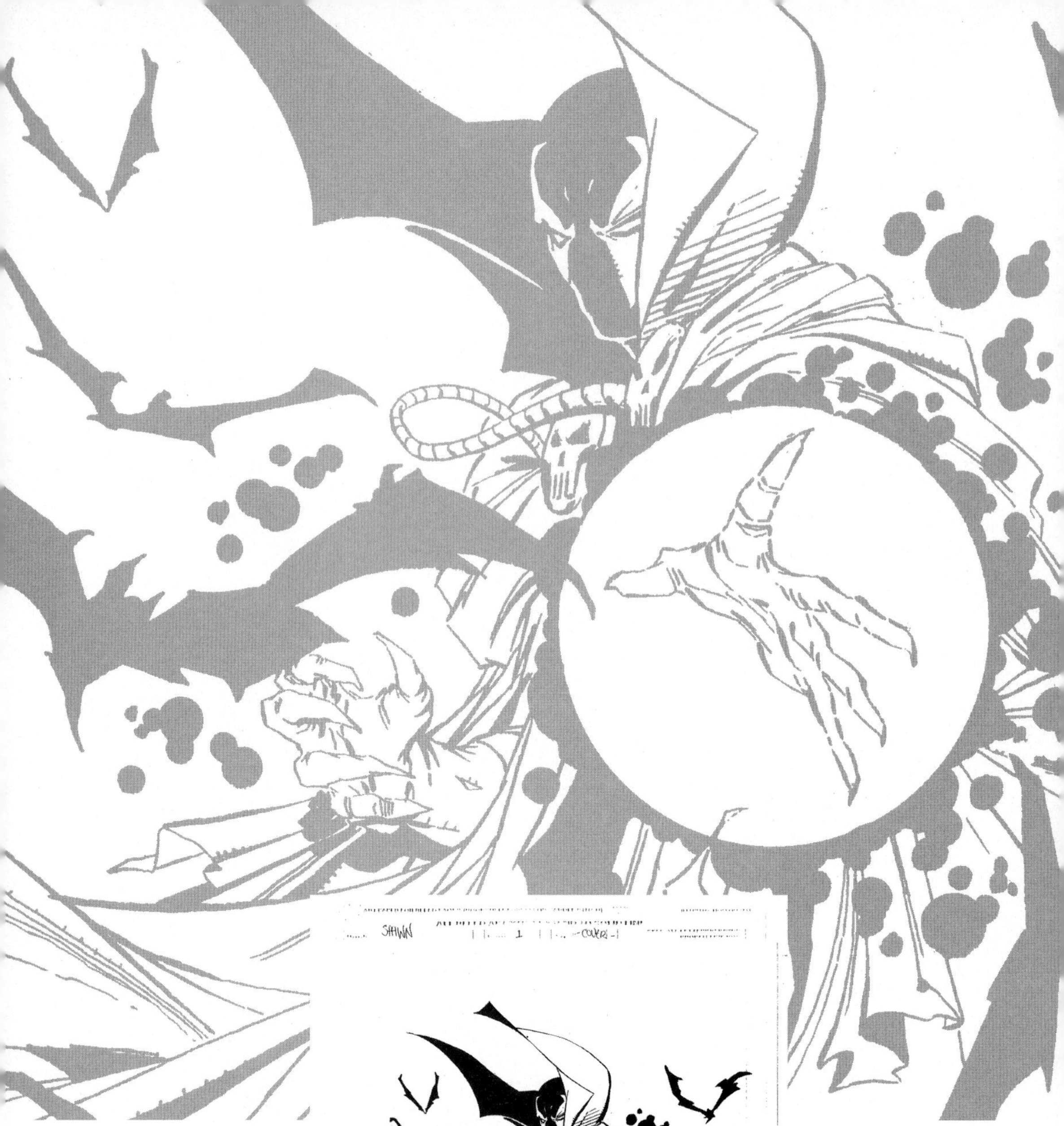

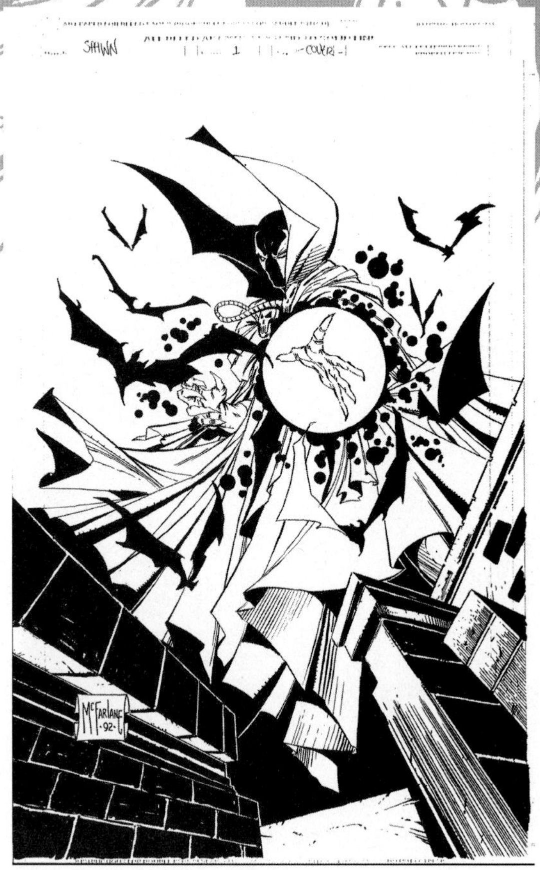
SPAWN
McFARLANE
-92-

Spawn #1
pull-out poster, inks

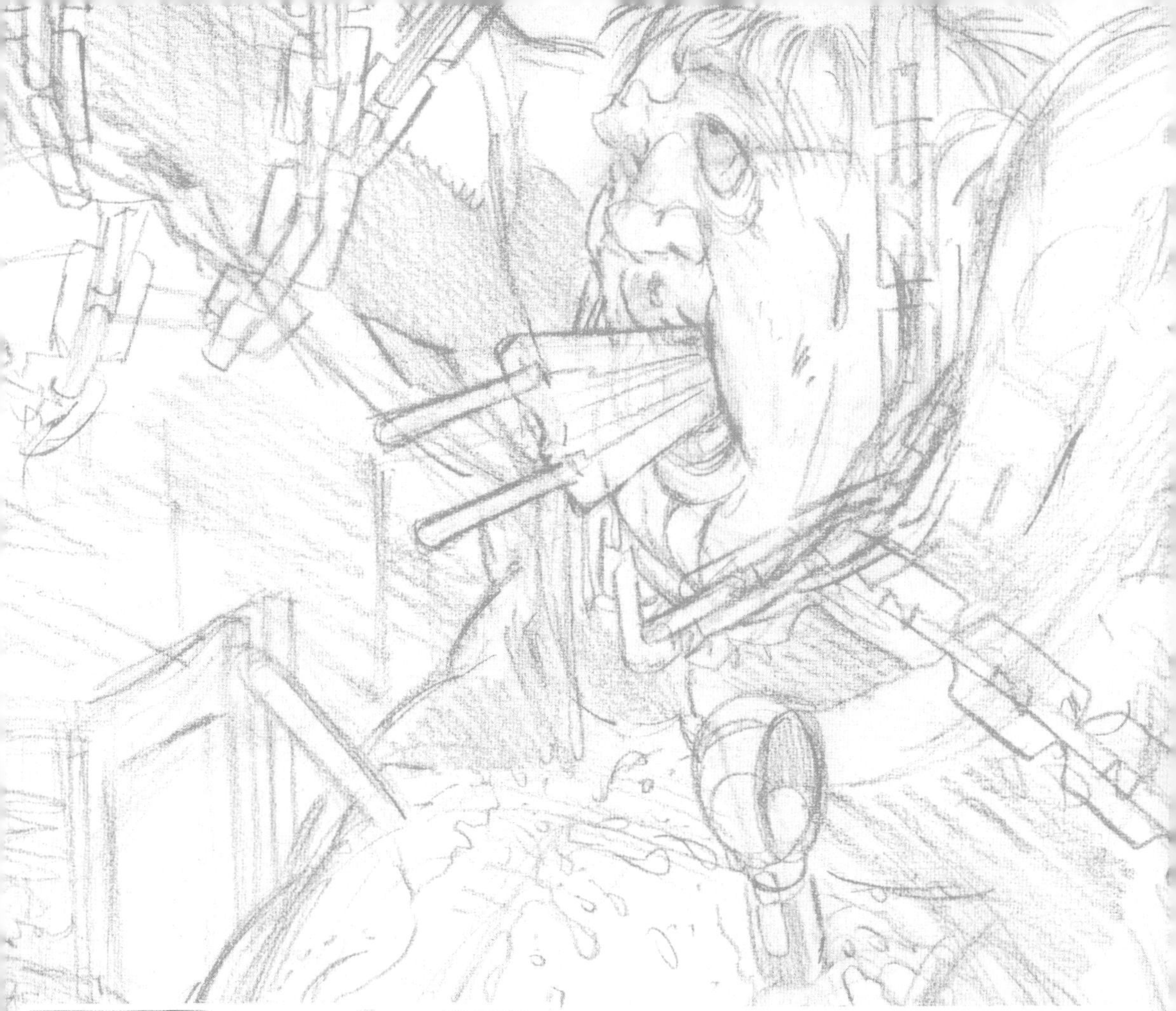

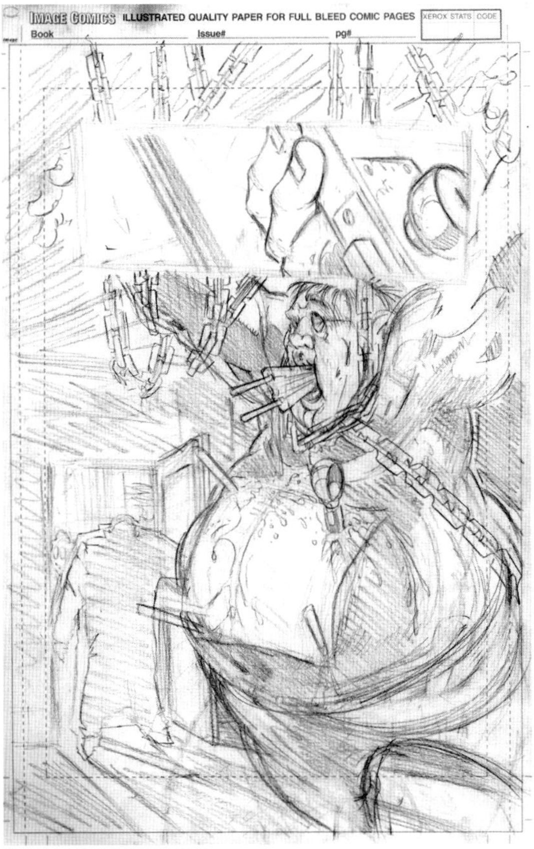
IMAGE COMICS ILLUSTRATED QUALITY PAPER FOR FULL BLEED COMIC PAGES
XEROX STATS
CODE
Book
Issue#
pg#

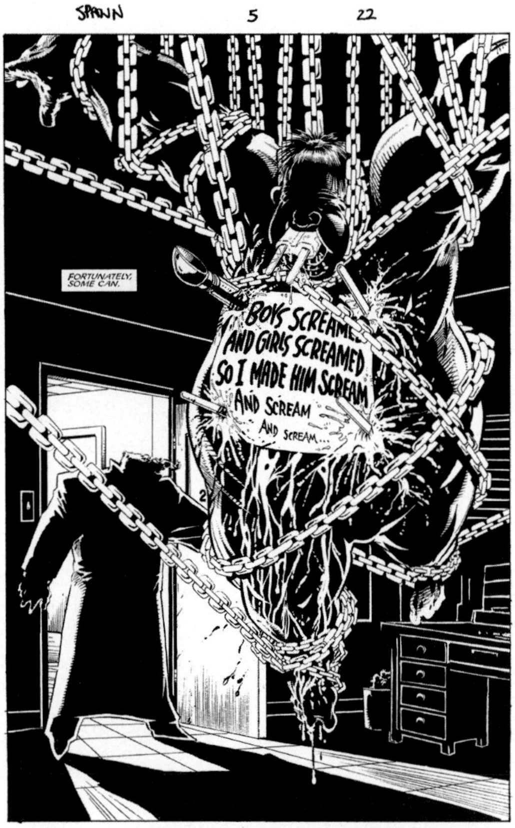
SPAWN
5
22
FORTUNATELY, SOME CAN.
BOYS SCREAME
AND GIRLS SCREAMED
SO I MADE HIM SCREAM
AND SCREAM
AND SCREAM...

Spawn #5, page 22,
rough sketch and final inks

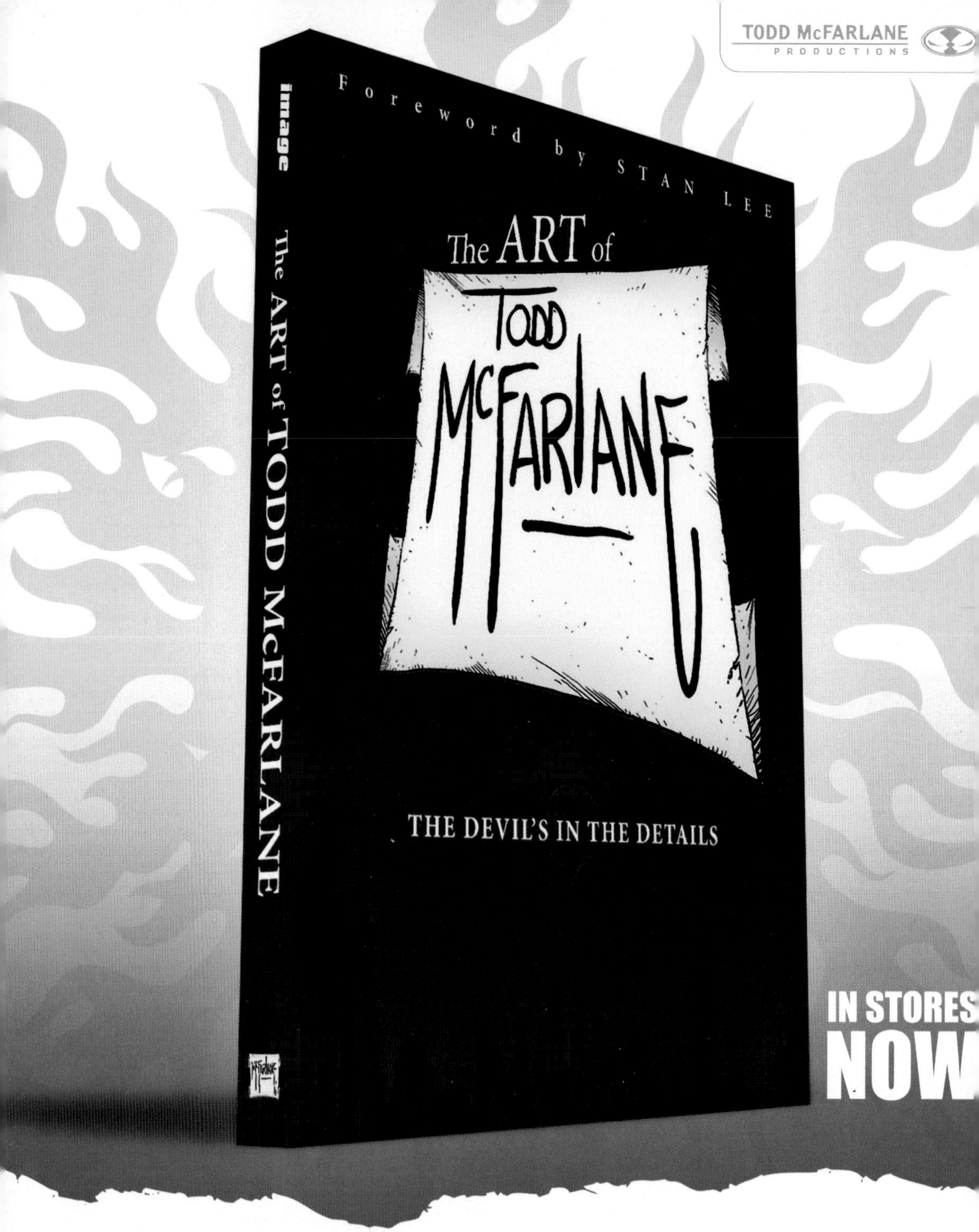

TODD McFARLANE
PRODUCTIONS
image
The ART of TODD McFARLANE
Foreword by STAN LEE
The ART of
TODD McFARLANE
THE DEVIL'S IN THE DETAILS
IN STORES NOW